The French Republic

THE FRENCH REPUBLIC

∾ History, Values, Debates ∾

EDITED BY

*Edward Berenson, Vincent Duclert,
and Christophe Prochasson*

Cornell University Press
Ithaca and London

This work, published as part of the program of aid for publication, received support from the French Ministry of Foreign Affairs and the Cultural Services of the French Embassy in the United States.

Cet ouvrage publié dans le cadre du programme d'aide à la publication, bénéficie du soutien du Ministère des Affaires Etrangères et du Service Culturel de l'Ambassade de France représenté aux États-Unis.

This work has also received support from the Humanities Institute at NYU.

Chapters 1, 2, 3, 4, 5, 6, 7, 10, 11, 12, 13, 14, 15, 16, 21, 22, 23, 25, and "American Perspectives on the French Republic" first appeared in *Dictionnaire critique de la République* (Paris: Flammarion, 2002, 2007), and appear here with the generous permission of Éditions Flammarion.

Part of the introduction, chapters 2, 4, 6, 7, 12, 13, 14, 15, 23, and the conclusion by Vincent Duclert have been translated by Arthur Goldhammer.

First published 2011 by Cornell University Press
First printing, Cornell Paperbacks, 2012

Printed in the United States of America

Library of Congress Cataloging-in-Publication Data

The French Republic : history, values, debates / edited by Edward Berenson, Vincent Duclert, and Christophe Prochasson.
   p. cm.
   Some contributions translated from the French.
   Includes bibliographical references and index.
   ISBN 978-0-8014-4901-7 (cloth : alk. paper)
   ISBN 978-0-8014-7784-3 (paper : alk. paper)
   1. France—History—1789– 2. Republicanism—France—History. 3. Political culture—France—History. 4. France—Intellectual life. I. Berenson, Edward, 1949– II. Duclert, Vincent, 1961– III. Prochasson, Christophe.

   DC55.F695   2011
   944—dc22   2010053812

Cornell University Press strives to use environmentally responsible suppliers and materials to the fullest extent possible in the publishing of its books. Such materials include vegetable-based, low-VOC inks and acid-free papers that are recycled, totally chlorine-free, or partly composed of nonwood fibers. For further information, visit our website at www.cornellpress.cornell.edu.

Cloth printing   10 9 8 7 6 5 4 3 2 1
Paperback printing   10 9 8 7 6 5 4 3 2 1

Contents

THE FRENCH REPUBLIC

Introduction

Transatlantic Histories of France

Edward Berenson and Vincent Duclert

Translated by Arthur Goldhammer

The Republic first appeared in France as a system of government and model of sovereignty on September 25, 1792, and subsequently developed into nothing less than a comprehensive worldview and way of organizing and understanding history. Two centuries of political controversy have turned the Republic into an all-encompassing structure, a totality, which makes the work of historians who seek to make sense of it as difficult as it is exciting. How can one write the history of something so vast, so comprehensive, and so desired—desired particularly by historians themselves, many of whom took part in the republican project? How can one restore the historical dimension and recover the critical perspective needed to study a world at once so close to us and so distant, so immediate and yet opaque—a world that is past as well as present, individual as well as collective, private as well as public, and consensual as well as controversial?

It was in these terms that Vincent Duclert and Christophe Prochasson described the ambition of the *Dictionnaire critique de la République,* which they edited for Éditions Flammarion in Paris and published in 2002.

Reprinted in 2007, this multiauthor volume, part encyclopedia, part critical history, forms the basis of the present work. The *Dictionnaire* was intended primarily as a historiographical survey, because there has always been a special relationship between the Republic and history. Indeed, the Third Republic defined itself as a historical project, or at any rate a historical discourse, whose purpose was to define both the French nation and French society. To study the Republic, we had to analyze this historical frame in order to move beyond it and define an object of study independent of republican politics and ideology. Historical as well as historiographical analysis seemed to us the best way to understand the Republic, "which is in principle simply a form of executive power, with a head of state who enjoys neither life tenure nor hereditary status," but which has become, in the words of the historian Maurice Agulhon, a political form defined "by a specific political content of liberty and laicity." Having developed *in* history, the Republic was constructed *by* history, constituting itself as a universal language for describing a past that transformed facts into ideas, men into symbols, and practices into experiences. The Republic can be seen not only as a set of values, institutions, heroes, images, symbols, and realities but also as a set of contradictions, repudiations, and episodes of violence, which the *Dictionnaire critique* of 2002 attempted to describe and understand.

To that end, the editors enlisted the help of a hundred or so historians, including seven British and American scholars (who contributed ten articles) for whom the French Republic was inevitably a more fluid structure, less constrained by political and intellectual habits, than it was for their French colleagues. For these British and American historians, implicit and explicit comparisons with their own national histories, the claims of French universalism, issues of democracy, and the recurrent contradictions between humanist republican discourse and authoritarian republican practice were central to their contributions to the 2002 volume. Their articles, most originally written in English, revealed a certain convergence of themes and touched on many topical issues not only of historiography but also of public discussion and controversy. The commonalities among them, and a distinctiveness in relation to many of the French-language contributions, led one of the original editors to join with Edward Berenson in conceiving the idea of a new volume on the subject in English, to be published in the United States.

The purpose of this new project was not simply to make these texts by British and American historians available to Anglophone readers but rather to develop a novel approach to the history of the Republic. We decided to do so by structuring the new book around the ten original British and American chapters paired with a nearly equal number of French pieces selected from the *Dictionnaire*. We then commissioned twenty new articles designed to highlight the interests and perspectives of U.S. historians of France while including three pieces by French scholars, two of them sociologists, not appearing in the volume of 2002.* Our intention was to begin by constructing the object itself through an examination of "republican values" (drawing mostly on articles from the *Dictionnaire critique*

* The following articles appeared in French in either the original *Dictionnaire* of 2002 or the revised version of 2007: "The First Republic," "The Republicans of the Second Empire," "War and the Republic," "The Republic and Vichy," "Fraternity," "Democracy," "Laicity," "Citizenship," "The Press," "The USA, Sister Republic," and "The Republic and the *Indigènes*." The following were written in English and translated into French for the original *Dictionnaire*: "The Enlightenment," "The Second Republic," "The Third Republic," "Liberty," "Equality," "Universalism," "Times of Exile and Immigration," and "American Perspectives on the French Republic." The rest of the chapters are new to this volume.

and published here in English translation) and then to offer a critique, even a deconstruction, of that object through an examination of the flaws, blind spots, and omissions in the "republican model." The result is a distinctive new work, inspired to be sure by the *Dictionnaire critique de la République* but developing its own historiographical perspective and demonstrating the richness of Anglo-American research on the French Republic.

As this research makes clear, the history of France has exploded its national, hexagonal bounds. French history has become an international history, an object of study especially important to British and U.S. historians. In 2004, when Nancy L. Green and Edward Berenson organized the annual meeting of the *American* "Society for French Historical Studies" at the Bibliothèque Nationale de *France,* they found themselves overwhelmed with proposals for papers and panels. Immediately, the *British* "Society for French History" sought to join in, and ultimately a conference program representing historians of France from sixteen different countries was created.

This multinational collection of scholars defined French history differently from the way it had been defined—until very recently—in France. Our international group understood "France" in an international way—not, that is, as a nation-state outlined by its hexagonal boundaries, but as a former empire deeply implicated in the history of Africa, Asia, and the Americas. As for the Hexagon itself, many of the 550 people who spoke at the conference saw it as having been refigured by the descendants of its former colonial subjects, who now reside there in very large numbers. And just as these once-immigrant peoples have altered French society, so have they moved historians to reformulate the subjects of their research. The hottest topics at the conference, as in much recent historiography—especially Anglophone historiography—were immigration, Islam, colonialism, empire, and, as this volume attests, the ways these new subjects of research have redefined the nature and meaning of the Republics and republicanism in France. Articles newly commissioned for this volume reflect these historiographical trends, including those, for example, by Herrick Chapman ("The State"), Alice L. Conklin ("The Civilizing Mission"), Joan Wallach Scott ("Parité"), Mary Dewhurst Lewis ("Immigration"), and John R. Bowen ("The Republic and the Veil").

Together, these articles, plus some of those reprinted from the original *Dictionnaire* (e.g., Emmanuelle Saada's "The Republic and the *Indigènes*" and Cécile Laborde's "Citizenship"), depart significantly from the ways the French Republics and republicanism had long been portrayed. According to what became an orthodox view, French republicanism produced a form of government and society in which each individual enjoyed full equality in the eyes of a democratic state uninterested in its citizens' particularistic distinctions—their religion, ethnicity, gender, and social class. If in practice, the French Republics sometimes treated their citizens unequally, favoring employers over workers, Catholics over Jews, men over women, whites over nonwhites, the reasons—so the Republic's advocates and historians long maintained—had to do with the flawed human beings in charge at a particular moment, not with the institutions of the Republics themselves. If leaders had consistently lived up to the Republic's ideals, such problems would have been rare. Solutions, then, turned on better education, better leadership, better media, and the like. The "republican model" needed to be intelligently and consistently applied; it required no major overhaul.

This perspective is less persuasive to the current generation of historians in France than it was to its elders. To historians trained in the United States, its persuasive force is virtually nil. Which is not to say American scholars think the French Republics have done more harm than good or that their ideals should not be taken seriously. When compared to other kinds of regimes, the French Republics look good to most U.S.-trained historians. But Americans have grown up in a society whose republic accepted slavery and racial discrimination, gave religion—especially Protestantism—a prominent role in public discourse, and recognized group identities as much as individual ones. The current generation of U.S. historians seldom idealizes its republic—though many of them doubtless idealize other aspects of the American experience—so it is unsurprising that they do not overestimate the qualities of the French Republic. For that reason, many of the articles in this book cast a critical eye on the French Republic's attitudes toward and treatment of women, immigrants, people of color, Muslims, and others. But our authors do not sing a one-note samba of criticism—far from it. Steven Englund ("Antisemitism, Judeophobia, and the Republic"), for example, finds Third Republic–era anti-Semitism mild in comparison with its counterpart in Austria and Germany. Philip Nord judges the Third Republic relatively open and egalitarian in relation to other contemporary Western governments, though he is fully aware of the French regime's flaws. Lloyd Kramer ("Times of Exile and Immigration") examines the qualities that enabled republican France to attract generations of political and intellectual refugees unwelcome in their own countries. Stéphane Gerson ("The Local") depicts the vitality of local life, while Jerrold Seigel ("Intellectuals and the Republic") pays homage, not uncritically, to the French Republic's engaged men of letters.

If U.S. historians of France have beamed their scholarly spotlight on French republicanism, the interest is mainly intellectual and professional. It is what they study, not what they live. Americans are for the most part uninvolved personally and directly in the raging debates of present-day France, debates over whether and how to integrate Muslims into French society and a republican political order supposedly blind to religious, ethnic, and racial particularities. Nor are they directly involved in discussions about whether Islamic girls and women should be allowed to don headscarves in school, wear the burqa in public, refuse treatment by male doctors, and swim in pools segregated by sex. They do not, in general, weigh in about how to remember and acknowledge the legacy of slavery and the claims of French citizens whose ancestors had been enslaved. Nor do they engage in arguments over how to talk about race and racism in a society whose official ideology denies the salience of racial distinctions and even forbids the publication of statistics that classify people and phenomena according to race. Americans' distance—geographical, emotional, electoral, and economic—from these controversies makes dispassionate reflection somewhat easier for them than for their French colleagues. But it also deprives them of the immediacy of understanding and passionate engagement that can nurture scholarship at its best. French historians who specialize in contemporary history (1789 to the present) or present-day history (*histoire du temps présent,* 1945 to 2011) do so from the perspective of citizens of a republic whose values, practices, histories, and memories are the subject of rancorous debate. Sometimes such debate can narrow scholarship by reinforcing political correctness, ideological partiality, and an inclination to read present-day concerns onto the past. But occasionally it can launch historical inquiry into once-invisible realms.

If U.S. historians of France are shielded from French society's intense questioning of republicanism, the better to engage with it intellectually, they are also distanced from any consideration of republicanism at home. Although in the 1980s and 1990s, specialists in U.S. history debated the meaning and nature of republicanism in eighteenth- and nineteenth-century America, this debate—and even the concept itself—had a limited "career," as Daniel T. Rogers put it in an influential article in the *Journal of American History* in 1992. That is, both the debate and the concept of republicanism as a frame for historical analysis experienced a rise, a period of maturity, and, like any individual's career, ended in retirement. It is not that U.S. historians have abandoned the concept of republicanism, but rather that term's ubiquity in 1980s scholarship made its use so promiscuous that its apparent utility ultimately disappeared. Republicanism, as Rogers writes, had been applied to so many historical phenomena, used to tie neatly together so many analytical loose ends, that it finally resembled a concept like "modernization": it came to mean too much and hence too little.

If historians of the United States no longer turn to the concept of republicanism in framing their work, for U.S. historians of other countries, as for ordinary citizens, republicanism as a political philosophy, set of practices, and collection of ideals has never—at least in recent memory—possessed much relevance, or even meaning. There is no contemporary public debate about republicanism, and the term is mentioned only in relation to the ideology of one of the country's two dominant political parties. But the ideas and ideals of present-day members of the Republican Party or GOP bear little relation to the eighteenth-century notions of "virtue," "disinterestedness," and "commercial corruption" that scholars of American republicanism—J.G.A. Pocock, Gordon Wood, John Murrin—had in mind. The contemporary GOP resembles even less the leftish workingmen's republicanism that once figured prominently in the books of U.S. social historians who came of age in the 1980s (e.g., Sean Wilenz, Daniel Walkowitz, and Jonathan Prude).

Republicanism in the United States is so much taken for granted that there is little need to mention it. Americans have, after all, never known any other kind of regime, and only rarely have they felt the need to call it into question. Instead, different political formations and ideologies have appropriated republicanism for their own purposes—Populists to laud the "general interest" as opposed to the "selfish machinations' of corporate titans; Southerners to defend their "agrarian and pastoral" landscape against the "corruption" and "extravagance" of the industrial world of the North.

The French situation could not be more different. There, republicanism has had to fight a great many uphill battles, battles against Jacobin and Bonapartist dictatorship, monarchical restorations, Catholic reaction, and the proto-fascism of the Vichy regime. Each of France's first four Republics (1792–99, 1848–52, 1870–1940, 1945–58) found itself menaced and ultimately overthrown by antirepublican forces.* And even the Fifth Republic (1958 to the present) has faced two existential threats, the first early on when rebellious French military leaders in Algiers threatened a coup d'état against Paris, and later, in May 1968, when a loose coalition of workers and students brought the country to a halt. The radicals of '68 rejected both Charles de Gaulle's muscular Republic and François Mitterrand's proposed restoration of a more traditional parliamentary-style regime. The irony of France's current situation, as Martin Schain suggests below ("The Fifth Republic"), is that never before has a French Republic appeared so institutionally stable while facing so many challenges to its commanding ideologies and practices: challenges from xenophobes opposed to republican France's relatively open borders; from populists antagonistic to European integration and U.S.-led globalization; and from multiculturalists eager to press the claims of group identity against the abstract individualism of the republican state.

For U.S.-trained historians and others in the English-speaking world, this is heady stuff and a welcome, if often disturbing, respite from the stale American debate between liberals and conservatives, between advocates of an activist state and those who want government "off our backs." If our ingrained cultural liberalism can make it difficult to understand the French state and society's limited tolerance for religious individualism, group rights, and hyphenated identities,

---

* Even though the Fourth Republic was immediately succeeded by the Fifth, the former had collapsed in the wake of a threatened military putsch, and though the ascension of Charles de Gaulle in 1958 assumed a veneer of republican legality, it was only a veneer.

U.S.- and British-informed experiences can give us insight into those very things—especially as we thicken and deepen a transatlantic and cross-Channel discussion with French colleagues like those represented in this book. Distinctive as the Anglo-American viewpoints often are, they are not necessarily opposed to those of our French counterparts. As readers will see, the American Philip Nord ("The Third Republic") is closer in perspective to the Frenchman Stéphane Audoin-Rouzeau ("War and the Republic") than to U.S. colleagues like John R. Bowen ("The Republic and the Veil") and Bonnie G. Smith ("Gender and the Republic"). The latter two are more skeptical of the accomplishments of the French Republics than is either Nord or Audoin-Rouzeau. Likewise, the French sociologist Éric Fassin ("Order and Disorder in the Family") agrees more with Smith than either do with the British historian Jeremy Jennings ("Liberty," "Equality," "Universalism") or with the American Steven Englund. Complicating our mix is the geographical dispersal of our contributors. The French scholars Emmanuelle Saada and Frédéric Viguier live and work in the United States, while the Americans Green and Englund teach in Paris, and the French political theorist Cécile Laborde in London. The Frenchmen Fassin and François Weil are specialists on U.S. society and history, while Berenson has taken to British and American history, in addition to French.

These complexities of ideas, method, and location mean, among other things, that there is no single way to read this book. Some will want to approach it in order, proceeding in part 1 from the Enlightenment through the five French Republics (and their twentieth-century wartime interludes) before delving into the more pointed matters of "Principles and Values" in part 2 and "Dilemmas and Debates" in part 3. Others will want to read the book thematically, following, for example, the question of universalism through the chapters by Jennings, Saada, Bowen, Conklin, and Scott. Still others will know the work of some of the scholars represented here and want to zero in on them. Whatever order they choose, readers will find an innovative blend of Anglophone and Francophone scholarship and an international history of the French Republics and republicanism with implications that transcend the geographical and intellectual boundaries of France.

Part I

TIME AND HISTORY

1

The Enlightenment

Johnson Kent Wright

Alphonse Aulard once claimed that the French Revolution could not be said to have had *intellectual* origins at all, for an obvious reason: prior to 1791, there were simply no republicans in France. Rhetorical exaggeration aside, this captures what is still perhaps the conventional wisdom about the fate of republicanism and republican ideas during the Enlightenment. On this view, the leading French *philosophes*—Montesquieu, Voltaire, the Encyclopédistes, Holbach, the Physiocrats alike—agreed that republican government was a thing of the past, rendered obsolete by both the sheer size of modern states and the complexity of their functions. Far from any kind of republic, the ideal modern regime, for the Enlightenment, was one form or another of "enlightened despotism"—which, in practice, amounted to a pragmatic compromise with absolute monarchy, whose immanent demise in France none of the *philosophes* foresaw. The one possible exception, Jean-Jacques Rousseau, proves the rule. For it was precisely Rousseau's nostalgic republicanism, nurtured by his Genevan background, that led to his ostracism from the Enlightenment; nor did Rousseau himself ever dream that the Bourbon Monarchy might one day give way to a republic. For all these reasons, Aulard maintained that the advent of the First Republic thus owed nothing to the Enlightenment, for which it would have been anathema. Instead, the Republic's arrival resulted from the abject failure in 1789 of the constitutional monarchy, a form of government far closer to what the *philosophes* might have approved.

If such remains the conventional view of the Enlightenment attitude toward republics and republicanism, recent scholarship has made it look increasingly inaccurate. Close inspection of the real record of eighteenth-century political thought suggests that the notion of a consensual royalism on the part of the *philosophes*—much less advocacy of "enlightened despotism"—is largely a myth, and that opinion about republicanism was far more various, and sympathetic, that the above account suggests. Moreover, what is at stake in considering eighteenth-century ideas about republicanism is not merely the issue of political legitimacy or advocacy—how many or few "republicans" there were in France before Varennes—but also the very *definition* of the term. For it now seems clear that the Enlightenment represented the great transitional epoch in the long history of republicanism in the West—the moment when an old and august tradition of political thought underwent a fascinating process of *modernization,* with dramatic historical consequences. Indeed, contrary to what is suggested by Aulard's formula, a grasp of both the variety and the development of republican ideas in the Enlightenment seems crucial for understanding the fate of the great experiments in constitution making during the Revolution.

A century earlier, when the Bourbon Monarchy was at the peak of its international power and prestige, republicanism naturally had a negligible presence in France. In fact, this was likely the moment of lowest ebb for the entire early modern tradition of European republicanism. As a political ideology rooted in Greco-Roman political writing and history, republicanism first emerged in late medieval and Renaissance Italy, where it served to legitimate the resistance of the northern Italian city-states to emperors and popes alike. The sixteenth century saw its diffusion around much of the rest of Europe, as part of the ideological arsenal deployed against absolute monarchy in the epoch of its ascendancy. By the end of the seventeenth, the upheavals that had overthrown Spanish and English absolutism had generated particularly radical versions of republicanism in the United Provinces and England—which, with the older Italian tradition, became the major sources for the revival of republicanism in the eighteenth century. At the same time, the Dutch Revolt (1568–1648) and the English Revolution (1640–60) failed to create stable republics—the latter, spectacularly so. English republicanism, in particular, remained essentially an ideology of protest in the face of restoration, typically utopian or nostalgic in character. Much the same could be said of the far fainter echoes of republican ideas heard in France late in the reign of Louis XIV (1638–1715). Not surprisingly, the earliest premonitions of a republican revival in France were to be found among the Sun King's *aristocratic* critics intent on defending the lost "liberty" of the French nobility. These dissidents included Fénelon, whose enormously influential *Telemachus* used the device of a "virtuous" kingship from classical antiquity to criticize the regime of Versailles. Equally striking was the comte de Boulainvilliers, whose historical writings made the scandalous case that the "feudal government" established by the Frankish nobility in their original conquest of Gaul was the realm's only legitimate form of rule—"feudal government" understood as a kind of aristocratic republic, expressly assimilated to the "mixed governments," monarchical and noble, of classical antiquity and the English Commonwealth tradition.

If he was a kind of classical republican, Boulainvilliers was manifestly not an Enlightenment thinker. There is no doubt as to who was responsible for launching the Enlightenment debate about republics. As his most authoritative American commentator, Judith Shklar, has argued, "Montesquieu did for the latter half of the eighteenth century what Machiavelli had done for his century: he defined the terms in which republicanism was to be discussed." The centerpiece of *On the Spirit of the Laws* (1748) was a universal taxonomy of three forms of government: republican, monarchical, and despotic; there were, in turn, two forms of republic, determined by the location of sovereign power: aristocratic or democratic. Both forms were animated by the same affective "principle," *virtue* or "love of the republic" (specified as "love of equality" in democracies, and a "spirit of moderation" in aristocracies). Indeed, it was Montesquieu who did more than anyone else in the eighteenth century to establish the equation between republicanism and civic "virtue." This is not to say that Montesquieu was in any sense an advocate of republicanism. On the contrary, while *On the Spirit of the Laws* offered no theory of historical development as such, there were numerous hints in the book that Montesquieu regarded republican government as having been superseded by the rise of large, commercially oriented monarchies in modern Europe, which were governed by a different "principle" altogether—that of "honor."

This was not, however, quite the last word on republicanism in *On the Spirit of the Laws*. There were two other occasions in the text in which one of the central tokens of early-modern republican thought—the idea of a "mixed government"—made very memorable appearances. One was the famous analysis in Book 11 of what Montesquieu regarded as the uniquely libertarian constitution of England, which superimposed a novel doctrine of the "separation of powers" on a more traditional conception of "mixed government." Elsewhere in the book, Montesquieu described England as a "republic disguised as a monarchy." But even more striking was the philosopher's account of modern monarchy itself, whose "nature" was founded on a set of "intermediary, subordinate, and dependent powers" firmly rooted in institutional structures (the clergy and *parlements*), and a powerful noble class completely missing in despotic governments. As Montesquieu wrote, "the most natural intermediate and subordinate power is that of the nobility. It enters, in a sense, into the essence of monarchy, whose fundamental maxim is, *no monarchy, no nobility; no nobility, no monarchy*." Montesquieu stopped short of assimilating modern monarchy to "mixed government" altogether. But there is no doubt that a republican-style "mixture" was central to his conception of the idealized monarchy of his age.

On the Spirit of the Laws thus bestowed a rich but ambiguous publicity on thinking about republics. Montesquieu offered a vivid portrait of republican government proper, even as he cast doubt on its contemporary relevance. Meanwhile, the shadow of a republican-style "mixture" of governmental forms fell across both his analysis of the English constitution and modern monarchy itself. These themes then set the agenda for a second phase in the development of republican ideas, as the early Enlightenment passed into its maturity. Here it is possible to discern a sharp divergence of opinion, not so much over the legitimacy or even the definition of republican government—Montesquieu's analysis remained authoritative throughout this period—as over the contemporary relevance of each. In other words, the High Enlightenment saw something like a reenactment of the decisive intellectual contest of half a century earlier, the famous "Quarrel of the Ancients and the Moderns." The "moderns," in this instance, were those thinkers inclined to render explicit the historical analysis largely buried in Montesquieu's work. In doing so, they came close to rejecting Montesquieu's own contemporary appropriations of republican ideas. Voltaire, the Physiocrats, and those who wrote on republics and republicanism for the *Encyclopedia* were all "modernists," in this sense. The *Encyclopedia* articles—Jaucourt's "République," in particular—were probably the most influential statements of the case for the historical obsolescence of republican government, above all on the grounds of the sheer size of modern states. Similar arguments could be found in writings of Voltaire, Quesnay, and Mercier de la Rivière, each of whom, meanwhile, wrote scathing critiques of the sort of governmental "mixtures" associated with *On the Spirit of the Laws*. At the same time, it is important not to exaggerate the antirepublicanism, as it were, of these or any other "modernist" thinkers of the High Enlightenment. Neither Voltaire, the Encyclopédistes, nor the Physiocrats were anything like conventional apologists for absolute monarchy. Indeed, the normative basis for the political thought of all three turned on conceptions of popular sovereignty derived from contemporary social contract theory—very explicitly so in the case of Diderot's own articles on politics in the *Encyclopedia,* and even the Physiocratic theory of "legal despotism." Moreover, none of these was immune to at least some of the attractions of republicanism. Voltaire could, on occasion, give it the warmest appreciation, as in his famous "Republican Ideas" of 1765, written as the result of immersion in Genevan affairs. Diderot may well have ended his intellectual career fully convinced of the possibility of creating a French republic. And in the late 1770s and 1780s, Physiocratic political economy, in a classic illustration of unintended intellectual consequences, provided the seedbed for the emergence of the first fully modern conceptions of republicanism in France.

In the meantime, however, these "modernists" had long since been answered by a formidable set of "ancients" no less indebted to Montesquieu, thinkers profoundly convinced of the contemporary relevance of his analysis of republicanism. Among these, Rousseau might be thought to need no introduction. In fact, it is only recently that scholars have begun fully to explore his relation to the wider traditions of early-modern republicanism. This delay, otherwise inexplicable, doubtless has something to do with the position of Rousseau's thought at the crossroads of both of the major progressive political traditions of his time, traditions whose concepts and values he blended in a unique and unprecedented way.

On the one hand, Rousseau was perhaps the most original eighteenth-century theorist of "natural rights," a modernist preoccupation little indebted to ancient republicanism. His first major work, the *Discourse on the Origins of Inequality* proceeded via a stringent critique of earlier contract theorists—Pufendorf, Locke, and Hobbes above all. Later, his influential *On the Social Contract* offered what was in effect the first genuinely democratic contract theory, equating political legitimacy with high levels of egalitarian participation in public decision-making. On the other hand, there is no doubt about Rousseau's republican credentials, born of a nostalgic attachment to his native Geneva and a profound admiration for the city-state civilization of classical antiquity. He had made his debut as a thinker with a passionate attack on the corrosive effects of the modern arts and sciences on public virtue and private morality, doing so in the name of "Spartan," republican simplicity; the *Discourse on the Origins of Inequality* depicted human history as a Polybian nightmare, chronicling the inexorable decline of forms of government into the embrace of "despotism"; the democratic republic outlined in *On the Social Contract* was inspired by classical example from top to bottom. The theoretical linchpin of the whole system, which made possible this unique blend of natural-rights theory and classical republicanism, was the conceptual innovation of the "general will," which required not just that laws be "general" in their application—a principle of equality before the law—but also in their source, which amounted to one of popular, participatory sovereignty.

Rousseau was without question the most original republican thinker of the High Enlightenment, but he was far from alone. The same years saw the mature work of the abbé Gabriel Bonnot de Mably, whose thought reflected a far more traditional version of republicanism than that of Rousseau. The elder brother of the philosopher Condillac, Mably had begun as a royalist, but then reversed course, producing philosophical histories of ancient Greece and Rome, holding up the "mixed governments" of an egalitarian Sparta and republican Rome as the acme of political achievement. In 1758, at the height of clashes between the court and the *parlements* in France, Mably's republicanism found a particularly radical expression. *On the Rights and Duties of the Citizen,* a text prudently left unpublished for thirty years, imagines a whispered conversation between an English Commonwealth man—a composite of Harrington and Sidney—and a French proselyte, in which the former first expounds a theory of popular sovereignty and resistance to monarchy, and then presents a scenario for a gentle revolution (*révolution ménagée*) in France: parliamentary resistance would be used as a lever to secure a convocation of the Estates General, which would then preside over a transition from absolute to constitutional monarchy, conceived of as a species of "mixed government." In other work of the same period, Mably advanced a neo-Stoic theory of political "virtues" and schemes for the redistribution of property that would later earn him a reputation as a proto-communist. His optimism, however, about the prospects for the successful overthrow of absolute monarchy in France did not last. By the time he completed his mature masterpiece, *Observations on the History of France,* in 1771, Mably had decided that the trajectory of French history revealed the impossibility of any escape from the era's decadent despotism. But the event that sealed Mably's ultimate pessimism—Chancellor Maupeou's "coup," which temporarily stripped French *parlements* of their power—seemed altogether different to other thinkers of similar political temper. Among these was the young Bordeaux lawyer Guillaume-Josephe Saige, who produced one of the most radical pamphlets to emerge from the Maupeou controversy. Saige's *Catechism of the Citizen* joined Rousseau's theory of the "general will" to Mably's notion of a de facto French constitution that made the French king and people mutually dependent. This mélange yielded a hybrid form of republicanism destined to a play a crucial role during the "pre-Revolution," some fourteen years later.

These developments, important as they were, did not constitute the Enlightenment's final word on republicanism. The last two decades before the Revolution saw a third phase in the development of republican ideas, unexpectedly producing a synthesis of the "modernist" and "ancient" positions described above. Two changes in the wider historical context made this synthesis possible. One was the rapidly declining fortunes of the Bourbon Monarchy in the last third of the century. Defeat in the Seven Years' War (1756–63) led to the fiscal crisis that eventually proved fatal to the absolutist state; the Maupeou "coup" of 1770–71 proved a public relations disaster, conjuring up the silhouette of an oppositional "patriot" party; and efforts at fiscal and administrative reform from above all ended in failure—most strikingly, those proposed by the king's controller-general A. R. J Turgot in the mid-seventies. Growing disaffection with the Bourbon Monarchy was then complemented by an external event, the success of the American Revolution, which of course provided a sudden and convincing demonstration of the relevance of republicanism to the modern European world. The famous French debate over the American state constitutions amounted to a political education in the realities of what might be termed "actually existing republicanism."

The result of this altered context was that the late Enlightenment in France saw the emergence of what can properly be called modern republicanism, as opposed to the classical versions sponsored by Rousseau or Mably. Premonitions of modern republicanism, in this sense, can be found in the later political thought of major Enlightenment figures such as Diderot and Holbach, both deeply impressed by the American Revolution, which to them demonstrated the feasibility of creating large-scale republics. But modern republicanism found its fullest expression in writings of the 1780s by a younger generation of *philosophes,* most of whom were destined to play leading roles in the Revolution: Roederer, Clavière, Sieyès, and Condorcet. For all the differences among these figures, their thought now tended to converge on two fundamental assumptions, both of which up-ended earlier views about republics. First, the argument against republics based on the size of modern states now disappeared once and for all: these new writ-ings abounded with theories of political representation, which became a central token of all modern understandings of republicanism. Second, the belief in the incompatibility of the ideals of republican government and the realities of modern economic life, still a key feature of the "classical" outlook of Rousseau or Mably, vanished as well. On the contrary, for Roederer, Clavière, Sieyès, and eventually Condorcet—all students of modern (liberal) political economy—a republican re-gime guaranteeing high levels of participatory self-rule, and buttressed by a Rous-seauian politics of civic "virtue," was the perfect and necessary complement to a market economy. A coherent, cumulative tradition of modern republicanism—much less its reality—was still a long way off, of course. But its shape could al-ready be glimpsed by the start of the prerevolutionary turmoil in 1786.

Contrary to an old legend, then, there was no lack of republicans or republi-can ideas in France before 1791 or even 1789. On the eve of the Enlightenment, republicanism of the standard early-modern kind was indeed virtually missing in France, its echoes confined to the outer reaches of the disaffected nobility. The early Enlightenment, and especially Montesquieu's *On the Spirit of the Laws,* considerably amplified these echoes, placing republicanism at the center of po-litical debate. The High Enlightenment that followed saw a striking divergence of opinion in which one current of thought expressed doubts about the relevance of republican government to the vast, commercial polities of the modern world, while another presented a French variant of classical republicanism, linked to the radical natural-rights tradition and offering a revolutionary understanding of French history. Finally, as the Bourbon Monarchy began to stumble toward revolution, the late Enlightenment produced the first programs of modern repub-licanism, uniting a thoroughly Rousseauian theory of political legitimacy with a fully modern understanding of political economy. The traditional assumption that France was lacking in models of republican government in 1791 can thus be set aside, or even reversed. If anything, the Enlightenment bequeathed too many such models. Each conception of republicanism considered above—aristocratic, classical, modern—was destined to a play major role on the revolutionary stage. Together, they produced a drama that was itself only the prologue to the long and tumultuous history of republican government in modern France.

References

Baker, Keith Michael. "Transformations of Classical Republicanism in Eighteenth-Century France." *Journal of Modern History* 73 (2001): 32–53.

Belissa, Marc, Yannick Bosc, and Florence Gauthier, eds. *Républicanismes et droit naturel: Des humanistes aux Révolutions des droits de l'homme et du citoyen.* Paris: Editions Kimé, 2009.

Furet, François, and Mona Ozouf, eds. *Le siècle de l'avènement républicain.* Paris: Gallimard, 1992.

Linton, Marisa. *The Politics of Virtue in Eighteenth-Century France.* Basingstoke, UK: Palgrave, 2001.

Mossé, Claude. *L'antiquité et la Révolution française.* Paris: Albin Michel, 1989.

Nelson, Eric. *The Greek Tradition in Republican Thought.* Cambridge, UK: Cambridge University Press, 2004.

Rosenblatt, Helena. *Jean-Jacques Rousseau and Geneva: From the First Discourse to the Social Contract, 1749–62.* Cambridge, UK: Cambridge University Press, 1997.

Shklar, Judith N. "Montesquieu and the New Republicanism." In Gisela Bok, Quentin Skinner, and Maurizio Viroli, eds., *Machiavelli and Republicanism,* 265–79. Cambridge, UK: Cambridge University Press, 1990.

Sonenscher, Michael. *Sans-Culottes: An Eighteenth-Century Emblem in the French Revolution.* Princeton, NJ: Princeton University Press, 2009.

Whatmore, Richard. *Republicanism and the French Revolution: An Intellectual History of Jean-Baptiste Say's Political Economy.* New York: Oxford University Press, 2000.

2

The First Republic

Patrice Gueniffey

Translated by Arthur Goldhammer

The four Republics that France has known since 1848 have one thing in common: each devised a constitution at the outset and abided by that constitution for the duration of the regime. In this respect the First Republic stands out. Even if we discount the many discontinuities that marked its history, it encompassed at least three distinct political forms: a parliamentary dictatorship (1792–95); a limited-suffrage republic (1795–99); and a plebiscitary regime, inaugurated after Napoleon Bonaparte's coup d'état of 18 Brumaire (November 9, 1799). This coup led to the installation of Bonaparte as life consul in 1802 and thus laid the groundwork for another form of government, a new hereditary monarchy. Still, the imperial regime (1804–14) should perhaps be included in the history of the First Republic, because Napoleon never denied that his Empire was rooted in the Revolution. So we have at least three regimes and four constitutions: 1793, 1795, 1799, 1802, and perhaps 1804 (First Empire) and 1815 (the Hundred Days).

The First Republic was not a distinct, coherent system of government but a historical process whose chronological beginning and end are not well defined. Indeed, the Republic was never proclaimed and never abolished. When the National Convention met for the first time on September 21, 1792, it formally abolished the monarchy but said nothing about the nature of the regime that was to succeed it. Although the Republic already existed in fact, it made its formal entrance quietly a few days later when public laws began to be promulgated in the name of the "French Republic." Much the same was true of the First Republic's close. Long after it had become a ghost of its former self, it still existed officially: the *sénatus-consulte* of 14 Thermidor, Year X (August 2, 1802), stipulated that Bonaparte was appointed for life to the position of First Consul of the Republic, and the following *sénatus-consulte* of 28 Floréal, Year XII (May 18, 1804), entrusted "the Government of the Republic" to an emperor. In reality, the history of the First Republic did not end until 1814, with the return of the Bourbons.

The fall of Louis XVI began the history of the Republic, and the accession to the throne of Louis XVIII ended it.

⚘

If it is difficult to define the precise limits of the First Republic, it is no doubt because of the uncertainty that surrounded concepts such as "republic" and "republicanism" at the time. Claude Nicolet rightly referred to these terms as "wandering words." According to sixteenth-century theorists, the term "republic" could be applied to any organized state, regardless of its form, republican or monarchical, elective or hereditary. The philosophers of the eighteenth century introduced nothing fundamentally new. To be sure, Rousseau had limited the use of the word to regimes "guided by the general will" (in which the people themselves vote on the laws), but this condition implied nothing about the form of the government responsible for enforcing the law: officials could be either elected or hereditary, and Rousseau wrote that if the general will reigned, then "monarchy itself is republican." Montesquieu did not move much beyond this classical definition, using the word "republic" to refer to any state in which leaders govern not as they please "but in keeping with fixed and settled laws."

Historically, republicanism belonged to the past. It lived on in memory only, in the heroic examples of Greece and Rome as well as that of the "leveling" and regicide English Revolution of the seventeenth century. Sometimes this memory was magnificent but remote, while at other times it could be harshly critical; in both cases, it remained a dead letter except for a few scattered places such as Italy and Switzerland, whose constricted oligarchies were hardly likely to set imaginations on fire.

In 1776, American independence rescued the republican idea from the recesses of memory and the pages of philosophical treatises. History seemed to rise from its ashes. "Americanophilia" became the passion of the age, proof of the rebirth of republicanism. The European elites of the late eighteenth century were fascinated by this new nation, apparently delivered from the burden of history and prejudice, untainted by privilege, and relatively egalitarian. Americans, it seemed, had applied to a vast virgin territory theories about the rational foundation of societies. It was as if one had traveled back in time to witness the birth of Athens or Sparta. As imagined through visions of America, however, the essence of the republic lay not so much in its institutions as in its manners: austere, rustic, and egalitarian. The political system, too obviously based on that of England, was not particularly attractive to continental Europeans, especially after the adoption of the federal constitution of 1787, whose representative system, bicameral legislature, and strong executive seemed to threaten precisely that which had aroused such admiration and enthusiasm: a society that governed itself through its manners.

Although many people admired the rebirth of the republican model in America, no one seriously imagined that this exceptional experiment could be duplicated in Europe. The New World was also *another world,* as remote as antiquity. It was not just an ocean that separated the Europe of privileges and kings from democratic America; it was the depth of history. An abyss opened up between the two continents.

᧩

That abyss was nevertheless overcome; the monarchy itself helped fill it in. Had the royal family not attempted to flee on June 21, 1791, the Revolution would have remained what it had been since 1789: republican by reason and royalist by sentiment.

The advent of the Republic does not in fact date from August 10, 1792. The French Revolution was republican from the first: the proclamation of equal rights, the collective appropriation of sovereignty, and the establishment of representative powers signaled the birth of a new order in which, in the words of one contemporary, "the constitution was no longer in the monarchy, but the monarchy in the constitution." To be sure, the king remained in place, and most people remained attached to him, but there was a vast difference between the old system, in which all power was vested in the will of a single individual, and the new regime, in which the law made by all was enforced by a king subject to the national will. Could the word "king" still be applied to an official who was in fact nothing more than a sort of hereditary president of the Republic?

The crisis that erupted in June 1791 did not bring forth legions of republicans. The majority still wanted to maintain the monarchy after the flight of the royal family, but this was now a choice dictated by reason rather than affection. The spell had been broken. The profound trauma inflicted by the flight to Varennes is a good indicator of this: republicanism appeared first as a passion, fed by bitter feelings of abandonment and treason. The hatred of the monarchy was obsessive, but there was as yet no alternative political model. "No more king!" screamed the republicans of 1792. Yes, but what was to be put in his place? No one was in a position to answer this question, since everyone had taken to heart the lesson of the century: a republic was impossible to establish in a large country.

The Republic began as a passion, not a project—all the more so because the insurrection of August 10, 1792, which overthrew the monarchy, also toppled the institutions that had been in place for the past three years. The work of the Constituent Assembly—Enlightenment philosophy translated into law—vanished into the black hole of "the ancien régime." This sealed the fate of the two sources of legitimacy that the Constituents had contrived to yoke together in spite of themselves: the old, monarchical legitimacy and the new, republican one. True, the king of 1789 was no longer the absolute monarch of the Old Regime, but the change had been carried out with a flesh-and-blood king inherited from the past, who remained the sacred incarnation of sovereignty. It was easier to reduce his prerogatives than to destroy his symbolic authority. The Revolution had created a bicephalic order, which linked two things: a faceless figuration of national unity in a representative body whose legitimacy stemmed from popular suffrage, and a hereditary monarch who personified national continuity and whose legitimacy derived from a dynastic "election" shrouded in the mists of time.

The France of 1789 was thus a body with two heads. The France of 1792 was a headless body. In the interval between the fall of the monarchy and the beheading of the monarch (on January 21, 1793), the principle that had for centuries made it possible to unite so many diverse peoples and reconcile so many contrary interests had disappeared, and with it went the principle that was supposed to ensure the cohesiveness of the new society of individuals that the Revolution had brought into being. The nation suddenly dissolved.

The first thing to go was the government, and, even more, the very idea of law. By throwing out the Constitution of 1791, the insurgents of August 10 rejected not only the existing constitution but also the principle on which any future constitution would have to rest. They destroyed the idea that the law can compel and can be changed only by legal means. They substituted the rule of force for the rule of law, and minority dictatorship for government by the majority. To overthrow the constitution by violent means was in effect to devalue any future legality and establish the principle that the will of the people, or at any rate of those who claim to speak in the name of the people, is superior to any contract or commitment. After August 10, there could be no willing obedience, no voluntary submission to orders. From then on, there was no procedure for attributing power, which, no longer embodied in institutions, now belonged to whoever could convincingly claim to be the instrument of revolutionary legitimacy. To make matters worse, now that the monarchy had been toppled, *all power* was up for grabs. As long as the king remained the head of state, any appropriation of power was bound to remain incomplete. An inaccessible position of power remained at the top of the State, and this had the virtue of limiting ambitions and attenuating conflicts. After August 10, violence was unleashed by the collapse of legality together with the elimination of obstacles to ambition. Every party could aspire to gain complete power, yet the winner could no longer count on the protection of the law. Since all claims to legitimacy were now open to challenge, every faction felt it had no choice but to eliminate its rivals.

Violence was no less prevalent in the social sphere than in the political. Society dissolved along with the state that had formerly shaped its identity and maintained its cohesion. Everything that tended to create bonds among individuals fell to pieces. The collapse was all the more rapid because the violent destruction of the government made people think that the Republic would either mark a new beginning or end in failure. Hence it was necessary, they believed, to destroy everything in order to rebuild on a new foundation. Nothing was exempt: neither the most deeply rooted beliefs nor the most basic social formalities. Why prohibit formal dress, the use of the formal *vous,* or the terms "Monsieur" and "Madame" as modes of address unless it was to banish civilization judged as unjust and unequal and to reduce society to a pre-civil state of nature? These actions were a minor-key counterpoint of the de-Christianization policy and the adoption of the republican calendar with its ten-day weeks. This uprooting of all entrenched values had its moments of paroxysm: Lavoisier's murderers screamed in his face that the "Republic has no need of scientists," and the revolutionaries of Nantes allegedly executed their enemies by tying a naked man and naked woman together before drowning them in a ritual known as "republican marriage." Nothing that made man sociable and human—the stuff of which societies are built—was to be left standing. People had to be taken back to the pre-social stage, to "point zero," and from there they were to reinvent humanity. It was back to square one, as an entire nation hurled itself into the void, dreaming of disappearing into *nothingness.*

The memory of the Republic of 1793 long stood in reproach of the republican idea. But was it not rather the Revolution itself that was the real issue? If the history of the republic as *principle* began not in 1792 but in 1789, the history of the First Republic as *regime* did not begin in 1792 but rather in 1795. The fall of Robespierre on 9 Thermidor (July 27, 1794), followed by the gradual dismantling of the regime of public safety that he had created, allowed the Revolution to return to the task it had begun in 1789: to provide France with new institutions.

A new era seemed to have begun, a "happy era" in which, as the *rapporteur* of the new constitution would put it a year later, "we could cease to be gladiators of liberty and become its founders."

The Constitution of Year III (August 22, 1795) marked the restoration of the supremacy of law over force and will, including the will of the people. To be sure, the Constituents of 1789 already embraced this principle. But the Thermidorian Constitution was not yet another revolutionary constitution superimposed on those of 1791 and 1793. On the contrary, it showed the extent to which those who had survived the ordeal of the Terror had rejected many of the principles that they had held to be untouchable and even sacred after 1789, such as the importance of a unicameral legislature and a weak executive. By creating two legislative chambers and a strong executive—known as the Directory—they repudiated the logic that had led to a concentration of sovereign power in a single omnipotent assembly. For the first time, the two problems of legitimacy and liberty were seen as distinct, and the concern was to find a way to arrange the powers of government so as to provide a guarantee against despotism. Having suffered through the unchecked exercise of a power that was supposed to emanate from the people, the revolutionaries let go of the illusion, of which 1793 had marked the culmination, that it was possible to establish a perfectly transparent government whose interests and goals would coincide perfectly with those of the society from which it emanated. Only after the Terror did they discover that citizens needed to be protected *from* government, even from a government of the people, rather than protected *by* a government supposedly of the people.

Of course the policies of the Thermidorian regime were a long way from reflecting its principles. Its history began on a sour note (the "two-thirds" decree, which restricted the right to vote in order to ensure that the new institutions would be controlled by former members of the Convention) and ended suddenly on 18 Fructidor, Year V (September 4, 1797), when the Directory, unable to prevent voters from repudiating the government, canceled the result of recent legislative elections. Then, with the army's support, the Directory deported several dozen elected officials: the First Republic had lasted twenty months.

There were few defenders of the emergency measures that the Directory adopted early on, thereby condemning itself to continue to rely on them until its final collapse. And the Conventionals' thirst for power and corrupt ways did not argue in their favor. But that is not the essence of the matter. They had established a Republic that inevitably depended on free elections, but it was also a Republic that faced, because of memories of the Terror, a growing number of enemies now free to express themselves because restrictions on freedom of speech had in fact been loosened. The institutions were republican; the majority of the French was not, or in any event, no longer. The regime had lost the consensus its institutions needed to fulfill their functions. These institutions could not survive without resorting to force, which both destroyed their credibility and mortgaged their future. In fact, institutions alone could not resolve the problems of a society in which new divisions further complicated the cleavages that had been tearing it apart since 1789.

France in 1796 or 1798 was not a nation but a battlefield on which two legitimacies, two peoples, and two histories faced each other. The nation was elsewhere, on other battlefields: the battlefields of the war that since 1792 had pitted the armies of the Revolution against the armies of Europe. The war, waged at first to defend French soil, turned offensive in 1794, when it was transformed into a war of conquest in the name of "natural frontiers," themselves breached soon enough. Historians have seldom understood what it really meant to substitute the doctrine of natural frontiers for the Girondin dream of 1792 for universal emancipation. The idea of natural frontiers combined the quest for security with the pursuit of power; as such, it enabled revolutionary France to follow in the footsteps of the old royal diplomacy. And this is not just a metaphorical statement: the soldiers of the Revolution followed the same routes that royal armies had taken before them, routes marked by the sites of brilliant victories won by illustrious generals. In the end, the war deprived the ancien régime of the history from which it derived its legitimacy, and added it to the patrimony of the Revolution. The epic of conquest from Convention to Empire became the laboratory in which the nation, which politics had proved powerless to invent, came into being, developed its own mythology, and rejoined the two histories that 1789 had torn asunder.

That is why neither Bonaparte's seizure of power on 18 Brumaire (November 9, 1799) nor even the transformation of the consular regime into a quasi monarchy in 1802 marked the end of the First Republic. To be sure, if one defines a republic in terms of its institutions, by 1800 the regime was no more than a phantom. But it survived the disappearance of its forms. Its history continued in the irreversible triumph of the revolutionary principle of equality before the law. It also continued in the work that the Consulate and even the Empire did in the fields of law and institution-building. To be sure, these accomplishments were the culmination of reforms begun much earlier, in some cases even during the Convention, but they could be completed only by an authoritarian regime that shared the old hope of establishing a stable, rational state and that had ensured its safety from a scheming opposition. Last but not least, the history of the Republic continued in wars of conquest, which are so often attributed to Napoleon's personal ambition. "In my hands," the emperor very rightly said, "war was the antidote to anarchy." Not only did it preserve civil peace by exporting the bellicose passions that the Revolution had aroused and a decade of troubles had not entirely quenched, but it also continued and even accelerated (owing to the scope and magnificence of French victories) the national romance that portrayed France as enamored of both the Revolution and its previous history. In other words, France became a nation by making Europe dance to the sound of its cannon.

In 1814, Napoleonic Europe and the imperial regime crumbled, but when the Bourbons returned to the throne, it was less as victors than as vanquished, for they were obliged to submit to the new France that had previously driven them out and whose incomparable splendor remained in spite of military defeat. This time the Revolution was finished: the moderation of Louis XVIII after his return is the proof. To be sure, Napoleon's ultimate adventure, the episode of the Hundred Days of 1815, revived resentment and hatred. Even so, the republican principle had won. The abortive counterrevolution of 1815–16 demonstrated better than anything else that the ancien régime was no longer a credible alternative. The question of legitimacy had been resolved, but the question of republican institutions remained.

References

Aulard, François-Alphonse. *Histoire politique de la Révolution française: Origines et développement de la démocratie et de la République (1789–1804)*. Paris: Armand Colin, 1901.

Dupuy, Roger, and Marcel Morabito. *1795: Pour une République sans révolution*. Rennes: Presses Universitaires de Rennes, 1996.

Furet, François. *Revolutionary France (1770–1880)*. Translated by Antonia Nevill. Oxford, UK; Cambridge, MA: Blackwell, 1992.

Furet, François, and Ran Halévi. *La monarchie républicaine: La Constitution de 1791*. Paris: Fayard, 1996.

Nicolet, Claude. *L'Idée républicaine en France (1789–1924)*. Paris: Gallimard, 1982.

3

THE SECOND REPUBLIC

Edward Berenson

For more than a hundred years after the collapse of the Second Republic in 1852, historians treated the events of France's shortest republic as something of an embarrassment. The Revolution of 1848 and its aftermath marked a "turning point that didn't turn," an episode that revealed the French people's inability, at midcentury, to govern themselves. Tocqueville portrayed his country as veering wildly from revolution to reaction to revolution again, unable to find stable democratic institutions compatible with social order and private property. Karl Marx, also a keen observer of French society, condemned its elites for sacrificing political liberty on the altar of private property and for embracing Louis-Napoleon Bonaparte's promise to protect them from the Reds.

Views such as these held sway until the 1970s, when a new generation of historians led by Maurice Agulhon rejected this bleak view of the Second Republic. Rather than representing the failure of democracy and socialism, 1848 and its aftermath now became, as Agulhon put it, "the apprenticeship of the Republic." The years from 1848 to 1852 were, he wrote, a time when France's still largely rural population prepared for the republican and democratic regimes they have enjoyed, save for the brief interlude of Vichy, since the 1870s.

Although scholars no longer take a dim view of the Second Republic, they still see its brief four-year existence as emblematic of France's political volatility in the nineteenth century. The preceding two regimes had each lasted less than twenty years, and Louis-Philippe d'Orléans's "bourgeois" or July Monarchy (1830–48) was itself the product of revolution in July 1830, when a loose coalition of journalists, workers, and students overthrew Charles X, France's final Bourbon king. This revolutionary pedigree earned Louis-Philippe unflinching hostility on the Right, as Legitimists, or advocates of the deposed monarchy, refused to recognize his reign. As for the Left, its early hopes for a "republican monarchy" quickly gave way to disillusionment over political repression, the refusal to extend voting rights, and the apparent ascendancy of a parvenu elite. The regime faced major urban insurrections in 1831 and 1834, a series of attempted coups d'état, one by the future Napoleon III, and the alienation of workers and, eventually, sizable portions of the middle class.

Meanwhile, artists, intellectuals, and writers systematically undermined the regime. Honoré Daumier lampooned it with his devastating caricatures and cartoons, one showing Louis-Philippe's head shaped like a pear; historians taxed it as mundane in comparison to the recent revolutionary and Napoleonic past; religious thinkers condemned its crass bourgeois materialism and ill-treatment of working people; a new "feminism," a term coined in 1836, challenged its deafness to women's rights; republicans criticized its suppression of individual liberty and unwillingness to address social inequality; and socialists found it excessively individualistic, the handmaiden of bankers, industrialists, and financiers determined to keep workers in their place. When Louis-Philippe's long-serving minister, François Guizot, told critics to "enrich yourselves" to qualify for voting rights instead of agitating for electoral reform, his comment seemed to encapsulate all that was wrong with the regime. It fell in the wake of growing demands for political rights and a severe economic crisis (1846–47) that seemed to confirm the intellectuals' critiques.

On February 22, 1848, thousands of workers and students erupted in protest against a government decree forbidding a huge Parisian political banquet scheduled for that day. When Prime Minister Guizot called in the National Guard the next morning, the citizen militia refused to fire on the crowd. At this point, the king began to panic, dismissing Guizot and then trying without success to appoint a new prime minister capable of soothing the crowd. When the royal palace itself came under attack, Louis-Philippe gave up the fight. On February 24, just two days after the rioting began, he abdicated in favor of his nine-year-old grandson, whose reign lasted less than a day.

The people now occupying the streets of Paris wanted a republic, and on the evening of February 24, 1848, a group of left-wing deputies and journalists made their wish come true. Representatives of the two leading republican newspapers, the moderate *National* and the democratic *Réforme*, proclaimed a new provisional government carefully balanced between the two tendencies. Socialism received a nod in the persons of Louis Blanc, the theorist of collective ownership, and Alexandre Martin, an activist worker known simply as Albert.

In theory, all eleven members of the Provisional Government shared executive power equally. In reality, some were more equal than others. Destined to dominate the group were Lamartine at foreign affairs; Ledru-Rollin, minister of the interior; Crémieux, justice; and Marie, public works. The first two leaned left, the latter two right. Despite their disagreements on social questions, all four shared with the rest of the Provisional Government the conviction that all adult men should have the right to vote. They believed that "universal" suffrage would consecrate a new unity of democratic wills so strong as to overcome differences of class and status. If social divisions, in their view, evaporated into an ether of republican faith, questions of gender remained outside the political realm. A small number of women activists demanded full universal suffrage, not just manhood suffrage, but these early feminists were dismissed out of hand. When the journalist Jeanne Deroin campaigned for a legislative seat in 1849, she faced mockery and contempt.

Beyond manhood suffrage, all members of the Provisional Government agreed on two other general principles designed to distinguish the Second Republic from the First: the abolition of slavery in the colonies and a ban on capital punishment for political offenses. This time, there would be no guillotine, no Terror, and no slave revolts. The Provisional Government's consensus broke down, however, over the question of economic reform, and most immediately, over how to alleviate unemployment. Blanc wanted workers to take the economy into their own hands by establishing collectively owned enterprises known as producers' cooperatives. But moderates rejected such a "socialist" plan.

The Provisional Government attempted to resolve the impasse with two compromises. The first established National Workshops to provide jobs for those out of work. This new institution bore a superficial resemblance to the "social workshops" that Louis Blanc had proposed, but in reality National Workshops were little more than traditional forms of charity and poor relief. The second compromise gave Blanc not the Ministry of Labor he had hoped to direct, but the presidency of a government "Commission for the Workers," mandated to study the social question. This "Luxembourg Commission," so called because it met in the Palais du Luxembourg, former home of the Chamber of Peers, did much to publicize grievances, advance solutions, and keep working people mobilized. It did little, however, to change their daily lives.

Contributing enormously to the popular mobilization were more than two hundred political clubs comprising one hundred thousand members. These organizations debated political and social issues and attempted to push the Provisional Government to the left. The most prominent clubs, attracting four thousand to five thousand members each, were those led by the former insurrectionists Blanqui and Barbès, the communist Cabet, and the poor man's doctor, Raspail. Though women attended club meetings, the leading organizations forbade them to speak. In response, women revolutionaries such as Deroin, Adèle Esquiros, and Suzanne Voilquin formed several clubs of their own. Most notable was the Société de la Voix des Femmes, an organization that coalesced around a feminist newspaper of the same name. One feminist club, the Vesuvians, advocated military service for women and an equal share of household work for men.

Despite the clubs' efforts to postpone parliamentary elections until the peasantry could be "educated," balloting for a new Constituent Assembly took place on April 23. The overwhelming majority of those elected were long-standing

monarchists who declared allegiance to the Republic during the short-lived
"springtime of the people." These *républicains du lendemain* were willing to
tolerate, even endorse, a republican government, but not the social republic of
Blanc, Blanqui, and Raspail's dreams. On May 15, these and other radical leaders
found themselves in serious trouble after an abortive putsch failed to replace the
moderate republic with a more socialistic regime.

By now, the Provisional Government had given way to an Executive Commission of five members, and power had shifted to the Assembly, whose majority was increasingly eager to be done with socialism and workers' demands.
A decree of June 22 ordered those enrolled in the National Workshops to either enlist in the army or move to the provinces. This dramatic measure may
or may not have been intended as a provocation; it nonetheless triggered a
working-class revolt of unprecedented ferocity.

The fight lasted four days and stands as the modern world's first significant
episode of "class warfare," a label used by Tocqueville, Marx, and many others at
the time. General Eugène Cavaignac, the former governor-general of France's
Algerian colony, methodically suppressed the insurrection in his new capacity as
"chief of executive power." His "saturnalia of reaction," as the defrocked priest
Lamennais called it, cost the lives of at least four thousand insurgents, most of
them killed in acts of retribution after the fighting had ceased. Another fifteen
thousand were arrested and many later deported to Algeria, the scene of Cavaignac's earlier military campaigns against Arab resistance to French rule. The indigenous population of Algeria, it should be noted, had been excluded from the
"universal suffrage" of 1848.

Once the Parisian rebels had been subdued, Cavaignac instituted a variety
of repressive measures, including restrictions on freedom of assembly and the
press. But the Republic remained in place, especially in the provinces, where a
series of local elections imbued ordinary people with a democratic culture and
the experience of political participation. If Paris was the scene of repression and
military rule, provincial France had become more republican and democratic
than ever before.

Soon Paris returned to a semblance of normality, and the Assembly proceeded to draft a new constitution. That document, ratified on November 4,
1848, combined French and American models. From the French Revolution,
the new constitution adopted the idea of a sovereign unicameral legislature, and
from the American experience, a powerful President legitimized by the votes
of all adult men. The Assembly scheduled the presidential election for December 10, and three serious candidates entered the race: the centrist Cavaignac; the
moderate leftist Ledru-Rollin; and the Bonapartist heir, Louis-Napoleon.

Against all expectations, Bonaparte won by a landslide—nearly 5.5 million
votes against only 1.4 million for Cavaignac and 400,000 for Ledru-Rollin. Given

the still overwhelmingly rural character of the French population and the geographical distribution of the vote, it is clear that most of his support came from peasants. Many of the latter were moved by a vibrant Napoleonic legend that benefited the otherwise obscure Louis-Napoleon. Other peasants, destined to vote for the Left in subsequent elections, supported Bonaparte as an expression of independence from local notables who sided with Cavaignac. The elites divided their votes between Cavaignac and Bonaparte, while urban workers, hostile to the general, voted either for Ledru or Bonaparte, known for the vaguely socialistic writings of his youth.

After taking office, Louis-Napoleon appointed a ministry dominated by former Orléanist and Legitimist politicians; it included not a single republican. Under these circumstances, two utterly distinct political groupings took shape: a coalition of conservatives and moderates, known as the Party of Order; and an alliance of democrats and socialists, who called themselves *démoc-socs*. The Right sought limits on speech and assembly, restrictions on the right to vote, and the elimination of anything perceived as a threat to private property. The Left formed a proto-party called Solidarité Républicaine, whose goal was to organize political action in each *département,* and especially to reach the peasantry with a message of political and social equality.

The two parties confronted each other in the legislative elections of May 13, 1849. Although the outcome constituted a clear victory for the Party of Order, which won 500 of the 750 seats, most of the remaining 250 places went to the *démoc-socs.* Cavaignac republicans were almost completely shut out. Though conservatives outnumbered leftists by more than 2 to 1 nationwide, throughout the mostly rural Center and South, *démoc-socs* had more than held their own. Of the forty-six departments from Burgundy to the southern border, the Left won an absolute majority in sixteen departments and between 40 and 50 percent of the vote in another seventeen. These results terrified the Party of Order, which believed that if the *démoc-socs* continued to conquer the peasantry they would win the presidential and parliamentary elections scheduled for spring 1852.

To prevent such a victory became the raison d'être of the Right, whose leaders used the levers of government to repress the *démoc-socs.* The Party of Order equated socialism with theft and accused the Left of seeking to undermine the family and abolish private property. *Démoc-soc* leaders did a disservice to their cause when, on June 13, 1849, they took to the streets in protest of the government's military efforts on behalf of the pope, banished from Rome by Mazzini and Garibaldi. In lending support to insurrectionary demonstrations, leftist leaders gave conservatives a pretext for heightened measures of repression.

Though most leaders of the Parisian Left landed in jail or exile after the fiasco of June 13, the *démoc-socs,* now firmly entrenched in the provinces, remained a vital force. Remnants of the press freedoms established in 1848 permitted left-wing newspaper editors to continue publishing their journals and to make their headquarters informal centers of political organization. After clubs and electoral committees were banned, cafés served as meeting places and reading rooms, where patrons could be exposed to news and political ideas. People who traveled for a living—salesmen, insurance agents, railroad employees, coach drivers, and mailmen—also helped spread *démoc-soc* ideology and news of the day.

By mid-1849, the *démoc-socs* possessed a largely coherent, if not fully workable, doctrine. They advocated a social republic that would give all French men political rights and social justice, a republic that would use the magic of democracy to make socialism real. By socialism, they meant producers' cooperatives, a state-guaranteed right to work, progressive taxation, cheap credit, the nationalization of transport and communications, and universal education. Far from abolishing private property, they sought to democratize ownership by holding mortgage rates down, both for farmers buying land and for workers establishing cooperative enterprises. No one would be expropriated, and no violence would be necessary. Liberty and equality would stand on a foundation of fellow feeling, which the *démoc-socs* often expressed in Christian terms. The Gospel, they liked to say, had introduced the fraternal democracy they aimed to create. These ideas anticipated the democratic socialism of later times, while highlighting the challenges facing any political system that seeks to bend the market to its will.

Démoc-soc ideology continued to penetrate the French countryside throughout the remaining years of the Second Republic, but repression had deprived the Left of a national organization and leadership. Under those apparently favorable circumstances, certain old warhorses of the Party of Order now asserted their independence from the President, a man they belittled in private. Louis-Napoleon was not, however, as inept as conservative stalwarts like Adolphe Thiers believed. Bonaparte understood that in a country far more accustomed to kings and emperors than to republics, a President anointed on the strength of five million votes could wield a great deal of power. Though he collaborated with the Party of Order on a bill to impose religious domination over public education (the Falloux law of March 1850), the President showed mounting signs of independence. He cultivated the military and traveled around the country in regal style.

The Party of Order, meanwhile, stepped up its repression of the Left. After two new *démoc-soc* electoral victories in March and April 1850, conservatives voted on May 31 to remove one-third of France's adult men, mostly workers and peasants, from the electoral rolls. To further emasculate the Left, conservatives found ways to put most opposition newspapers out of business and to round up provincial *démoc-soc* leaders, whom they accused of conspiring to overthrow the government. As a result, much of what remained of the left-wing movement went underground, forming secret societies, clandestine networks, and samizdat publications.

With the *démoc-socs* apparently under control, conservatives turned on themselves, as Legitimists, Orléanists, and Bonapartists divided into separate, mutually hostile factions. Shrewdly, Bonaparte played the monarchist factions against each other, using their renewed rivalry to emasculate the parliament and place his growing number of loyalists in key positions of power. The President then launched a campaign to undo the section of the constitution that barred him from a second term. It was a sophisticated effort that borrowed many of the *démoc-socs'* most successful propaganda techniques. In the end, Bonaparte gained a healthy majority in favor of revision, but he fell short of the three-fourths majority the constitution required. Now, with less than a year left in his term, the President faced the choice of stepping down in May 1852 or illegally extending his reign.

In the wee hours of December 2, 1851, the anniversary of Napoleon I's coronation, Louis-Napoleon staged his own 18 Brumaire. He dissolved the Legislative Assembly, dispatched heavily armed troops to every corner of Paris, and arrested about a hundred men deemed capable of organizing resistance to his coup. Some fighting occurred, and barricades went up, but nothing resembling February or June 1848 developed. By December 4, the capital had been subdued.

But before Louis-Napoleon could celebrate, the provinces rose up against his blatant violation of the constitution. It was the nineteenth century's largest rural rebellion—some hundred thousand strong—and one of the most significant, if least known, peasant revolts in all of French history. Throughout central and southern France, farmers and village artisans organized themselves into makeshift military columns and then marched to the nearest *sous-préfecture*. For the most part, gendarmes were strong enough to halt the rebels' advance, but several *sous-préfectures* and one departmental capital—Digne of the Basses-Alpes—temporarily fell into rebel hands. The most successful acts of rural resistance occurred in regions with active secret societies; the larger the society, the more extensive the rebellion. Since secret societies took root largely within the "Red" areas of France, there is a general, though imperfect, correlation between the electoral strength of the *démoc-socs* in 1849 and the centers of insurrection in December 1851.

As is often the case with key historical events, contemporaries who commented on the insurrection of 1851 shaped the way it would be understood for a long time to come. Conservatives saw the rural rebels as furies from hell who rose from the bowels of the countryside to rape and pillage the rich. Republicans, by contrast, called the uprising a necessary effort to restore the constitutional legality so outrageously violated by their President. The one group emphasized violence and mayhem, the other order and decorum. In reality, the rebellion was remarkably tame, though not entirely without violence. And there was an element of class warfare in this event. The rebels aimed not to restore the republican status quo ante but to establish a new kind of republic, a democratic and social republic dedicated to improving the lives of the poor.

The rebellion was not, of course, destined to succeed. By December 10, government troops had mostly stamped it out, arresting more than twenty-six thousand people. The repression was harsh and swift, as Mixed Commissions of military, prefectoral, and judicial officials condemned thousands to penal colonies abroad and imprisonment at home. Louis-Napoleon had triumphed, but at the cost of a military campaign against his own people.

With one-third of France under a state of siege, the Prince-President held a plebiscite to legitimize his rule. Though full manhood suffrage had been restored, it was anything but a free and open vote. Still, Bonaparte did not hesitate to use his apparent support (7.5 million people had voted yes) to establish a near-dictatorial regime. On December 2, 1852, the Prince-President declared himself Napoleon III, Emperor of the French. Once again, a promising republic had degenerated into a Napoleonic empire. But this time the republican message had spread far and wide; when the Bonapartist second coming collapsed eighteen years later, France's age of kings and emperors ended as well.

References

Agulhon, Maurice. *The Republican Experiment, 1848–1852.* Cambridge: Cambridge University Press, 1983.

———. *The Republic in the Village: The People of the Var from the French Revolution to the Second Republic.* Cambridge: Cambridge University Press, 1982.

Berenson, Edward. *Populist Religion and Left-Wing Politics in France, 1830–52.* Princeton, NJ: Princeton University Press, 1984.

Margadant, Ted W. *French Peasants in Revolt: The French Insurrection of 1851.* Princeton, NJ: Princeton University Press, 1979.

Marx, Karl. *The Eighteenth Brumaire of Louis Bonaparte.* New York: International Publishers, 1967.

McPhee, Peter. *The Politics of Rural Life: Political Mobilization in the French Countryside, 1846–52.* Oxford: Oxford University Press, 1992.

Rosanvallon, Pierre. *The Demands of Liberty: Civil Society in France since the Revolution.* Cambridge, MA: Harvard University Press, 2007.

———. *Le peuple introuvable: Histoire de la représentation démocratique en France.* Paris: Gallimard, 2002.

Scott, Joan Wallach. *Only Paradoxes to Offer: French Feminists and the Rights of Man.* Cambridge, MA: Harvard University Press, 1996.

Seigel, Jerrold. *Marx's Fate: The Shape of a Life.* Princeton, NJ: Princeton University Press, 1978.

Tocqueville, Alexis de. *Recollections: The Revolution of 1848.* New York: Transactions, 1987.

Tudesq, André Jean. *L'élection présidentielle de Louis Napoléon, 10 décembre 1848.* Paris: A. Colin, 1965.

4

The Republicans of the Second Empire

Sudhir Hazareesingh

Translated by Arthur Goldhammer

The republicans of the Second Empire found themselves in rather sad shape by the early 1850s. Crushed by the coup d'état of December 2, 1851, destroyed as an autonomous political force, and sentenced to long prison terms, deportation, or exile in London, Brussels, Geneva, or Guernsey, they were reduced to bemoaning their fate in personal diaries, subdued private meetings, and ephemeral secret societies, which were quickly infiltrated by the imperial police. Although the "liberal Empire" of the late 1860s permitted them to engage in political activities more openly than before and energized the press, pamphleteers, and students, in other respects it was scarcely more favorable to them. Bonapartism remained firmly entrenched throughout France, especially in the provinces and countryside, and the practice of running "official candidates" guaranteed the regime a comfortable margin. Indeed, the crushing political defeat suffered by the "republican party" in the plebiscite of May 1870 seemed to set it back twenty years. Stuck in an impasse, the republicans seemed caught between hopes of an improbable return to the "old beards" of 1848 and the impossible utopia of a social revolution, which was soon drowned in the blood of the Paris Commune.

This Sisyphean imagery plainly haunts the article that Emile Littré published in *Philosophie positive* in 1879, which expresses an extremely harsh judgment of the broad outlines of the republican experience since 1830. Going so far as to deny all legitimacy to the Revolution of 1848, the philosopher emphasizes the absolute necessity of repudiating a past filled with violence, political incoherence, and "metaphysical" thinking. The Opportunists, adroitly led by Jules Ferry and Léon Gambetta, would take up this call for a break with the past and therefore reject the experiences of the Second Empire in the name of "positivist" principles. When the republicans finally regained power, moreover, they chose July 14 as the date of their new national holiday (first celebrated in 1880), in a deliberate throwback to the cult of the Great Revolution that seemed to confirm the marginalization of the 1850s and 1860s in national memory. The Second Empire was now characterized as a period of "Caesarism," a pejorative label that symbolized a number of different things: adventurism and political humiliation; a geographical split between enlightened cities and a backward countryside ("land of mountains, land of idiots," as one celebrated republican pamphleteer put it); and, above all, the moral and cultural debasement of the entire nation. In a speech to the Five Academies in October 1871, Jules Simon maintained that republicans bore a share of responsibility for these disasters: "Should we not confess that, despite the heroes and martyrs of the final hour, we were beaten before Sedan [site of France's defeat in the Franco-Prussian War, 1870–71]? Yes, we bore within ourselves the cause of the defeat. Yes, we were almost as culpable as we were unfortunate."

A politically engaged historiography thus long sustained the idea that the Second Empire was a period of failure that served primarily as a symbol of republican impotence and decadence against which subsequent success could be highlighted to good effect. Fortunately, history is today reasserting its rights, and recent research on the history of the Second Empire has substantially revised our picture of this crucial period. New approaches have shed a good deal of light on the republicans' intellectual and cultural inventiveness. Though defeated politically and forced to survive in often difficult conditions, they nevertheless discovered a myriad of ways to assert their identity. In particular, they developed a variety of new associations and forms of sociability. These included circles such as Jean Macé's Ligue de l'Enseignement, societies of freethinkers, and local workers' groups, many of which would play a crucial role in the republican conquest of power in the 1870s. Above all, republican sociability took on more and more of the flavor of a cult. Like the Catholics, who discovered during the Second Empire the delights of practicing their religion in public, republicans ecstatically embraced rites of their own: they celebrated republican memory in a variety of ways, from political anniversaries (especially February 24) to illegal importation of busts of Ledru-Rollin, Félix Pyat, and even Robespierre. There were also rites connected with so-called trees of liberty, planted under the Second Republic only to be cut down by Bonapartists after 1851, but which lived on in memory (and in some cases in the form of precious relics). There was the cult of Marianne, which, as Maurice Agulhon has shown, really took off during the Second Empire. And there were civil funerals, which became places for republicans to meet and join in spiritual communion, despite the energetic efforts of the prefect of police, Maupas, to prevent them from doing so. Even the Paris Commune would acknowledge the importance of organizing "public ceremonies" to "strike the imagination of the people."

Intellectual creativity did not lag behind. Among the best-known republican political thinkers of the 1860s and 1870s were Étienne Vacherot (whose best seller *La démocratie,* earned its author a term in Sainte-Pélagie prison), Charles Dupont-White (a leading writer on public affairs, whose major work was *L'individu et l'État*), and Jules Barni (the author of *La morale dans la démocratie*). These men drew political ideas and concepts from a rich variety of traditions, including not only French political ideologies from earlier in the century (including the thought of the Doctrinaires, Saint-Simonism, and early socialism) but also English and German political philosophy: Dupont-White was the translator of John Stuart Mill, and Barni of Emmanuel Kant. Beyond these individual thinkers, it is important to insist above all on the "European" character of republican political thought in this period: for French republicans, Europe was a place of asylum, and several countries, including England, Belgium, and Switzerland, offered concrete examples of liberal and republican practice in their political systems. Equally important was the extent to which the European setting allowed republicans to cast their thought on a broader scale: republican thinking about issues of war and peace was genuinely universal, especially in Barni's work with the Ligue pour la Paix et la Liberté. There was already talk in this period of a United States of Europe. If the idea was ahead of its time, these bold republicans adopted the universalist political traditions of the 1830s (and in particular of the "Young Europe" movement) to lay the groundwork for a project that would find concrete embodiment a century later.

We find a similar ferment in philosophy. The republicans of the Second Empire exhibit a remarkable conceptual fluidity. For example, there was no agreement on "fraternity": Littré rejected it, and Vacherot relegated it to the status of a "feeling," whereas for the Paris Commune it was an essential component of the republican trinity (along with "liberty" and "equality"). Indeed, the Commune ordered the destruction of the Vendôme Column, which it saw as a "perpetual assault on one of the three great principles of the French Republic, namely, fraternity." No Communard, Jules Ferry nonetheless applauded "universal" (male) suffrage in the early 1880s, treating it as the basis of political education and an instrument of social reconciliation. By contrast, Eugène Pelletan waxed ironic about the ignorance of peasants and their inability to distinguish between the living and the dead, citing the example of a commune that allegedly voted for Cambronne, even though he had been dead for some time. This led Vacherot to wonder whether it might not be better to postpone universal suffrage until the people were better educated. If republicans disagreed about fraternity, after 1851, they all seemed to concur about liberty—this was easy, since the imperial regime denied them the rights to associate, to assemble, to think, and to write; it even ordered the motto "liberty-equality-fraternity" removed from public buildings. As a group, republicans agreed with Adolphe Thiers in insisting on "necessary liberties," by which they could claim the right for each individual to act, without state interference, in accordance with the dictates of his conscience (within the limits of the law). But how far could and should that liberty go? Disagreement emerged in the course of tough political fights among moderates, radicals, and revolutionaries in the final years of the Empire. These divisions would reemerge during the war of 1870–71 and above all during the Communes in Paris and the provinces—most notably in connection with social and religious issues, in which we see early signs of the militant anticlericalism that would reach its apogee during the Third Republic. Behind these debates there was nevertheless a clear convergence toward a neo-Roman definition of liberty, the purpose of which was to free the individual of all arbitrary domination. In the splendid words of the neo-Montagnard Alphonse Esquiros, mastermind of the Ligue du Midi during the Franco-Prussian War, "One commits oneself in order not to be a slave."

I will return to the question of liberty later in this essay. Indeed, it is essential if we are to appreciate not only the internal vacillation of the republicans but also their synergies and convergences with other families of political thought. Images of division, fragmentation, and prostration were not in fact the heart of the matter. We should bear in mind that the republicans of the Second Empire shared the same intellectual and political field as the liberals, the Catholic traditionalists, and the Bonapartists: they mingled with one another and appealed to the same historical memories and references. In the course of a more or less permanent dialogue, they raised the same questions about democracy and often reached similar judgments about certain fundamental matters. Let us consider four examples of these elective affinities, chosen to reflect different levels of analysis: the philosophy of the state, the discourse of the nation, the question of decentralization, and the role of republican elites in the provinces.

The philosophical defense of the state during the Second Empire and early Third Republic was the work of Charles Dupont-White, a subtle and original if somewhat eccentric thinker (and politically impossible to classify, although he was fundamentally republican in his political commitments and actively opposed the coup d'état of December 1851). For Dupont-White, the state represented the principle of superiority in distance, the detachment from narrow parochial interests: it guaranteed equality of all before the law and made sure that local (social and religious) "castes" did not use their power to oppress the weakest members of society. (In this respect he was what would today be called a Jacobin.) Initially, after opposing the seizure of power by Louis-Napoleon, Dupont-White caustically criticized the political authoritarianism of the imperial regime. But his attitude toward the Second Empire was far from irreconcilable. He was clearly pleased that it had maintained Napoleonic centralization (imperial pamphleteers always cited him on this issue, moreover). He applauded Napoleon III's restoration of "pride" in the state. And most important of all, he attacked the anarchy of the late Second Republic and the ideological battles among republicans in 1870–71, saying aloud what many moderate republicans thought privately: "A bad monarchy is better than a bad republic." Many moderate liberals and republicans would have been perfectly comfortable with an imperial parliamentary government if the Second Empire had not blundered into the suicidal folly of the Franco-Prussian War. Illustrious republicans who accepted the Empire, such as Émile Ollivier and Lucien Prévost-Paradol, should be seen as trees that hide the forest.

Republican thought about the "nation" is just as interesting. On this score, some writers distinguished between the period before 1870 and that after, arguing that republicans shifted from sentimental antimilitarism to a more rigid and doctrinal "nationalism." Others contrast republican "patriotism," which is said to have been political and civic in nature, and Bonapartist "nationalism," which is supposed to have been bellicose and aggressive. These distinctions are rather arbitrary and generally serve only to bolster the "rosy" legend of a French nation created solely by the Republic, as against the "dark" legend of Bonapartism as a degenerate chauvinistic form and nothing more. In reality, the "patriotic" discourse of Bonapartists and that of republicans had much in common and rested on a shared heritage of memories, political forms, and national institutions inherited from the revolutionary tradition. The civic celebrations of the Second Empire, especially the national holiday of August 15, illustrate this convergence. When the Empire confronted tsarist Russia in 1855, republicans applauded in the name of the struggle against "feudalism," and republicans and Bonapartists alike feted the Italian war of 1859, this time in the name of "liberating nationalities." This Jacobin-Bonapartist patriotism—to hazard a phrase—could take a variety of forms: nostalgic, when republicans throughout France joined with their fellow citizens to pay homage to the "Médaillés" of Saint-Helena, those "glorious relics" of the Grand Army honored by Napoleon III; jingoistic, when republicans joined the Empire in praise of what would soon be called France's *mission civilisatrice* (civilizing mission) to the colonies; heroic, and at times impudent, when republicans took up where the Empire left off in denouncing Prussian barbarism and calling for volunteers, in Gambetta's words, "to defend the soil of the old kingdom of France."

Let us turn next to decentralization, which was the most important political issue in France in the 1860s. The debate on this issue matters not so much for the "external" contribution of republicans on the question of local liberties (which in any case would be abruptly eliminated with the death of the liberal Empire in 1870) as for its "internal" ideological value. Indeed, it was in pondering the issue of local liberties under the Second Empire, and especially under the influence of the Nancy Project of 1865, that republicans began to question their fundamental political values and ultimately to reformulate their basic philosophy of citizenship. Three distinct approaches emerged: Dupont-White's centralizing doctrine has already been mentioned; Proudhon's federalism, which would inspire the Commune (whose elder statesman, Charles Beslay, observed: "It is through the complete liberty of the commune that the republic will take root in France"); and what Ferry called the "municipalist" doctrine, which would reconcile the two components of republican citizenship—a central state to uphold the general interest and a vibrant and active communal sphere in which citizens and municipal officials work together for the public good and provide an apprenticeship in democracy. The commune was thus the *petite patrie,* and the central state the *grande patrie.* This distinction would become a commonplace under the Third Republic, and the municipalist doctrine would inspire the great reform of 1884, which finally established the practice of electing mayors. Note that the municipalists borrowed ideas from liberals and even Bonapartists (the issue of decentralization divided nearly all the political families), and municipalist thought also reflected an important political reality of the 1860s: the growth of the republican party in large and medium-sized cities and the emergence of an urban bourgeois elite, which would assume local power under the Third Republic. In this area perhaps more than any other, we see the ideological recomposition of the republicans at work: it was a twofold process, involving both internal differentiation (which led to purification and clarification of the doctrine) and conceptual openness to the outside (as republicans borrowed ideas from others).

We are thus a long way from the post-1870 myth of a frontal opposition between republican doctrine and Bonapartist "Caesarism." Far from the sound and fury of Paris, the vehemence of irreconcilables such as Auguste Blanqui and Henri Rochefort, and the imprecations of the likes of Edgar Quinet and Victor Hugo, men from both camps could maintain cordial relations and even work together. A significant example of this common ground can be seen in the workers' societies, which flourished in the 1860s with encouragement from the Empire. Here, moderate republicans and liberal Bonapartists joined forces to defend their corporate interests, contribute to the moral and material emancipation of workers, and work toward reconciliation of capital and labor. In 1865, and again in 1870 (in the midst of the Franco-Prussian War), a substantial number of republicans were elected to municipal councils across France. The Empire often chose the most moderate of these figures to serve as mayor: men such as Édouard Ordinaire, a staunch opponent of Bonapartism, who would never renounce his republican convictions but was nevertheless appointed as the top official in his commune, Maisières (Doubs), for almost the entire duration of the Empire. Gambetta subsequently named him prefect under the Government of National Defense (1870). These local administrators, who form the subject of a remarkable prosopographic analysis by Vincent Wright, are also interesting to study from the standpoint of relations between republicanism and Bonapartism. Although it turns out that nearly all of these Gambettist prefects were "historic" opponents of December 2, they were also capable of pragmatism and even conservatism: after 1871 they became "republicans of order." Furthermore, four out of ten republican prefects were Freemasons, and republicans and Bonapartists rubbed shoulders in many provincial Masonic lodges. To cite just one example of this equable ecumenism, when the *Parfaite Union* lodge of Montauban met in 1861, it boasted four republican members, three Orléanists (devotees of Louis-Philippe's "bourgeois monarchy"), three men "loyal to the government," three advanced liberals, two legitimists (supporters of Henry V, the Bourbon pretender), and one socialist. To the end of the Empire, the Montauban lodge chose as its "Venerable" Adrien Praix-Paris, a deputy and mayor of the town. This zealous Bonapartist would serve as deputy from Tarn-et-Garonne from 1869 to 1898.

By the end of the Empire there existed an undeniable duality in the republican community. On the one hand, there was a crystallization of the culture of protest: wasn't the republicans' last major political act to say no to the liberal Empire in May 1870? This no reflected a visceral hatred of Bonapartism, which is easy to understand. But the foolishness of this posture was not lost on the most lucid members of the republican camp, who had more in common with liberal Bonaparists and "third party" centrists than with the most radical elements of their own camp, most notably the Blanquists and neo-Jacobins, to say nothing of the revolutionary socialists of the Workers' International. For the first time, however, the moderate republican Left felt that it was held hostage by the more "advanced" forces: this leftism was destined to continue in the years ahead, and it remains an essential element of the culture of the Left in France—for better and for worse.

Myth has always been a prodigious political force in France, and the years of the Second Empire have left republican culture deeply imbued with mythologies—especially negative mythologies. First, the republican identity was reified as an identity of "resistance," which accounts for the extraordinary popularity of Victor Hugo in the early years of the Third Republic. He was mythologized as a man who symbolized the absolute refusal to compromise with the "Caesarist" regime (and, after 1871, to ratify the transfer of Alsace and Lorraine to Germany). The Second Empire also witnessed the birth of virulent opposition on the part of some republicans to the church and traditionalist Catholicism (later joined under the unflattering appellation "clericalism"). Above all, the period 1851–70 inaugurated the long tradition of institutional hostility to a "strong" executive, which resurfaces in every great political crisis in France and is almost a recurring motif in each generation of the Left. At times this results in embarrassing errors, most notably the denunciation of General de Gaulle as a "fascist." This negative identity of the republicans, this "all-or-nothing" culture, is in some ways reminiscent of contemporary aberrations of the French Left, especially in regard to the European Union.

But the great republican myths have also been a positive source of commitment and identification in this period, especially in regard to the question of liberty, the supreme principle from which all republican political philosophy derives. Here we find the idea of the state as the incarnation of a sovereignty that, in Barni's words, "cannot belong to a master who does with it as he sees fit." The idea of justice was also a major achievement of the Second Empire period: it is no accident that among the leading Dreyfusards (supporters of French army Captain Alfred Dreyfus, who was unjustly convicted of espionage in 1894) we find men such as Arthur Ranc, Auguste Scheurer-Kestner, and of course the indomitable Georges Clemenceau, all men formed in the harsh school of imperial proscription. But besides these great principles, Second Empire republicans were above all skilled in the practice of ideological flexibility and cultural creativity. Indeed, what we find is not a sharp break between Bonapartism and republicanism but any number of continuities. The liberal version of the Empire offered a framework for reflection and even a number of concrete ideas and practices for rethinking republican citizenship. To mention just a few examples in no particular order: messianic nationalism, the colonial idea, the apprenticeship of universal suffrage (with respect to which the Bonapartist regime did what the Forty-Eighters were never able to accomplish, establishing a voting place in each commune), a revolutionary but socially conservative discourse toward the peasantry, free and regular municipal elections, civic holidays as a ludic form of sociability, association of a depoliticized regional tradition with the cult of the nation, and social and economic modernization. The Third Republic also kept the administrative system it inherited from the Revolution and Empire. The reversal on this point was significant: after vehemently attacking "law-and-order prefects," republicans wisely decided to keep them, along with the Conseil d'État, which was championed after 1871 by that great admirer of Napoleon and of French centralization, Léon Gambetta. Let us therefore borrow a celebrated phrase from Édouard Durranc, but with less irony than he intended: "How beautiful the Republic was under the Empire!"

References

Agulhon, Maurice, and Janet Lloyd, eds. *Marianne into Battle: Republican Imagery and Symbolism in France, 1789–1880.* Cambridge: Cambridge University Press.
Hazareesingh, Sudhir. *From Subject to Citizen: The Second Empire and the Emergence of Modern French Democracy.* Princeton, NJ: Princeton University Press, 1998.

————. *Intellectual Founders of the Republic: Five Studies in Nineteenth-Century French Political Thought.* Oxford: Oxford University Press, 2001.

Hazareesingh, Sudhir, and Vincent Wright. *Francs-maçons sous le Second Empire: Les loges provinciales du Grand-Orient à la veille de la Troisième République.* Rennes: Presses Universitaires de Rennes, 2001.

Lalouette, Jacqueline. *La libre pensée en France 1848–1940.* Paris: Albin Michel, 1997.

Les révolutions du XIXe siècle 1852–1872. 10 vols. Paris: Éditions d'Histoire Sociale, 1988.

Nord, Philip. *The Republican Moment: Struggles for Democracy in Nineteenth-Century France.* Cambridge, MA: Harvard University Press, 1995.

Price, Roger. *People and Politics in France, 1848–1870.* Cambridge: Cambridge University Press, 2004.

Tchernoff, Iouda. *Le parti républicain au coup d'état et sous le Second Empire.* Paris: Pedone, 1906.

Wright, Vincent. *Les préfets de Gambetta.* Edited by Éric Anceau and Sudhir Hazareesingh. Paris: Presses Universitaires de Paris-Sorbonne, 2007.

5

The Third Republic

Philip Nord

The Third Republic lasted seventy years, a feat of longevity unmatched in France's postrevolutionary history. Yet, until recent years, the Republic has not had a good press. Criticism has taken a variety of forms.

The regime's constitution and political mores have been a primary target. By tradition, republicans had a strong preference for the unicameral legislature. In the 1870s, however, when the Third Republic's constitutional laws were under debate, republicans, though gaining ground on the electoral front, did not enjoy a majority. The more moderate among them made common cause with former Orléanists, together hammering out a constitutional compromise with three principal features: a cabinet of ministers responsible before a Chamber of Deputies elected by universal manhood suffrage; a Senate whose members were elected indirectly; and a weak, but not entirely ceremonial, presidency. This tripartite structure attempted to balance a powerful Assembly against an upper house biased in favor of rural constituencies, and a President named by the legislature. Mindful of Louis-Napoleon's abuse of the position under the Second Republic, neither republicans nor ex-Orléanists favored a strong executive.

Over the course of the regime, the constitution underwent certain revisions. The Senate arrogated to itself the authority to overturn cabinets and made use of that right on critical occasions in the 1930s, most notably in 1937, when it voted out Léon Blum's first Popular Front government. The President's authority, by contrast, diminished. The Constitutional Law of 1875 invested the office, under the appropriate circumstances, with the right to dissolve the Chamber. The regime's first President, the Maréchal MacMahon (1873–79), made use of that prerogative in May 1877, disbanding the lower house and calling for new elections. MacMahon, a soldier of reactionary views, did not like the Chamber, which he judged too republican in composition. He was hoping to conjure a more pliable legislature, but the elections returned an unambiguously republican majority.

MacMahon bowed before the results. The weapon of dissolution was discredited as an instrument of reaction and never used again.

The Republic's constitution has been described as all brakes and little motor. Overambitious cabinets fell victim time and again to a conservative Senate or unstable majorities in the Chamber, and the head of state lacked sufficient authority to impose discipline. The result: revolving-door cabinets and, worse, a general immobilism that France was able to live with in the halcyon days prior to the Great War but not in the turbulent decades thereafter. It did not help that the regime's political mores were of dubious character, or so it seemed to many contemporaries. Periodic financial scandals roiled public life from Panama (1892) to Stavisky (1934). The Chamber earned a reputation as a cozy club, populated by "pals" more concerned with vote getting and backroom deals than with high-minded matters of state.

What kind of society, it might well be asked, would put up with such a sorry state of affairs? The Republic's critics had an answer ready to hand: a stalemate society. The construction of the regime in the 1870s was not just constitutional but electoral, a corps of city-based militants fanning out to the countryside and over the course of the decade rallying a rural majority to *l'idée républicaine.* No man threw himself into the effort with greater vigor than Léon Gambetta, who toured the nation campaigning for the cause, earning himself the nickname "the traveling salesman of the Republic." The coalition of middle-class and peasant constituencies that resulted—the so-called republican synthesis—assured the regime's survival, indeed, its longevity, but over the long run, the synthesis turned out to be problematic. The republican bourgeoisie was composed in the main of middling businessmen and professionals, men who valued thrift, property, and enlightened thinking. What drew peasant voters to the Republic, at least in part, were promises of material progress and a modest sufficiency, earned by individual effort but fostered and guaranteed by a supportive state that had the little man's interests at heart. The republican vision of a nation of smallholders had a basis in reality. French men and women, in increasing number down to the end of the century, rose to the ranks of the propertied. The vision also possessed a cultural dimension, one that found expression in the Republic's celebration of littleness, of the family business passed on from generation to generation.

It is not hard to figure out what might be problematic about these arrangements. Regime critics chalked up all sorts of ills to the Republic's cult of the little man. A social order that revolved around independent ownership left little room for the wage earner stuck in a factory job with minimal prospects of individual advancement. There was not much hope for serious welfare reform in a regime anchored in constituencies preoccupied with thrift and budgetary restraint. The fetishization of *la petite entreprise* discouraged the kind of entrepreneurial risk-taking essential to economic innovation and expansion, and more than that: it dissuaded husbands and wives, preoccupied with preservation of the family patrimony, from producing a numerous progeny. A sullen because marginalized working class, glacial economic and demographic growth—such were understood to be the consequences of France's stalemate society. And France would pay for them: in leftist extremism and political instability on the home front, in diplomatic and military decline abroad.

✑

Looking back from the postwar decades of the 1940s and 1950s, such a somber view of Third Republic history might well have made sense. France had spent the 1930s mired in an undeclared civil war and then succumbed to a terrible defeat in 1940. The immediate postwar years witnessed a disappointing return to the parliamentary instability and political cronyism of the old Third Republic.

The clouds parted, however, in subsequent decades, and the reasons for the national détente are not hard to find: the postwar baby boom, the so-called Trente Glorieuses, the end of empire overseas, and Gaullist stabilization at home. As the nation's woes dissipated, there was less need to invoke the Third Republic and its flaws to explain a disappointing present. Indeed, it became possible to take a fresh and more sympathetic look at the regime. The result was a complex, bifurcated history of the Republic. That postwar history spoke of an initial golden age lasting through the Great War, followed by stalemate and decline, standard themes that retained a critical place in the narrative but did not come into play until the interwar decades. If in this account, the Republic ended in disaster, done in by its own weaknesses, it had begun with enormous promise and achievement.

On this account, the republican synthesis is understood less as a repudiation of industrialism than as the faithful expression of a social order still overwhelmingly rural and small-town in character. The regime was representative of the majority of the French in this respect and in a second sense as well. The Republic's parliamentary institutions were underpinned by a political culture—a set of institutions, symbols, and ideas—that won the allegiance of, and was in return energized and appropriated by, a vast, participating public. It is often said that the French are an individualist people resistant to collective action. Hence the weakness of the trade-union movement in the early Third Republic and of political parties as well, at least compared to Germany and Great Britain. On closer inspection, however, it turns out that associational activity drew in huge numbers of "individualist" participants. Cooperatives, freethinking societies, Masonic lodges, *amicales,* chambers of commerce, and a myriad of leagues (the Ligue de l'Enseignement is a prime example) structured a web of democratic sociability that helped sustain republican values. In addition, two less formal institutions bear mentioning in this connection, the café and the newspaper. Both worked to initiate citizens into the political domain, the former as a site of electioneering, the latter as an instrument of public debate, and both as intermediaries between the quotidian and the grander rhythms of national life.

All such activity came encrusted with a powerful mythic overlay. The "founding fathers" of the Republic, it was believed, were carrying forward a vast project of human emancipation with ancient roots. France, as the homeland of the Enlightenment and of 1789, had made itself the bearer of that project, a beacon of liberty to all mankind. There were a great many ways to dramatize this story: in written form, of course, but also in songs and ceremonials, monuments and statuary. By such means, citizens might be surrounded with everyday reminders of the great story both French and human of which they were a part. A simple walk in the city became a lesson in itself, as the stroller threaded his way among statues of *philosophes,* revolutionaries, and present-day humanitarians. Amid this forest of symbols, the Republic itself was ever present, most often represented in female form, whether as a pagan goddess or as a youthful French maiden, Marianne.

Such symbolism spelled out in no uncertain terms what the regime imagined it stood for: democracy and liberty, reason and enlightenment, science and progress. France meant to bring these goods to the world, and it intended to carry out its universalizing mission by example and instruction. War was the method of unregenerate old regimes, ruled by aristocracies and military castes. An irenic France would know how to defend itself against aggressors, but arbitration and agreement, not blood and iron, were its preferred modes of action.

What is striking is how much of this project came to be realized. On the symbolic front, the regime acted with dispatch, recognizing in 1879 "La Marseillaise" as the national hymn, the next year enshrining the *quatorze juillet* (the 14th of July) as a national holiday. More concretely, on the matter of liberties, republican majorities vastly extended individual liberties, enacting laws in the 1880s that guaranteed freedom of speech and the press and relaxed the policing of public meetings and regulations governing cabaret life. In 1882, the state stopped appointing town mayors, leaving that task henceforth to municipal authorities. The regime's record on associational freedoms, however, was more uneven. Trade unions were legalized in 1884, simple enough, but then came the association law of 1901. In general, it simplified and liberalized procedures for organizing voluntary associations, political parties included. Indeed, in years following, France's first formal parties were founded, most notably the left-wing republican Parti Radical in 1901 and the Socialist SFIO in 1905. There was a major exception to the liberalizing trend, however: Roman Catholic religious congregations found themselves subjected to such intrusive state surveillance that a good number ended up moving abroad or disbanding altogether.

Overall, the republican state pulled back from the regulation of public life, although unevenly. Retreat, however, was not the order of the day when it came to citizen making. In the early 1880s, first as minister of public instruction then as prime minister, Jules Ferry oversaw construction of a nationwide primary-school system that was designed to ensure basic civic education and that guaranteed all citizens a primary education at public expense. Officials poured state resources into school building and teacher training on an unprecedented scale. The result was threefold. The schooling offered was exam-based, intended to allow bright students of modest background a path of upward mobility through the accumulation of diplomas. The scholarship boy on the rise in life was not just a propagandistic invention. He existed (though not in the numbers the regime advertised), and Édouard Herriot is often cited as a case in point. From a middling, provincial background, he climbed through education into public life, becoming a perennial prime minister in the interwar years. He was a poster boy for the regime's educational promise, so much so that one historian has dubbed him "la République en personne" (the Republic personified). The nickname is a reminder that the education the Republic's new school system tendered was above all civic and patriotic. It was secular as well. Ferry, married to a Protestant and himself a man of positivist, science-oriented views, considered the midcentury Catholic Church a bastion of obscurantism. He made certain to exclude it, to the degree such exclusion was possible, from the realm of public instruction. The process of citizen making, which the school initiated, continued during a young man's period of compulsory military service. Conscription became universal in 1889, although the actual length of service required varied across the life of the regime. The army styled itself the "school of the nation," and it played a not inconsiderable role steeping generations of French youth in patriotic values.

However inclusive the new republican edifice, it did not extend an equal welcome to all: women remained disenfranchised, Catholics subject to discriminatory legislation, wageworkers left largely to fend for themselves. The Republic encouraged self-help: mutual-aid societies, cooperatives, and the like. It was prepared to countenance trade unions and even, up to a point, strike action. Indeed, striking workers, confronted with obdurate employers, were disposed to welcome state arbitration. On the other hand, compared to (say) imperial Germany, the French Republic was slow to act in welfare matters, failing to legislate an old-age pension bill, for example, until 1910, more than twenty years after the first Reich legislation, and, even then, the benefits provided were modest. The Republic, moreover, haunted by memories of the Paris Commune, quickly, and often forcibly, repressed all forms of militancy that hinted of revolution. A CGT (Confédération Générale du Travail)-sponsored general strike in 1906 was severely put down, and the army summoned to quell the 1907 winegrowers' strike in the Midi. Finally, there is the question of the Republic's willingness to tolerate regional difference. The regime set itself the task of constructing a national culture, a project it embarked on with a missionary zeal. Not for nothing were its schoolteachers known as the "hussars of the Republic." There is no doubt that the pursuit of a French language–based cultural uniformity went hand-in-hand with hostility to local dialects and folkways, though recent historical work has demonstrated that in practice the Republic's agents were flexible when dealing with local customs and habits. All in all, if the regime did not deliver in full on its promises of liberty and equal citizenship, it nonetheless represented a major advance over its predecessors, Louis-Napoleon's Second Empire and MacMahon's government of Moral Order (1873–79). Even compared to contemporary states, France had little to be ashamed of. The Republic opened public life to religious minorities—Protestants and Jews—to an extent unusual anywhere in the world. It did not practice, at least within its continental borders, the kind of ethnic and racial discrimination that the United States practiced against blacks, England against the Irish, and Germany against Polish-speakers. Perhaps most important, much of what the Third Republic accomplished in its first decades has stood the test of time, outliving the regime itself. It codified a set of political symbols that even today retain the power to stir public emotion. The liberties it offered now belong to many of those once excluded from their benefits. And its educational ideal, anchored in principles of universalism and laicity, still excites passionate attachment and debate.

Three "episodes" from the Republic's golden age bring into relief just how complicated was the mix of qualities the Republic stood for. The regime inherited from its predecessors a modest overseas empire. It built on such beginnings, multiplying France's holdings tenfold. The process began in Indochina, moved on to Central and North Africa, and reached its culmination just after the Great War with the acquisition of Syria and Lebanon, former Ottoman territories "mandated" by the League of Nations. In the end, France found itself master of eleven million square kilometers of new territory inhabited by sixty million subjects.

This imperial expansion was the Republic's work. Overseas administrators, often men of deep republican conviction, understood themselves as bearers of a *civilizing mission,* charged with sweeping aside the primitive institutions of yesteryear—feudal chiefdoms, slavery, ignorance—and bringing in their stead the goods of progress—modern medicine, education, railroads. All this was meant to elevate subject peoples in preparation for a future citizenship. And indeed, small portions of the empire, the four communes of Senegal for example, took part in French national elections. Does it need saying how short of its proclaimed goals the republican imperial project fell, how tainted it was by racism and condescension?

Still, two additional points must be made. First, the empire was a major source of strength, an important recruiting ground in the First World War, a base of operations in the Second. In the 1920s, France set about the *mise en valeur* (economic development) of its imperial holdings with an exploitative fervor, which paid dividends in trade during the Depression years, when dealings with continental Europe withered. Second, the legacy of the empire was more ambiguous than might at first glance be supposed. The brutal colonial wars in Indochina and Algeria, which finished off the Fourth Republic, belonged to that legacy, but so too does a vast, worldwide Francophone community, which has enriched and complicated the culture of metropolitan France.

If the empire reveals the Third Republic's complex character, so too did the Dreyfus affair. In 1894, Alfred Dreyfus, an army captain of Jewish origin, was convicted of selling military secrets to the Germans. He was packed off to Devil's Island, and the case appeared closed until 1897, when information surfaced exculpating the unfortunate Dreyfus. The army brass maneuvered to block a reopening of the case, and the military's dishonest stonewalling was abetted by popular nationalist leagues that deployed a lethal compound of anti-Semitic rhetoric and street action to keep public officials from stepping in. On the other side, a coalition of intellectuals and progressive politicians pressed for a reconsideration of Dreyfus's case. The army retried Dreyfus in 1899, finding him guilty again, although this time with extenuating circumstances. The President of the Republic then issued a pardon, with Dreyfus exonerated altogether in 1906.

The affair was a remarkable event on several counts. It was a curtain-raiser for a populist anti-Semitic Right destined to play a major and destructive role not just in France's history but in Europe's as a whole. It also made plain that certain important elements of the army and the Catholic Church, which had aligned themselves with anti-Dreyfusism, were uncommitted to democratic principle and procedure. Despite the betrayal of these and other key institutions, the Republic proved more than a match for its opponents. Dreyfus's cause was first taken up by a new figure, the intellectual. The intellectual acted in the name of grand principle, not petty partisanship. He (less often she) did not so much take to the streets as buttonhole opinion through newspaper articles and manifestos. In a democratic culture that took the rights of man to heart, such conscience pricking achieved its effect, stirring a somnolent public to life. The intellectuals' prodding rallied republican sentiment and helped create a new partisan coalition, the so-called Bloc des Gauches, which included not just regime stalwarts like Clemenceau but portions of the labor and socialist Left as well. Disfavored as it was, the working class proved its loyalty to the regime.

The third episode is the Great War. France lost 1.4 million dead. No major belligerent, relative to the size of its population, suffered greater losses. Why French soldiers fought and fought on, even at such staggering cost, may not be altogether fathomable, but the Republic is part of the explanation. It had schooled its sons in lessons of patriotic sacrifice, and that willingness to serve—for this was a war that enjoyed widespread consent—reached its high-water mark in the almost yearlong battle of Verdun. To be sure, the spirit of sacrifice had its limits; witness the mutinies of 1917. Yet even then, it was as citizen-soldiers that the mutineers acted. They were neither revolutionaries nor defeatists, but common men who would no longer tolerate military strategies so wasteful of their lives. Unlike the Russian imperial forces in 1917, the French army did not disintegrate. A second point: France's wartime government was civilian-led throughout, and it succeeded, through fair means and foul, in maintaining national discipline. The German Reich followed a different path, resorting to military dictatorship in 1917–18 before collapsing into revolution.

In these various respects, France's war experience bore the Republic's imprint and may be counted the regime's finest hour; yet the cost of the effort was awesome, casting a dark shadow over the nation's interwar history. Historians have generally treated the Great War as a watershed, marking a cruel end to the Republic's golden age. Thereafter, France's troubles multiplied and festered, culminating in the cataclysms of 1940. The interwar decades look so grim precisely because they have most often been seen in the terrible light of the "strange defeat" at German hands. From this angle, the period appears one long run-up to disaster.

The Republic has been indicted for the debacle on multiple counts, the first economic and social. Here, the stalemate-society argument comes into full play. The economic crisis of the 1930s ravaged the regime's principal social clienteles, peasants and small businessmen, eating into its base of support. Unemployment levels, though lower than those of Germany and the United States, were high enough, coupled with underemployment, to fuel the anger of the "marginalized" working classes. Organized labor's perennially tepid support for the regime now took on major consequences. The result was an erosion of the Republic's social underpinnings, a process that strengthened antirepublican forces on the right- and left-wing extremes.

The Republic might have dampened such opposition had it acted with dispatch and effectiveness to handle the economic crisis, but it did not. Instead, important members of the majority became implicated in a major financial scandal, the Stavisky affair, which broke open in early 1934. The scandal provoked the first pitched battle in the undeclared civil war of the thirties. Angry taxpayers, war veterans, and right-wing rabble-rousers took to the streets on February 6, 1934. The crowd moved on the Chamber of Deputies but was beaten back by the police, leaving several dead. The event was thrilling to the Far Right, galvanized by the antiparliamentary possibilities of mass street action. Extremist leagues had led a fitful, on-again, off-again existence since the Dreyfus affair. February 1934 afforded them a fresh lease on life, especially the fast-growing Croix de Feu.

Much the same was true of the Left, which had been divided between Socialists and Communists since 1920. The latter disdained the Republic—and the

Socialists with it—as instruments of bourgeois domination. The events of February 1934 and the rise of fascism in general prompted a softening of the party line, which made possible a rallying of left-wing forces into an electoral coalition of Socialists (SFIO), Communists (PCF), and radicals known as the Popular Front. Its victory in 1936 gave rise to the first Socialist-led administration in France's history. No less remarkable, the new prime minister, Léon Blum, was of Jewish origin.

Blum's government had high ambitions for social reform, some of which it achieved—most notably the forty-hour week and paid vacations for workers. But political misjudgments and dissension among the coalition partners, to say nothing of the ongoing financial instability and opposition from powerful enemies in the business world and the Senate, doomed the Popular Front within a year. The conservatives and centrists who replaced it rolled back some of its most popular reforms, evoking angry strikes in November 1938, answered by a crushing show of repressive force.

Street violence and the rise of the political extremes—such was the legacy of the Republic's sclerosis in the 1930s. And the situation would deteriorate further before the decade was out. Portions of the Republic's political class began to lose confidence in the effectiveness of parliamentary institutions. Too paralyzed to act, deputies abdicated to the prime minister, authorizing the 1938 Daladier administration, for example, to impose legislation by decree. Xenophobic sentiment, on the rise throughout the thirties, imposed its poisonous effects at the highest levels. In 1934 and 1935, Parliament enacted laws limiting the ability of foreigners and even naturalized citizens to become doctors and lawyers. Resident aliens were placed under special police surveillance from 1938. A year later, the regime set up a system of internment camps, intended at first for refugees fleeing the brutal denouement of the Spanish civil war. Worst of all, the prevailing climate of hand-wringing anxiety sapped the nation's will to face up to Adolf Hitler. Daladier ceded to the dictator's intimidation at Munich in 1938, allowing the Germans to gobble up portions of Czechoslovakia, a democratic state formally allied with France. By decade's end, the corrosive currents of antiparliamentarism, xenophobia, and weaseling pacifism had reduced the Republic to a shallow shell of its former self. No wonder, in the aftermath of the debacle of May-June 1940, that the antirepublican Vichy regime had such an easy time installing itself, so well prepared was the ground. Historians now characterize the Republic's final years as "Vichy before Vichy."

Such an assessment of the late Third Republic is harsh in the extreme. A more modulated evaluation of the regime's performance must be made. To begin, France was not a stalemate society, no more so than, say, Japan, which also had (and, in comparative terms, still has) a sizable rural population with an important smallholding sector. During the thirty years from the turn of the nineteenth century to the Depression, France experienced a surge of industrial growth. The economy went slack in the 1930s but then took off again after 1945 in another multidecade burst of expansion. Interwar France had a modern industrial sector and a modern working class. Its economy performed better than its much-touted British counterpart and would continue to do so after the Second World War.

What then of the regime's paralysis in the thirties? Four points are relevant here. First, the French welfare state, with its distinctive pro-family and pro-natalist agenda, was well under construction before the Second World War. Social insurance laws of 1928 and 1930 brought a huge, worker-run mutual-aid sector under state supervision; legislation of 1932 did the same for employer-organized *caisses d'allocations familiales;* and the Code de la Famille (1939) streamlined family-welfare provisions and included measures designed to jump-start a flagging birthrate.

Second, however vacillating its political leaders, France did more than most European states to prepare to fight the German menace. At the outbreak of the war, France (and its allies) measured up to the Nazis in war matériel, thanks in large part to a rearmament program begun under Blum and pushed forward by his successor, Daladier. France's defeat in 1940 resulted as much from a lack of reliable allies as from France's internal weakness. At the outbreak of the First World War, the Russians pinned down important German forces in the East; in 1939, the Nazi-Soviet pact turned the USSR from a potential partner into Hitler's confederate. In retrospect, it is easy enough to say that French policymakers in the thirties should have set aside anti-Communist passions, lining up a Soviet alliance (whatever the cost to France's East European allies), and so confronting the Germans with the kind of two-front war that had worn them down thirty years before. But were the Republic's statesmen so unusual in their anti-Communist fixations? Without Soviet backing in 1939–40, France had to rely that much more on the Western democracies: on isolationist America, on neutralist Holland and Belgium, and on Great Britain, the appeaser that roused itself for France only in 1939, when it was much too late. Was the Republic alone to blame for not being supported by its putative friends? And what other state in Europe or North America was prepared in 1940 to ward off the blows of Hitler's Blitzkrieg?

The Republic was able to act with as much vigor as it did in part because the regime's institutions were more flexible than often supposed. This is the third point. The constitution of the Republic no doubt raised obstacles to forceful executive action. Prime ministers who attempted to finesse parliamentary obstructionism through direct appeals to the public more often than not got themselves into trouble. For this reason, radio played a minor part in the nation's political life in the 1930s in contrast to its role in the Anglo-American world. There was no equivalent in France to the authoritative tones of the BBC or to the charm and intimacy of Roosevelt's fireside chats. And yet, for all its divisions and squabbling, the French parliament was prepared to stand down in the late thirties and authorize Daladier wide leeway to take action by decree. The prime minister pledged himself to a program of national renewal and brought into government impressive talent, both young and old. The electorate responded to such muscle flexing with approval, as shown by the brand-new techniques of public-opinion polling. These various developments may be taken as symptoms of a general breakdown in parliamentary authority, but they may just as well point to the opposite conclusion: that the Republic, confronted with a crisis of unprecedented proportions, was beginning to evolve in new directions to meet the challenges that beset it. There is truth in both propositions, but enough in the latter to raise doubts about just how dysfunctional the regime really was.

The fourth and final point turns on Daladier's general popularity in 1938, the readiness of citizen-conscripts to answer the call to arms in 1939, and the common soldier's evident will to fight and die once Germans invaded French soil (as attested by battlefield losses of one hundred thousand in a campaign lasting less than two months). Such facts do not suggest a nation stripped of all cohesiveness, its sense of identity eaten away by a decade of civil discord. To be sure, economic dislocation, the Popular Front experiment, and high levels of immigration (France took in more foreign immigrants in the interwar decades than did its Anglo-American counterparts) fed an ugly, xenophobic backlash. That backlash menaced the Republic via militant extraparliamentary agitation, but the regime held its own against the street. Indeed, the Republic took active measures not just to contain the Far Right but to rein it in. In 1936, the Popular Front dissolved ultraright leagues like the Croix de Feu (which, however, resurfaced in another form). And in 1939, the Marchandeau law prohibited violent public expressions of racism. Unlike so many regimes elsewhere in Europe, the Third Republic stood its ground.

What the nationalist resurgence did do was to push the nation's political center of gravity rightward. It was more legitimate at the decade's end than at its beginning to carp against foreign influences, to complain of the incompetence of Parliament, to advocate a militant and illiberal anticommunism. In this way, the general rightward lurch of the thirties opened the door to Vichy, but it would take a cataclysmic military defeat before that threshold was crossed.

The passage of time has allowed a more positive evaluation of the Third Republic to emerge. The regime's early decades have benefited most from the change of interpretive climate, taking on the patina of a golden age—an assessment on the whole confirmed in these pages, although not without an effort to identify the ambiguities and complexities of the "republican achievement." The late Third Republic, by contrast, has not benefited from a similar reevaluation. Most historians have stood by the traditional, declinist understanding of those years. The approach here has been more tempered. In a comparative context, the Republic did better than most contemporary regimes forced to confront the general crisis of the interwar years. In certain respects, the drift of French public life doubtless paved the way for the authoritarian nationalism of Vichy. But it is possible to discern, in the regime's interwar record, anticipations, not just of Vichy, but of a new, expert-driven welfare state, of a Fifth Republic destined perhaps for an even longer life than the Third.

References

Agulhon, Maurice. *Marianne au pouvoir: L'imagerie et la symbolique républicaines de 1880 à 1914*. Paris: Flammarion, 1989.

Audoin-Rouzeau, Stéphane, and Annette Becker. *14–18, Retrouver la guerre*. Paris: Gallimard, 2000.

Azéma, Jean-Pierre, and Michel Winock. *La IIIe République (1870–1940)*. Paris: Calmann-Lévy, 1976.

Berstein, Serge. *Edouard Herriot, ou, La République en personne*. Paris: Presses de la Fondation Nationale des Sciences Politiques, 1985.

Conklin, Alice. *A Mission to Civilize: The Republican Idea of Empire in France and West Africa, 1895–1930*. Stanford, CA: Stanford University Press, 1997.

Dutton, Paul V. *Origins of the French Welfare State: The Struggle for Social Reform in France, 1914–1947*. New York: Cambridge University Press, 2002.

Hoffmann, Stanley. "Paradoxes of the French Political Community." In Stanley Hoffmann et al., eds., *In Search of France: The Economy, Society, and Political System in the Twentieth Century*. New York: Harper & Row, 1965.

Jackson, Julian. *The Popular Front in France: Defending Democracy, 1934–1938*. New York: Cambridge University Press, 1987.

Rémond, René, and Janine Bourdin, eds. *Edouard Daladier, chef de gouvernement, avril 1938-septembre 1939*. Paris: Presses de la Fondation Nationale des Sciences Politiques, 1977.

Weber, Eugen. *Peasants into Frenchmen: The Modernization of Rural France, 1870–1914*. Stanford, CA: Stanford University Press, 1976.

6

War and the Republic

Stéphane Audoin-Rouzeau

Translated by Arthur Goldhammer

The French Republic was born in war. The abolition of the monarchy, unanimously approved by the deputies of the National Convention on September 21, 1792, and the next day's decision to date all public documents from Year I of the Republic, were preceded, on September 20, by the victory at Valmy of the revolutionary armies over the forces of Prussia and Austria. Another war was launched inside France against Vendeans and Bretons who remained loyal to the Catholic monarchy.

The wartime birth of the Republic shaped the representations and practices of the *res publica*. Although the Second Republic initially thrived on the fraternity of peoples and the romantic spirit of the Revolution of February 1848, it, too, experienced an episode of internal warfare with the pitiless repression of the uprisings of June 1848. The Third Republic, like the First, was born in wartime, on September 4, 1870, but this time the occasion was marked by a French defeat at Sedan, where the Prussian army had crushed the imperial army. The new regime's first test was the "defense of the nation," followed by yet another episode of internal warfare: the crushing of the Paris Commune in the "Bloody Week" of May 1871.

The defeat at the hands of the enemy and the occupation of French soil solidified the republican dogma of resistance inherited from the French Revolution, a dogma that would be a decisive factor in the French victory in World War I. The great world conflict revived the century-old tradition of the embattled Republic, while casting an immense shadow on the nascent century. The pacifism of the 1920s and 1930s and the Resistance of the 1940s were thus consequences of World War I and its memory, which was as much republican as it was national. The "Great War" is therefore particularly deserving of a place in a critical history of the Republic and of France.

"The Republic cannot lose!" Although this comment comes from a film (Claude Chabrol's *Le Cheval d'Orgueil,* 1980), the character who uttered it, a

Breton deputy dispatched to the front during the Great War, nevertheless sums up quite well what was at stake in that war for the regime born in 1870. The Third Republic was the product of an unprecedented defeat, but given the magnitude of the military disaster bequeathed to it by the Second Empire (1852–70), the national catastrophe could not be blamed on the Republic. When war erupted in 1914, the situation was quite different: this time, how could the Republic not be held solely accountable for any military defeat? Had not the regime's detractors long cast doubt on its ability to avoid defeat in case of conflict with Germany? On the eve of the battle of the Marne, the historian Jacques Bainville voiced the deep suspicion of right-wing nationalists toward the Republic: "The French will not fail to comprehend this dreadful lesson. Those who have already understood it, those who knew that Democracy and the principles of the Revolution were bound to lead us into defeat, were the first to march. Our armies are full of men who saw this war coming, who were absolutely certain that the Republic would lead France to ruin" (*Journal inédit,* 1914). To be sure, the "feeling of fragility" (that is, the sense that the Republic would crumble in war) also existed on the left (e.g., Marcel Sembat), although the conclusions the Left drew from this were diametrically opposed to those of the nationalist Right. In any case, no particular steps were taken to ensure that the regime would function in wartime.

Four and a half years later, however, no one could deny that French territory had been staunchly defended, though at the terrible cost of nearly nine hundred dead per day: in this sense, the Great War proved to be a decisive moment of truth for the Republic. As Fabienne Bock wrote, this was "the first—and only— major crisis in France that did not lead to an abrupt change of regime."

Thanks to a deep and lasting consensus regarding the duty to defend the nation, both at the front and in the rear, the parliamentary Republic ultimately carried the day. In the immediate postwar years, liberal democracy, in the words of Jean-Marie Mayeur, "was seen as the great winner in the war." This regime spread over a vastly wider area than ever before, and as a result, the consequences of the military victory for the Republic's underlying legitimacy were considerable: "As a victory for the Republic, the war strengthened the regime," notes Mayeur, who also rightly remarks that republican institutions survived intact and the government did not invoke dictatorial powers. Yet things may have been more complicated than they appear. Can we really be certain that the outcome of the Great War was as favorable to the republican regime as this simple logic might suggest? Did the armistice of November 11, 1918, mark a Pyrrhic victory for the French Republic? These questions must be raised.

Let us begin by recalling the price paid in terms of civil liberties lost and basic republican principles compromised. War suspended all political activity, including local and national elections. France's political parties more or less went dormant. Add to these developments the state of siege (which gave substantial police powers to the military authorities), courts-martial, the influence of the general staff (at least until 1916), and finally what Olivier Forcade has called the wartime "information system," which featured censorship of the press, authorized by the law of August 5, 1914. As Jean-Jacques Becker rightly observes, "Democracy [was] in question."

And yet the "first surprise" was that democracy "succeeded in reestablishing itself." Thus in 1925, Pierre Renouvin was able to write in *Les formes du gouvernement de guerre:* "Among the major belligerent states, France was the one that remained most faithful to its traditions and constitutional principles throughout the crisis." Indeed, civilian government fairly quickly regained control: as early as September 1915, civilian leaders stripped military authorities of their police powers outside the military zone; these leaders also ended courts-martial in April 1916 and revised the military justice system to afford greater rights to the defense. To be sure, the state of siege was not lifted in the military and coastal zones until October 1919, at which time censorship was also ended. Well before that date, however, civilian power had regained the upper hand over the military in a series of stages marked by the battle of Verdun, the failed offensive of April 16, 1917, and the crisis following from the mutiny of frontline troops.

The Republic also did not renounce its principles with respect to parliamentary control. Certainly, Parliament abandoned its pre-1914 politicking: wartime governments enjoyed very substantial votes of confidence, and the fall of Paul Painlevé in November 1917 marked the first time that a government had been toppled since the summer of 1914. Despite this, Parliament, as the center of gravity of the republican regime, continued to play a major role and to influence the conduct of the war. Parliamentary oversight, which had disappeared until an extraordinary session was convened on December 22, 1914, thereafter remained in place without interruption (it remained in permanent session until the end of the war). What is more, this oversight proved extremely meticulous, because the work of the legislature was turned over to *grandes commissions,* key elements of the Third Republic's political system that gave some members access to technical information.

Legislators proved capable of decisive action to adapt their methods to the new situation created by the war. In addition to the traditional public sessions, they established "secret committees" (eight in the Chamber and four in the Senate between June 1916 and October 1917). Oversight of the military was established by reverting to old ways: the Third Republic in this respect followed (symbolically, at any rate) the lead of the Convention, which had sent "representatives on mission" to the troops during the French Revolution. Some deputies were mobilized as soldiers, and while their political role should not be overestimated, they did create a minimal link between the representatives of the nation and the troops in combat. In short, a veritable "wartime parliament" was created.

Although the balance of power among the various branches of government was not fundamentally altered, a certain strengthening of the executive did run counter to republican parliamentary tradition. This was particularly noticeable under Clemenceau, who became prime minister in the final year of the war. The "Tiger" assumed the position of minister of war as well and surrounded himself with a military as well as a civilian cabinet. An undersecretary of state attached to the prime minister's office coordinated the action of all ministries. Other changes that altered the traditional equilibriums of the republican regime include the development of an advisory cabinet around Clemenceau; the institution of undersecretaries of state and general commissioners attached to the prime minister's office; the elimination of secret committees; and the regulation of commerce in food and other commodities after February 1918. Of course, the "dictatorship of Clemenceau" is a myth. As prime minister, he "governed in full legality, with complete respect for the constitution," in the words of Fabienne Bock. It is true, however, that the Tiger's personal influence and efforts to win the public's (including soldiers') support over the heads of the legislature did mark a departure from republican tradition as it stood at the turn of the century. After the war, adversaries of the victorious Republic had no difficulty arguing that even though it had won the war, it did so ultimately by sacrificing certain of its fundamental principles.

Yet it was probably the Union Sacrée that introduced the most pernicious seeds of instability into the overall economy of the republican regime. Thanks to the work of Jean-Jacques Becker, we now know exactly what the Union Sacrée of 1914–18 entailed. It did not put an end to all opposition, much less reconcile old adversaries, but it did suspend political, social, and religious confrontation in the name of national survival. At the governmental level, the "truce among the parties" was given concrete form on August 26, 1914, when the center-left Viviani Ministry was expanded to include the socialist Left (Guesde and Sembat) as well as centrist republicans who had been defeated in May 1914 (Ribot, Delcassé, Millerand, and Briand). The whole republican family was thus united and, after rallying in support of the war, agreed to take charge of running it. But only the republican family was included: the antirepublican, monarchist, clerical, nationalist Right remained outside. At almost the same moment, on August 20, 1914, Maurice Barrès published his famous article in the *Écho de Paris,* in which he recalled "the abject times" of the Dreyfusard Republic and asked "how a France so pure" had been able to emerge "from that sewer"—a reminder that fundamental cleavages remained intact. All sides believed that they were laying the groundwork for postwar victory.

But the Union Sacrée evolved according to a dynamic of its own. When Denys Cochin entered the Briand government in November 1915, the Catholic and monarchist Right joined in managing the defense of the nation, at least until August 1917. The presence of a member of the Catholic Right, which did not support the Republic, alongside Émile Combes, the anti-Catholic architect of the separation of church and state, raises a crucial question: To what extent did the Union Sacrée disturb the fundamental forces of French politics, potentially destabilizing if not the republican regime then at least the image of the Republic and the mobilizing energies behind it? This is a question about political culture, or, more precisely, about republican political culture.

As Jean-Jacques Becker has shown, the Union Sacrée yielded huge benefits for the Right, for cultural reasons. In fact, the Right succeeded in "capturing the consensus"—so much so that it sought to turn the wartime consensus into a permanent ideology and a social ideal. When the Radical Party allied itself with the parties of the Right in 1915 and then broke with the Socialists in September 1917, center-left radicalism was the big loser in the "rightward drift" of the Union Sacrée. In fact, the war deprived the Radicals of their identity. Thus the central pillar of the Republic—and of republican culture in France—was permanently weakened. The Right's victory in the November 1919 elections—the Radicals lost both votes and seats, while the Socialists lost only seats—was particularly symptomatic in this regard: the pendulum swung back to the Right for the first time since 1876, and it moved quite a spectacular distance. The first postwar elections therefore did not strengthen the hand of the Republic's staunchest champions. On the contrary, the greatest electoral benefits went to its most lukewarm partisans. More troubling still was that the extreme Right did not participate, while some Radicals and even a few independent Socialists loyal to the Union Sacrée did. The victorious National Bloc was not simply a coalition of right-wing parties. The traditional left/ right cleavage was thus blurred by the formation of a coalition—the National Bloc—which laid down an implicit dividing line between parties that were "in" the nation and parties that excluded themselves from it.

The electoral dimension of this shift no doubt pointed to a deeper change, and one that was more worrisome for the Republic. The "wartime culture" that shaped the system of representations in France during the war promoted right-wing values for the four and a half years of the conflict and indeed beyond—or, if not right-wing values, then at least values alien to the heritage of the Left, as that heritage was understood by the end of the nineteenth century. The cult of military heroism, the focus on the army, the flag, and the nation at war, to say nothing of the revival of religion—all of these things were a windfall for the parties of the Right, and especially the nationalist Right, whose ideas and values dovetailed with those dominant during the war. This was the Right's revenge. Even the "gender barrier," itself exacerbated by the separation of front and rear and the guilt that people in the rear felt with respect to those at the front, "functioned" on behalf of the most traditional values of virility: the war's apparent "emancipation" of women was illusory, and more so in France than elsewhere.

Similarly, the war muted the clash over religion, and this, too, seems to have worked against republicanism. The church saw the Union Sacrée as a way of rejoining the national community, indeed of reconciling France with the church. Catholics, fortified by their belief that France was "the eldest daughter of the church" and that God favored "the Franks," found it easy to support the defense of the fatherland. The path was smoothed, of course, by the decision to suspend the battle against the teaching congregations at the beginning of the war as well as by the great wave of religious fervor that swept over the country as a result of the conflict. The Catholic decision to link the emblem of the Sacred Heart to the flag of the Republic attests to the depths of the desire to rejoin and reconquer the nation after being excluded during the first decade of the twentieth century. This reconquest should be seen, however, in light of what happened in the trenches, where soldiers of Catholic and anticlerical background discovered one another and found that they had much in common: the religious issue, which had loomed so large in French politics before the war, was permanently drained of much of its virulence. The Cartel des Gauches, a center-left alliance, would pay the price for this change in French political culture when it attempted to revive anticlerical sentiment in 1924.

Further evidence of this change can be seen in the new syncretism of the monuments to the dead, most of which were erected in the period 1919–23. Many feature images of Marianne, the symbol of the Republic, holding a fallen soldier in her arms. Frequently, however, the fallen are stripped of their uniforms, and the woman holding them is as much the Virgin as she is the Republic. As Annette Becker has shrewdly remarked, Marianne became the Pietà—a Pietà wearing a Phrygian cap. Since Christian and Republican iconography had previously seemed quite incompatible, such syncretism is surprising; what made it possible was the joining of religious and republican fervor during the war. The two were combined in a "cult of the nation" unlike anything that had gone before, a cult that allied two traditions, both of them patriotic to be sure, but based on largely opposing premises.

Once the civic spirit of republicanism was combined with traditional Catholic themes, however, a fundamental political cleavage was permanently narrowed. The "religious issue" did not disappear, but a political dividing line that had long been decisive in French politics lost much of its pertinence. This development in turn weakened the traditional cleavage between left and right. To some extent, the Republic lost its bearings. We see this too in the desire to transcend political differences after the war—an ambition particularly apparent in the veterans' movement: the men who had been in the trenches, who formed the heart of the electorate in the interwar years, were among those who felt most strongly that the old issues had become obsolete. Nostalgia for the Union Sacrée played a role in Raymond Poincaré's formation of a cabinet of national union in 1926. All of these signs suggest that the old political debate had been exhausted, but instead of leading to a new consensus, this exhaustion merely diminished the Republic's ability to mobilize support. Was it still something that people were willing to fight for?

Indeed, the Republic could only suffer from the dashing of the great hopes that the culture of wartime had fostered. Those hopes were deeply imbued with a secular form of millenarianism, a lay eschatology built around the desire to rid mankind forever of the scourge of war. France had fought the war to end all wars, and this goal became an article of faith, with strong support on the left— the perfect continuation of republican pacifism, a movement that had been temporarily diverted by the outbreak of war. Witness the eschatological language in which a Radical newspaper, Le Progrès of Lyon, described the secularized coming of the Messiah on November 12, 1918: "This war has killed war.... War is dead, and we are the ones who killed it. Let us sing La Marseillaise with new fervor in tribute to this incalculable victory.... Let us celebrate the finest of festivals of humanity.... Let nothing be done that is not noble, magical, and divine!" On October 5, 1919, in Clermont-Ferrand, the Socialist Alexandre Varenne shared the same hope: "A new world will emerge from the war, which in my opinion marks a date as important as the birth of Jesus Christ." Yet it was already clear in 1919, and it would become even clearer in the 1920s, that the better world envisioned by the wartime culture would not be achieved anytime soon: the mass mourning of the postwar years was accompanied by the dashing of eschatological hopes after four and a half years of belief that a better world was on the way. The ensuing disappointment inevitably reinforced the feeling that the Republic was in the process of losing the peace.

Should we be surprised, then, that the victorious Republic lost at least some of its powers of attraction? As evidence of this loss, Maurice Agulhon noted the waning appeal of images of Marianne after 1918. Studies of local commemorations should shed much light on the question of who exactly was credited with victory. Was it the Republic? Or the nation, which was not exactly the same thing, especially after the nonrepublican parties of the Right joined the defensive effort? Thesis research currently underway on the celebration of victory in the *département* of Puy-de-Dôme shows the astonishing degree to which the Republic was forgotten in speeches, political debates, and commemorations in the immediate aftermath of the war: victory was attributed to the nation and its soldiers, not to the Republic, not to the regime itself. Even in this *département,* whose emotional investment in the Republic prior to 1914 had been unusually strong, the republican idea had lost some of its luster in the four and a half years of war. To be sure, local socialists were quick to point out what victory owed to Marianne, but they were virtually alone: in commemorative speeches given shortly after the war, Radicals surprisingly attributed success to the nation and its soldiers, not to the republican regime, of which they had been, and remained, the major pillar. Evidence from other *départements,* such as the Somme, through which the front passed and which emerged from the war ravaged by the fighting, corroborates these findings: Radical Party candidates in November 1919 chose to celebrate the victory of "eternal France" rather than of the Republic.

Of course it is possible to give quite contrasting assessments of the postwar image of the parliamentary Republic. The regime could take pride in having organized, as Clemenceau put it in his speech of November 20, 1918, "the finest day our race has ever known," a day on which France welcomed its "triumphant banners, drenched in blood and tears and torn by shrapnel, the glorious apparition of our illustrious dead." Indeed, it was the dead who marched down the Champs-Élysées on Bastille Day 1919. The following year, in November 1920, the Republic celebrated itself with considerable pomp as it laid the heart of one of its founding fathers, Léon Gambetta, before the tomb of the unknown soldier at the Arc de Triomphe: 1871 was avenged. But behind the facade of ideal victory, the Republic had permanently lost part of its original spirit, though the loss was still not apparent. At the very least, republican values had been diluted, and it was against this background that criticism of the parliamentary system mounted in the 1920s. Should we not therefore look for some of the deeper causes of the political crisis of the next decade in this hidden loss? Furthermore, even if the entire responsibility for the war and its disasters was laid at the door of authoritarian regimes, the fact that democracies had resorted to such violent means for such an extended period of time and used all the resources of science to compound the destruction had inevitably undermined the republican belief in man's continual progress. After 1918, the deepest roots of republican ideals remained blighted by the brutality of war. Did the trauma of the Great War cause the French to lose faith in the Republic? Marianne had indeed emerged victorious from the conflict, but it was as if the war, or a certain idea of the war, had sounded her death knell.

Paradoxically, however, the Republic succeeded in establishing Armistice Day, November 11, as the only national holiday other than Bastille Day to achieve lasting "success." Indeed, it was on November 11, 1940, that the first large demonstration of collective refusal to accept defeat in World War II took place on the Champs-Élysées, as the French for the first time demonstrated resistance to the German occupier and protested the assassination of the Republic by Vichy. The marchers were Parisian university and high-school students, that is, children of survivors of the Great War. This was a sign that the "second generation" had indeed appropriated the symbolism of November 11.

Has that appropriation diminished since that time? Probably less than one might think. Although in the 1970s President Valéry Giscard d'Estaing proposed eliminating May 8 (the holiday marking the victory over the Nazis in World War II) to dramatize France's reconciliation with Germany, there was never any question of tampering with November 11. More recent experience appears to confirm that the date of the 1918 armistice is still the most meaningful in France's calendar of commemorations, which is no doubt why the President of the Republic decided in 2007 to place greater emphasis on the ceremonies of November 11. In March 2008, ninety years after the armistice, France buried the "last *poilu* [World War I soldier]," Lazare Ponticelli, in a unanimous outpouring of emotion that was reminiscent in some ways of the Union Sacrée of the war years. Can this have been anything other than a sign that in the French Republic the immense massacre of 1914–18 retains a particularly sacred character?

References

Agulhon, Maurice. "Marianne en 1914–1918." In Jean-Jacques Becker et al., eds., *Guerre et cultures, 1914–1918,* 373–84. Paris: A. Colin, 1994.

Audoin-Rouzeau, Stéphane. "La Grande Guerre: Le deuil interminable." *Le Débat* 104 (March-April 1999): 117–30.

Audoin-Rouzeau, Stéphane, and Annette Becker. *14–18, Retrouver la guerre.* Paris: Gallimard, 2000.

Becker, Annette. *La guerre et la foi: De la mort à la mémoire, 1914–1930.* Paris: A. Colin, 1994.

Becker, Jean-Jacques. *1914: Comment les Français sont entrés dans la guerre.* Paris: PFNSP, 1977.

———. *La France en guerre, 1914–1918: La grande mutation.* Paris: Complexe, 1988.

Becker, Jean-Jacques, and Serge Berstein. *Victoire et frustrations, 1914–1929.* Paris: Seuil, 1990.

Bock, Fabienne. *Un parlementarisme de guerre, 1914–1919.* Paris: Belin, 2002.

Duménil, Anne. "La commission sénatoriale de l'armée." In O. Forcade, E. Duhamel, and P. Vial, eds., *Militaires en République, 1870–1962,* 313–24. Paris: Publications de la Sorbonne, 1999.

Forcade, Olivier. *"La censure politique en France pendant la Grande Guerre."* Ph.D. diss. Université de Paris X-Nanterre, 1998.

Fryszman, Aline. "La victoire triste? Espérances, déceptions et commémorations de la victoire dans le département du Puy-de-Dôme au sortir de la guerre (1918–1924)." Thesis, EHESS, 2009.

Leroy, Hervé. "La perception de la victoire dans le département de la Somme, de l'armistice du 11 novembre 1918 aux cérémonies du 11 novembre 1920." Mémoire de maîtrise, Université de Picardie, 1993.

Mayeur, Jean-Marie. *La vie politique sous la IIIème République, 1870–1940.* Paris: Seuil, 1984.

Prost, Antoine. *Les anciens combattants et la société française (1914–1939).* Paris: PFNSP, 1977.

Renouvin, Pierre. *Les formes du gouvernement de guerre.* Paris: Les Presses Universitaires de France; New Haven, CT: Yale University Press, 1925.

7

The Republic and Vichy

Julian Jackson

Translated by Arthur Goldhammer

August 25, 1944. Liberated Paris. General de Gaulle arrives at the Hôtel de Ville and is welcomed by the National Resistance Committee (CNR). When invited to proclaim the Republic to the people gathered for the occasion, de Gaulle flatly refuses: "The Republic," he says, "has never ceased to exist. Vichy always was and always will remain null and void." For twenty years, French collective memory shared this Gaullist version of history, according to which, apart from a few collaborators, the vast majority of the French were resisters, and the government of Vichy was merely a puppet state. In other words, Vichy was "German." Robert Aron would attempt to rehabilitate Vichy to a certain extent in his 1954 book, *Le régime de Vichy,* which distinguished a "good" Vichy from a "bad," the former associated with Pétain and the National Revolution between 1940 and 1942, the latter with Laval and collaboration between 1942 and 1944. The book deserves credit for treating Vichy as a historical phenomenon, but it failed to challenge the idea that the vast majority of the French resisted: Aron's strategy was to treat the Vichy regime as part of the resistance effort.

Aron's arguments were demolished in 1972 by Robert Paxton in a work that has since become famous. By showing that all the leaders of Vichy—Pétain no less than Laval—sought to collaborate with the Germans, Paxton destroyed the "two Vichys" thesis. He also showed that Vichy had a political agenda of its own, which it pursued without the slightest pressure from Germany. Hence Vichy was indeed "French." Paxton's book came out just as a new generation in France was beginning to question the myths of its parents. The film *Le Chagrin et la Pitié* (The Sorrow and the Pity, 1969) depicted a France in which much of society had collaborated.

Paxton's book dealt with the Vichy *regime,* but in the 1980s historians turned increasingly to the question of French *society* during the Occupation. The work of Pierre Laborie revealed a country in which public opinion was vacillating and disoriented, as far from the optimistic legend of a resisting France as from the dark legend of a collaborating France. Following this lead, other historians began to study daily life (women, social groups), culture (film, theater, literature), and intermediate structures between state and society (civil servants, police). They also began to investigate the burning question of anti-Semitic persecution. Robert Paxton, Michael Marrus, and Serge Klarsfeld analyzed Vichy's role in Germany's "final solution." But in July 1992, on the occasion of the fiftieth anniversary of the "roundup" of Jews by French police and internment at the "Vel' d'Hiv" (a stadium for bicycle races), President François Mitterrand rather surprisingly became a defender of the Gaullist myth and refused to acknowledge French responsibility in the Holocaust. In his view, "the French nation did not engage in this sad business with the government of Vichy." Paradoxically, it was a Gaullist president, Jacques Chirac, who for the first time, in 1995, formally accepted France's responsibility. Nevertheless, the question continues to haunt the public imagination, so much so that historian Henry Rousso warned against a "Judeocentric" approach to the period, which sees the Vichy regime solely in terms of persecution of the Jews and overlooks the persecution of Communists and other groups. In addition, historians such as Asher Cohen and Renée Poznanski have pointed out that many Jews were sheltered by non-Jewish French citizens. In short, there is general agreement today that a "French Vichy" did indeed "exist," but there is still debate as to its significance and relation to the history of republican France.

To answer this question, let us go back to the beginning. We start with a straightforward observation: Vichy emerged from the ruins of a Republic that had proved unable to avoid a catastrophic military debacle. On June 15, 1940, Prime Minister Paul Reynaud, having taken refuge in Bordeaux along with his government, asked General Weygand to order the French army to surrender. This purely military action, which did not involve the resignation of the government, should have enabled leaders to leave metropolitan France in order to continue the fight from foreign soil, with troops still ready for battle, as the queen of Holland did when she took refuge in London. But Weygand, who wanted the government to sign an armistice, rejected the Dutch solution for France.

Weygand's defiance (which Pétain supported) sealed the fate of the Reynaud government and of the dying Republic. In strictly legal terms, Weygand, who had never done more than pay lip service to the Republic, acted improperly, but in the circumstances of 1940 his argument was not without substance. What influence would "republican legitimacy," as symbolized by Reynaud in exile, have had against the legendary Marshal Pétain, perhaps France's greatest World War I military hero, who remained in France?

On June 16, Reynaud, capitulating to reality, resigned to make way for Pétain. Three weeks later, on July 10, 1940, the National Assembly, meeting in Vichy, granted Pétain "full powers" to promulgate "a new Constitution...[which] must guarantee the rights of Work, Family, and Fatherland." Only eighty deputies voted against the measure. Only a single senator, Marcel Astier, protested, shouting: "Long live the Republic all the same!" Even General de Gaulle in London chose to speak for "honor and country" rather than in the name of the Republic. The Republic having lost its legitimacy in defeat, Pétain derived his standing from his glorious past. In quasi-religious terms ("I give myself" to France), he presented himself as the savior of the nation and protector of a people bewildered by defeat, disoriented by the failings of its elites, and traumatized by the painful ordeal of exodus. The French had been citizens of the Republic; now they became the wards of a grandfatherly redeemer who could be both severe ("It is from yourselves that I want to save you today") and comforting ("My children...gather round me"). The simple and direct tone of Pétain's speeches deliberately avoided the hollow promises of his predecessors, including "We will win because we are stronger." As Pétain put it, "I hate the lies that have done you so much harm." The *pays réel* turned against the *pays légal.*

What did Pétain do with his power? A new constitution was drafted in 1941, but it was never promulgated. To the end, Vichy remained a provisional government. The Republic was never formally abolished, but it surreptitiously disappeared, just as it had been born surreptitiously in 1875: Pétain became head of "the French State" rather than of the French Republic. To the consternation of hard-core antirepublicans, Vichy retained the tricolor flag, the national anthem ("La Marseillaise," although Pétain let it be known that his favorite verse was the sixth, which begins: "Sacred love of the Fatherland"), and the Bastille Day holiday (although playing down its significance), but it also tried to create its own calendar (with May 1 as Labor Day, May 8 as Joan of Arc Day, and the last Sunday in May as Mothers' Day) and its own symbolism (*la francisque,* the oath of the Legion, etc.).

So much for forms and symbols. What about social and political content? In the summer of 1940, everyone who had been excluded from the Republic hastened to Vichy to seize the opportunity created by the political void. The city swarmed with politicians, intellectuals, journalists, and commentators, each of whom had a remedy to propose for what ailed France. Among them were Maurrassians (followers of Charles Maurras, the royalist and prewar leader of the ultranationalist Action Française), fascists, social Catholics, authoritarian

Catholics, union leaders, scout leaders, *cagoulards* (members of extreme right-wing paramilitary groups), social planners, and Personalists (followers of the philosopher Emmanuel Mounier). Who came out on top in this power struggle? In fact, there would never be a definitive winner. All factions remained in contention, continuing to vie for a power that began to unravel as time went by. Vichy, which had been chosen as capital because its numerous hotels could accommodate ministers and bureaucrats, was a small city. The atmosphere was stifling, and conspiracies added spice to a dull existence. Hotel corridors were rife with rumor and intrigue. Between July 1940 and April 1942 there were no fewer than seven ministerial shake-ups. In the words of Stanley Hoffmann, Vichy was a "pluralist dictatorship."

At the top was "the court" of the Marshal, a cold and cunning octogenarian. Foremost among the courtiers was his physician, Dr. Ménétrel, who doubled as his private secretary and screened his many visitors. Laval would later say: "I foresaw everything, except that France would be governed by a doctor." In theory, Pétain was both head of state and head of government (*président du Conseil,* or prime minister), but in reality the governments were headed by the deputy prime minister: Pierre Laval in 1940, Admiral François Darlan in 1941. On the fringes of the government hovered a diffuse group of journalists, study groups, committees of experts, and institutes keen to participate in the national revival and therefore eager to influence government policy. Among these one should mention the École des Cadres (Leadership School) of Uriage, where the Personalist philosophy of Emmanuel Mounier held sway; the cultural group "Young France," founded by Pierre Schaeffer; Alexis Carrel's Foundation for the Study of Human Problems; and the Economy and Humanism Group created by the Dominican Louis Lebret. As the economist Charles Rist put it, Vichy was "total confusionism."

In reality, however, the leading personalities of the regime were mostly former servants of the Republic. There was Laval, a veteran of republican politics, and Darlan, who owed his entire career to his connections with the very republican Georges Leygues. There were high *fonctionnaires* of the Republic such as Yves Bouthillier, an inspector of finance (minister of finance from July 1940 to April 1942); Marcel Peyrouton, a former top colonial civil servant (minister of the interior from July 1940 to December 1940); and René Bousquet, a rising star in the prefectoral corps and protégé of the republican Sarraut brothers (secretary general of the police from April 1942 to December 1943). There were intellectual pillars of the Republic, such as the jurist Joseph Barthélemy (minister of justice from January 1941 to March 1943) and the historian and journalist Lucien Romier (minister of state from January 1941 to December 1943). These were not men who had been "excluded" from the Republic; rather, they had been "disappointed" by it. Their presence at Vichy owed something to the "great fear" of the French bourgeoisie, which still had not recovered from the shock of the Popular Front ("better Hitler than Blum"), but it also attests to what had become of the liberal tradition in France since the end of the nineteenth century. (Léon Blum was the prewar leader of France's Socialist Party and prime minister in the leftist Popular Front government of 1936–37.) There is an obvious link between the presence at Vichy of such eminent republicans as Romier and Barthélemy and the work of the moderate republican Charles Benoist, who in the 1890s began to warn about the eroding power of bourgeois elites—of "competence"—in favor of professional politicians drawn from the provincial petite bourgeoisie. Against the rising tide of mass society, these conservative liberals sought refuge in the cult of the leader and authority. Highly symbolic in this regard was the intellectual itinerary of the writer Daniel Halévy, who evolved from Dreyfusism to Maurrassism and ended as an admirer of Marshal Pétain in 1940. Vichy was in some respects the revenge of the Orléanist "men of competence" against the radical "new strata."

Keeping this overview in mind, we can schematically divide the history of the Vichy regime into four periods:

- July 1940–December 1940. For these six months, Laval was in power. But since he was occupied exclusively with foreign policy—negotiations with Germany—he left domestic policy to "traditionalists" (including the Maurrassian Raphaël Alibert, minister of justice, and the very Catholic Jacques Chevalier, minister of national education), who wanted a "national revolution." Dreaming of an "organic" society based on natural communities—family, profession, region—they celebrated the artisan, the peasant, and the housewife. The "fascist" choice of a single party was rejected in favor of a "Legion of Combatants." Youth organizations were encouraged, but the Nazi model of a single-party youth movement was rejected. Vichy adopted the slogan "Youth united but not unique." This pleased the Catholic Church, which gained ground in the schools. "Fascists" such as Marcel Déat and Lucien Rebatet exiled themselves to Paris.
- December 1940–April 1942. After losing Pétain's confidence, Laval was unceremoniously dismissed on December 13, 1940. Following a brief interlude in which Pierre-Étienne Flandin (another moderate republican) presided over the government, the "Darlan era" began. Darlan's team was full of "young wolves" who dreamed of modernizing France in collaboration with Germany. As graduates of the *grandes écoles* and members of the most prestigious corps of bureaucrats, they had ties to the worlds of industry and finance: for example, François Lehideux had worked for Renault and Jacques Barnaud for the Banque Worms.

Today one would call them technocrats, but at the time people spoke of a mysterious thing called "synarchy." After Darlan, the next most powerful man in the government was Pierre Pucheu, the minister of the interior, a graduate of the École Normale Supérieure who had worked for Pont-à-Mousson, a top metallurgical firm, before joining Jacques Doriot's fascist French Popular Party (PPF). In collaboration with Paul Marion, another former member of the PPF, who became secretary of state for propaganda, Pucheu sought to beef up the regime. The two men attempted to regiment the youth movements and mold the Legion into a more effective unit. Marion set up a group of "propaganda delegates," which he saw as the nucleus of a single party. The government took a dim view of any initiative over which it did not have tight control. Thus Mounier was banned from giving lectures at Uriage. In other words, Vichy was tempted to take a fascist turn but did not entirely succumb.

- April 1942–December 1943. In April 1942, Laval returned to power. The Germans increased their pressure. They requisitioned young Frenchmen to work in Germany under the Compulsory Labor Service (STO). They demanded the deportation of Jews and insisted on a more effective repression of the Resistance. For the Vichy government, the problem was no longer to transform France but rather to manage a situation growing more difficult by the day. This did not displease Laval, who shared neither the nostalgia of the traditionalists nor the dreams of the modernizers; he nursed visions of an authoritarian Republic. More comfortable with republican clientelism than with natural communities or vague efforts to create a single party, he attempted to revive his old republican networks. But support melted away, and in reality the regime relied more and more on the fascist-style Militia, which Joseph Darnand created in January of 1943.

- December 1943–August 1944. At the end of 1943, Pétain attempted to get rid of Laval in order to lay the groundwork for an agreement with the Allies. The Germans reacted immediately. They not only insisted on keeping Laval but also demanded a ministerial shake-up. Parisian "ultras" joined the government: Philippe Henriot became minister of information; Darnand, minister of maintaining order; and Marcel Déat, minister of labor. In these final months, Vichy became an ordinary police state whose only purpose was to track down the "terrorists" of the Resistance.

✏

It was a long road from the nostalgic utopianism of 1940 to the repressive ferocity of 1944. Nevertheless, continuities in Vichy policy should not be underestimated.

All Vichy leaders shared certain fundamental values. They accepted an end to democratic individualism in favor of elitist and authoritarian policies. They rejected "class struggle" for a policy of "social peace" (strikes were prohibited and trade unions suppressed). They wanted to strengthen the family. They believed in the need to eliminate what they called "anti-French elements" (Jews, Communists, and Freemasons). The repressive aspects of the regime intensified over time. Pétain's speech of August 12, 1941, denouncing an "ill wind" marked an important step, but the tendency was present from the beginning. The first Jewish Statute was issued on October 3, 1940. Arrests of Communists began in the fall of 1940. By late 1940, fifty-five thousand people were held in concentration camps.

Above all, all the Vichyites believed firmly in a German victory and in the need to collaborate with Hitler in the name of realism. But these "realists" were in fact fantasists, because they thought it would be possible to remake France despite the presence of Germans on French soil. They believed in "France alone" (Maurras), as if the country could be isolated from the effects of the war in Europe. Films from the Vichy era show an old-fashioned, static, timeless society in which the war and the Germans do not appear. But the regime's intentions were undermined by social and political realities. In October 1940, the hiring of women by the civil service was prohibited. Two years later, that law was suspended because of the shortage of manpower in France. In 1943, prefects were even encouraged to hire women as a way of alleviating the effects of the STO on the labor market. Vichy talked incessantly about the family at a time when there were 11 or 12 million prisoners of war, leaving hundreds of thousands of families without fathers. The gap between Pétainist discourse and the daily reality of the French people grew steadily wider.

Having destroyed local democracy in October 1940 by replacing the elected General Councils with administrative commissions appointed by the government, Vichy never succeeded in establishing its own lines of communication to the people. The Legion turned out to be too sectarian to play that role, and the propaganda delegates never developed as an institution. By attacking republican values, Vichy drove the Resistance (and de Gaulle) to a revival of republican discourse. It was in the name of rediscovered republican values that de Gaulle attempted to close the parenthesis of Vichy in August 1944.

It would be wrong, however, to believe in the comforting illusion that Vichy was only a parenthesis. In both its precursors and successors, Vichy belongs to the history of France, and even to the history of republican France. With respect to precursors, we have already seen how the regime revealed the decay of democratic values among French liberals. But the ideology of the National Revolution also drew on the natalist discourse of the interwar years and on the virulent French anti-Semitism of the 1930s. All of this explains why the historian Gérard Noriel was able to speak of the "republican origins of Vichy." Vichy also left traces on its successors. The Fourth Republic was in some ways shaped by men who had participated in Vichy before taking their distance from the regime. Such was true, for example, of the celebrated economist François Perroux, who was a very loyal Pétainist before becoming one of the architects of French planning after 1945. It was true as well of François Gravier, whose book *Paris et le desert français* (1947) became the bible of postwar decentralizers. And it was true of Hubert Beuve-Méry, one of the intellectual stars of the Uriage Leadership School, who became one of the most respected voices in postwar France as director of the newspaper *Le Monde*. In short, if Vichy was in large part the work of men disappointed in the Third Republic, the France of the Fourth Republic owed a great deal to men disappointed in Vichy.

References

Baruch, M.-O. *Servir l'état français: L'administration en France de 1940 à 1944.* Paris: Fayard, 1997.

Burrin, P. *Living with Defeat.* London: Arnold, 1996.

Faure, C. *Le projet culturel de Vichy: Folklore et révolution nationale.* Lyon: Presses Universitaires de Lyon, 1989.

Hoffmann, S. "The Vichy Circle of French Conservatives." In *Decline or Renewal: France since the 1930s.* New York: Viking, 1974.

Jackson, J. *The Dark Years.* Oxford: Oxford University Press, 2001.

Monnet, F. *Refaire la République: Andre Tardieu, une dérive réactionnaire, 1976–1945.* Paris: Fayard, 1993.

Noiriel, G. *Les origines républicaines de Vichy.* Paris: Hachette, 1999.

Paxton, R. *Vichy France.* New York: Knopf, 1972.

Peschnaski, D. *Vichy: Control et exclusion.* Brussels: Editions Complexe, 1997.

Pollard, M. *Reign of Virtue: Mobilizing Gender in Vichy France.* Chicago: University of Chicago Press, 1998.

8

The Fourth Republic

Rosemary Wakeman

The Fourth Republic, according to the historian Pascal Cauchy, is the poor parent of contemporary French history, "little-liked, born a bit by chance … out of the desire to forget defeat, foreign occupation, and an authoritarian regime" (3). The squabbling politics of the years 1946 to 1958 that led to an astounding twenty-six governments are often judged incomprehensible and largely irrelevant to the larger schema of French history. If the Fourth Republic is given any notice by scholars, it is generally to condemn the regime as dysfunctional and unable to deal effectively with the extraordinary problems facing France in the postwar era. To add to this humiliation, the Fourth Republic is often brushed aside in contemporary historiography by the Trente Glorieuses, or "Thirty Glorious Years," of sweeping postwar economic and social transformation. Yet the Fourth Republic may have more claims on our scholarship than previously thought. Historians now argue that it was at the epicenter of extraordinary changes in France. These twelve years from October 1946, when the Fourth Republic's Constitution was ratified, to the regime's demise in June 1958, were the stage for the full flowering of the Cold War, the painful process of decolonization, the French economic miracle, the construction of Europe, and a social metamorphosis that created a new French middle class. The Fourth Republic was able to weather these storms, however briefly, by constructing a polymorphous political center at the core of governance.

Most historians identify an initial stabilization of "liberated France" under a provisional government from 1944 to 1946, followed by an era of reconstruction from 1946 to 1951 that saw the opening salvos of the Cold War. These years were marked by the shift from the Resistance and the tripartite coalition of Communists, Socialists, and the Catholic-oriented Mouvement Républicain Populaire (MRP) to the Third Force (center-left) politics that dominated the regime's early political landscape. The role of de Gaulle's theatrical resignation in January

1946 in protest against a *gouvernement d'assemblée* has been downplayed in recent historiography, which instead concentrates on the politics surrounding the purge of Vichyites and collaborators, and on postwar reconstruction. Scholars in both France and the United States have uncovered the civil wars that lay just beneath the veneer of liberation and national unity. These unresolved conflicts continued to divide France throughout the Fourth Republic and muted the vainglorious optimism associated with the Trente Glorieuses.

The year 1947 provides good evidence of the underlying tensions that frequently bubbled to the surface and forced the Fourth Republic to deal with unending crises. Three years after the Liberation, continued rationing of basic foodstuffs, the odious black market, and soaring inflation fueled frustrations. Government-imposed price reductions only added to the economic crisis by strengthening the black market and encouraging farmers to hold back their grain. The conditions of daily life became desperate. Bread riots were followed by strikes and large-scale demonstrations on May Day throughout France. Rampant fears of a Communist takeover, fueled by the advent of the East-West Cold War, moved Prime Minister Paul Ramadier to expel a furious Maurice Thorez and the Communist Party from the tripartite governing coalition. The dismissal of Communist ministers exacerbated the social conflict, expanding the strike wave throughout the public sector, industry, the banks, and transport, and brought the economy to a standstill. Still immensely popular thanks to their crucial role in the Resistance, the Confédération Générale du Travail (CGT) and Communist Party championed working-class interests and used the unrest to solidify their voting base. Meanwhile, news of the Cominform's creation in Eastern Europe merged with fears of Communist subversion inside France in an atmosphere of growing, although largely unfounded, panic. It set the stage for the Third Force centrist alternative to *tripartisme* that vowed to save the Fourth Republic from leftist extremism. Socialists, the center-right Union Démocratique et Socialiste de la Résistance (UDSR), the old Radical Party, the Christian Democratic MRP, and a host of centrist politicians joined forces. But the threat to the Fourth Republic came likewise from the right and the reappearance of Charles de Gaulle with his newly formed Rally for the French People (Rassemblement du Peuple Française, or RPF). De Gaulle railed against the Communists and denounced the Fourth Republic's "little parties who were absorbed in the intrigues of their own little world" (qtd. in Rioux 127). Votes for the RPF surged in the municipal elections of October 1947. In the words of Socialist Party head Guy Mollet, the Fourth Republic's mission was to "defend democracy and the Republic against Gaullist or communist 'totalitarian danger' and to assure financial stability and social justice" (Cauchy 43). By reformulating institutional and political practices around the center, France aimed to maintain its independence in the new geopolitics of the Cold War and retain its position as a colonial power.

The MRP became the mainstay of the Fourth Republic, and progressive Catholics provided some of its most talented leaders, among them Robert Schuman, who led the campaign for European integration. The revival of Christian Democratic, or in France, Catholic, politics was sustained by the popularity of postwar humanism. Its universalist principles focused on the human condition and on the values of dignity, equality, and tolerance. This moral and intellectual perspective provided the ideological adhesive for French national unity, a fragile field in the early postwar years. In the context of a shattered nation, the optimism and hopefulness of humanist discourse held enormous power. It brought together intellectuals from a variety of backgrounds, from the religious to the secular, the technocratic to the Marxist. These writers expounded humanist principles in the two most powerful journals of progressive opinion, *Le Temps Modernes* and *Esprit*. Among the main proponents of this moderate humanist politics, the MRP led the defense of parliamentary democracy against de Gaulle's call for robust executive power. The Republic's coalitions championed passage of a new constitution, the right to work and strike, and the right to health and quality of life, education, and political asylum. The regime endorsed the ideal of human brotherhood and sanctioned the social projects of the Popular Front and the Resistance. In 1945, French women voted for the first time. These measures formed part of the broad political consensus that permeated Western Europe after the war.

It was a high-minded project indicative of the Liberation's hopes and dreams, and it was bound to disappoint. The Fourth Republic's new constitution was defeated in a first referendum and then passed with only a slim majority on the second try. In a coup de grâce against executive authority, power was "democratized." The National Assembly and its wrangling parties took charge. The opposition of both left and right political extremes and the hydra-like composition of the centrist Third Force alliance created the conditions for permanent governmental instability. The Socialist Party (SFIO), the MRP, Radicals, and Independents all attempted to steer a temperate course through a boiling sea of domestic and foreign difficulties. The always-fragile coalition governments produced an endless succession of premiers and cabinets all broadly identical in composition. Around them flowered a host of cantankerous political movements and interest groups. The negative reputation of the Fourth Republic falls on the shoulders of the backroom political squabbling that resulted, the tactic of *attentisme* and remaining in power "by evading the issues" (Rioux 195), and the ministerial crises that increasingly alienated the French public.

In France's postwar historiography this image formed the core of a historical narrative in which France undergoes an almost seamless twentieth-century political decline from the Third Republic through the Second World War and Occupation to the postwar era. Recently, however, historians have argued that the stigma is undeserved. Paradoxically, the Third Force Socialists and MRP succeeded in creating a broad centrist coalition at the governing core that defended the Republic against its foes and, perhaps even more important, solidified the French public's acceptance of republican values as the basis for national unity. The endless political reshuffling on the surface of the Fourth Republic's political life hides this deeper, more fundamental success from view. None of the Cold War rhetoric or the strikes and clashes in the streets seriously threatened this republican consensus. Despite its apparent volatility, the regime succeeded in carrying through a coherent program of reconstruction, planning, and economic modernization that stabilized France's international position.

One reason for this underlying stability was the continuity of key political figures, men such as Schuman and Georges Bidault for the MRP, Paul Ramadier and Vincent Auriol for the Socialists, René Pleven for the UDSR, Henri Queuille for the Radicals, Antoine Pinay for the conservatives, and eventually Jacques Chaban-Delmas for the Gaullists. These were the political figures most associated with the Fourth Republic. Their practice of republicanism was double-edged. An increasingly skeptical public accused them of playing musical chairs in cabinets that on average lasted six months. Yet at the same time they provided continuity and a measure of stability amid unrelenting crises. As President of the National Assembly in 1946–47 and then President of the Republic from 1947 to 1954, the socialist Auriol personified the Third Force attempt to reconcile political factions and rule from the center. Elected to the presidency by a wide margin, Auriol was viewed as the backbone of the regime, upholding political authority in the face of incessant ministerial crises (a dozen in seven years). Historians now argue that the experiences of Vichy, the Occupation and Resistance, and the purges inspired a revised political culture in which politicians from a variety of castes proved more dynamic and receptive to change than has been previously assumed. Conservative René Pleven, for example, held a number of cabinet posts and became prime minister in 1950. An ardent supporter of European integration, he pushed through the ratification of the Schuman Plan for the European Coal and Steel Community and proposed the European Defense Community. Pleven kept with tradition in defending French colonial rule in Indochina and was defense minister in 1954, when the defeat at Dien Bien Phu ended French hegemony in the region. The Resistance hero and head of the MRP, Georges Bidault, served the Fourth Republic in a variety of capacities—as prime minister, foreign minister, and defense minister—and supported a program of social reform and a state-managed economy. As an Atlanticist, Bidault was one of the founding fathers of European-American cooperation. Like Pleven, he insisted on maintaining French ties to colonial empire.

The elections of 1951 swept away the Third Force and inaugurated the well-known slide to the political right as the Socialists joined the opposition and the Gaullists took their place alongside the Radicals and MRP to form a new center-right coalition. Although the MRP remained in power, it had lost its luster as herald of Liberation principles. Humanistic ideals now played a secondary role to pragmatism and administration by *haute fonctionnaires*. The overhaul of France's administrative machinery and a more open recruitment of civil service elites signaled a broad change in governance. While politicians bickered endlessly in the National Assembly, a technocratic corps took up positions in an expanding state bureaucracy, determined to avoid the sectarian strife of the past, to modernize backward business elites, and transform France into a forward-looking nation. The creation of the École Nationale d'Administration (ENA) in 1945 consolidated the state's selection and training of senior officials and created a meritocracy at the highest levels of public administration. Their dirigiste policies shifted France toward a more modern public service framework akin to Great Britain's budding welfare state.

The French technocratic approach has been extensively studied and at times criticized as bureaucratic authoritarianism. Yet throughout Europe, states took upon themselves the task of overseeing economic reform. Their most basic aim was to control the swings of the capitalist economic cycle and avoid plunging their countries into another devastating depression. Reconstruction and modernization were also considered the ultimate safeguards against political extremism, and especially against communism. The grand *commis* (high-ranking civil servants) embraced Keynesian state policies and American aid in the form of the Marshall Plan. The Commissariat Général du Plan and its Modernization Commissions, inspired by civil servant Jean Monnet and a growing technical elite, were vital to the resurgence of the economy and to France's emergence as a modern nation. These commissions produced a series of five-year plans for economic development and became a rare arena for social and political consensus. The First Five-Year Plan for Modernization and Equipment (the Monnet Plan, 1947–53) made reconstruction the priority. The Second Plan (1953–58) focused on the industrial infrastructure and on agriculture.

Given the relative success of these plans, many historians argue that the Fourth Republic revealed a firmer grasp of economic and political realities than the British governments of the same period. France was transformed from a byword for economic Malthusianism into a modern industrial power. Labor-management missions to the United States sponsored by the Marshall Plan introduced the French to American-style production and marketing strategies. Productivity and modernization became the dominant themes. The banking sector, public utilities, car and aircraft manufacturing, and the coal and steel industries were all nationalized and modernized. They produced an outpouring of technological wizardry from the Caravelle airplane to the Citroën DS (or Déese) that became the symbols of the age. François Bloc-Lainé was the most celebrated spokesman for this growth-oriented *économie concerté*. But modernizers were found among public officials, politicians of the Left and Right, labor leaders, industrialists, and intellectuals. There was general agreement that a new French identity could be forged through a managed economy and social reform led by dynamic public administrators working for the providential state.

Their numbers included Paul Delouvrier, Guy de Carmoy, and Pierre Mendès-France as well as Étienne Hirsch, Jean Fourastié, and Alfred Sauvy. Jean Monnet and Robert Schuman established joint management of the coal and steel industries with West Germany and laid the groundwork for the European Common Market. The reality of German resurgence and European economic integration were as much behind the modernization drive as concerns about rectifying the failures of the past. Indeed, the innovations instigated by the Fourth Republic's political and technocratic elite represented a radical departure from the do-nothing Third Republic and stalemate society of the prewar years. They were instrumental to the specifically European path to state-managed modernization and capitalism. In this sense, France was a first-rate example of the European success stories of economic modernization backed, supervised, and planned by government.

Yet despite this enthusiasm for modernization, social tensions and stark inequities remained. France remained a society of scarcity in the early 1950s, and social divisions remained deep; there were winners and losers in the wrenching process of modernization. Despite its political exile, the Communist Party continued to offer a counterhumanistic alternative to the Fourth Republic's "bourgeois" society, an alternative that held tremendous appeal. Protests against "coca-colonization" and the Marshall Plan articulated fears about American domination. Strikes continued throughout the 1950s over salaries and living standards. Although the currency was stabilized, inflation remained a curse in the initial postwar years, and Finance Minister Pinay's efforts to defend the consumer achieved only partial success. By mid-decade, recession and unemployment reached levels not seen since the Liberation.

The postwar economic crisis became particularly acute in 1953, when public-sector employees suffering from low salaries and declining purchasing power came close to leading a general strike. Led by rank-and-file militants of the syndicalist Force Ouvrière, almost four million workers paralyzed the country by walking out in August at the height of vacation season. Adding to the Fourth Republic's social ferment was a massive housing crisis that brought homeless advocate abbé Pierre and thousands of infuriated French out in protest the same year. The government's favoring of modern industry over declining sectors of the economy provoked a virile reaction among small-time shopkeepers and traditional small-business people, who organized under the leadership of populist Pierre Poujade.

Begun as a protest against the income tax and price controls imposed by Pinay to limit inflation, *poujadisme* flowered into a full-blown reaction to industrialization, urbanization, and American-style modernization, widely perceived as threats to the identity of rural France. From their nerve center in the Lot, the Poujadists fanned out into the center and the southwest in support of *les petits.* Protests by winegrowers in the Midi and cattle farmers in the west turned violent. Roadblocks and barricades went up; prefectures were besieged. Yet for all the turmoil neither the strikes of 1953 nor the Poujadist protests that followed constituted a vast social movement, nor did they threaten the regime. Still, there is no doubt that the Fourth Republic was shaken by the multifaceted unrest. The Third Force political coalition collapsed; stalemate and disillusion followed in its wake. In June–July 1953, France's political leaders found themselves unable to form a viable governing coalition. Despite the tireless efforts of President Auriol, the deadlock lasted a full thirty-six days. In the end, the investiture of the center-right Joseph Laniel as prime minister provided a temporary, though relatively effective, solution. This outcome showed that the Fourth Republic was able to survive its calamities by steering a hardheaded centrist agenda that aligned with the general conviction that republicanism offered the best hope for national unity.

Following the crises of 1953 and 1954, Pierre Mendès-France, a reform-minded member of the Radical Party, became the face of the Fourth Republic. Named prime minister in June 1954, the Radical leader took office on an emergency platform. "Mendès" or "PMF," as he was known, enjoyed broad popularity with the French public for his pragmatic leadership and appeared to be the one politician who could liquidate the war in Indochina and reconcile French republican political culture with the modern transformations of the postwar era. He negotiated France's withdrawal from Indochina in the nine-power Geneva Conference of May–July 1954 and, at the same time, took the first steps toward Tunisian and Moroccan independence. Mendès attempted to crack open the regime's ossified political practices and do away with *attentisme.* He embraced the media and appealed to the nation in his Saturday evening radio broadcasts rather than relying on venal political maneuvering. He sponsored constitutional reform to strengthen executive powers. And rather than bargaining with established figures over ministerial portfolios, Mendès appointed youthful figures to government positions, including François Mitterrand (Interior Ministry), Jacques Chaban-Delmas (Public Works), and Jean Berthoin (Education Ministry). Like many of his Fourth Republic contemporaries, Mendès advocated European integration and a European Defense Community. In his May 14, 1954, "Appel à la jeunesse," published in the news magazine *L'Express,* he proposed far-reaching economic modernization through a dynamic public sector and investments in new industries, education, and scientific research. Although the "Mendès moment" lasted a mere seven months, its impact on France was profound. It signaled a change in France's political culture and the rise of a new generation to lead the Trente Glorieuses.

By the end of the 1950s, the "baby boom" had increased the Hexagon's population from around forty million in 1950 to nearly forty-five million in 1958. In the early 1950s, life in France was still based in the countryside and in small towns. Labor still meant work on farms, in artisan crafts, in retailing, and in transport as much as work in factories. But in the postwar years, the French broke with tradition by moving to towns and cities in droves. The old rural village patterns gave way to nuclear families and urban living, particularly in the country's largest towns and cities. The decentralization of government and of nationalized industries transferred jobs from Paris to the provinces and remade old provincial capitals into new centers of a modernizing France. The new middle classes embraced the prosperity of the Trente Glorieuses, with its seductive consumerism and the comforts of private family life. Many moved into the new public housing projects and early *grands ensembles* being built on urban peripheries throughout France, while city centers were cleared of crumbling neighborhoods and built anew. Although housing construction proceeded at a snail's pace during the reconstruction years, between 1953 and 1957 nearly a million new residences went up. French families invested in household appliances, new clothing fashions, and personal hygiene products, enjoying the benefits of the new leisure society. From 1947, Renault factories churned out the 4CV model, the first mass-produced car in France. Immensely popular, it was emblematic of the 1950s and the country's turn toward mass consumption. By the end of the 1950s, some six million cars ruled the roads, and one household in four owned an automobile. In all, the consumer index grew by 40 percent between 1949 and 1957. These vast changes in lifestyle, and the overall improvement in social conditions, stemmed in large part from the consensus policies of the regime.

In addition, France under the Fourth Republic absorbed the effects of mass culture and the media. Advertising, glossy photo-magazines such as *Paris-Match,* the radio, and, slowly, television broadened the appeal of celebrity and consumer culture. From 1952, French families enjoyed such weekly television game shows as *La Tête et les Jambes* and the musical variety programs *La Joie de Vivre* and *Trente-six Chandelles.* Weekly news magazines such as *L'Express* enjoyed a large and relatively affluent readership. Founded by Radical Party luminary Jean-Jacques Servan-Schreiber and by Françoise Giroud, who directed *Elle* magazine, *L'Express* joined much of France's new media in supporting the state's modernizing policies. Women's magazines such as *Elle* introduced French women to new ideas about fashion, hygiene, and domestic consumption. In general the growth of the magazine and media industries created a new national community, a "neo-bourgeois space" (Kristen Ross) that forged French identity and lifestyles in the fast-moving currents of the Trente Glorieuses.

In 1967, Servan-Schreiber published *The American Challenge,* a call to match the economic powerhouse across the Atlantic. But the captivating style and energy of Americanization was problematic for France: it was both embraced enthusiastically and rejected as dire threat. The massive influx of American films, music, and consumer culture that accompanied the Liberation became a torrent in the 1950s. Although there were spectacular instances of anti-Americanism, such as the protests and riots against General Ridgway in 1952, the aversion to Americanization never became a widespread cultural phenomenon. It was closely tied to the Cold War and the stance of left-wing intellectual elites. Opinion polls in the 1950s actually revealed the French to be among the least anti-American in Western Europe. In 1953, 61 percent of respondents declared themselves sympathetic with the United States. France was able to hold its own against the Yankee icon and the "American way of life." A distinctly French version of the modern emerged in the 1950s. Existential beatniks in black cruised the Left Bank in Paris and descended into basement clubs to hear the jazz avant-garde. Intellectuals from Jean-Paul Sartre to Françoise Sagan achieved mythic status. Students and tourists flocked to the cafés of Saint-Germain-des-Prés to spy the mandarins of postwar French intellectual life. By the end of the decade, French rock 'n' roll rebels cut their first records, and Johnny Hallyday was set to become one of the most prolific and successful rock stars of the late twentieth century. France had its own version of glamour. Celebrities from Yves Montand and Jean-Paul Belmondo to Brigitte Bardot mesmerized French fans and achieved international fame. The years of the Fourth Republic were a golden age of French cinema, from the high-quality poetic genre inherited from the prewar period to film noir and the first inklings of the New Wave revolution. Ciné-clubs and film journals abounded, each contributing to intense debates over film style and ultimately to modern film criticism. This rich *cinéphilie* infused the conventions of Hollywood with a distinctly French flair. The 1950s were, then, a period of intense cultural creativity in which a distinctly modern French identity was being forged.

Far from a dysfunctional abyss, the Fourth Republic was then a force for republican resurgence and for the modernization of social, political, and cultural life. But important as they were, these attributes could not save the regime. The intensifying economic and colonial crises increasingly personalized political power around such figures as Antoine Pinay, Joseph Laniel, and Pierre Mendès-France. The war in Indochina, the mounting Algerian crisis, and the formation of "Europe of the Six" dominated their governments. Despite the lack of widespread public opposition to the regime, its demise came quickly in a last, short phase from 1956 to 1958, dominated by the Algerian War. This brutal crisis highlighted all the Fourth Republic's contradictions. If there was no great sentiment against it, virtually no one found the inspiration to save it. Still, even if the

Algerian crisis ultimately brought it down, the Fourth Republic might better be seen as the victim of rapid growth and modernization, of social transformations that may have come too fast. The tensions they wrought played as large a role in its demise as did the inability to cope with Algerian nationalism and the end of France's colonial rule.

References

Bourg, Julien. *After the Deluge: New Perspectives on the Intellectual and Culture History of Postwar France*. Lanham, MD: Lexington Books, 2004.

Cauchy, Pascal. *La IVe République*. Paris: Presses Universitaires de France, 2004.

Elgey, Georgette, Marie-Caroline Boussard, and Matthieu Rey. *Histoire de la IVe République*. 5 vols. Paris: Fayard, 1993–2000.

Guilleminault, Gilbert. *Le roman vrai de la IIIe et de la IVe République, 1870–1958*. Vol. 2. Paris: Robert Laffont, 1991.

Judt, Tony. *Past Imperfect: French Intellectuals, 1944–1956*. Berkeley: University of California Press, 1992.

Kelly, Michael. *The Cultural and Intellectual Rebuilding of France after the Second World War*. New York: Palgrave Macmillan, 2004.

Kuisel, Richard. *Seducing the French: The Dilemma of Americanization*. Berkeley: University of California Press, 1993.

Rioux, Jean-Pierre. *The Fourth Republic, 1944–1958*. Cambridge and Paris: Cambridge University Press and Éditions de la Maison des Sciences de l'Homme, 1987.

Ross, Kristen. *Fast Cars, Clean Bodies: Decolonization and the Reordering of French Culture*. Cambridge, MA, and London: MIT Press, 1996.

Rousso, Henry. *The Vichy Syndrome: History and Memory in France since 1944*. Translated by Arthur Goldhammer. Cambridge, MA: Harvard University Press, 1991.

9

The Fifth Republic

Martin Schain

For well over a decade after the birth of Fifth Republic (September 28, 1958), social scientists and journalists considered it a fragile regime. Viewed in the context of French republican history, this new regime appeared to be a stopgap affair, a temporary solution to a crisis of decolonization. The new constitution was so strongly formulated to meet the priorities of the regime's founding figure and first President that observers frequently labeled it "the de Gaulle Republic." It is striking, therefore, that fifty years later, amid the most serious economic crisis since the Great Depression, the regime now appears both stable and uncontested. For the first time since the French Revolution, a key focus of French politics is no longer the regime itself.

Like each of its four predecessors, the Fifth Republic emerged from civil strife linked to the breakdown of the preceding regime. The last years of the Fourth Republic may have seen economic success, but political failure both at home and abroad overshadowed the country's other gains. The Suez invasion of 1956 ended in humiliation and undermined the legitimacy of the Socialist-led government in power. The governments that followed were seen as ineffective in subduing the growing rebellion in Algeria, and the Republic itself was accused of lacking the institutional strength to exert leadership in a time of crisis. By May 1958, the regime had lost the support of France's major political forces, especially the Communists on the left and the Gaullists on the right. These developments indicated the need for constitutional change designed to strengthen the government's ability to lead.

The immediate cause of the downfall of the Fourth Republic was a military coup in Algeria, which took place in the context of a governmental crisis in Paris. At the beginning of May 1958, General Raoul Salan, commander of French forces in Algeria, wired the President of the Republic with a thinly veiled threat. "It would be impossible," Salan wrote, "to predict [the army's] reaction" if the new prime minister were not firmly committed to the maintenance of

French Algeria. If most Muslim Algerians wanted separation from France, the overwhelming majority of European Algerians sought to keep Algeria French. To maintain French rule, Europeans, whether military or civilian, appeared increasingly favorable to the army's seizure of power there. When France's new premier-designate, Pierre Pflimlin, pledged to negotiate a cease-fire with leaders of the Algerian independence movement (without specifying a date), French military officials in Algiers resolved to overturn the Republic. On May 13, as the National Assembly in Paris debated the investiture of Pflimlin's government, military leaders in Algiers seized the governor-general's headquarters and established a civil and military Committee of Public Safety (*salut publique*). They then demanded the establishment of a Government of Public Safety in Paris as well.

For two weeks, France hovered on the brink of civil war. As troops from Algiers took control of Corsica in preparation for an assault on the mainland, government leaders found themselves powerless to oppose the impending coup. At this point, General Charles de Gaulle, the former Resistance leader, who had been largely absent from the Fourth Republic, announced his willingness to serve a "useful" role. On May 28, the generals in Algiers endorsed de Gaulle's move, telegraphing President René Coty that paratroopers would invade Paris two days later if he failed to appoint de Gaulle prime minister. Coty complied, accepting the "conditional" resignation of his cabinet and, after a series of tense negotiations, the investiture of de Gaulle. On June 2, de Gaulle became the Fourth Republic's last premier, as an overwhelming majority of the Assembly effectively voted the regime out of existence.

Within a day of de Gaulle's investiture, the new government passed an enabling act outlining a procedure for creating a new constitution. In less than two months, the cabinet prepared a first draft, which it then submitted to a Constitutional Consultative Committee, and finally to the Conseil d'État. The core ideas for the constitution were rooted in the long constitutional debate in France since the Revolution. But the key elements of the quasi-presidential system that emerged in the summer of 1958 stemmed from a study organized by Michel Debré during the Second World War and from a speech by de Gaulle in September 1946. It was no surprise, therefore, that Debré played a pivotal role both in organizing the process and in writing the constitution of what became the Fifth Republic. In a referendum of September 28, 1958, nearly 80 percent of the electorate (with 85 percent of eligible voters participating) approved the new charter.

Every new constitution is meant to deal with the perceived problems of governance in the existing system. Although the Fourth Republic was eminently successful in guiding the country through the post–World War II economic recovery (a process one analyst called "the invisible revolution"), governmental ineffectiveness and the political inability to manage and resolve key issues undermined the legitimacy of the regime. A great many analysts located the core of the problem in the weakness of executive authority and related that weakness to the executive's dependence on parliamentary majorities that tended to dissolve rapidly once a government was in place. The inability to maintain parliamentary majorities, in turn, was linked to both the large number of political parties and their weak organization. All governments had to be coalition governments, and the political glue that held them together proved extremely thin. Adding to the regime's instability was the permanent outsider status of the country's largest (in terms of electoral support) and best-organized political party, the Communist Party, judged unacceptable as a coalition partner by both the Right and the Left after 1947. While this situation posed a particular problem for the Left, it created a deeper problem for the legitimacy of the political system. The 20–25 percent of French voters who routinely supported the Communists found themselves and their party permanently barred from office and essentially alienated from the regime.

In general, the Fifth Republic's new political system featured a more radical solution to the problem of authority than had any of France's four previous republican regimes. It created a powerful executive (President and prime minister) that—once in place—was well protected from the vicissitudes of changing parliamentary majorities. Indeed, the prime minister was no longer required to have a parliamentary majority and could be forced to resign only in the event of a formal no-confidence vote in the National Assembly. In addition, the executive now controlled the legislative agenda and the legislative process in unprecedented ways. A new constitutional separation between rule making and legislating placed whole categories of lawmaking directly in the hands of the executive (rule making), and gave it the prerogative to force Parliament to vote on its own proposals, rather than those initiated or amended in the National Assembly. It also permitted the executive to enact legislation without parliamentary approval by declaring the "responsibility of the government" on the passing of a bill. In such a case, the bill (*projet de loi*) is passed without a vote unless an absolute majority votes no confidence in the government. The only way, in other words, to reject such a bill would be to bring the government down.

Although the 1958 Constitution gave the President the right to appoint both the prime minister and all other cabinet members, in a formal sense the prime minister enjoyed considerable independence and power. The Constitution attributed virtually all of the enhanced legislative powers elaborated above to the prime minister, whom the President could not formally dismiss. The one clear, independent (and controversial) authority that the Constitution granted the President was the emergency power (Article 16) to act unilaterally "when institutions of the Republic, the independence of the nation, the integrity of its territory or the fulfillment of its international commitments are under serious and immediate threat, and when the proper functioning of the constitutional public authorities is interrupted." Beyond these emergency powers, the President enjoys the right to dissolve Parliament and call for new elections whenever he wants, provided only that he consult with the prime minister and parliamentary leaders first.

In these ways, executive power is guaranteed constitutionally, unlike other parliamentary systems (the British, for example), in which executive power is contingent on reliable, well-organized parliamentary majorities. Thus the most important difference between the new French system and the old is the formal separation in certain key ways of the executive from the legislative branch. To remain in office, neither the President nor the prime minister needed the support of a parliamentary majority. The prime minister, moreover, did not have to be an elected member of Parliament, and the President was named by an electoral college of about eighty thousand people largely independent of the National Assembly.

Although proclaimed as a solution to the instability and immobilism of the Fourth Republic, the Fifth Republic confronted a series of challenges to its legitimacy that left its durability uncertain until the 1970s. During its first four years, the new regime faced two military revolts (three, if we include the revolt in 1958); an underground terrorist movement directed by former high military officials; at least three assassination attempts against President de Gaulle; two periods of emergency government during which the normal functioning of Parliament was suspended; numerous shuffles and changes of government and the successful censuring of the government by parliamentary majority; and a major constitutional revision of dubious legality. The Algerian problem, moreover, was finally settled by referendum, rather than by more conventional parliamentary processes.

Throughout its first year, de Gaulle's government found itself preoccupied with the complexities of launching a new political regime and especially with the Algerian revolt. In September, de Gaulle announced a tentative direction for negotiations with the Algerian nationalists, offering them the possibility of self-determination in the near term and the ultimate prospect of choosing their own future. Such negotiations enjoyed strong support in the National Assembly but faced violent opposition from supporters of Algérie Française in both Algeria and metropolitan France. In Paris, the Gaullist party split into supporters and opponents of the President's plans, while Georges Bidault, the influential leader of the centrist Christian Democrats (MRP), rejected the proposals. The respected minister of finance, Antoine Pinay, resigned. The new Republic's very existence was threatened when both the armed forces and civil service in Algeria strenuously opposed any hint of independence for the colony, raising doubts about their loyalty to the regime. De Gaulle reacted by replacing certain generals and trying to force the allegiance of the civil service.

In late September, pro–Algérie Française riots broke out in Algiers, killing several police officers. The paratroopers dispatched to quell the rebellion seemed sympathetic to the rioters, who began to construct barricades (hence, "the revolt of the barricades"). By the end of the month, the army finally dispersed the insurgents, but only after being ordered to do so by de Gaulle in a televised address. On February 3, 1960, the President was granted the authority to use decree power (under Article 38 of the Constitution) to take all necessary measures to maintain order, safeguard the Constitution, and deal with the Algerian situation.

De Gaulle employed these powers both to move forward on the Algerian problem and to pacify the army, using positive and negative means. On the one hand, he renewed his commitment to the development of an independent French atomic force (*force de frappe*), which the army wanted; and on the other, he transferred unreliable senior officers to posts outside of Algeria. Toward the end of the year, the President announced a referendum, set for January 1961, to approve new Algerian political institutions. The results, both in mainland France and Algeria, overwhelmingly supported de Gaulle's approach. But they triggered a putsch in Algeria later known as "the Revolt of the Generals." To counter it, de Gaulle invoked emergency powers under Article 16 for the first (and only) time in the Fifth Republic's history. In the end, the generals were able to mobilize little public support, but they moved underground, establishing the Secret Army Organization (Organisation Armée Secrète, or OAS), which then initiated a campaign of terror that included several attempts on de Gaulle's life. Undaunted, the President proceeded to negotiate an independence agreement with Algerian nationalists, ultimately approved at Évian in March 1962 and ratified by referendum a month later in France.

The Fifth Republic's founding crisis had, at long last, come to an end. But, paradoxically perhaps, de Gaulle's political support was beginning to wane. With Algeria settled, other issues emerged, especially the question of European unification. De Gaulle's caution on this matter roused strong parliamentary opposition. To placate it, he forced his unpopular prime minister, Michel Debré, to resign, replacing him with the young and relatively unknown Georges Pompidou. This move did not, however, prevent a no-confidence vote in May 1962, when a large minority in the National Assembly nearly overturned de Gaulle's government. This development represented the strongest parliamentary challenge to the President's authority to date; it moved de Gaulle to tilt the balance of power in his direction. When the Assembly reconvened in October, he exploited a near-fatal assassination attempt to propose (in a televised address) that the Constitution be amended to institutionalize enhanced presidential powers for him and his successors. He wanted to replace the electoral college with a presidential election by popular vote. He resolved to make this change by circumventing Parliament and taking a referendum directly to the public at large, an approach most jurists considered illegal. In fact, de Gaulle meant his amendment to mark a line in the sand between the Fifth Republic and France's previous parliamentary regimes. A powerful presidency, legitimized by a majority of French voters, de Gaulle believed, would prevent his country from reverting to the ineffective political systems of the past. The National Assembly reacted by passing a motion of censure (for the only time during the Fifth Republic), forcing Prime Minister Pompidou to resign the next day. De Gaulle then dissolved the National Assembly and called for new elections in November.

De Gaulle's referendum of October 28, 1962, proposing a popularly elected President of the Republic, won easily, as did the newly established Gaullist party (UNR-UDT) in legislative elections a month later. These victories meant that de Gaulle had prevailed in an important *épreuve de force* against the political remnants of the Fourth Republic. The President's actions had given the institutions of the Fifth Republic a stronger democratic base, making it unlikely that the French political system would revert to its traditional forms. Nevertheless, the Gaullists were not the only parties to emerge stronger from the 1962 legislative elections. Both the Communist and Socialist vote increased substantially over that of 1958. Perhaps more important, the two parties increased their parliamentary representation by cooperating in choosing which candidates would withdraw in the second round of the elections (*désistements*), when all candidates gaining more than 12.5 percent of the first-round votes have the right to stand again. In electoral districts in which both the Communist and the Socialist candidates passed into the second round, one agreed to withdraw so the other could benefit from the combined left-wing vote. The most important losers were the right and center-right parties, many of whose deputies switched to the Gaullists.

De Gaulle's victory in the referendum, and indeed the success of the Gaullist parties, represented personal victories for the French President far more than expressions of allegiance to the institutions of the Fifth Republic. We know from opinion surveys at the time that support for the regime itself was almost nonexistent among parliamentarians of the Left, and even among Gaullists, support was highly conditional. For these reasons, de Gaulle stood as both the great strength and asset of the Fifth Republic as well as its greatest weakness. When his personal popularity dropped, so did support for the regime.

Although de Gaulle would be reelected in 1965, his authority waxed and waned during the seven years between his victory in the referendum of 1962 and his resignation in 1969. The independence of Algeria and the defeat of the OAS testified to de Gaulle's strength and authority. Yet when he attempted to order striking French miners back to work in 1963, his popularity plunged to 42 percent, and he was forced to back down. Strike movements began to expand after that, and in the first popular election for President, in 1965, de Gaulle was forced into a runoff election with the moderate leftist candidate, François Mitterrand. De Gaulle had attracted less than 44 percent of the first-round vote. Though he ultimately won with 55 percent in the second round, his failure to be coronated in the first round placed him in a category of an "ordinary" candidate. The 1967 legislative elections once again revealed the President's declining support; although the Gaullists consolidated voters on the right, they lost seats overall. The Left, meanwhile, and particularly the Communists, gained substantially.

The most important and enduring challenge to de Gaulle and the "Gaullist Republic" emerged in the spring of 1968. The student movement in April and May garnered important public support and was directed above all at the Fifth Republic's Achilles' heel, its personal identification with de Gaulle. When workers began to strike as well, the spreading movement—the largest strike wave in French history—became a direct challenge to the Fifth Republic, a challenge so powerful that neither the opposition parties nor the trade unions could control it. By the end of May, the government seemed to have lost control as well, as two opposition leaders—Mitterrand and Pierre Mendès-France—proposed to create a provisional government, following the precedent of earlier French revolutions. Amid this chaos, de Gaulle secretly traveled to Germany, where he assessed the loyalty of the French army stationed there under the command of his old adversary, General Massu. On returning home, the President called for legislative elections in June. The Left's effort to establish a provisional government enabled the Gaullists, under Pompidou's leadership, to frame the impending election as an effort to defend the Republic. In the end, the Gaullists won an overwhelming victory, allowing them to save the regime. But with Pompidou in the forefront, the electoral success did little to burnish de Gaulle's declining authority. A year later, he turned a referendum over an obscure institutional change into a vote of confidence/no confidence in his leadership. When the referendum went down, he promptly resigned.

The *événements* of 1968 demonstrated what social scientists had hypothesized for some time: that the legitimacy of the Republic was stronger among voters than among political elites. During the next decade this situation began to change, as the parties of the Right shifted their loyalty from de Gaulle to the Republic itself. Though the left-wing parties reemerged after 1968 stronger than ever under Mitterrand's leadership, they operated within, rather than against, the institutions of the Fifth Republic. In 1981, more than twenty years after the founding of the regime, Mitterrand was elected President of the Republic on a platform supported by the combined parties of the Left. For the first time in the Fifth Republic's history, a transfer of power, an *alternance,* had taken place. That it had occurred peacefully and without any threat to the regime demonstrated the solidity and legitimacy of the Fifth Republic. (After that, until 2007, majorities shifted with every legislative election.) In assuming the presidency in 1981, Mitterrand noted that the Fifth Republic's institutions were not of his making, but that they suited him very well. In effect, he admitted that his 1964 critique of de Gaulle's regime, *Le coup d'État permanent,* had been wrong. The Fifth Republic was not, as Mitterrand had argued, merely a fig leaf covering de Gaulle's "personal power." Once in control of the state, the Left made no attempts to substantially alter the institutional arrangements of the Fifth Republic, despite the many reforms they sponsored after 1981. In fact, since that time, no important political party, on the left or the right, has rejected the constitutional arrangements of the Fifth Republic.

The Constitution would be altered in important ways during the next twenty-five years, but always by amendment, and generally in ways that added support and legitimacy to the regime—mainly by augmenting parliamentary prerogatives relative to the executive. As a result of a constitutional amendment in 1995, Parliament now meets by right most of the year, a change that has enhanced the role of committee leaders in the legislative process, and amendments passed in 2008 brought parliamentary committees directly into the legislative process by making the legislation reported out of committees the basis for parliamentary approval. Even the executive's ability to force legislative passage by declaring the responsibility of the government has been sharply limited. Since 2008, it applies only to finance laws.

In addition, since 1981, there has been an attempt to bring the presidential and legislative elections (and majorities) closer together. The Constitution was amended in 2000 to reduce the presidential term to five years, the same as the legislative mandate of the National Assembly. Finally, the Constitution was amended in 1974 and again in 2008 to make the once weak Constitutional Council into a distant cousin of the U.S. Supreme Court. The Council now enjoys the ability to check the actions of both the executive and the parliamentary majority. The 1974 amendment allowed the parliamentary opposition to bring any piece of legislation before the Council before it was promulgated; the amendment of 2008 gave the Council appeal jurisdiction in court cases in which the defendant claims that a law violates "rights and liberties" guaranteed by the Constitution. All of these amendments came from governments of the Right.

The essential result of these and other developments is that, fifty years on, the Fifth Republic has achieved what no other modern French regime had done. It has built stable institutions and earned legitimacy in the eyes of elites and public alike. Given the unexpected durability of the Fifth Republic, how precisely can we explain its institutional strength? How can we understand its success compared with the failures of the four previous republican regimes? For most scholars, a key part of the explanation turns on three features of the Fifth Republic's political system: two-round elections, single-member districts, and a President elected by nationwide popular vote.

Very quickly after the establishment of the Fifth Republic, the Communists and the Socialists realized that two-round elections with single-member districts worked to their disadvantage against a more unified party on the right. If both Communist and Socialist candidates competed in the second round, they divided the left-wing vote, allowing the conservative contender to win. After 1962, it became common for the weaker of the remaining leftist candidates to withdraw voluntarily before the second round, ensuring a two-way election between a candidate of the Left and one of the Right. As a result, the Left's parliamentary representation grew faster than its electoral support. On the right, the appeal of General de Gaulle attracted a growing number of centrist deputies to the Gaullist parties after 1962. Before long, the expansion of the Gaullist Party overwhelmed the old parties of the center-right, virtually snuffing them out. By 1968, a single conservative party, the Gaullist UNR-UDT, won a majority in Parliament for the first time in the history of any French Republic.

This trend toward the outlines of a two-party system was augmented and enhanced by the initiation of a popularly elected President in 1962. The prize of the presidency became the centerpiece of party efforts after 1962, and negotiations within the Left and the Right focused on agreements about candidacies for the first round and on whom to support in the second. The events of 1968 derailed these efforts, but by 1973–74, strong political parties had emerged on both the right and the left. Strong parties meant that a smaller number of stable political parties dominated electoral politics: by 1973, 76 percent of the vote went to two major groupings, the Communists and Socialists on the left and the Gaullists and their allies on the right. Strong parties also meant that the most important national organizations gained control over the candidates presented in their name, and that party groups in Parliament voted together in a disciplined way. Finally, strong parties meant that national parties gained control over the alliances formed by their local affiliates and increasingly organized their national alliances around party programs.

Against this party-oriented interpretation, some scholars have argued that the decline of ideology provides the key to the Fifth Republic's stability, as narrowing ideological differences have supposedly promoted centrist politics and diminished challenges to the regime itself. There is little evidence, however, for this point of view. By the early 1980s, ideological divisions between left and right had grown stronger rather than weaker, making French politics even more bipolar than before. During the 1970s, the Socialists had moved to the left, forming an electoral alliance with the Communists based on common objectives. Socialist leaders then expelled local units that had traditionally concluded local alliances with the center. The Left's "common program" advocated a "rupture" with the political economy of capitalism, and the Socialist-Communist alliance acted on this program when it gained power in 1981. Within the Right, economic liberalism became the dominant ideology, and when conservatives won a parliamentary majority in 1986, they proceeded to undo much of what the Left had done. Ideological commitment became the basis for the reorganization of the Left in opposition, and then became crucial for the Right when it returned to opposition in 1988. Indeed, as ideological differences among voters diminished in many ways, they grew stronger among political party elites.

Thus the normalization of the Fifth Republic is directly related to the "divine surprise" of party development. Although the Fifth Republic's Constitution was conceived as a substitute for strong and dominant political parties, exactly the opposite has occurred. Party leaders in Parliament have used constitutional tools to enhance their domination over their deputies, consolidating their own power and that of the parties they represent. Overall, emerging practices, as well as constitutional amendments, have gradually changed the system to better integrate Parliament, and to create new institutional capabilities in Parliament and the courts to challenge executive power.

As in every other European parliamentary democracy, stability and political effectiveness now depend on relatively strong political parties capable of representing the ideas and interests of their constituents and making the state more responsive to problems the electorate wants to address. Challenges to the party system have not undermined the stability of the Republic (at least in the short run), although they have weakened governmental and opposition effectiveness. After 2002, the governing coalition of the Right effectively withstood a challenge from the extreme Right, as well as divisions within its own ranks, to win the presidential and parliamentary elections again in 2007. The Left's electoral loss in 2007 made the Socialists both leaderless and vulnerable to a resurgent ecological movement. Nevertheless, no political party now questions the legitimacy of the Republic, and, as in other European parliamentary democracies, both government and opposition have maintained disciplined caucuses in Parliament.

References

Bell, D. S., and Byron Criddle. *The French Socialist Party: The Emergence of Party Government.* Oxford: Clarendon, 1988.

Bowen, John. *Why the French Don't Like Headscarves: Islam, the State, and Public Space.* Princeton, NJ: Princeton University Press, 2007.

Culpepper, Pepper D., Peter Hall, and Bruno Palier. *Changing France: The Politics the Markets Make.* Basingstoke, UK: Palgrave, 2006.

Hoffmann, Stanley, Charles Kindleberger, Laurence Wylie, Jesse R. Pitts, Jean-Baptiste Duroselle, and François Goguel. *In Search of France.* Cambridge, MA: Harvard University Press, 1963.

Perrineau, Pascal, and Luc Rouban. *Politics in France and Europe.* New York: Palgrave, 2010.

Schmidt, Vivien A. *Democratizing France.* New York: Cambridge University Press, 1990.

Stone, Alec. *The Birth of Judicial Politics in France: The Constitutional Council in Comparative Perspective.* New York: Oxford University Press, 1992.

Suleiman, Ezra. *Elites in French Society.* Princeton, NJ: Princeton University Press, 1978.

Wahl, Nicholas, and Jean-Louis Quermonne, eds. *Le régime présidentiel en France.* Paris: Presses de la FNSP, 1995.

Weil, Patrick. *How to Be French: Nationality in the Making since 1789.* Translated by Catherine Porter. Durham, NC: Duke University Press, 2008.

Part II

Principles and Values

10

LIBERTY

Jeremy Jennings

Few words in the vocabulary of politics have been more subject to misunderstanding or abuse than the word "liberty." French republicanism has not been immune from this problem. Fortunately, in a lecture of 1819, Benjamin Constant gave precise form to a distinction between different types of liberty that had long been the subject of discussion. Liberty, Constant contended, has two forms: the "ancient" and the "modern." Stated in its simplest terms, "modern" liberty amounts to the right to go about one's life and business, to associate with others, to practice a religion, and to express an opinion without constraint. "It is the right," Constant wrote, "to be subjected to the laws, and to be neither arrested, detained, put to death or maltreated in any way by the arbitrary will of one or more individuals." Later Isaiah Berlin was to rework this description, characterizing it as "negative" liberty. The liberty of the ancients, by contrast, amounts to the full participation by citizens in the public life of their community. This liberty, however, is combined not only with a disregard for the virtues of private life but also with "the complete subjection of the individual to the authority of the community." Thus, Constant concluded, as a citizen the individual "decide[s] on peace and war; as a private citizen, he [is] constrained, watched and repressed in all his movements." Isaiah Berlin familiarized our present-day audience with this form of liberty when he redescribed it as "positive" liberty.

Constant's ambition in his famous lecture was to provide an explanation of how and why the French Revolution had descended into terror and tyranny. The great mistake, he said, was to have followed Rousseau in transporting "into our modern age an extent of social power, of collective sovereignty, which belonged to other centuries." The challenge for the future therefore was to establish a "liberty suitable to modern times," and this entailed the recognition that "individual independence is the first need of the moderns." More specifically, Constant's distinction between ancient and modern liberty highlighted tensions within French republicanism that both predated and postdated his lecture. Which of the two definitions was French republicanism to favor? More intriguing still, could French republicanism succeed in embracing both, learning, as Constant himself desired, "to combine the two together"?

Following writers of the Scottish Enlightenment, such as David Hume and Adam Smith, Constant correctly observed that the advent of modern liberty was intimately associated with the rise of commerce and of the commercial spirit. An individual's worth was no longer to be judged according to his role as a citizen or his devotion to the common good but rather as a property owner, producer, or trader. As a possessor of inalienable rights, the individual asked of government no more than that it should protect these rights and leave him free from un-necessary and burdensome interference. Gone were the heroic, warlike virtues of the Greek and Roman citizen; they were replaced in the modern world by the private qualities of honesty and hard work, which in turn would produce peace and prosperity for all. Virtue, in short, was privatized, while the activity of politics lost its moralizing function, having been reduced to a form of arbitra-tion between conflicting individual interests. At the same time, modern liberty presupposed the abandonment of a unitary conception of truth, especially when it came to religion. It was for this reason that the essence of liberty lay in tol-eration, made manifest not only through religious observance but also through freedom of speech and of the press more generally. Jean-Fabien Spitz described the outcome of this long process of political and intellectual evolution as follows: "With regard to the liberty of the subject within the State, it consists of the exer-cise of rights guaranteed by the law but does not entail any active participation in the government of the State." There can be no doubt that in 1789 the members of the Constituent Assembly sought to institute such a modern conception of liberty. Attacking the abuses of the ancien régime, their ambition was to protect the individual from arbitrary government. They did so not only by recognizing the rights to security, property, and resistance to oppression in the Declaration of the Rights of Man and of the Citizen, but also by endorsing in the same document a definition of liberty as "the power that belongs to all men to do everything that does not harm the rights of others." Problems arose immediately however, as the Constituents sought simultaneously to sketch out the form of government most capable of protecting such individual rights and liberties. This modern conception of liberty was associated above all with England and the English system of gov-ernment, which philosophers beginning with Montesquieu believed to rest on the existence of precisely those intermediary powers—principally, the aristocracy—from which France now sought to rid itself. Thus, by the end of the summer of 1789, the attempt by the *monarchiens* to secure the preservation of individual liberty through a system of representative and constitutional government on the English model had been rejected. Many members of the Constituent Assembly, moreover, doubted the merits of a commercial society. Invariably they believed that their contemporaries lived in a fallen or degenerate condition. Like Jean-Jacques Rousseau before them, they believed that the wealth France had accumulated over the centuries was a misfortune, if not a curse.

What happened next is too well known to need recounting: the revolutionaries who created the First Republic turned their back on England and modern liberty. Instead, these republicans determined to emulate the political forms of Greece and Rome, while returning to an earlier, uncorrupted simplicity of morals. Here, the example of wholesome Americans forging a new civilization from the virgin wilderness did much to sustain their enthusiasm. The goal of politics, as Mona Ozouf has noted, became the re-creation of a new Adam, the rediscovery of a new innocence, the reconstitution of a virtuous people. According to Robespierre, the Revolution would accomplish the complete regeneration, both physical and moral, of the French population.

This misplaced nostalgia for premodern times came replete with a theoretical justification of a return to ancient liberty. Constitutional debates after 1789 abound with references to the "general will," an unerring, indivisible source of all political authority. The author of this notion, as one deputy expressed it, was "'the greatest publicist of the century'": Rousseau. His conception of an unerring general will was transposed onto the nation, whose sovereignty (i.e., power and authority), the revolutionaries said, lay in the unity of its members. This was a nation, furthermore, to be shorn of privilege and inequality. Purged of these evils, what had the nation to fear from itself? There was, then, no need for the guarantees against arbitrary government embedded in the English political model, because the government and the people were now, so leading revolutionaries believed, one and the same. Any expressions of particular, individual wills violated an inherently unified general will and thus by definition were factious, even criminal.

No republican gave clearer expression to this conception of politics and the place of ancient liberty within it than Robespierre. The good individual was the good citizen, and the good citizen was the good patriot. The common good always took precedence over individual interest; the public realm always outweighed the private realm. A man who lacked public virtues, Robespierre announced, could not have private virtues. Accordingly, the individual will was to be subordinated to the demands and duties of civic virtue. For that reason, the newly relegitimized objective of the individual's moral regeneration as citizen could best be secured in a communal, rather than economic, setting. It is this belief that explains the Jacobins' obsession with civic festivals. Of these, the most important and threatening was the Cult of the Supreme Being, the replacement religion that was to purge the individual of everything that separated him from the civil body. All divisions and differences would disappear before the universal religion of Nature.

The problem, of course, was that this vision of the sublime future left a great many people unconvinced. Opponents refused to go away, dissenting voices continued to speak, and measures for reform produced unforeseen practical disasters. For the revolutionaries, the only explanation of these dissonances could be the continued existence of individual selfishness and wickedness. The Jacobin response was to deploy with mounting intensity a rhetoric that contrasted virtue, truth, purity, and the undivided people with vice, enemies, corruption, and factious individuals. With the latter, the true patriot could make no compromise, for, as Robespierre proclaimed, "when the people themselves are corrupted, liberty is already lost."

With astonishing prescience Robespierre understood exactly what was required to restore liberty: terror. Here he made the all-important distinction between revolutionary and constitutional government. "Constitutional government," he clarified, "is concerned principally with civil liberty and revolutionary government with public liberty. Under a constitutional regime, it is sufficient to protect individuals against the abuse of public power; under a revolutionary regime, the public power is compelled to defend itself against all the factions that attack it.... Toward the enemies of the people, it owes only death." Revolutionary government, in brief, was to be government without limits: it was to be absolute, inflexible power; its goal was nothing less than the moral salvation of the people in the name of virtue. It was to be "the despotism of liberty against tyranny."

It is no unimportant coincidence that Robespierre proclaimed his hatred not just of the English system of government but of its mercantile and commercial culture, the very bedrock of Constant's modern liberty. This republican antipathy toward English liberty continued well into the nineteenth century, as works such as Ledru-Rollin's *De la décadence de l'Angleterre,* published in 1850, amply illustrate. Far from being the country of liberty, as both Montesquieu and Voltaire had maintained, England, on this view, was one enormous oligarchy. Its famed defenses against the arbitrary abuse of power—with regard to freedom of the press, trial by jury, the right of assembly, and the famous act of habeas corpus—were powerless to protect the people's individual liberties from the infringements of England's landed and industrial aristocracy.

The Terror, as Mona Ozouf has observed, stripped this argument of its appeal, and over time, French republicans came to recognize that the Republic would be securely established in France only by shedding its terrorist past. Doing so took various forms, but one "explicit break with Jacobinism," Ozouf argues, was the recognition that "liberty is more desirable than virtue." Of republican politicians such as Jules Ferry, Ozouf remarks: "When it came to fixing the relationship between liberty and the good...they always chose to subordinate the good to liberty, membership to independence."

Throughout the nineteenth century, a series of statements illustrate the extent to which republicans sought to move toward a new, less virtue-focused, understanding of liberty. One of the most important and concise, written in 1848 as a civic catechism for the new Second Republic, is Charles Renouvier's *Manuel républicain de l'homme et du citoyen*. If the text itself betrays both the heated debates of the period and Renouvier's personal passion that the Republic should embody both justice and fraternity, it also provides a formal, legalistic definition of liberty. The republican catechism informs the reader that "liberty is the power to do everything that does not harm others, everything that does not take away the rights of others." Our "principal liberties," said to be "natural" and the responsibility of the Republic to guarantee for its citizens, are taken to be "liberty of conscience, freedom of speech, the freedom to write and to publish." To these are added three more important liberties: individual liberty, defined as the right not to be accused, arrested, or detained without proper authority; political liberty, defined as a citizen's right to obey only those laws authorized by his representatives and to pay only those taxes to which he has consented; and, finally, freedom of association, which applies in particular to religion and politics.

Complications, not surprisingly given the context, begin to arise when Renouvier considers the liberties associated with the right to property. "The fundamental goal of a well-ordered Republic," he writes, "is to guarantee the security of each person through the protection of his person, his rights and everything that belongs to him." This includes a citizen's property, which is described as "the fruit of a man's labor." Accordingly, Renouvier concludes that a law violating the right to property "would greatly diminish the liberty of man and would place the citizen in a position of too great a subordination vis-à-vis the Republic." Somehow, such liberty has to be reconciled with republican demands for equality and fraternity, and Renouvier goes to great, if futile, lengths to demonstrate how this can be done—largely by merging the beliefs of Christianity with the cause of the Republic.

Later, Renouvier's disillusionment with the descent of the Second Republic into Bonapartism led him to develop a more mature philosophy of the Republic grounded on the work of Immanuel Kant. Here he was not alone, as the writings of one of republicanism's foremost neo-Kantians, Jules Barni, reveal. Like Renouvier, Barni published his own *Manuel républicain* (1872), which built on Barni's earlier work, *La morale dans la démocratie* (1868).

Barni did not disguise his desire to escape from ancient liberty's misplaced equation of politics with morality. This, he announced, "had been the error of the republics and the philosophers of antiquity," an error perpetuated by such eminent eighteenth-century writers as Rousseau and Mably. Neither, in Barni's view, had embraced "the modern spirit," which, he argued, inclines toward "granting autonomy and liberty to the individual conscience, to freeing it from the intemperate yoke of politics, and confining the latter within the limits of the law." It followed that the first duty of the state was to respect and protect the "natural rights" of all citizens and therefore that liberty should be defined in terms of the absence of arbitrary restraint upon and interference in the actions of individuals. "Liberty," Barni observed, "is, in essence, the capacity that allows man to direct his own actions, to dispose of himself, in a word, to be his own master rather than the property of another." Barni gave this description of liberty further definition by specifying that it included the right of each person to "think and speak freely, to work freely and freely to make use of the fruit of his labor."

At least three features of Barni's account of republican liberty merit further comment. Each tells us much about how republicanism was to develop in the Third Republic. The first is Barni's conviction that liberty must not be confused with "license." Liberty, that is, had to be informed by a comprehensive set of republican values that obliged every citizen to seek personal moral improvement and to respect the "human dignity" of others. The conservative, not to say bourgeois, character of this moralized vision of liberty is shown in the central place allotted to hard work, sobriety, chastity, and the sanctity of the family. Next, rejecting the arguments of Pierre-Joseph Proudhon, Barni unequivocally includes the right to property as a fundamental individual liberty, as the source of a society's prosperity. It is crucial, Barni added, for governments to respect this fundamental right. Charity and self-help, rather than government intervention, would provide solutions to the misery of the poor. Finally, Barni extended liberty of thought to include "liberty of conscience," and therefore concluded that the principle of liberty must entail the separation of church and state.

Here then is the definition of liberty that came to predominate among republicans from the 1870s onward. It sought to detach liberty from the threat of revolutionary tyranny and dictatorship and to ally it with a stable, property-owning democracy. It also provided republicans with a program of political reform. Equally important, by prioritizing the claims of liberty over the claims of equality, it sought to delegitimize radical and socialist understandings of liberty within the republican movement. So, for example, if Renouvier had agonized over the practical implications of including the rights to work and assistance within a republican conception of liberty, Barni saw only the "ruin" and "despotism" that would follow from "the organization of work by the State."

It was this unwillingness to see liberty in terms of greater economic equality that led many on the left to turn away from what they increasingly saw as a bourgeois republic. We should briefly consider this alternative republican conception of liberty, which, as the socialist Louis Blanc proclaimed, is "not only the right but also the ability accorded to man to develop his faculties." For Blanc, as for so many socialists who rallied to the Second Republic, unrestricted economic competition destroyed such liberty, producing only what he termed "the most barbarous despotism." If Blanc recognized the importance of freedom of the press, conscience, and assembly, he also believed that France's understanding of liberty had to be pushed much further, to encompass what he described as "the liberty of life," "the liberty to choose a job," and "the liberty of abundance." Liberty was meaningless unless it abolished the servitude arising from poverty, hunger, and economic exploitation. Only when all our needs and desires had been satisfied would it be possible to speak of "the free man." Thus by "liberty" Blanc meant not the narrow conception of liberty as the absence of restraint—what is the liberty of the unemployed worker deprived of a salary?—but something more extensive, a vision of liberty that could be realized only in a just society and in the *social* Republic. Many on the left— for example, those who later joined the Parti Communiste Français after 1920— remained wedded to this conception of liberty throughout the twentieth century.

Increasingly, however, this view represented only a minority view of republicans. This was certainly so by the end of the Second Empire. The experience of Bonapartism convinced the majority that liberty would exist only when imperial power and personal despotism had been brought to an end. The republicans' primary concern, therefore, shifted from the social question toward the establishment of political liberty through a new set of republican institutions. Barni, for example, recommended administrative decentralization and an extension of municipal liberties. Jules Ferry did the same, proclaiming in 1869 that "France will not have liberty for as long as she lives under the constraints of administrative centralization." To this requirement he added the establishment of an independent judiciary and the abolition of the standing army. It is intriguing that as republicans sought to establish liberty on the solid foundations of a stable political regime, they turned increasingly to the forms of governance that the Jacobins had rejected as a regime of aristocratic corruption. "We must banish from our Republic," Jules Ferry proclaimed in 1884, "all memories of the republican cities of ancient Greece." Despite such statements, leaders of the Third Republic did not entirely betray the revolutionary heritage of 1789. If, in their view, liberty could exist only when "earthly Caesarism" had been banished, so too they believed that "intellectual Caesarism" had to be overcome. This meant an assault on the power of the Roman Catholic Church, and later the separation of church and state in 1905. Only "the secular State" could protect individual liberty from "perpetual Roman occupation." Such views show that, for all their social conservatism, the republicans of the Third Republic maintained the belief that individual liberty could not be divorced from intellectual emancipation. Here their conception of liberty showed itself to be deeply impregnated not just with the spirit of the eighteenth-century Enlightenment and the Revolution of 1789 but also with the powerful tradition of nineteenth-century philosophical positivism. In this way, "freedom of education" found its way into the pantheon of republican liberties.

Anticlericalism therefore stood side by side with the pursuit of stability and order at the center of the republican program. It was this combination that led Jean-Pierre Machelon to speak of "la République contre les libertés." In his view, the Third Republic was no golden age for individual liberties: striking workers, anarchists, religious congregations, and civil servants (not to mention women) felt the full force of state repression, as the fundamental liberties of certain categories of individuals were disregarded in the name of social peace and stability.

How do these ideas and practices inform republican conceptions of liberty today? One view is that the economic market, combined with globalization, is fatally undermining the republican model, and, as a result, the emphasis now falls exclusively upon the rights of the individual to the exclusion of civic virtue. Modern liberty has not been combined with ancient liberty, but has extinguished it. What predominates today is the liberty of the producer and the consumer rather than the liberty of the citizen. Similarly, recent demands for the recognition of the rights of religious and ethnic minorities—the right to difference—challenge the very principles of liberty embraced by the secular state. Faced with these challenges, republicans of all shades of opinion have had to rethink what they mean by liberty in a de facto multicultural and economically individualist society. If some have seen salvation in a more thorough espousal of the conception of "modern" or "negative" liberty associated with the Anglo-American tradition, others have sought to reinvigorate the earlier, "ancient" perspective, which sees the attainment of liberty as inseparable from civic involvement and citizen participation.

References

Barni, Jules. *Manuel républicain.* Paris: Germer Baillière, 1872.

Blais, Marie-Claude. *Au principe de la République: Le cas Renouvier.* Paris: Gallimard, 2000.

———. *La solidarité: Histoire d'une idée.* Paris: Gallimard, 2007.

Blanc, Louis. *Le Socialisme: Droit au Travail.* Paris: Michel Levy: 1848.

———. "La Liberté." *Le Nouveau monde: Journal Historique et Politique* (8): 1850.

Constant, Benjamin. "The Liberty of the Ancients compared with that of the Moderns." *Political Writings.* Trans. and ed. Biancamaria Fontana. New York: Cambridge University Press 1988.

Ferry, Jules. *La République des citoyens.* Paris: Imprimerie Nationale, 1996.

Hazareesingh, Sudhir. *Intellectual Founders of the Republic: Five Studies in Nineteenth-Century French Political Thought.* Oxford: Oxford University Press, 2002.

Machelon, Jean-Pierre. *La République contre les libertés?* Paris: Presses de la Fondation Nationale des Sciences Politiques, 1976.

Nord, Philip. *The Republican Moment: Struggles for Democracy in Nineteenth-Century France.* Cambridge, MA: Harvard University Press, 1995.

Ozouf, Mona. "Liberté." In François Furet and Mona Ozouf, eds., *Dictionnaire critique de la Révolution française.* Flammarion: Paris: 1992.

———. "L'Idée républicaine et l'interprétation du passé national." *Annales* 53 (6): 1998.

Renouvier, Charles. *Manuel Républicain de l'Homme et du Citoyen.* Pagnerre: Paris: 1848.

Robespierre, Maximilien. *Œuvres de Maximilien Robespierre,* X. Paris: PUF: 1967.

Spitz, Jean-Fabien. *La liberté politique: Essai de généalogie conceptuelle.* Paris: PUF, 1995.

———. *Le moment républicain en France.* Paris: Gallimard, 2005.

11

Equality

Jeremy Jennings

"In theory, equality is a simple idea." This was the view of the French Conseil d'État in its report *Sur le principe d'égalité,* published in 1998. In truth, very few people have believed in complete or formal equality. An exception would be the socialist Étienne Cabet, in whose utopia, *Voyage en Icarie,* every conceivable form of social and economic inequality was to be eradicated. There was to be no private property, everyone giving their labor to the community on equal terms, drawing whatever they needed from a central storehouse. Everyone was to dress alike and to live in the same houses. If the family unit was to be retained, there was to be equality between the sexes. Life was to be simple and austere. Given that this is a conception of equality that has received little support (and which has proved unworkable whenever put into practice), the important questions—for French republicans as for everyone else—have been, rather, Which equalities (or, conversely, which inequalities) are of importance? What matters most: equality before the law or equality of wealth and income? Equality of opportunity or equality of outcome? Which should take precedence: political, economic, social, or legal equality? What, if any, is the relationship between political and economic equality? Are claims for equality compatible with the recognition of individual rights? Does equality threaten or extend liberty? Even the most vigorous defender of inequality will normally embrace some aspect of egalitarianism. Not surprisingly, therefore, over the last two hundred years and more, republicanism in France has put forward a variety of sometimes conflicting interpretations of equality. So too it has not been immune from the fundamental dilemmas that arise from the questions set out above.

Our starting point must be the Revolution of 1789. As was first noted by Pierre-Louis Roederer, in *L'esprit de la Révolution de 1789,* and then by Alexis de Tocqueville, in *L'ancien régime et la Révolution,* the driving passion of the Revolution was that of equality and not liberty. Its principal motive was not to free lands and persons from all servitude, nor to free industry from all restraint, but rather to put an end to privilege. As the abbé Sieyès announced: "By their very nature, all privileges are unjust, odious and in opposition to the supreme goal of political society." Such was the fervent hostility to privilege, and the inequalities that it embodied, that the assault upon it demanded not just the abolition of those privileges associated with the First and Second Estates, the church and the aristocracy, but the destruction of all those privileges held by cities, provinces, bodies of magistrates, and corporations. On the night of August 4, 1789, the privileges of all these bodies and institutions were abolished, producing for the first time a body of equal citizens living under a set of laws common to all. This was confirmed by the Declaration of the Rights of Man and of the Citizen, which proclaimed: "All men are born free and equal in their rights." Article 6 of the Declaration further indicated that the law was to be the same for all and, most important, that "all citizens...are equally eligible for all public positions, places and employments, according to their capacities and without other distinction than that of their virtues and their talents." Article 13, recognizing the injustice of the nobility and clergy's tax privileges, stipulated that taxation "be equally apportioned among all citizens according to their means." Equality therefore was to be achieved by and through the law, which itself was to embody equality through its generality and universality. Equality was conceived as an equality of rights, its most tangible expression being that access to public offices could not longer be bought. All of these principles, although they predated the birth of the First Republic, became part of the heritage of republicanism and, in various forms, have appeared in subsequent republican constitutions.

Several points, however, should be noted. First, equality was not listed among the "natural and imprescriptible rights of man." These were restricted to liberty, property, security, and the resistance of oppression. The tension between the demands of liberty and equality was already established. Next, in 1791 the Loi Le Chapelier, in wishing to make impossible a return to the reactionary spirit of corporation and privilege, made illegal all those intermediary trade and professional bodies that might protect the common interests of groups of workers. The individual (male) citizen was to stand equal, if alone, before the law, and shorn of all particularistic affiliations. Steadily weakened over time (for example, by the Third Republic's recognition of trade unions) and now the subject of increasing challenge, this principle still demands that in law the Republic treat all citizens equally, irrespective, for example, of their ethnic or religious identity. Third, civil equality quite definitely did not entail political equality. The promise of equal participation in the formation of the general will was quickly withdrawn, as constitutional theorists—with Sieyès foremost among them—sought to reduce the political influence of ordinary people with a variety of ingenious proposals, most notably the distinction between active and nonactive citizens. Only later would the Republic embrace the principle of universal suffrage, which did not apply to women until after the Second World War. Finally, civil equality did not require or entail economic equality. If, following the night of August 4, what constituted property was radically transformed (one could no longer own offices as property), the right to property, and therefore the right to unequal ownership of wealth, was sacrosanct. This right could only be taken away under the exceptional circumstances of public necessity.

How, if at all, did the arrival of the republicans to power change this perspective on equality? The *Declaration of the Rights of Man and of the Citizen* voted by the Convention in June 1793 reaffirmed the commitment to civil equality and strengthened the attachment to political equality through Article 29, which stipulated: "Each citizen has an equal right to take part in the formation of the law and to choose his representatives and agents." Likewise, the Jacobins included detailed reference to the rights and prerogatives of property, and this was so for the simple reason that they believed property acted as a guarantee of liberty. Indeed, in this new republican order, it was property rather than privilege that defined a person's worth.

But this *Declaration,* unlike that of 1789, listed equality as one of the citizen's natural rights and did so by placing it before both liberty and property. What did this signify? First of all, we have to remember that the Jacobins opposed the agrarian communism advocated by the so-called Enragés. Such a wholesale redistribution of wealth they regarded as both undesirable and impractical. Yet the austere moral vision of the Jacobins led them to despise luxury and avarice. They admired the hardworking peasant and artisan and loathed the usurer and the economic parasite. Robespierre was prepared to advance a restrictive definition of property as "the right belonging to each individual to enjoy and to dispose of that quantity of goods guaranteed to him by law." This right also entailed "the obligation to respect the rights of others." The ideal of the Jacobins, then, was not strict equality but rather a situation in which all those who labored would have enough to own a few tools, a plot of land or a workshop, and enough to support their family with dignity.

Two further points arise from this understanding. By linking property with labor the Jacobins unleashed an idea that was to prove very powerful in the hands of later radical egalitarians within the republican movement. Secondly, the actual disparity of wealth that existed in society made it very difficult to justify the newly established legal status of property before the property-less. In practice, if not in theory, the sansculottes believed they had the right to take and remove the property of others in order to satisfy their needs. Individual interests could be sacrificed in the name of equality of treatment.

Initially, revolutionaries responded to the discontent of the poor by maintaining that private property should not be abolished but shared more equally. But in 1796, Gracchus Babeuf's *Conspiration des égaux* took republican thinking a decisive step in the direction of radical equality. Henceforth, the egalitarian demand to do away with the distinction between rich and poor citizens would be couched in terms of the end of personal ownership and the call for what the *Manifeste des égaux* called "real equality." "From time immemorial," the document proclaimed, "it has been repeated hypocritically that men are equal, but from time immemorial the most degrading and monstrous inequalities have insolently weighed upon the human race." Equality was now raised to the status of "the first need of man." The Revolution of 1789 has been betrayed, but the goal of the next Revolution, "a greater and more solemn revolution which will be the last," would be to do away with class distinctions and inequalities of income through the instrument of revolutionary dictatorship.

Babeuf's abortive rising came to nothing and the demands for real equality were silenced as the republican movement itself was virtually extinguished over the next few decades. It is important to realize, however, that even for Babeuf and his associates the term "property" essentially meant land. Suggestions for the redistribution of private wealth therefore usually took the form of demands for the periodic redivision of land—the Jacobins, for example, opposed primogeniture for this reason—rather than the socialization of the means of production. These notions began to change significantly in the early decades of the nineteenth century as it became increasingly obvious that it was the bourgeoisie that appeared to be the principal beneficiary of the newly emerging industrial system. The eradication of pauperism, on this view, demanded radical measures. Here the challenge for republicans of the Left was to displace the fashionable doctrines of liberal political economy, and this in turn meant denying the superiority of England's industrial society. Accordingly, celebrated left-republican writers such as Flora Tristan, Jules Michelet, and Ledru-Rollin painted a vivid picture of England as the country of inequality, its workers ground down by the inhumanity of industrial exploitation. Republican socialism was sustained in this view by the rising of the starving workers in Lyon in 1834. To this was then added, especially from 1840 onward, a secularized religious impulse that saw the attainment of equality as the key component in the advance toward the rediscovered goal of fraternity.

No one better embodied this republican attachment to equality than Louis Blanc. Liberty without "the immortal sisters, equality and fraternity," would only produce "the liberty of the savage." This, he believed, was what existed under the capitalist system of unbridled competition, with England cast as the supreme example of "the principle of national egoism." Blanc's response, set out most famously in *L'organisation du travail* of 1840, was to recommend the establishment of workers' cooperatives, the funds for which would be forwarded by the government. This was not to be a system of enforced collectivization nor of state-imposed equality but one where equality would emerge through the principle and practice of association. "Each member of the social workshop," Blanc wrote, "would have the right to dispose of his salary at his own convenience, but the obvious benefits and incontestable excellence of life in common would not delay the birth of a voluntary association of needs and enjoyments" among members of the workers' cooperatives. Similarly, the economic success of the workshops would gradually drive private capitalists out of business. The end pursued was unambiguous: a society in which "all men have an equal right to the complete development of their unequal faculties, the instruments of production belonging to all like the air and the sky." The guiding moral principle of the new society was to be the supremely egalitarian "From each according to his abilities, to each according to his needs."

With the establishment of what were called National Workshops in February 1848, Blanc had the opportunity to put these egalitarian principles into practice, only to see the workshops dissolved soon afterward. But now, for the first time, republicans saw the opportunity for establishing a Republic that would embody not just the political equality of the ballot box but also social equality through the newly formulated "right to work" and "right to assistance." Here there is no better guide to the passions of those who participated in the 1848 Revolution than the debates of the National Assembly as its members sought to define the principles of the new constitution. How could they create a social and democratic Republic? How could the Republic secure the progressive improvement of the physical and intellectual condition of the people? On these questions there was simply no agreement, as time and time again representatives grappled with the problem of reconciling the claims of liberty, equality, and property. As the tide turned against the radicals, their conservative opponents coalesced around the arguments of Adolphe Thiers against the right to work. His ideas helped produce a Preamble to the Constitution limiting the Republic's responsibilities to "fraternal assistance" designed to "guarantee the existence of those citizens in need, either by finding them work within the limits of its resources or, where there is no family, by supporting those who are not fit to work." The cause of social equality was decisively beaten.

Where did this now place the concept of equality in republican discourse? For guidance we can turn to Charles Renouvier's *Manuel républicain de l'homme et du citoyen*. This key document's starting point was that all men "are born equal in rights." The emphasis then fell upon the civil equalities declared in 1789: "The law of the Republic admits of no distinction of birth among citizens or of any hereditary power." No one could claim ownership of any civil or political function. The law was to be the same for all. Economic equality, however, was rejected because it threatened liberty. "The Republic," Renouvier wrote, "does not want the perfect equality of conditions, because it can only be established by depriving citizens of their liberty." The trick therefore was to combine liberty with equality, and this was to be done, in true *quarante-huitard* fashion, through fraternity: "It is fraternity that will lead the citizens brought together through their assembly of representatives to reconcile their rights and in such a way that they will remain free and, as far as is possible, become equals." What substance could be given to this aspiration? If Renouvier endorsed the claim for "the right to work and to subsistence through work," he gave pride of place to what was to become one of the great republican leitmotifs: "the right to receive an education." To the extent that this education depended upon the Republic, Renouvier noted, "it must be the same for all." It was to be not merely a technical education but also a moral and civic education: its aim was "the elevation of the soul and the molding of the heart." Henceforth it was to be education, tied to the doctrine of laicity, which would be the motor of republican equality.

The retreat within the republican mainstream from demands for greater social and economic equality was only confirmed by the experience of the Second Empire and then by the need to establish the Third Republic on a foundation of bourgeois support. Again, this is easily demonstrated by reference to Jules Barni's *Manuel républicain* of 1872. Liberty is there described as "the first principle of republican government," with equality defined as its "necessary consequence." What followed from this was equality before the law, civil equality, political equality, "no more privileges, castes or classes" but not "the leveling of all fortunes." If the provision of education was the first duty of the Republic, personal taxation was to be modest. The first duty of the citizen was respect for the law, and this was to be accompanied by a willingness to subordinate private interests to the public interest. The good citizen was to display "the virtue of abnegation." At no point, as Barni himself observed, was the word "socialism" mentioned, although "the social question" was not forgotten. The aim was to ensure that "the workers and the bosses, the rich and the poor, no longer form—as they too often do today—two warring classes." As Barni succinctly expressed it: "The love of equality is not the hatred of all superiority." This desire to temper the demands for social and economic equality helps explain the republicans' widespread enthusiasm for the doctrine of solidarity associated with the politician Léon Bourgeois at the end of the nineteenth century.

Yet the most telling (and long-lasting) example of Barni's (and republicanism's) willingness to compromise his understanding of equality emerged in his efforts to deny equal political rights to women. "Without doubt," Barni commented, "they are not called upon to participate like men in the business of politics." As he wrote elsewhere, women were the equals of men "as moral persons," and everything should be done to "emancipate women from all forms of degrading tutelage," but "in general the life appropriate to women is not the life of politics but that of private life." "Their true place," Barni continued, "is not at the forum but at the domestic hearth." This position was widely held among republicans, with very significant consequences. Jean-Pierre Machelon described the unequal status of women during the Third Republic as follows: "At a juridical level, the inferior situation in which women found themselves was principally made manifest through their political ineligibility, through restrictions upon their civic role and through their legal exclusion from certain functions and public employments. Strictly speaking, universal suffrage and equality before the law only applied to half of the population." The Constitution of 1946, which guaranteed to women rights equal to those of men, at last removed this iniquity.

How then might we try to summarize the conclusion of this long evolution of republican thinking on equality? Equality within the dominant republican discourse as well as practice has come to mean equality of rights rather than of opportunity or outcome. It is characterized by formal equality before the law rather than by economic or social equality. It forbids formal inequalities that arise out of race, religion, or gender. In the key area of schooling, it means that all pupils, irrespective of their beliefs and background, are to be treated equally and that reward is attained through merit. Political equality exists in the form of universal suffrage. The state is under an obligation to treat all citizens equally; inequalities of treatment can only be justified in terms of the general interest.

Is such an understanding of equality a credible one? Today it is possible to identify at least three serious challenges to it, challenges that come from both within and outside the republican movement. The last thirty years have seen growing economic inequalities, as the crisis of *l'État providence* (the welfare state) has been accompanied not only by the increased power of a (globalized) market but also by the appearance of new inequalities in the form of social and educational exclusion. As the distinctive French social model comes under increasing strain, the Republic, it has been argued, can aspire at best to achieve equality of opportunity, as the attainment of equality in income and wealth is an unrealizable (as well as dangerous) chimera. But is even the former a realizable aspiration? If republicanism in both theory and practice has sought to refashion its conception of equality in response to these new economic realities (for example, through the creation of education priority zones), there are those who argue that the state is becoming increasingly powerless to implement redistributive policies designed to produce equality of life chances. On this view, we should lower our egalitarian expectations even further and turn primarily to the market as the most efficient, if not the most just, means of distributing resources.

Next, the republican understanding of equality faces new criticism from those who believe that minority ethnic and religious groups might require differential rights and treatment if they are to enjoy the status of equals. Equality, on this multicultural view, demands the recognition of difference and group identities. The response of orthodox republicanism is that the Republic recognizes the rights and claims of individual citizens and not communities. Yet over the last two decades, a growing number of republicans has sought to make the republican conception of equality more responsive to the claims of cultural identity and difference. In this context, the reports of the Haut Conseil à l'Intégration make for fascinating reading. Over time they have come to adopt an increasingly flexible and pragmatic approach toward the claims of Muslims in France to be treated differently, while at the same time seeking to remain true to the egalitarian principles of the "republican pact." There are, however, those who argue that in a de facto multicultural society equality should now be abandoned in the name of *equity*. Danilo Martuccelli describes the difference between the two as follows: "Equality places the accent upon those elements common to abstract individuals and not upon their differences or collective particularisms. . . . It is otherwise with the notion of 'equity,' which recognizes the political relevance of the cultural specificity of individuals and groups and of accepting the idea of a differential treatment for members of these collectivities." Equality of rights therefore has to be understood in terms of the specific and particular situation of each individual rather than in terms of equality of treatment. In this view, there should be an *equality of respect* for different cultures.

Finally, the republican conception of equality has earned criticism from those who wish to see political parity (*parité*) for women as the goal of a just society. Here the subject of debate is too well known to require detailed recapitulation. The equals of men in political rights only since 1946, women remain unequal in terms of political participation and representation: the principle of *parité* therefore requires quotas in order to secure real political equality. The orthodox republican response is to argue that such positive discrimination would itself threaten the core republican principle of the equality of citizens. Why, indeed, should a special case be made for equality between men and women? The response is to argue that if equality is to mean more than simple formal equality before the law, some practical provision has to be made to secure that end. Otherwise, the active citizen will remain the male. The broader significance of this debate, as with demands for *equality of respect* for cultural minorities, is that the insistence on *gender equality* forces republicanism to confront the issue of whether equality should always be premised on identical treatment. It also demonstrates that, in the contemporary world, the question of equality cannot be restricted to the civil, political, and economic issues with which republicanism in France has been preoccupied over the last two centuries.

References

Conseil d'État. *Sur le principe d'égalité*. Paris: La Documentation Française, 1998.
de Baecque, Antoine, et al. *L'an 1 des droits de l'homme*. Paris: Presses du CNRS, 1988.
Fitousi, Jean-Paul, and Pierre Rosanvallon. *Le nouvel âge des inégalités*. Paris: Seuil, 1996.
Gaspard, Françoise, et al. *Au pouvoir citoyennes! Liberté, égalité, parité*. Paris: Seuil: 1992.
Machelon, Jean-Pierre. *La République contre les libertés?* Paris: Presses de la FNSP, 1976.

Ozouf, Mona. "Egalité." In François Furet and Mona Ozouf, eds., *Dictionnaire critique de la Révolution française: Idées,* 139–62. Paris: Flammarion, 1992.

Renouvier, Charles. *Manuel républicain de l'homme et du citoyen.* Paris: Pagnerre, 1848.

Roman, Joël. *La démocratie des individus.* Paris: Calmann-Lévy, 1998.

Scott, Joan Wallach. *Parité: Sexual Equality and the Crisis of French Universalism.* Chicago: University of Chicago Press, 2005.

Sewell, William H. *Work and Revolution in France: The Language of Labor from the Old Regime to 1848.* Cambridge: Cambridge University Press, 1980.

Sieyès, Emmanuel. *Qu'est-ce que le Tiers Etat?* Paris: PUF, 1982.

Smith, Timothy B. *France in Crisis: Welfare, Inequality, and Globalisation since 1980.* Cambridge: Cambridge University Press, 2004.

Wieviorka, Michel, ed. *Une société fragmentée: Le multiculturalisme en débat.* Paris: La Découverte, 1996.

12

Fraternity

Anne-Claude Ambroise-Rendu

Translated by Arthur Goldhammer

What is fraternity in politics? A virtue? A form of naïveté? The poor relation of the revolutionary triad: liberty, equality, fraternity? A metaphor destined to embody proletarian hopes of justice and the remote ideal of a universal Republic? In any case, not a human right but an idea "as embarrassing as it is indispensable," as a philosopher put it in an article published in *Le Monde* in May 2002. Why embarrassing? Because although political action can create conditions favorable to the flourishing of fraternal sentiments, it cannot ensure that such sentiments will exist, nor can it verify, much less compel, their existence.

The inception of "fraternity" as a partly political, partly moral concept can be traced to the French Revolution, but it attracted little notice at the time. Fraternity made its official appearance in 1791, in supplementary articles of the Constitution, which envisioned it as the fruit of upcoming national celebrations. It was part of the official program of the Festival of the Federation, during which Lafayette swore an oath on the Champ-de-Mars to remain faithful to the people of France, to whom he was linked by "indissoluble bonds of fraternity." The Constitution of 1793 ignored fraternity, however, as did the Charter of 1830, and the word did not reappear until 1848, when it figured in the new Constitution as the third term of the republican motto. In constitutional language, fraternity has long played a minor role. But the rarity of the word tells us nothing about the actual importance of the idea. We must look beyond words and ask how the notion of fraternity was actually put to use. Concrete embodiments of the concept are everywhere: the opening of a previously closed society in the French Revolution; the great demonstrations of unanimity, such as the Festival of the Federation in 1790 and the proclamation of the Constitution of 14 September 1791; the sans-culotte dream of an egalitarian world; the ideal of universality and emancipation heralded by the abolition of slavery; and the pedagogical ambitions of the Enlightenment philosophers Condorcet and Lakanal—all can be interpreted as manifestations of the fraternal idea. According to Alfonse Aulard, the great late nineteenth-century historian of the French Revolution, the custom of greeting others as "brothers and friends" originated in April 1791. But fraternity really triumphed along with equality under the dictatorship of the Montagnards, the radical revolutionaries whose leaders would establish the Reign of Terror. It was the Revolution that conceptualized fraternity in purely secular terms and made it a facet of the republican ideal.

The state was nevertheless discreet about the use of fraternity in official texts and symbolism. There are several reasons for this discretion: the ambiguity of the word, its hint of overweening ambitions, its religious and Masonic overtones (one finds it frequently in the sermons of patriotic and, later, constitutional priests), and its origins among the Cordeliers and fraternal societies, birthplaces of *sans-culotterie,* the radical artisans and shopkeepers of Paris. What is more, its meaning and connotations changed as political life turned increasingly brutal. If the word initially connoted universality, factional conflict narrowed its definition to exclude traitors to the fatherland from the fraternal embrace. And when it became a political instrument, it acquired ironic connotations, as section members invoked it each time one of their comrades was purged, removed from office, or expelled.

The fraternal idea made a comeback in politics (and even more in law) with the Revolution of 1848. After the long hiatus of the Consulate, Empire, and Restoration, the communitarian movements of the July Monarchy laid the groundwork for this revival. Étienne Cabet, the Christian theorist of peaceful communism, advocated the organization of small fraternal collectives. Cabet's theories appealed not just to adepts of his communist movement but to a much larger audience of tradesmen impressed by the advantages of cooperative organization.

A more combative fraternity emerged with the banquet campaign and the episodes of fraternization between National Guardsmen and insurgents. With the triumph of the Republic it at last became possible for fraternity to make its official entrance. Universal suffrage marked the coming of age of the people: rather than a government of fathers taking their children in hand, the Republic was portrayed as a band of brothers. The intuition of the revolutionaries was proved right: fraternity was impossible without liberty and equality, because only free and equal human beings qualified as brothers. On April 20, 1848, three days before the election of the Constituent Assembly, a Festival of Fraternity was held in Paris. It was a great success: men, women, young people, groups, individuals—everyone fraternized. In November, the Constitution officially enshrined fraternity as a basic principle of the regime: "The Republic rests on the principle of liberty, equality, and fraternity."

Moreover, the newly proclaimed Republic saw itself as "generous, or, more simply, humane": it abolished slavery in the colonies and the death penalty for political crimes. Reflecting the humanitarianism of the victors of the February uprising and rejecting the arbitrariness of the three previous regimes as well as the Revolutionary Tribunal of Year II of the French Revolution (1793–94), the abolition of the death penalty represented a remarkable advance. In addition, the Constitution would give content to the word "fraternity" by spelling out various forms of public assistance and support. The Republic acknowledged its duty to ensure "by way of fraternal assistance…the existence of needy citizens." The legislative measures proposed to establish the reign of fraternity included limitation of the duration of work, guarantee of the right to work and to associate, and establishment of councils of ombudsmen to hear workers' complaints.

Fraternity manifested itself everywhere in egalitarian protocol. For example, official letters concluded with the formula "Greetings and fraternity," which did away with class distinctions and hierarchies. Eugène Varlin, the militant socialist and revolutionary leader, would use this same formula to end his letters twenty years later. Fraternity thus fulfilled the promise of linking the idea of individuality closely to the idea of humanity, adding an authentic social right to the usual civic rights. The victors of February thus found it possible to believe that they had consummated the marriage of socialism and republicanism.

"Fraternity is the law above the law," said Michelet. For him and most other nineteenth-century historians and philosophers who hated individualism and everything divisive in revolution and democracy, fraternity was the central principle of the French Revolution. By attributing an ethical foundation to the Revolution, Michelet hoped to resist the temptations of individualism and atomization. For him, fraternity both completed and transcended the other two terms of the republican motto, liberty and equality. Secularized fraternity was the brotherhood of justice and a call to personal responsibility.

The socialists Louis Blanc and Philippe Buchez put fraternity ahead of liberty and equality because it came from God rather than man. Blanc, who admired the oaths sworn by the *fédérés,* deplored the disappearance of fraternity "in the tempest unleashed by the thinkers of the Mountain." But Buchez accepted the fraternization of the Terror and the sacrifice of the present generation as the price to be paid for the realization of an ideal: the happiness of subsequent generations.

In 1831, the philosopher Pierre Leroux saw in the concept of fraternity a promise of moral reorganization, a way of bridging the gap between liberty and equality, but only on the condition that the three terms were "combined in a philosophy named: Religion." "So, embrace a religion," he urged his readers, or give up the idea of reconciling one man's liberty with another's. Buchez and the "utopian" socialist Saint-Simon, like the Catholic reformers Lamennais and Lacordaire, also believed that fraternity must be based on Christianity. And in 1899, one Buram, the author of *Petites réflexions sur la devise républicaine,* incorporated fraternity into a humane and universal religion based on the biblical injunction to "love thy neighbor as thyself."

Thus we begin to see what fraternity meant in the first half of the nineteenth century. Whether understood as Christian or revolutionary, it was crucial to the dream of a new type of political regime. Strict republicans were wary of the concept because behind it, they believed, lurked the threat of socialism, whereas socialists invoked it as a challenge to individualism and a promise of infinite rewards.

Since 1848, fraternity has often been reaffirmed. The Third Republic availed itself of the inaugural celebration of July 14, 1880, to revive the triad bequeathed to it by its predecessor. But its inscription on the facades of public buildings was mainly a symbolic consecration. Republicans remained suspicious. Committed to the defense of the rights of man (individual liberties, equality before the law, respect for private property), they did not know what to make of the concept of fraternity, which some denounced as a fraud and others rejected along with equality as a direct legacy of the Terror.

Fraternity figured explicitly in both the Preamble and Article 2 of the Constitution of October 4, 1958. To be sure, it symbolized the survival of the spirit of revolution in the institutions of the Republic, but it also meant something more. The decision to include or omit the word and the way its meaning was interpreted revealed different conceptions of social and political organization and thus contradictory notions of what the Fifth Republic ought to be. The regime deserves credit for having gradually reinstated fraternity as a fundamental principle of certain aspects of current public law.

For Marx, the fraternal effusions of 1848 merely reflected the euphoric illusions of the moment, temporarily concealing the reality of class struggle. But the Workers' International referred to workers as brothers in order to foster "not just the feeling but the fact of fraternity." Varlin addressed the members of the French Section as "brothers and friends."

During the Second Empire, Victor Hugo presented *Les misérables,* his vast paean to the humble and poor, as "a book whose basis is fraternity." The Commune revived the word in all its various connotations: fraternity of peoples, fraternity with strikers, fraternization with the troops, and appeals from workers to their "peasant brothers." More than that, it attached new concrete meanings to the idea. The whole effort to achieve a revolutionary reorganization of work reflected the insistence on fraternity. The closing of placement offices, the aid offered to workers' cooperatives and associations of female workers, and the planned expropriation of absconding owners for the benefit of workers' collectives were all facets of the effort to redefine the meaning of fraternity.

The Third Republic's reluctance to embrace the concept of fraternity moved the workers' movement to promote it in the 1880s in all phases of its activity: ideology, organization, and action. Syndicalists, anarchists, and socialists declared themselves brothers but eventually yielded to Fernand Pelloutier's influence and adopted the less emotionally charged term "comrade." The fraternity of workers was fourfold. First, it was central to their daily struggle for better working conditions and mutual assistance. Second, it had the broader sense of fraternity of all mankind, which would be realized when the oppressive capitalist system was finally overcome. Third, it extended, through the international workers' movement, to all peoples of the earth. And finally, Jaurès and his socialist allies expressed confidence that "the great socialist fraternity"—which ultimately was nothing less than the unity of all mankind—would eventually unify the Left.

In the twentieth century, the term "fraternity" fell out of favor, and its meaning narrowed. "Fraternization" supplanted "fraternity" in the context of proletarian struggle. In a compilation of proletarian music published by the Jeunesses Communistes in 1929, a song entitled "Fraternization" called upon soldiers and sailors to join the workers in establishing a regime of soviets: "Debout! Tous avec nous! Des puissants, la force se brise/Quand le soldat, uni avec nous,/Garde ses armes et fraternise!" (Arise! Everyone with us! The powerful become powerless when the soldier stands with us, arms in hand, and fraternizes!)

Beyond the fraternity of working people, the legacy of 1848 also established a call for fraternity among nations. This form of fraternity would foster popular emancipation, liberation of oppressed nationalities, and the ideal of international peace. Parisians demanded (but did not obtain) a commitment from the Provisional Government (February–June 1848) to support the Poles, the favorite "brothers" of the French. Lamartine, the de facto foreign minister at the time, favored a more moderate approach: France would not export its Revolution and refused to commit itself to supporting rebellions elsewhere. This policy, which may have been realistic and was certainly prudent, had the merit of exorcising memories of Year II. France not only gave up the guillotine and the Terror; it also renounced wars of conquest. It would be a pacific Republic, respectful of the fraternity of peoples. Faced with a choice between the proclamation of 1790 affirming that France renounced all wars of conquest and all violations of the liberty of other nations, and the proclamation of 1792, which committed France to the fraternal support of any people that wished to free itself from tyrants, the Second Republic preferred the former.

Fifty years later, Buram's pamphlet on the Republican motto also condemned war as "the most anti-fraternal crime that the evil spirit could have imagined," and for good measure denounced the great conquerors: Cyrus, Alexander,

Caesar, and Napoleon. This did not prevent the Third Republic from pursuing its colonial adventure, though it did deny being xenophobic or nationalistic. In an 1881 article on France's "Islamic policy," Pierre Lafitte attacked any racist or nationalistic conception of development, which he said would amount to a denial of the fraternity of mankind.

In the trenches of World War I, a new kind of fraternity was born of the dangers that everyone faced in common and the extremely difficult living conditions, moral as well as physical, that everyone faced. Jan Patocka would call this the "solidarity of the shell-shocked." This spirit survived among veterans in the interwar years and supplanted the pacific fraternity of the internationalists. In 1917, however, the mutinies on the front lines led to some desultory fraternization with strikers and pacifists in the rear, while rumors from Russia spoke of fraternization across the lines by opposing armies. This contrast would persist in the postwar euphoria, with some happy about the victory and others simply relieved by the end of hostilities.

We see an echo of this division in 1923, when Georges Millandy, a champion of moderation, wrote a very pacifistic "Chant des peuples": "À tous la grande voix du Monde/A commandé: "cessez-le-feu!"…L'amour triomphe de la haine! La force cede à la bonté/Les esclaves jettent leur chaîne,/Ils comprennent enfin ce mot: Fraternité!" (To all the Great Voice of the World/Gave the order, Cease fire!…Love triumphs over hatred! Force surrenders to goodness/Slaves throw off their chains/At last they understand the word: Fraternity!)

The Popular Front (1936–37) offered another opportunity to greet the advent of fraternity with song. Eugène Bizeau's "Chanson de Paris" celebrated the good news: "La Chanson de Paris, c'est la chanson humaine/Préparant l'avenir épris de liberté,/Qui servira la paix comme une souveraine/Dans un siècle d'amour et de fraternité" (The song of Paris is the song of humanity/paving the way to a future in love with liberty/Which will serve peace as a sovereign/In a century of love and fraternity.)

On May 18, 1848, the Club de la Fraternité Républicaine published an essay on the creation of assistance and retirement funds for workers. Its author, a typesetter, urged his readers to abandon speculative theory and tackle the "workers' issue" in order to make sure that "the holy trinity of the Republic [liberty, equality, fraternity] does not turn into a bitter mockery of the poor." What this text tells us is that "fraternity" had entered the lexicon of people concerned with social issues. Its use in this context became commonplace, but in the wake of Léon Bourgeois's Solidarist movement, the concept would acquire a new name: solidarity. The switch from fraternity to solidarity deprived the former of the near monopoly it had enjoyed for a century in the legitimation of social rights.

The shift in terminology signals a crucial change in political philosophy. "Solidarity" did not carry the same emotional charge as "fraternity." It entered the public arena just as class consciousness was dawning among workers, and as sociology, positivism, and secularized moral teachings were gaining influence. Late nineteenth-century republicans were convinced that fraternity could never serve as a basis for social rights, and preferred the more concrete idea of solidarity, which was a basic principle of their social philosophy. A new conception of the relation between citizens and the state took hold.

It was also part of the mission of the twentieth-century welfare state to alleviate the inevitable tensions between liberty and equality. But something was lost in the shift from fraternity to solidarity. The demand for solidarity could be satisfied by a certain redistribution of wealth and greater social justice, whereas fraternity, a more demanding concept, implied real relationships with others and virtually unconditional attention to their needs. Indeed, Félix Grindelle made this point as early as 1924, when he remarked that the Declaration of Rights of 1789 and the motto "liberty, equality, fraternity" had envisioned a transformation of man's inner life. Without illusions, he added: "About fraternity I would speak more eloquently if I were myself more fraternal." Fraternity was not just an experience but a sort of utopian ideal, never to be achieved, for which the Republic remains eternally nostalgic. Its nostalgia for the fraternity of 1848 found reinforcement in the dreadful ordeal of another kind of fraternity, what David Rousset, speaking of the concentration camps, called "the fraternity of abjection."

In the spring of 2002, two presidential candidates used the word "fraternity" in their campaign posters: Christine Taubira, the candidate of the centrist Radicaux de Gauche, and Bruno Mégret, an ultranationalist of the extreme Right. Their common use of this term shows that the concept of fraternity continues to encompass radically different views and remains an elusive and multifarious ideal.

References

Amadou, R. "Liberté, égalité, fraternité: La devise républicaine et la franc-maçonnerie."
    Special issue, *Renaissance Traditionnelle* (1977).
Borgetto, M. *La notion de fraternité en droit public français: Le passé, le présent et l'avenir de la
    solidarité.* Paris: Librairie Générale de Droit et de Jurisprudence, 1993.
Buram. *Liberté, égalité, fraternité: Petites réflexions sur la devise républicaine.* La Rochelle:
    Imprimerie Nouvelle, Noël Texier, 1899.
David, M. *Fraternité et révolution française.* Coll. Histoire. Paris: Aubier, 1987.
————. *Le printemps de la fraternité: Genèse et vicissitudes, 1830–1851.* Coll. Histoire. Paris:
    Aubier, 1992.
Grindelle, F. *La Déclaration des Droits de l'Homme et du Citoyen, la charte républicaine et la devise liberté, égalité, fraternité: Étude historique et exégétique.* Alençon: Imprimerie Corbière
    et Jugain, 1924.

13

Democracy

Patrice Gueniffey

Translated by Arthur Goldhammer

The relationship between republicanism and democracy is singular: republicanism was not always democratic, and if today the spread of democracy seems irresistible, it is hardly the case that republicanism is everywhere seen as the form of government indispensable to democratic societies. Indeed, several European democracies remain monarchies. Democracy is thus a notion at once concrete and vague: concrete, because its defining conditions are readily identifiable, but vague, because its territory is without precise limits. The closer one approaches, the farther its frontiers seem to recede. Democracy is a system, and an expectation that can never be fully satisfied.

Let us first consider democracy as a system of political and personal rights. It is, in Benjamin Constant's words, "the right of each person to state his opinion, to choose his line of work, to dispose of his property and even to abuse it, and to come and go without having to seek permission or explain his reasons or his actions. It is the right of each individual to join with others to discuss common interests, to worship as they please, or merely to spend their time as they see fit or even as suits their fancy." In the political order, it is also a set of arrangements for ensuring that each person has a share of influence: guarantees of basic liberties, freedom to vote, regular and open elections, government of the majority with respect for the rights of the minority, and so on. In other words, democracy includes the institutions characteristic of today's Western governments.

But democracy is not just a political system; it is also a social state. Nineteenth-century historians, Tocqueville chief among them, had their reasons for tracing this form of democracy back to the Middle Ages, when the establishment of towns with the support of the monarchy began the emancipation of the Third Estate and initiated a process that would continue for centuries. Although this genealogy of democracy cannot withstand detailed historical scrutiny, it nevertheless illustrates the depth and venerability of the change that undermined the traditional order from within—a traditional order in which individuals were prisoners of the status they occupied in a hierarchy that defined their prerogatives and obligations and subjected them to the external authority of king and church. This traditional order gradually gave way to an order based on autonomy, on the freedom to do and to judge for oneself. In the Age of Enlightenment, everything changed: the old hierarchies and distinctions lost their legitimacy, even if they did not vanish altogether from life or law, while the *philosophes'* efforts on behalf of freedom of conscience and religious toleration emancipated individuals from their former subjugation to civil and especially church authorities. The democratic idea burst forth everywhere in the eighteenth century, from Voltaire's campaigns against religious persecution to debates over freedom of enterprise and commerce. The benefits expected from these various kinds of freedom reflect the advent of societies in which people felt less and less constrained by the hierarchy of orders and increasingly equal and autonomous: indeed, the concept of "self-interest" was really a synonym for this autonomy.

To be sure, the old order still had many champions among adepts of "aristocratic ideology," but the concessions that a traditionalist writer like Henri de Boulainvilliers (1658–1722) felt obliged to make to the idea of equality shows the extent to which it ruled men's minds even before it triumphed in fact and penetrated the realm of law. In this sense, the principal effect of the abolition of privileges that took place on the night of August 4, 1789—the event that marked the advent of a society of free individuals equal before the law—was the important step taken toward aligning legality with legitimacy.

The history of democracy as a political regime began much later. Until the end of the eighteenth century, the term referred to direct democracy as practiced in the city-states of antiquity, and the concept aroused ambivalent sentiments. Although admiration of this glorious past was *de rigueur,* and although this admiration extended to a system compatible with the principle of natural equality because it granted all citizens direct control over their collective destiny, this ancient heritage was by no means seen as a model to imitate. Indeed, admiration for democracy was accompanied by suspicion. In the first place, the "liberty of the ancients" depended on material conditions that belonged to an irrevocably vanished past: the ancient city-states were small in size and limited in population, so that it was possible for all the people to meet in public assemblies, and citizens were served by a large population of slaves, so that they were free to devote as much time as they wished to public affairs. These material conditions were reinforced by moral considerations: political participation was seen as the very essence of civic virtue. Whether in the agora or on the battlefield, whether by casting a ballot or sacrificing oneself, the citizen who participated in the life of the city achieved a higher form of existence than the person whose horizons did not extend beyond his own private interests. Wariness of democracy in the eighteenth century also stemmed from the lessons of history: small democratically governed cities had always been prey to tumult and passions, to internal dissension and factional struggle, and to decisions inspired by enthusiasm or imposed by intrigue. Reason had often been defeated in them, and in the eyes of Enlightenment philosophers it was reason that validated law—to the point where reason was considered to be more important than the identity of those making the laws. Did not Condorcet say as late as 1789 that laws made by an enlightened monarch were preferable by far to decisions taken by an ignorant populace?

Last but not least, the disappearance of the conditions that had made direct democracy possible was merely the sign of a deeper change. Indeed, the crucial eighteenth-century argument against democracy was of a philosophical order: it turned on the transformation of the idea of liberty, which gradually migrated from the public, collective, political sphere to the private or individual sphere. Liberty had previously been identified with direct, collective participation in sovereignty, so that participation was far more important than guarantees of personal freedom and security. A man was not free if he was merely "king in his own castle." He could achieve freedom only in conjunction with his fellow citizens, for whom he would, if need be, sacrifice his interests and even his life. Modern liberty is the exact opposite of this ancient liberty. This does not mean that the moderns are indifferent to political liberty, only that liberty, for them, is no longer identified with participation in sovereignty. They remain attached to political liberty, as an end in itself, but largely as a means to the tranquil enjoyment of their own individual liberty and freedom to engage in their own private affairs. The liberty of the ancients unfolded in public space; for the moderns, it is achieved in private space.

For all these reasons, representative government—today synonymous with democratic political regimes—was taken in the eighteenth century to be a system distinct from democracy. In fact, representative government was not as alien to democracy as theorists of the time tended to think. To be sure, representative government imposed limits on citizen intervention, but for that very reason it granted access to a kind of liberty that until then had seemed possible only in the ancient world. By applying to political affairs a division of labor imposed by the increasing unavailability of citizens for public life, and by creating the conditions for rational deliberation, representative government brought democracy within reach of the moderns. This new version of democracy had lost both its admirable qualities (self-government by the people) and its apparent defects (the frequent irrationality of its decisions).

To be sure, there were elitist aspects to the representative ideal. The goal was not so much to represent, through elections, the diversity of existing interests and opinions but rather to organize enlightened debate about matters of common interest. Bear in mind that no one at the time thought of the political realm as divided into parties, that is, adverse forces expressing different but equally legitimate points of view with respect to matters of general interest and seeking to command a majority in favor of their opinion. The problem was not to amass votes in order to determine a legislative majority and minority. Divided legislatures were always taken to be symptoms of a sick political body. Instead, the hope was that the initial diversity of opinion could be reduced by eliminating errors through deliberation, in order to arrive ultimately at the general will: the one true answer to each question put to a vote. In Enlightenment theory, representative government was a system in which decisions were taken only after due deliberation by enlightened representatives, who were supposed to be capable of renouncing their own beliefs in order to yield to the clear expression of the general will and who were also not bound by any promises to their constituents and thus free to engage in the indispensable effort of reflection prior to reaching a judgment. Representation was an enlightened substitute for the people. Early in the French Revolution, Sieyès maintained that each deputy was elected by a locality, but he was to think of himself as representative of the nation, not of his electors.

This rationalist approach to collective decision-making justified not only the delegation of sovereign power but also limits on participation in the form of indirect elections and property qualifications for voting. (Only those who paid more than a particular, legally defined amount of property taxes possessed the right to vote.) Apart from the brief interlude of Jacobin power, the representative system would incorporate limitations of this kind until the adoption of universal (male) suffrage in 1848. It is important to note, however, that judgments about the effects of property qualifications, especially of those established during the French Revolution, are often false. Critics tend to refer to the Restoration (1814–30), at the beginning of which less than a hundred thousand people enjoyed the right to vote. But doing so overlooks the fact that in 1790 the Revolution's relatively minimal property qualifications permitted more than four million people to vote. What is more, critics often forget that electoral qualification based on tax payments was in fact democratic, because they ignored status differences and allowed for social mobility. The property qualification was not a permanent exclusion, and in the minds of those who adopted it in 1789, the progress expected to result from revolutionary reforms would lead to a gradual increase in the number of voters, ultimately broadening the definition of citizenship and culminating in universal suffrage. The *cens,* as the tax determining eligibility to vote was called, was a provisional response to the unequal distribution of enlightenment and material independence, which were taken to be essential prerequisites of true citizenship. If the *censitaire* regime is evidence of the power of philosophical rationalism, it also illustrates the connection that existed from the outset between equality and legitimacy.

A similar observation can be made with respect to representative doctrine, which was elaborated in opposition to direct democracy but reshaped from within by a purely democratic means. In the first place, contemporaries saw elections as a way of preserving equality by subjecting all legal authority to popular consent. In addition, the possibility of replacing political leaders was intended to prevent people in authority from developing interests distinct from those of the people. Finally, elections increased the number of citizens allowed to exercise responsibility for government. Regular elections were meant to teach the French the principles of liberty, to familiarize them with the issues of politics, and to create citizens conscious of their duties and capable of managing public affairs. No one at the time imagined that the representative system would lead to the formation of a specialized "political class" distinct from the rest of society. Indeed, it was believed that representative government would prevent this from happening and allow an ever-growing number of citizens to exercise political responsibilities one after the other. Although eighteenth-century representative theory was elaborated in opposition to direct democracy, the ancient ideal remained: no polity was worthy of the name unless each citizen had an opportunity to participate in government. The democratic spirit persisted within a system that was often seen as its opposite, or at any rate as a corruption of the ideal.

The modern political formula, combining universal suffrage with representative government, did not take hold immediately. The year 1789 established representation without universal suffrage; 1793 proclaimed universal suffrage but undid representative government. These were the inaugural episodes of the two democratic traditions that would pit heirs of the French Revolution against one another through the middle of the nineteenth century.

Criticism of democratic institutions on the basis of democratic principles began with the inception of democracy itself. In 1789, many people invoked the Declaration of the Rights of Man in calling for an end to the denial of political rights to domestic servants and indigents, while a much smaller number—really only a few isolated voices—insisted on equality for women. The new political leaders were accused of having established an "aristocracy of wealth" on the ruins of the aristocracy of birth and, worse still, of having undermined popular sovereignty by instituting a representative system that favored an oligarchy of elected officials responsible to no one but themselves. Demands for universal suffrage accompanied calls for direct democracy in one form or another—such as the right to recall "unfaithful" representatives or to pass laws by referendum. Without these, it was argued, there could be no authentic democracy, meaning a regime in which the people, all the people, govern themselves by exerting strict control over the actions and decisions of their parliamentary representatives (the need for which no one denied). Condorcet's draft constitution as well as the text ultimately adopted in June 1793 granted expanded powers to citizens, thus marking the ephemeral victory of proponents of direct democracy. The spirit of these texts can be summed up in two words: unity (of the people and its representatives) and transparency (of society and power, with power identified more strictly than ever with society, which was in a position to dictate its will to government). The important point is not that these demands, which were partly inspired by the Old Regime's tradition of imperative mandates and partly dictated by a desire to transcend representative democracy, often reflected tactical political considerations, but rather that they show the extent to which the very *idea* of democracy posed a permanent threat to the legitimacy of the institutions that embodied it. Democracy contains the seeds of protest against democratic institutions and the limits that they must lay down in order to function effectively, and therefore, a fortiori, against the exclusions inevitably imposed on access to political rights. Democracy is remarkably vulnerable to a dynamic of perpetual deepening and outbidding. It is not just a political system and a social state but also an idea, or, more precisely, a promise of perfect liberty and equality that can never be fully satisfied. Yet with every defeat and every victory, its horizons become ever more remote and inaccessible. Democracy permanently calls for its own transcendence: in that respect above all, it is by nature revolutionary.

During the Revolution, these vulnerabilities embedded in democracy helped produce the Terror, whose experience durably condemned universal suffrage, and to an even greater degree direct democracy, both of which were now linked to memories of an era associated with the unimpeded rule of an ignorant and barbarous multitude. These memories, together with Napoleon Bonaparte's use of plebiscitary democracy, encouraged the identification of modern democracy with representative government. But the crisis of representation did not end with the French Revolution. What began with the election of the first representatives still endures today. It is consubstantial with the history of representative government and attests to an ambiguity at the heart of modern representative democracy: The more modern individuals become disengaged from civic life, the more necessary it becomes to represent them. But the very process of representation only heightens a disengaged people's suspicion that representative government is unfaithful to democracy itself.

Today, democracy is not just a republican value. It is the express condition of all legitimacy, regardless of the form political institutions take. The republic (and indeed monarchy where it still exists) is nowadays *contained within democracy,* as one of its modes of organization. For a long time, democracy had been *contained within the republic,* as one of its forms. One factor played a paramount role in this inversion: the rise of the idea of individual rights, a development that political theory long ignored. For example, the republican tradition from Machiavelli to the thinkers of the English Revolution largely ignored the question of rights and conceived of liberty not in terms of individual rights but rather of the common good. In other words, liberty was a property of the whole rather than of its parts, and the participation essential to its perpetuation was not so much a consequence of an individual right as a moral requirement associated with the capacity to put the general interest above any personal interest. The republic was based on virtue, not on the rights of citizens. In this respect, modern republican thought, which had such a profound influence on the American revolutionaries of the late eighteenth century and even on the French, was not "democratic," at least not in the modern sense of the word. The republican discourse of virtue did not disappear with the advent of the question of rights, nor was it a monopoly of the Jacobins of 1793. It survived in the democratic age of the Republic, embodied in an institution—*l'administration,* or state bureaucracy, which was responsible for maintaining strict equality among citizens—and in a feeling—patriotism, which allowed individuals separated by their rights to share a sense of membership in a free community outside of which their rights would have been a mere fiction. Indeed, if the universalism of the rights of man tends to loosen community bonds and deracinate individuals, belonging to the nation—and the sentiment of such belonging—"re-roots" individuals defined rationally in terms of rights and turns them into citizens: the nation re-creates citizens and Frenchmen, whereas the rights of man produce inhabitants of a world virtually without borders.

The territory of democracy has been growing steadily, in France and elsewhere, for two centuries. The French Revolution had confined it within the strict limits of political liberty and equality before the law. The nineteenth century gave it a new dimension with the emergence of the social question, and in particular the worker question, which had not yet surfaced during the French Revolution. The individualization of contemporary societies has broken through all the dikes while at the same time accelerating the process of civic disengagement. Benjamin Constant saw disaffection with public action as a factor favorable to liberty and public tranquility owing to the extinction of political passions. To be sure, democracy becomes more stable as citizens cease to think of themselves as participants in government and place increasing value on the selfish and tranquil enjoyment of personal freedom. But there are two sides to everything, and there is a limit to the benefits of civic disengagement. Beyond a certain point, the indifference of citizens, as Constant himself recognized, becomes a threat to liberty. The danger lies not in the destruction of democratic institutions but rather in the possibility that citizens will give up their sovereignty to an oligarchy that would arrogate all power to itself while leaving the people with only the appearance of sovereignty, that is, the duty to obey.

References

Constant, Benjamin. *Écrits politiques.* Edited by Marcel Gauchet. Paris: Gallimard, Folio, 1997.

Gauchet, Marcel. *La révolution des pouvoirs: La souveraineté, le peuple et la représentation, 1789–1799.* Paris: Gallimard, 1995.

Rosanvallon, Pierre. *La démocratie inachevée: Histoire de la souveraineté du peuple en France.* Paris: Gallimard, 2000.

———. *Le peuple introuvable: Histoire de la représentation démocratique en France.* Paris: Gallimard, 1998.

———. *Le sacre du citoyen: Histoire du suffrage universel en France.* Paris: Gallimard, 1992.

Skinner, Quentin. "On Justice, the Common Good, and the Priority of Liberty." In Chantal Mouffe, ed., *Dimensions of Radical Democracy: Pluralism, Citizenship, Community,* 211–24. London and New York: Verso, 1992.

14

Laicity

Jean Baubérot

Translated by Arthur Goldhammer

The (French) Republic is secular (*laïque*), and (French) "laicity" is republican.*
In France, this might seem to be an obvious fact needing no lengthy commentary.
For instance, Claude Nicolet's *L'idée républicaine en France* (1982) devotes only a
few pages to the theme of laicity and republicanism. "Legal and territorial unity,"
Nicolet argues, "also require unity of another kind: moral or spiritual: this is the
function of laicity." He then adds: "This is too well-known to dwell on at any
length." Later he returns to the same refrain: "The history [of laicity] is too well-
known to dwell on."

But is the case really that closed? Aren't these dismissive remarks rather a
sign of the difficulty of writing a critical history of republican laicity? It is untrue
that the history of laicity is "too well-known." Rather, it is crushed beneath the
weight of memory, which is a very different thing.

The dialectic of remembrance and amnesia—a dialectic characteristic of
memory in general—has been all the more inescapable in this case because two
related but hostile collective memories have told the same story in two different
ways, in terms of laicity's conquest on the one hand and anti-Catholic "persecutions" on the other. These two contradictory memories continue to permeate
the French imagination. But because historical scholarship has corrected certain

---

* Rather than translate the French term *laïcité* as "secularism," it seems more accurate to use
the admittedly awkward word "laicity," which has a broader meaning than "secularism" and
therefore better describes the French case. Unlike "secularism," "laicity" refers to three phenomena all at once: freedom of conscience, the nondomination of any religion over state and society,
and the principle of nondiscrimination for religious reasons. The first theoretical definition of
laïcité came in 1883 when the philosopher Ferdinand Buisson described it as a situation in which
"the State remains neutral with respect to all religions, free from all clergymen," and so can promote "equality before the law [and] freedom for all religions." On the whole, the 1905 law on the
separation of church and state (still valid today) corresponds to this definition, and this conception
has remained the dominant influence in French legislation concerning religion since then.

points, a new version of the story has emerged, in which historical laicity is presented as a "compromise" solution. This new version is linked to the end of the conflict between the Republic and Catholicism as well as to the difficulty of accepting the multicultural character of France today, so that the danger now is an excess of irenic understanding rather than an exaggeration of hostility. The conflict between two Frances did indeed exist, but so did a conflict within the secularist camp at the decisive moment.

The notion of "republican laicity" must therefore be problematized and its pertinence evaluated. Did the Republic really break with the monarchy and/or empire? Didn't French laicity borrow from abroad? And what Republic are we talking about? The Third, which laicized the public schools (which became purely secular institutions) and separated church and state? Or the First, whose secularizing measures were repeatedly treated as almost…sacred icons?

In fact, the proper referent is rather the Revolution taken as an indivisible "bloc" (G. Clemenceau). But should we not distinguish between republican measures as such and those of the Constituent Assembly and its abortive efforts to establish a constitutional monarchy? Its work was of great importance, but ambivalent. Important, because it abolished religious crimes (such as heresy, blasphemy, sorcery, and magic) in May 1791, eliminated discrimination against Protestants (in December 1789) and Jews (in September 1791), and constitutionally guaranteed "freedom for all to worship as they please" (in September 1791).

Yet that foundation stone was marked by ambivalence. Article 10 of the Declaration of 1789, which proclaimed, "No one shall be persecuted for his opinions, even religious opinions," nonetheless restricted the "manifestation" of those opinions in the name of "public order," a phenomenon not mentioned in any other connection. Aimed at religious minorities, this proviso was subsequently used against refractory priests (those who refused to accept the Civil Constitution of the Clergy—see below). In the meantime, the Assembly had placed "ecclesiastical properties" at "the disposal of the Nation," in exchange for a commitment to bear the costs of maintaining Catholic churches and clergy (November 1789). This implicit nationalization of the dominant religion was confirmed by the Civil Constitution of the Clergy (July 1790), which, without the pope's agreement, changed the structure of the Catholic Church and made it dependent on the new revolutionary state. (The Catholic Church was broken in two: "constitutional" and "refractory." The first conformed to the Revolution; the second did not.) In addition, monastic vows, deemed incompatible with the rights of man, were abolished (February 1790), and the Constitution of 1791 established a new form of "religion" by inaugurating "national holidays to preserve the memory of the French Revolution, foster fraternity among citizens, and attach them to the Constitution, the Fatherland, and the law."

Freedom of conscience and worship, continuation of state oversight of religion, accentuation of the Gallicanism (French independence of the pope) of the ancien régime, discredit of certain forms of religion, and establishment of a secular version of religious activity: here we have various types of laicization, and the Revolution took steps in each of these directions before the monarchy was abolished. What followed became part of its legacy: abolition of teaching and hospital orders (August 1792) and laicization of vital records (birth and death) and marriage on the eve of the proclamation of the Republic (September 20, 1792). Although the effort to make the Revolution the object of quasi-religious veneration and the blossoming of political and religious persecution were two sides of the same coin and became inseparable from the Terror, they also grew out of the earlier proliferation of civic oaths. These had become common in 1791 and contradicted the spirit of the Enlightenment, for such "irrational" practices had no place in an enlightened political system.

The real innovation of the First Republic was the separation of (constitutional) church and state in February 1795. In order to end the civil war against the Chouans in the Vendée and Brittany and soothe the religious passions of these traditionalist regions, the Convention agreed to take steps toward (limited) freedom of religion. The La Jaunaye accord of February 17, 1795, was followed by the decree of 3 Ventôse (February 21, 1795), which restored freedom of worship provided that services were held on private premises, without public manifestations or outward signs. Boissy d'Anglas declared: "Monitor what you cannot prevent, regulate what you cannot prohibit." The Convention had previously slashed the budget of the loyalist church to zero, a move that was tantamount to abrogating the Civil Constitution of the Clergy.

This separation subsequently became an iconic reference. One philosopher recently put it this way: "Marianne [the imaginary young woman with a Phrygian (liberty) cap who symbolized the Republic] then…changed the law to promote liberty and equality of all citizens." By contrast, Albert Mathiez's judgment was harsh: "Tolerance was tossed to the Catholics as alms." Both judgments miss the mark: the decree of 1795 denied state subsidies to religions but allowed them to hold services at will, albeit under police surveillance and with all ceremonies and observances kept strictly inside the church or synagogue's walls. Freedom of religion was thus sharply limited, and all the more so after the coup of 18 Fructidor, Year V (4 September 1797), when the government stepped up its repression of individual rights.

What is important in a revolution is what remains after the revolution ends. Napoleon's authoritarian recentering of the regime consolidated certain changes wrought by the Revolution, rejected others, and introduced innovations that ensured structural stability. The historiography of laicity sees the Napoleonic period as one of "regression," and it is true that the 1795 separation of church and state was abolished. But it is not unlikely that if the Restoration had come at the dawn of the nineteenth century, it would have reversed the Revolution's laicization further than Napoleon did: The emperor kept some of his predecessors' accomplishments in place.

Although the Concordat (the official agreement between Bonaparte and the pope, signed in 1801) reinstated the public standing of a reunified Catholic religion, it did not restore Catholicism as the official religion of France. The dogmatic union of church and state was definitively ended, since the Civil Code (1804) contradicted canon law on numerous points. The marriage ceremony was laicized, as were birth and death records, and citizenship was completely divorced from religious affiliation. The Napoleonic Organic Articles (rules of public order) revived the Gallican perspective of French state control over the church (not only royal and parliamentary but also revolutionary) and, among other things, established a number of "recognized religions" (Protestantism in 1802, the "Israelite religion" in 1808). The emperor's purpose was to bring the "succor of religion" to all the French and ensure their moral socialization. But other socializing institutions were also established, especially in the field of medicine and education. A law targeting "the illegal practice of medicine" was promulgated in 1803, and an imperial university created in 1806. Although Voltaire had admired the (relative) religious freedom of the English in the eighteenth century, France and Great Britain now switched positions in this respect: in England, nonconformist Protestants did not obtain political rights until 1828, Catholics in 1829, Jews in 1858, and atheists in 1886, while non-Anglicans were not admitted to "Oxbridge" until the 1850s, for example.

Thus not only the First Republic but also, before it, the short-lived constitutional monarchy and, after it, the Consulate and Empire created a situation that, while by no means equivalent to the laicity of the Third Republic, nevertheless incorporated certain of its structural characteristics. The founding fathers of the Third Republic always insisted on this fact. In the *Dictionnaire de pédagogie,* Ferdinand Buisson pointed to the neutrality of the state, freedom of religion, civil status and marriage, and equality of rights regardless of creed. He concluded that, despite certain "inconsistencies," "the lay state had become part of our mores" well before the laicization of the schools. Jules Ferry said much the same thing in the Chamber.

Although the Restoration attempted to turn back the clock (with an abortive effort to restore responsibility for recording civil status to the clergy and a temporarily successful effort to pass laws against sacrilege), it was unable to destroy the (relatively) laicized structure, nor was the Second Empire. Under both regimes (and later, in the 1870s), there were, however, recurrent conflicts between "the two Frances" owing at bottom to two distinct visions of French identity. For one group, Catholicism, the "religion of the vast majority of the French," according to the Concordat, was supposed to define "the soul" of France, the heart of its national identity. For the other, the only basis on which a modern France could exist was that laid down by "the principles of 1789," to which all religions would have to adapt if they wished to survive.

Was the Republic the prize in this conflict between "clericals" and "anticlericals?" The sequence of events suggests as much. But to say this is to forget that the Republic could have made a point of reconciling the two Frances. It was in that spirit that the Revolution of February 1848 gave birth to the Second Republic: the Catholic clergy blessed the trees of liberty, and the insurgents knelt before the Holy Sacrament. A similar spirit of reconciliation marked the policies of several "republican" governments between 1893 and 1898, in the period of "the New Spirit" (L'Esprit Nouveau). At the time, some hoped, while others feared, that France would witness the emergence of a sort of two-party system, with a French "Tory Party" dedicated to the defense of certain social interests and resistant to laicization.

Yet both of these attempts ended in failure. In opposing the Ralliement (the pope's acceptance of the French republican regime in 1892) the bishop-deputy Monsignor Freppel regretted "the illusion" of believing that "the Republic in France is a mere form of government...rather than a doctrine fundamentally at odds with Christian doctrine." The phrase "Republic in France" was intended as an allusion to the other republic, the American one, which was regularly invoked by both sides, even as late as the separation of church and state in 1905. Religion had been disestablished in the United States since 1791, yet it remained the cornerstone of American democracy. Without rehearsing Tocqueville's arguments, let me mention one structural difference: the Declaration of Independence (1776) asserted that human beings "are endowed by their Creator with certain inalienable rights." The French Declaration of Rights (1789) was issued "in the presence and under the auspices of the Supreme Being," who was treated as a sort of honorary chairman with no active role. To have made the deity the author of the rights of man would have been tantamount to establishing the Catholic Church as the interpreter of those rights, whereas the multiplicity of sects in the United States prevented the appropriation of the rights of man by any one of them. As a result, however, the rights of man in France were divorced from the "rights of God" and therefore virtually in conflict with religion. The Nation, which declared itself to be the source "of all sovereignty" (Article 3 of the Declaration) thus confronted (and later opposed) religion. The American nation was shaped by the plurality of denominations and individual states. Did the Third Republic adopt the revolutionary conception of the nation? Was "republican laicity" associated with a "French exception"?

Jules Ferry did not pose the problem in these terms. He ordered an investigation to find out how other democracies achieved freedom of conscience in school. In the English-speaking countries, schools taught a "common Christianity" comprising certain rather general moral and religious principles. In parliamentary debate, Ferry cited this example and advocated "religious neutrality of the schools, as it is called in other countries." But he also felt that, unlike in

Protestant countries, where he said that teachers were independent of the clergy, teachers in Catholic countries inevitably found themselves under "clerical surveillance and authority" in religious matters. Indeed, until the law of March 28, 1882, ministers of the "recognized religions" determined the content of courses of moral and religious instruction in the public schools.

Elsewhere, schools were "de-confessionalized" and became "unsectarian," but in republican France they were laicized through the introduction of a course of moral and civic education that made no reference to religion. This distinctive French development calls for three remarks. First, Belgium, in July 1879, had replaced religious instruction with moral instruction and laicized all teachers (which France would not do until 1886). When the Catholic party returned to power in Belgium in 1884, it rescinded this law. Was this failure due to the fact that Belgium was a kingdom and not a republic, or was it because the French state was more powerful (a legacy of the ancien régime and Napoleon as much as of the Jacobins)?

Subsequently, those who rejected "a combative law" but wanted "a broad statement of principle that would evolve as the country evolved" (F. Buisson) defeated more radical laicizers, such as Paul Bert. Thus a circular of November 1882 indicated that the problem of crucifixes in the classroom should be examined on a case-by-case basis. It was essential to respect "the wishes of the people" and not risk sowing "trouble in families and schools." Strict laicizers protested: the Republic was undermining the principle of equality before the law established by the Revolution. By the turn of the twentieth century, they were no longer willing to support gradual, accommodative laicization and were prepared to insist on a state monopoly of education.

In the end, the course chosen was to go after the teaching congregations (which had prospered in the nineteenth century), as Jules Ferry had done for a time. Prime Minister Émile Combes (June 1902–January 1905) renewed this fight in a much more radical way (thirty thousand congregationists chose exile). But while the congregationist school, seen as a locus of countersocialization, was effectively challenged, freedom of instruction was never compromised. Opposing the idea of granting a monopoly to lay (or purely secular) schools, Buisson declared that "one doesn't make a republican as one makes a Catholic.... There is no liberal education unless intelligence is confronted with diverse arguments and contrary opinions."

The laicization of the school was therefore a historical construct in which several possible "republican" solutions were in contention. This was even more apparent with respect to relations between church and state. The victorious Republic kept the Concordat in place for a quarter of a century. Prime Minister Waldeck Rousseau (1900) spoke of it in positive terms: "This treaty does not allow the Church to appoint priests, exercise autonomy, or hold councils in France." A regalian republican Gallicanism emphasized control of religion over separation of church and state, and,

1905 notwithstanding, we are witnessing a resurgence of this today with respect to religions that are deemed to be potentially "dangerous" (Islam and various cults).

The law of separation that the new prime minister, Émile Combes, proposed in 1904 can be seen in this light. It increased the state's power to regulate ecclesiastical affairs and was characterized as "the Concordat without the Pope." It is significant that both republicans and Catholics have forgotten that it provoked a conflict within the republican camp. Indeed, the project was even disavowed by the National Association of Freethinkers (which rejected the "administrative arbitrariness" and "police harassment" to which its adoption would have led) and by the parliamentary committee that considered it (by a vote of 13 to 12).

With that conflict out of the way, another arose. Buisson and the radicals stuck to their "republican" position: separation meant that the state no longer recognized the Catholic Church but only citizens to whom the Republic guaranteed the right to associate in celebration of their rites. A different idea carried the day, however, one borrowed from the United States (as Jaurès observed in parliamentary debate) and from laws governing the Presbyterian Church in Scotland. Article 4, urged on the Chamber by Aristide Briand (who fathered the law), placed church property at the disposal of associations that abided by "the general rules of organization of the religion in whose name they propose to practice." In plain language (and despite exceptions envisioned by Article 8), this meant that churches were to be assigned to Catholics in communion with the bishop of the diocese and the pope even when a majority of the faithful in the parish and its priest wanted independence and preferred to promote a republican form of Catholicism (in keeping with the wishes of certain political elements). At the heart of this new conflict within the republican camp, we find a clash between the model of direct relations between the citizen and the state, ignoring all intermediate bodies, and another model, which envisioned the grant of certain rights to intermediate bodies as one possible dimension of individual freedom. The victory of the latter model over the former in the law of December 9, 1905, is one of the best-kept secrets of the French Republic!

The champions of the second model posed the issue in pragmatic rather than theoretical terms. At the time, however, many Catholics recognized the advantages it held for them. Brunetière and other academics asked the Catholic hierarchy to accept a law that, they wrote, does not prevent us "from believing what we want or practicing what we believe." The majority of bishops were not hostile to this idea (Assembly of May 1906). But the pope rejected the unilateral repudiation of the Concordat that this law entailed and therefore ruled out any accommodation (encyclical of August 1906).

This papal veto gave rise to a conflict among Catholics that mirrored the conflict among republicans, but the pope's decision also revived hostility between the two camps and required several additions to the law of 1905. In fact, we need to speak of laws of separation in the plural, because there was more than one. Given the pope's rejection of the disposition of church buildings embedded in the law of 1905, a new provision enacted on January 2, 1907, allowed the Catholic clergy to occupy churches "without any legal title." Yet another measure, the law of April 13, 1908, resolved the remaining practical difficulties created by the church's intransigence. There was an unintended consequence in these different accommodations: they gave Catholics an advantage over the other religions that did conform to the law of 1905. And the accord of 1923–24 between the French Republic and the Holy See granted the Catholic Church yet another privilege: "diocesan associations"—the ability, unique to Catholics, to establish in every diocese an official religious organization under the bishop's authority. Hence we must dispose of the fiction that "republican laicity" established equality among religions. It affirmed the principle of equality by denying recognition to any religion, yet it violated that principle in a variety of ways. In Alsace and Lorraine, neither the school law of 1882 nor the separation law of 1905 was enforced, and even today Catholicism is privileged relative to other formerly recognized religions (in ways ranging from social security for priests to religious holidays), just as other members of the latter group are privileged relative to religions that were not previously recognized.

The violations did not nullify the principle, however. For some, the Concordat was the basis on which they hoped to restore France's Catholic identity as a nation-state. This was the intention behind the Ralliement. With separation, the Republic no longer recognized any religion (Article 2) and guaranteed that all could practice freely (Article 1). It was no longer possible for France to have a Catholic political identity, and the pope placed the "national Catholicism" of the Action Française (1926–27) on the Index shortly after the agreement concerning "diocesan associations." The lay camp had won the battle of the two Frances: the Constitutions of the Fourth and Fifth Republics both state that France is a "lay" republic.

Similarly, according to the preambles of both Constitutions, "the organization of public education, free and secular at all levels, is among the duties of the state." The Debré law (1959), which required all private schools with state contracts to adopt curricula identical to those of the public schools and to "respect freedom of conscience," did not violate the principle of laicity. It did, however, introduce the notion that each school has its "own character," an interpretation of the principle that provoked heated conflict, which ended when the Debré law was extended indefinitely in 1984. Meanwhile, the 1975 Veil law on abortion (with a "conscience clause" exempting physicians who opposed abortion as a matter of principle) was seen as a symbol of the laicization of mores. In 1983, President Mitterrand included representatives of various "spiritual and philosophical sensibilities" on the Conseil National Consultatif d'Éthique.

The conflict between the two Frances was thus resolved by opting for "liberal laicity," and the tensions that remain are those that can be found in any democratic society. Yet at another level, French laicity remains a source of conflict. Since 1989, a so-called republican school of thought has been more likely to invoke the ideals of the Revolution than the accommodations of the Third Republic (witness the 2004 law banning "conspicuous religious signs" in public schools). Fears of the rise of Islam (in France and elsewhere) have converged with fears of globalization, leading to rejection of what is referred to as "Anglo-Saxon communitarianism." The risk now is that France will identify itself with "Catho-laicity" and fall back on its national "roots" (Clovis and the French Enlightenment) in nervous apprehension at the prospect of a modern multicultural France. (The Christian baptism of the "pagan" chief Clovis ca. 496 is considered the mythical foundation of [Christian] France.) The situation is ambiguous, however, because Islam itself has benefited from the liberalism of the 1905 law (through the creation of Islamic subsidized chaplaincies, for example). France today finds itself facing the same problem as many other democratic societies: how to reconcile respect for freedom of conscience with the presence of large segments of the population with very different attitudes toward secularization.

References

Baubérot, J. "Cultural Transfer and National Identity in French Laicity." (trans. Colin Anderson) *Diogenes* 55/2, no. 218 (2008): 17–26.

——. *Laïcité 1905–2005: Entre passion et raison.* Paris: Seuil, 2004.

Buisson, F. "Laïcité." In Guy Gauthier and Claude Nicolet, *La laïcité en mémoire.* Paris: Edilig, 1987.

Cabanel, P. *Entre religions et laïcité, XIXe–XXIe siècle.* Toulouse: Privat, 2007.

Kuru, A. T. *Secularism and State Policies toward Religion: The United States, France, and Turkey.* Cambridge: Cambridge University Press, 2009.

Lalouette, J. *La séparation des églises et de l'état (1789–1905).* Paris: Seuil, 2005.

Larkin, M. *Church and State after the Dreyfus Affair: The Separation Issue in France.* London: The Macmillan Press, 1974.

Mathiez, Al. "La séparation des Eglises et de l'Etat a-t-elle existé réellement sous la Révolution française?" (1928). In Jean-Marc Schiappa, ed., *1905! La loi de séparation des Eglises et de l'Etat.* Paris: Syllepse, 2005.

Mayeur, J.-M. *La séparation des églises et de l'état.* 3rd ed. Paris: Éditions Ouvrières, 2005.

Milot, M. *La laïcité.* Montreal: Novalis, 2008.

Nicolet, C. *L'idée républicaine en France (1789–1924): Essai d'histoire critique.* Paris: Gallimard, 1982.

Portier, P., ed. *La laïcité, une valeur d'aujourd'hui.* Rennes: PUR, 2001.

15

CITIZENSHIP

Cécile Laborde

Translated by Arthur Goldhammer

Citizenship—a central reference in the normative structure and political imaginary of French republicanism—was constructed in France as a concomitant of the "nation-state." It was based on the ideas of individual autonomy and the primacy of the nation-state and articulated in conjunction with the ideals of universality and equality. Paradoxically, it was in a context of profound questioning of the sociological basis of citizenship that the theme forced its way into political debate in the 1980s. Attempts to elaborate a "French republican model" have revived interest in the history of discourses and practices associated with the idea, and this has in turn influenced contemporary thinking. It is therefore essential to gain some perspective on both past and present understandings. Indeed, the embrace of the nation-state ideal of citizenship has served to obscure the fact that this legacy is today largely inoperative. More than that, some of the tensions that exist in today's understandings originate in the ambivalence of what we have inherited from the past.

The heritage invoked in contemporary discourse is that of a nation-state model of citizenship. The citizen's dual relation to state and nation reveals the complexity of the interconnection among the political, social, and cultural in the republican conception of citizenship.

The relationship between the citizen and the state is constructed in terms of emancipation and allegiance. Democratic citizenship shaped the historical process that witnessed the crumbling of traditional community identities and the emergence of the individualist, contractual identity that is fundamental to modernity. The citizenship ideal is based on a double affirmation: of both individual autonomy and political equality, symbols of the emancipation that the acquisition of citizenship represents. In becoming a citizen, the individual abandons "minority" and achieves "majority." He is recognized as an autonomous, rational individual capable of emancipating himself from social, religious, and cultural determinisms. The revolutionaries of 1789, by breaking sharply with the particularistic and communitarian structures of the ancien régime, forcefully proclaimed the advent of this new individual, who was emancipated because he was decontextualized and endowed with fundamental rights attributed "without distinction as to origin, race, or religion." The status of citizen was therefore both universalistic and egalitarian from the beginning. By repudiating the theological and hierarchical basis of monarchical sovereignty, the Revolution consecrated political equality among citizens, all of whom shared equally in democratic sovereignty. The emancipation of the citizen was thus part of the historical process that brought the people into the arena of modern politics. Abolition of privileges, emancipation of the individual, and national sovereignty: these were the fundamental ideals that animated the Declaration of the Rights of Man and of the Citizen of 1789.

Citizenship as understood in France was therefore imbued with a demanding ideal of individual and collective self-government born of confidence in the powers of human reason, which stemmed from the Enlightenment. Human dignity was honored, but not without qualification. Indeed, lack of reason or autonomy (which could be construed in intellectual, sociological, or economic terms) could justify exclusion, for these qualities were laid down as essential criteria of political capacity. After the Revolution there were more or less avowed efforts to circumscribe the subversive effects of political equality on the nascent bourgeois order (most notably through property qualifications on the right to vote, which excluded the lower classes). Although nineteenth-century republicans made the fight for universal suffrage their central battle, they never entirely overcame the conception of citizenship in terms of *capacities,* so that the "education of universal suffrage" became crucial to their project. The exclusion of women from suffrage until 1945 tells us a great deal about the impasses of French citizenship, which was radical in its early implementation of "universal" (male) suffrage but oddly slow to emancipate itself from the most deeply rooted social prejudices (those associated with gender). Did republican citizenship function as a utopian critique of society, promising ultimate emancipation to all, or was it a norm that generated exclusions and that makes sense only in relation to the boundary it established between citizens and noncitizens? In any case, it seems to have been shaped by a fundamental tension: it both expressed the properties common to human nature (reason and autonomy) and defined the criteria of excellence by which those properties were to be judged (in ways that often reflected the values of dominant groups).

While the state, in the republican conception, emancipates the individual, it also demands unstinting political allegiance in return. The individual enjoys civil and social rights in the first place as an active citizen participating democratically in the elaboration of the general will. From this comes the essentially political tenor of French citizenship and its primary incarnation in the right to vote. The formalization of the act of voting is one aspect of the representation and celebration of political equality and the general will. And since the general will is said to distill universal, public interests from the chaotic welter of private, particular ones, it radicalizes the distinction between public and private. In this way, republican citizenship dissolved economic conflict and social pluralism in egalitarian unanimity. It did so because the Republic was wary of factions, privileges, and special interests. Hence citizen participation was more readily interpreted in terms of allegiance (and especially respect for the duties of citizenship) than in terms of participation, which was suspected of sowing division in the body politic. The emphasis on the figure of the active citizen engaged in public affairs was therefore paradoxically coupled with an absence of concrete participatory institutions, of which the structural weakness of political parties was merely a symptom. Ever since the Revolution, the problem of granting adequate expression to the will of the people has vexed one regime after another, generally alternating between elitist representation in Parliament and a Jacobin utopian ideal of somehow embodying the homogeneous people in the state.

The difficulty of combining political universalism with the diversity of opinions, interests, and identities raises the more general problem of representing social citizenship in a republican context. Although republicans had to concede that the Republic as a political form—universal suffrage plus education—could not by itself resolve the basic "social question," the social content of citizenship remained thin throughout the Third Republic. The workers' movement could not make up its mind whether to defend the interests of the working class or to embrace the idea of universalistic citizenship. It was only after 1945, thanks to the historic compromise that gave birth to the welfare state, that a genuine republican welfare state was constituted. Labor—represented by a dense social network comprising trade unions, workers' parties, associations, and churches—was recognized as an essential component of citizenship. Even though the republican state claimed to forge social bonds out of the material of politics alone, "abstract" republican citizenship could not continue to mobilize citizens unless it was linked to a powerful welfare state (capable of using the universalist rhetoric of the general interest to cover its interventions in a fragmented society). Broadly speaking, republican citizenship, in staging the confrontation between the individual and the state, was construed in both political and social terms: allegiance was political, and security was economic and social.

The bond between citizen and nation was established in 1789. With the advent of the Third Republic, the equivalence between citizenship and nationality was enshrined in law. Nationality functioned as both common culture and boundary. It was the place where universality was realized in practice, as the individual was emancipated from the grip of his or her primary group. In France, national citizenship was therefore associated with a broad project of socialization into a common culture inspired by Durkheimian sociology and its civic paradigm. The democratic nation assigned itself the role of socializing its members in this common culture, which sanctified the values of liberty, equality, and fraternity. Under the Third Republic, the school became the primary locus of civic integration, conceived in terms of access to universalistic values and modernity and oriented toward repression of identities other than citizenship, including religious affiliations.

But civic integration was also integration into a particular culture, which took shape at the same time: the culture of French national identity. The national culture, which spread gradually from the center (Parisian elites) to the periphery (geographically and socially remote groups), infused membership in the "community of citizens" with concrete emotional content. The rhetoric of "La Grande Nation," which drew on the universalistic ambitions of the Revolution and belief in the superiority of French civilization, permanently blurred the distinction between civic integration (universalistic in principle) and cultural assimilation (particularistic by definition), as recurrent debates over the law of nationality attest. To be sure, republicans liked to contrast the ethnic definition of the German nation (based on *jus sanguinis,* or acquisition by filiation) with the "civic" definition of the French nation (which attached great importance to *jus soli,* or acquisition by residence). In practice, however, they rarely recognized residence as in itself a sufficient criterion for access to citizenship, even when coupled with a declared desire to become French. After passage of the 1889 law on nationality, it was indeed socialization in a common culture that guaranteed the automatic "Francization" of children born in France to foreign parents. Thanks to confidence in the universality of its values and the awesome efficiency of its assimilative institutions—schools, army, parties, unions—republican France managed to reconcile its status as a land of immigration with the preservation of a relatively homogeneous culture within its borders.

But if national citizenship ensured the cultural cohesion of the community of citizens, it also served as a remarkably effective boundary, a "social enclosure." The end of the nineteenth century witnessed a massive effort to nationalize society, and with it came the "tyranny of the national," symbolized by the bureaucratization of identity and the issuance of national identity cards. The state took steps to regulate, monitor, restrict, and expel the foreign population. The distinction between citizens and foreigners became the *summa divisio* of politics: the egalitarian inclusion of nationals was counterbalanced by the necessary exclusion of the rest. "Naturalized" foreigners enjoyed the full panoply of citizenship rights—civil, political, and social. Although the identification of citizenship with nationality seems to have been complete in metropolitan France, it was shakier in the colonies. The French colonial syndrome, which was not very different from that of other colonial empires (unless in the ambition of the *mission civilisatrice*), would ultimately be "reimported" into France itself when immigrant populations from the former colonies became permanent residents of France in the 1970s and 1980s.

It was during this period, when the legacy of nation-state citizenship was constantly invoked in public discourse, that it paradoxically proved to be inoperative, and the tensions and ambivalences that had been associated with it in the past were suddenly laid bare by contemporary crises of republican citizenship. Although the most striking symptom of the crisis in nation-state citizenship is the culturalist shift in the focus of political debate to the questions of national identity and the integration of immigrants, this shift served only to reveal a pluralistic multiplication of forms of citizenship and a wide gap between the supply of and demand for political responses. The culturalist shift has made the "immigrant" the focal point of a debate about the "interior boundaries" of citizenship. In official discourse, universalist republican integration is opposed to differentialist multiculturalism, but this has merely masked the implicit culturalization of the citizenship debate.

In the 1980s, the development of new forms of social and economic exclusion, the erosion of national sovereignty, and the electoral breakthrough of the Front National, a party that succeeded in instrumentalizing the rhetoric of cultural difference for xenophobic ends, placed the issue of immigrant integration at the center of political debate. Within a few years, a normative consensus, forged in the debates of the Commission on Nationality and crystallized around the "headscarf affair" of 1989, led to the promotion of a "French model" of "republican citizenship," advertised as an alternative to the threatening specter of "multiculturalism," which was defined as the official recognition of cultural difference. Multiculturalism, it was alleged, would undermine the foundations of republican citizenship one by one: liberty (understood as individual autonomy from the group), laicity (or secularism, based on the neutrality of the state and privatization of identities), equality (understood as uniformity of treatment), and fraternity (implying transcendence of particularism in the name of the common interest). In the words of the High Council on Integration, the French universalist model favored "a logic of equality and not a logic of minorities," in contrast to both the anti-integrationist extreme Right and the proponents of a "right to difference" on the left. Updating the Durkheimian model of national integration, republicans urged "immigrants" (a term abusively applied to the second generation) to trade their "ethnic" identity for a "civic" identity and to embrace the meritocratic and universalistic institutions of French society. Republicans hoped thereby to repeat the "success story" of an earlier wave of immigrants (one of the main indices of which is a high rate of mixed marriages in the second generation). The influence of this universalistic paradigm of citizenship—which, though not monolithic, shaped the dominant public discourse—received a striking, and in some respects, paradoxical demonstration in the justification of two apparently "differentialist" reforms of the 1990s: the PACS, or Civil Pact of Solidarity, which granted legal recognition to homosexual couples, and "parity," which increased the representation of women in democratic institutions. In both cases, the democratic advance was presented in universalistic terms: the PACS was a status of which all couples could avail themselves and not just homosexuals, and parity was simply the political translation of the "natural" division of humankind into two sexes, not a measure of "affirmative action" in favor of women. These rhetorical devices served to delegitimize in advance any recognition of cultural (or ethnic or religious) difference that might threaten French national identity more than gender or sexuality.

Universalist discourse on integration is caught in an impasse because it is part of a diffuse tendency toward "culturalization" of the political, itself partly a consequence of the belief that French national identity is in crisis. Evidence of this crisis can be seen in debates about reforming the Code of Nationality, controlling immigration, dealing with undocumented immigrants, assessing the compatibility of Islam and laicity, and coping with ubiquitous feelings of insecurity. As a result, the "immigrant" has become a true "inner frontier" in the collective unconscious. The abstract discourse on integration, mobilized to halt the rise of the Front National, cannot compensate for the failure to integrate the sons and daughters of immigrants in concrete economic and social terms. It also masks the persistence of pernicious institutional racism. This explains why part of the Franco-Maghrebin community has more or less consciously adopted a strategy of asserting its identity, in some cases explicitly repudiating the republican model. In a context of territorialization and increased ethnicization of social tensions, these processes have fostered "culture war" rhetoric and contributed to a hardening of republican national identity. The universalist discourse of integration is difficult to square with implicit community-based management of social needs such as housing and education, the persistent use of code words such as "youths" and "delinquents" to refer to ethnic categories (Arabs and blacks), and a revival of the idea that nationality should depend on "capacities" (a disguised form of which can be seen in the declaration of intentions demanded in 1993 of young people born in France to foreign parents). More generally, republican citizenship was recentered on a vision of society more communalist than universalist, and associated with particular histories, memories, traditions, and locations. We see this in the tendency to treat the national past as a "heritage," in the defense of the "French exception" against intrusive "foreign models" (which are misunderstood and misrepresented), and in resistance to the "false universalism" of globalization. In its two-front war against both globalization and multiculturalism, republican citizenship is sometimes communalist, sometimes universalist. In both cases, it tends to reduce the inherent instability and conflict of social life to the single dimension of the nation-state.

The focus on identity actually masks a pluralist fragmentation of modes of citizenship at a time when there is a deep disparity between supply and demand. One response to this disparity has been to reaffirm the traditional values of the nation-state model. Intransigence on the subject of "immigration" is clearly a symptom of the general crisis of social integration and nation-state citizenship in France. The causes of this crisis are many: the weakening of traditional institutions of national socialization (family, school, unions, parties, army, and public services); the decline of the working class and workers' movement; the development of new forms of social precariousness and disaffection owing to persistent unemployment and the crisis of the welfare state; the slow disintegration of suburban towns, the rise of antisocial behavior, and the decline of civic spirit (manifest in phenomena ranging from youth violence to elite corruption); and the growing instrumentalization of citizenship rights. Taken together, these phenomena have contributed to a general feeling that social bonds are weaker than they used to be. On top of that, there has been a deep crisis of political will, eroded by the decreasing power of the state in a context of globalized trade and transnational movements, as well as a crisis of political representation, marked by growing abstention, declining allegiance to traditional political parties, and increasing distrust of elites. If the citizen feels bereft of citizenship, it is because the social and political content of citizenship has been steadily shrinking.

In this context of profound desociologization of citizenship, the "nation-state" has responded by reaffirming the virtues of republican civility and civic spirit in relation to education (symbolized by the "sanctuarization" of the school, the crucible of equality and meritocratic values), morality (insisting on the need for internalization of common "values"), and security (repression of antisocial activity and violence). The symbolic restoration of citizenship—focusing on learned respect for communal norms and invocation of values of universalism and equality—increasingly functions in a performative rhetorical register without real purchase on social reality. It is as if the discourse emphasizing the importance of the abstract political bond were intended to compensate for the crumbling of the social bond. At the same time, the term "citizen"—traditionally associated with the relation between the individual and the nation-state in a democratic political community—has undergone an astonishing conceptual inflation. The word, more commonly used in its adjectival rather than its substantive form, has been divorced from democratic practice and applied to vast realms of social experience: thus people speak of "citizen enterprise," "citizen consumers," and "citizen encounters," as if semantic dissemination could make up for the loss of substance in nation-state citizenship.

Another form of response to the disparity between political supply and demand has been a surge of civic militancy, in some cases outside the nation-state model. In reaction to the rhetorical insistence on values without real practical effect, citizens have seized on new ways to "speak their minds." One response has been to reject the nation-state model explicitly and to seek to promote a "new citizenship" independent of national institutions and identity. Rooted in substantive practices and engagement in social and economic life, the new citizenship is expressed through local associations; egalitarian demands couched in ethnic, religious, or cultural terms; and efforts to obtain for foreigners the right to vote in local elections. Coupled with timid forays in the direction of transnational and postnational citizenship, especially in connection with the European Union, the new citizenship rejects the exclusive republican focus on the link between national belonging and citizenship. Yet it has proven difficult to give democratic and social content to the idea of citizenship without borders.

A second approach to the redefinition of citizenship is linked to new social movements, such as the vast wave of strikes that engulfed France in November and December 1995. This movement expressed resistance to the disintegration of the welfare state and called for participatory democracy in response to the perceived elitism and arrogance of the government. By giving voice to the grass roots and insisting that citizenship meant more than just the right to vote, the 1995 movement aimed to promote a more participatory idea of the republican social contract, yet without giving up any of the established rights of nation-state citizenship. We see this idea in the defense of public sector jobs as a "French exception," in the insistence on equality and solidarity as fundamental social values, in the notion that defending the public sector is a form of resistance to a more general loss of job security, and in demands for reinforcement of the protective role of the state. This politicization of the public sector has made reform of the welfare state especially difficult. In some respects *l'État providence* has become structurally dysfunctional (owing to corporatism, rigidity, and inegalitarian effects), even as many of the institutions on which national solidarity depended have been dismantled.

Beyond the new social movements, another form of civic militancy can be seen in the outrage that greeted the electoral success of the Front National in the first round of the 2002 presidential elections. The rhetoric of the FN—populist rejection of the "system," allegations that the ruling class had abandoned people at the grass roots, an overtly ethnicized interpretation of the social crisis (arguing that only "native" French deserved the benefits of the welfare state and citizenship)—painted an extreme and pathological picture of the crisis of French citizenship. Some voters responded to this message because they felt that the Left had ceased to oppose capitalism and had adopted a "managerial" response to the problems of the day. To be sure, the mobilization of voters in "defense of the Republic" against the extreme Right restored some of the luster of the basic act of citizenship: voting. Democratic ideals (however minimal) could still arouse passion. But the future of the idea of citizenship in France will depend on the country's ability to find an effective response to social anxieties and to formulate a political project capable of restoring equilibrium to the discursive economy of citizenship.

References

Balibar, E. *Droit de cité*. Paris: Presses universitaires de France, 1998.

Déloye, Y. *École et citoyenneté: L'individualisme républicain de Jules Ferry à Vichy*. Paris: Presses de la FNSP, 1995.

Feldblum, M. *Reconstructing Citizenship: The Politics of Nationality Reform and Immigration in Contemporary France*. Albany, NY: SUNY Press, 1999.

Laborde, C. *Critical Republicanism. The Hijab Controversy and Political Philosophy*. Oxford: Oxford University Press, 2008.

Noiriel, G. *La tyrannie du national: Le droit d'asile en Europe (1793–1993)*. Paris: Calmann-Lévy, 1991.

Rosanvallon, P. *Le sacre du citoyen. Histoire du suffrage universel en France*. Paris: Gallimard, 1992.

Rudder, V. de, C. Poiret, and F. Vourch. *L'inégalité raciste: L'universalité républicaine à l'épreuve*. Paris: Presses Universitaires de France, 2000.

Schnapper, D. *La communauté des citoyens. Sur l'idée moderne de nation*. Paris: Gallimard, 1994.

Taguieff, P. A. *La force du préjugé: Essai sur le racisme et ses doubles*. Paris: La Découverte, 1987.

Weil, P. *How to Be French: Nationality in the Making since 1789,* trans. Catherine Porter. Durham: Duke University Press, 2008.

Wieviorka, M., ed. *Une societé fragmentée Le multiculturalisme en débat*. Paris: La Découverte 1996.

16

Universalism

Jeremy Jennings

Let us begin by recalling, as Marc Fumaroli has, an age in the eighteenth century when Europe spoke French. French was not only the language of international diplomacy but also the language of civilization, of the arts, and of the republic of letters. It was, as English now is, the universal language. To speak French was to be a party to the aspirations of humanity as a whole. Next, let us acknowledge that one of the most striking features of the Revolution of 1789 was that from the outset its participants believed that their actions were of universal significance and that what was at stake was a set of universal values. One example of this universalist mentality was the assumption that France was not born to follow the examples of others but was rather the example that should be followed. Another was the manner in which it was assumed that the truths being proclaimed in Paris were applicable to the whole of humankind. Seen from within the Revolution, the whole world was watching and listening as revolutionary events unfolded. So too, as the French nation was reborn, shorn of privilege, that nation was thought capable of infinite enlargement and of embracing the inhabitants of the entire earth. France was truly the *patrie* of humanity.

Republicanism had little difficulty continuing and developing this universalistic vision. According to Robespierre, France, through the Republic, would realize "the destiny of humanity": "Let France, formerly renowned as being among the countries of slaves, eclipse the glory of all the free peoples who have existed, become the model of nations, the dread of oppressors, the consolation of the oppressed, the adornment of the universe, and let us hope that, in sealing our work with our blood, we will see the shining dawn of universal happiness." Accordingly, the peoples of Europe (and beyond) would become full participants in humanity to the extent that they espoused the principles of France's Revolution and Republic. In the name of humanity and the universal Republic, therefore, these principles could be carried beyond France's borders, and by arms if necessary. For the French republican, love of the *patrie* and love of humanity were indistinguishable.

The belief that France and the Republic were the privileged vehicle of the future progress and emancipation of all was a commonplace among republicans in the period prior to 1870. Time and time again, the ideals of the universal Republic were invoked to challenge Europe's monarchical order and to liberate the oppressed in Poland, Ireland, and elsewhere. If this entailed a certain nostalgia for the military glories of Napoleon Bonaparte—Alphonse de Lamartine was not alone in speaking of "the tricolor flag which has traveled the world with the Republic and the Empire"—it also frequently placed the republicans among the partisans of war, at least until 1871. After the Franco-Prussian War, the same assimilation of the Republic with the universal was transformed, for many on the left of the republican movement, into pacifism, internationalism, and even defeatism. In 1914, the tide shifted again, as republicans on the left and others skeptical of war enthusiastically joined the fight. Nonpolitical philosophers, with Henri Bergson and Émile Boutroux at their head, rallied to the Republic, contrasting France's universal message of liberty and justice with German militarism and industrial power.

Republican universalism, however, was not for export only: it applied equally to the salvation of the indigenous peoples of France. Examples abound, but no one gave better expression to this sentiment than Jules Michelet. In the very first lines of his *Introduction à l'histoire universelle,* France was identified unambiguously as "the pilot of the ship of humanity," a status confirmed in exemplary fashion by the events that followed 1789. But that same messianism also informed the manner in which France had created itself as an individual personality and indivisible unity. The particularisms associated with "the old races, the pure races"—the Celts, the Basques, and the Bretons—had been overcome; the dark materiality of nature had ceded to civilization; provincialism and the local spirit had made way for the genius of Paris. "In this way," Michelet wrote, "was formed the general and universal spirit of the country....Mind triumphed over matter, the general over the particular, the idea over the real." More than this, Michelet continued, "the very idea of this country, the abstract idea which owes little to the senses, will lead her forward to the idea of the universal homeland and the city of Providence."

To equate Michelet's enthusiasm for the eradication of provincialism with the distrust of federalism evidenced by the republican tradition would be unjustifiably crude, but it is nevertheless true that, in political terms, republican universalism showed itself deeply wary of decentralization and of local particularisms. One issue of special interest here concerns language. Michelet himself acknowledged its importance when he wrote: "The history of France begins with the French language. Language is the principal sign of nationality." We do not need to revisit the controversy that surrounds the manner in which the Republic, from the Revolution of 1789 onward, responded to the existence of regional dialects and languages. Although some historians deny that the Republic treated dialects and languages with unrelenting hostility, it cannot be doubted that, for many, language reform and the imposition of French was an important means of realizing the universal aspirations of both the Revolution and the Republic. The people were to be freed from ignorance and religious superstition, and this aspect of republican universalism is still much in evidence today. It is enough to reflect on the cultural policies associated with the worldwide promotion of *francophonie* and on France's determined reluctance to ratify the European Charter for Minority Languages, to see how continued aspirations to embody universalism can operate at the expense of diversity.

Let us also recall, not just an age when Europe spoke French, but a time when Paris was the center of Enlightenment. We do not need to enter the argument of whether the *philosophes* were responsible for the French Revolution and all its ills. We need only recognize that their cosmopolitanism placed man—the abstract individual—at the center of the world and that they, like later republicans, believed in the power of man's reason to discover truths that were both invariable and of universal application. The most obvious manifestation of this belief lies in the rhetoric of the rights of man and the manner in which republicanism subsequently embraced it as a set of universal political and constitutional ideals. Freemasonry, a vital ingredient of nineteenth-century republicanism, was also steeped in the culture of Enlightenment universalism. So too was the philosophical positivism that inspired so many Third Republic political figures, as was the version of neo-Kantianism that became the Republic's quasi-official philosophy. To an extent, the preeminence of Kantianism still exists, as the work of contemporary philosopher Blandine Kriegel illustrates. For her, Kant figures as "the great philosopher of the republican idea," and the Republic alone conforms "to the demands of reason." Summarizing this aspect of the "republican horizon," Mona Ozouf writes: "In opposition to the propensity to think of humanity as being heterogeneous and divided into races, classes and even sexes, the republican idea recalls the possibility of rational communication between men and the unity of humanity."

It is easy to demonstrate the manner in which such philosophical universalism generates both adherence and enthusiasm among republicans today. Faced with what is seen as the upsurge of Islamic fundamentalism or "tribalism," universalism is deployed as one of the bastions in the defense of individual reason and human rights. Confronting what is characterized as the crass and vulgar materialism of American globalization, universalism stands for the elevated culture of Western civilization and humanism. Prominent, ideologically distinct, writers such as Alain Finkielkraut, Régis Debray, and Pierre Bourdieu take one or both of these positions.

Most important, this same philosophical universalism has had an impact on republican conceptions of citizenship. Clearly, this model of citizenship is complex and has been subject to change. Sophie Duchesne's empirical investigation, *Citoyenneté à la française,* describes two models that serve to characterize distinct self-representations of French citizenship, those of the *citoyen par héritage* and the *citoyen par scruples.* It is the latter that draws most heavily on republican universalism. Repudiating the equation of citizen with nationality, the citizen here minimizes the importance of a sense of group belonging, preferring rather to emphasize the universalistic dimensions of relations among all human beings. The citizen's principal obligation, therefore, is not toward a particular (French) state but rather takes the form of an acknowledgment among individuals of respect for others. Intolerance and racism are seen as the height of *incivisme.* This model likewise draws on the humanitarian ideals born in the Republic's revolutionary past but does so by referring to a conception of the French nation as the homeland of liberty. Fred Constant has detailed this conception of citizenship in *La citoyenneté.* According to him it has four components: citizenship as an expression of national identity, citizenship as a set of rights and obligations, citizenship as active participation in the life of the polity, and citizenship as a set of moral qualities. On this account, universalism is expressed through loyalty to a set of national institutions and a national history taken to embody universal values and through participation in the public political sphere as a means of transcending individual interests. Of possible greater significance is Constant's contention that, as a whole, this characterization of citizenship leaves us with a vision of the citizen as a "decontextualized figure."

This is precisely the description of citizenship set out by Dominique Schnapper, now a member of the Conseil Constitutionnel and one of the most thoughtful (and persuasive) advocates of a modified version of republican universalism. In her widely read *La communauté des citoyens,* she talks of "the citizen as an abstract individual, without particularistic identifications or qualifications, over and above any concrete characteristics." The important distinction she makes is between "the abstract citizen and concrete individuals," with citizenship taking precedence over ethnic and religious particularisms or clan and family solidarities. Elsewhere, she speaks of the distinction "between the specificities of the private man and the universalism of the citizen."

This republican definition of citizenship has several important universalistic dimensions. Crucially, as Marc Sadoun has noted, "the Republic does not conceive of citizenship without the education of the citizen: the individual is not born but becomes a citizen." It is, in short, the school that figures as the principal site or location of individual emancipation. It is here, leaving behind the dogmas and traditionalisms of family, regional, and religious life, that the individual enters the world of progress, justice, tolerance, and liberty. Quotations to illustrate this viewpoint can easily be found in such authoritative sources as the writings of Schnapper and Claude Nicolet, but for evidence of its enthusiastic support we can do no better than cite Régis Debray. "The republican State," Debray writes, "has as its goal in society that of acting in the name of the universal. For this reason it is in league with the School, the institution that itself has the goal of allowing all the young, whatever their social origin, access to the universality of Knowledge." "Republican idealism," he continues, "demands an intransigent rationalism."

Here, in the form of an extraordinary pedagogical optimism, we again see the impact of Enlightenment patterns of thought on republican universalism. Indifference to the past, its customs, and its languages, as well as to (most obviously) the dark forces of religious ignorance, joined with a faith in the almost limitless potential of education to create new enlightened and reasonable human beings. Examples abound of such pedagogical optimism among the first republicans, even if the desire to induct the people into "the empire of reason," as Robespierre termed it, was to take the curious form of the cult of the Supreme Being. Continued hostility to the earthly powers of the church pushed republicans toward the endorsement of a secular ethic and, after 1870, toward the development of a secular educational system. The former again rested on a set of universalist assumptions, namely, that stable and permanent moral beliefs could be established and that these beliefs could be discovered through the processes of reason and science. The development of the latter was more complex, and possibly less Jacobin, than is often imagined. It was only in 1923 that reference to teaching "duties toward God" was dropped from the program of educational instruction and that state education became officially nonreligious, even though after 1882 the emphasis had shifted from "moral and religious instruction" to "moral and civic instruction." In fact, the doctrine of laicity—understood as the idea that the school, in the name of individual autonomy, equal respect, and civic solidarity, should remain neutral toward such private practices as religious observance, and that these practices should be confined to the private sphere— has become a core element of republican ideology. The problem is that to many people such a rationalist universalism rooted in the philosophy of the Enlightenment now looks more and more like a form of European ethnocentrism, and thus like a form of domination rather than an invitation to liberation. This has especially been true of the extended controversy surrounding the wearing of the Muslim veil or *hijâb* in French state schools. It is in this context that there has been discussion of developing a more open and less militant form of laicity.

Of late, however, there has been a growing awareness among republicans that the very principle of laicity has been challenged, especially by those whom republicanism sees as the advocates of cultural or religious identity. In brief, this challenge is associated with what hard-line republicans term the logic of minorities and the multiculturalist illusion. Again, this negative response to what some would see as the legitimate claims of certain disadvantaged sections of society is informed by aspects of republican universalism, and specifically the idea that a synthesis between the liberty of the individual and the general interest is attained through, and only through, the development of the autonomous citizen. In this regard, the Republic acts as if groups and collective identities simply do not exist. Such an approach is grounded not in any sociological reality but rather in the belief that it is through the recognition of the inalienable rights of individual citizens and their identification with the general interest that the potential contradiction between the particular and the universal can be overcome. This is a doctrine littered with problems and one that contrasts sharply with what might be termed the sociological empiricism of Anglo-American constitutionalism and philosophy. During the Revolution of 1789 republicans used this doctrine to terrible effect. As Lucien Jaume has shown in his meticulous dissection of Jacobin ideology, it was assumed that the common good and general interest could be comprehended in a simple, clear, and objective fashion, and therefore that it was necessary that "the situation, opinion, interest and even the behaviour of the individual... should disappear behind the general will." Accordingly, a doctrine—that of the rights of man—designed to defend the individual from arbitrary rule became a vehicle for promoting the claims of the whole (the universal) against the interests of its parts (the particular).

As the obsession with national unity abated among republicans, this powerful tension within their movement became less evident, but the unease about groups—be they ethnic, religious, or cultural—has remained. It can be seen, for example, when republican critics such as Christien Jelen equate calls for recognition of cultural difference with a France reduced to the pandemonium of the tower of Babel, or when Joseph Macé-Scaron argues that "the communitarian temptation" leads to "the valorization of minority culture at the expense of our common humanity." More seriously, it can still lead—as Régis Debray again illustrates—to an animosity toward the claims of civil society. In this context, Debray goes so far as to contrast the republic with democracy, arguing: "The universal idea governs the republic. The local idea governs democracy."

Recently, the question of how to integrate immigrants into French society has given rise to extensive debate about the manner in which republican universalism should respond, if at all, to claims of group identity. The successive reports of the Haut Conseil à l'Intégration, for example, have valiantly sought to apply the principles of republican universalism to the problems posed by the immigration of large numbers of Muslims. For example, its report of 1995, entitled *Liens culturels et intégration,* states: "The French model of integration rests on a lack of differentiation among persons. In this sense it is universalist. Each person is deemed to be of value independently of the community to which he belongs."

The 1997 report similarly states: "France has always refused to recognize collective rights specific to groups and minorities. It is to each man and to each woman that she accords the plenitude of their rights, thereby allowing him or her individually to take a place in French society." Underpinning this reasoning is not merely a distaste for what is seen as the logic of exclusion and the ghetto (a strategy associated with the United Kingdom and the United States of America) but the firm conviction that the French model embodies the universal principles of liberty and equality. For example, it guarantees respect for religious liberty as well as equality between the sexes. On these issues there can be no compromise. Moreover, it is this stance that has led some republicans to suspect that there is a fundamental incompatibility between the values and social practices of Islam and those of the Republic.

On the other hand, critics, and even some sympathizers, of this universalistic model argue that it ignores social and economic realities, especially with regard to those who suffer from disadvantage and discrimination. Dominique Schnapper, for example, recognizing that "the universalist idea proclaimed by the supporters of the French model of integration" is best seen as an ideal rather than a reality, comments that "transcendence through citizenship appears to a humiliated people as something purely formal that has the function of consecrating the domination of the other under the guise of universality." Bertrand Guillaume makes the point more brutally. "One can easily see," he remarks, "that the position which makes a principle out of ignoring the existence of groups...can easily be transformed into an ideology of the general interest whose principal function is to hide the fact that the republican State serves the interests of dominant groups." If these issues arise from the manner in which the Republic has sought to integrate immigrants, we should next briefly consider the manner in which republican universalism has responded to the existence of the foreigner. Indeed, there is no more fascinating tale, as Sophie Wahnich has shown, than the way in which the Revolution's universalistic aspirations were replaced by the denunciation of the foreigner and by what Mona Ozouf has termed "xenophobic fraternity." If, from the outset, all those who accepted the principles of the universal republic were welcome as citizens, the rhetoric of fraternity quickly changed into that of enmity as these very same foreigners were recast as traitors and false friends. Of these, the English received pride of place as the enemies of humanity (a tradition later continued by Michelet among many others). After the fall of Robespierre in 1794, the language of universal fraternity was largely abandoned, only for fraternity to reappear much later in the modest guise of a faith in communal solidarity. However, in the wake of France's defeat in 1870–71 and the loss of Alsace and Lorraine, the imposing figure of Ernest Renan again opened the definition of the nation to include all those who possessed the "the will to live together." Since the 1870s, republicans of every persuasion have repeated Renan's definition, enshrining in republican discourse the principle that membership of the French body politic can rest solely on residence (*jus soli*) rather than on ethnic origin or religious affiliation. It thus serves to give further embodiment to the core republican doctrine of treating the human subject as universal. All, in short, are welcome into the nation as part of a common political project.

If anything, recent projects to reform French nationality law have reaffirmed this elective conception of nationality, placing renewed emphasis on the need to actively affirm membership on reaching the age of majority. One effect of this approach has been to exclude the children of immigrants from automatic citizenship. Here perhaps we should remind ourselves that, prior to independence, the indigenous population of Algeria could obtain French citizenship only if they renounced their Islamic status. Membership in the universal community of citizens, in other words, came at a price.

It is, of course, the capacity of republican universalism to exclude that has recently been the focus of its critics' attention. According to Farhad Khosrokhavar, for example, "henceforth abstract universalism serves less to integrate than to dehumanize the excluded and the outcasts," while republicanism itself is becoming "more and more intransigent and monolithic." Alain Touraine has extended this argument, contending that "it has been in the name of the republican spirit and citizenship that women were excluded from the vote for more than a century, that minorities have not been recognised, and that xenophobia and racism have developed." Not to recognize these realities, he adds, is to imagine that "France alone has the capacity to defend universal rights against particular interests and to identify the history of France with the aseptic triumph of a French Revolution without end, transforming the Terror into political liberation, the exploitation of the workers into a belief in education, and the rejection of minorities into the right to integration into the country of the rights of man." Such outright rejection of the claims of republican universalism remains a minority position, but many other theorists of republicanism share the view that the model and philosophy of republican universalism needs serious reinvigoration and rethinking. As we move into the era of globalization, multiculturalism, and the postnational state, can this be done? As Dominique Schnapper herself has remarked, many of those who think so pine for a France that can never reappear. If this is true, the challenge will be to divest republicanism of the false and unnecessary aspects of its universalism and to construct, as Joël Roman has argued, a Republic resting on a relative pluralism and a plural universalism. To that end, as Schnapper succinctly expresses it, the task will be to create "political institutions that will allow the reconciliation and the conjugation of the absolute of citizenship—the Republic—with the legitimate expression of particularistic allegiances in conformity with democratic values." This is no small challenge, but it is one on which the future of the French Republic as a viable political form might rest.

References

Birnbaum, Pierre. *The Idea of France*. New York: Hill and Wang, 2001.

Bouretz, Pierre. *La République et l'universel*. Paris: Gallimard, 2000.

Constant, Fred. *La citoyenneté*. Paris: Montchrestien, 1998.

Debray, Régis. *Que vive la République*. Paris: Odile Jacob, 1989.

Duchesne, Sophie. *Citoyenneté à la française*. Paris: Presses de Sciences Po, 1997.

Fumaroli, Marc. *Quand l'Europe parlait français*. Paris: Fallois, 2001.

Guillarme, Bertrand. "L'individu et le groupe." *Pouvoirs* 84 (1998): 31–44.

Haut Conseil à l'Intégration. *Liens culturels et intégration*. Paris: La Documentation Française, 1995.

Jaume, Lucien. *Le discours jacobin et la démocratie*. Paris: Fayard, 1989.

Jelen, Christien. *Les casseurs de la République*. Paris: Plon, 1997.

Kaltenbach, Jeanne-Hélène, and Michèle Tribalet. *La République et l'Islam*. Paris: Gallimard, 2002.

Laborde, Cécile. *Critical Republicanism: The Hijab Controversy and Political Philosophy*. Oxford: Oxford University Press, 2008.

Macé-Scaron, Joseph. *La tentation communitaire*. Paris: Plon, 2001.

Michelet, Jules. *Le Moyen Age*. Paris: Robert Laffont, 1981.

Ozouf, Mona. "L'idée républicaine et l'interprétation du passé national." *Annales* 53 (1998): 1075–87.

Roman, Joël. *La démocratie des individus*. Paris: Calmann-Lévy, 1998.

Schnapper, Dominique. *La communauté des citoyens*. Paris: Gallimard, 1994.

Weil, Patrick. *How to Be French: Nationality in the Making since 1789*. Translated by Catherine Porter. Durham, NC: Duke University Press, 2008.

——. *La République et sa diversité: Immigration, integration, discriminations*. Paris: Seuil, 2005.

Wahnich, Sophie. *L'impossible citoyen*. Paris: Albin Michel, 1997.

17

The Republic and Justice

Paul Jankowski

Of all the ideals that five French Republics have invoked since 1793, none has caused them more pain than justice. Each promised to celebrate it; each was accused of subverting it. How could they place justice at the service of the people while emancipating it from their government? The problem is still with us. Arbitrariness, the republicans held, had been the besetting sin of monarchical justice. When justice was secret, justice was arbitrary; and it was secret when a regime subtracted it from the light of day and the sovereign gaze of the people.

Such precepts antedated 1789 and the cause of revolution itself. During the Calas affair in 1762, when a Protestant father wrongly suspected of murdering his son went to the wheel, Voltaire, no republican, had declared: Almost everything "appears left to the arbitrary sentiment of the judges." Mirabeau, no republican either, saw in the *lettres de cachet* that had sent him to the Château de Vincennes the surest sign of arbitrary power. His sympathizers included the magistrates of the Parlements, among the first institutions of the Old Regime to go in 1789. Long before, medieval monarchs had periodically tried to rein in the excesses of baronial or seigniorial justice, and accusations of lawlessness usually attended collisions between royal and ecclesiastical jurisdictions. The crusade against arbitrariness had served many political causes before the republicans made it their own. Once they did, they never let go of it, but nor did their critics. For two centuries it became the driving force behind the republicans' reforms and their recriminations, the leitmotif of their claim to speak for the nation. Arbitrary justice, employed to serve the regime rather than the people, came to epitomize much of what they despised in regimes that kept them out of power. Victor Hugo saw the Second Empire itself as a crime, and its ruler as a criminal. "Anarchy," he wrote two years before Louis-Napoleon's coup, "is arbitrariness in the street, and arbitrariness is anarchy in power." Just as surely, republicans in power harvested repeated accusations of dictatorial or monarchical behavior, precisely because they abused or manipulated the judicial system they had inherited. A fragile hold on power might set off the polemicists: in 1848 the Second Republic began a new purge of the magistrates and in 1880 the Third Republic followed suit, inspiring inescapable parallels with the excesses of the First. But so might an inveterate penchant for assuming the worst of the judicial system. Dreyfusards and anti-Dreyfusards alike indulged it to the full during the affair that was only the most resounding in a cascade of such scandals. The Fourth Republic began amid accusations of vengeful justice in the purge of wartime collaborators and ended amid selective outrage at inhuman justice in military courts designed to suppress the Algerian rebellion. And during the Fifth, when *Le Monde* termed Mitterrand's short-lived antiterrorist investigators the "Musketeers of the Élysée," and *Le Quotidien de Paris* compared his wiretaps for presidential security to the ways of Charles X, the two dailies honored a tradition. Lawlessness, like secrecy, was monarchical: an act became legal "because I wish it so," Louis XVI had declared in 1787. Even when the Republic no longer divided the nation, the accusation of arbitrary justice could easily recall the days when it did.

From the beginning, republican jurists found it easier to diagnose than to cure the ills they encountered in the administration of justice. At one time or another they prescribed legislative supremacy, transparency, uniformity, trial by jury, the abolition of political crime, judicial independence, and equity; and at one time or another they reconsidered each. At the heart of the problem lay a philosophical and constitutional quandary: What was the proper place of the justice system in the disposition of powers in the Republic?

Was the justice system the servant of the legislative branch? The Revolution had been supposed to mark the triumph of positive law. The sovereign made the law; the judges applied it. Rousseau had said no less in *The Social Contract* and *The Discourse on the Origins of Inequality:* the law was the expression of the general will, and the magistrates served at the pleasure of the citizens. A circular of 1791 insisted that the role of judges was merely passive, and soon Robespierre would propose abolishing the term "jurisprudence." The framers of the Third Republic's constitutional laws saw in the subjugation of the judicial to the legislative branch a condition of their own lease on life as well as of popular sovereignty. Little room seemed left for judicial interpretation, for the intelligent translation of the laws that the people or its representatives enacted. "Deliver us from the magistrates!" a deputy exclaimed in the Chamber in 1883. In practice, republican regimes quietly but repeatedly restored judicial prerogatives. They had to—they needed the judges, not only to protect their own hold on power, but to keep order in lawless times. Elective judgeships disappeared; some judges recovered lifetime tenure; prosecutors found their powers reestablished. Late in the nineteenth century, even as the Third Republic consecrated the supremacy of the legislative branch, republican jurists and sociologists—Durkheim, Duguit,

Gény—discerned in judicial interpretation the legitimate application of positive law to social reality. Gény deplored the "fetishism of the written and statutory law." The popular legalism of 1789 never held uncontested sway. It found the soil of the Fifth, and most presidential, Republic the most hostile of all.

Should the judicial system then move more properly within the executive orbit—closer to the cabinet or the presidency, depending on the Republic? At first the Third Republic, like the First and the Second, affected not to observe any distinction between executive and legislative powers. The cabinet emanated from the Chamber and in any case required just as urgently, in the words of Waldeck-Rousseau, "loyal representatives and servants of the established order." The President of the Fifth Republic put it more bluntly, when he declared in 1964 that all authority, even judicial authority, came from the head of state. But any time the executive, often in the person of the minister of justice, took too eager an interest in the agents of the law it provoked storms of protest in the representative assemblies and the political class at large. Most of the political scandals of the Third Republic, and many of the Fourth and Fifth, followed scripts of this sort. Rightly or wrongly, enemies of the regime or the ministry discerned criminal complicities in high places followed by a punctual subversion of the judicial or police systems to cover them up. During the Dreyfus affair each side accused the other of suborning a different justice system, the military or the civilian, and during the trials of collaborators in the late 1940s the extremes accused each other of suborning the same one—namely, that of the courts set up at the Liberation in highly unnatural circumstances. They were protecting their friends, the critics and scandalmongers charged. Or they were making good on ill-gotten gains: during many of the serial corruption scandals that shook the Third and Fourth Republics, ministers or officials supposed to have dabbled in illicit traffics of one kind or another were supposed as well to have silenced the police and the magistrates. Or they were ridding themselves of enemies or unwanted friends, of a Ben Barka under de Gaulle or a Jean de Broglie under Giscard, and using the police to do so. Or they were striking out at hostile intruders: Mitterrand employed a personal *gendarmerie* to spy on intrusive journalists. Imaginary or not, such scandals dramatized the pitfalls of tying justice too closely to the executive branch: law and order became surrogate targets for anyone discontented by the powers in place.

Often, the urge to detach justice from power reflected an inveterate republican preoccupation with political crime. If justice served the regime—its legislative or its executive arm—then it might turn instruments of repression against the opposition. The likelihood grew when regimes succeeded one another at a dizzying pace, as they did between 1789 and the 1870s, and again between 1940 and 1946. In the summer of 1789, when émigrés began leaving Paris, the city set up a *comité de recherches,* a surveillance body whose intrusive attentions led it to open the mail of the newly designated miscreants, the enemies of the nation at home or abroad. At once, liberal revolutionaries began to fret, as they did even more when a new crime of *lèse-nation* and with it a new court came into being. Thereafter, whether sending a king to the scaffold or a magistrate into retirement, each successive regime endured the reproach of arbitrariness: to perpetuate its hold it had enslaved or manipulated the country's judicial system—the surest manifestation of despotism and usurpation. Which was the outrage, and which the pretext? The more enemies a regime bred, the more blindly it might strike out, adding grist to the opponents' mill and savagery to its repression.

For much of the nineteenth century liberal republicans wrestled with the problem. They sought to place political crime in a class apart from common crime, by surrounding it with protections that bordered on clemency. The Old Regime had done the opposite, by placing lèse-majesté atop the pinnacle of common crimes and punishing it more savagely than any other.

True to liberal principles, the Second Republic abolished the death penalty for all political crimes, including assassination, and the Third restored the protection of a trial by jury for political offenders, one the Second Empire had removed along with several others. But once again the powers shrank from the practical implications of such enthusiasms. The Third Republic, *pace* the Second, could not allow a political motive to exonerate a murderous act and sent Santo Caserio in 1894, like Paul Gorguloff in 1932, to the guillotine for taking a President's life. It had already exiled the royal princes and would soon introduce special *lois scélérates* to repress anarchists. In the face of seditious threats, the Third, Fourth, and Fifth Republics each resorted to unusual courts, the kind that tried General Boulanger and his associates in 1889, selected collaborators in 1946, and de Gaulle's would-be assassins in 1963. Extraordinary crimes called for extraordinary tribunals, the regimes maintained, but the proceedings uncomfortably recalled the royal commissions that the Old Regime had set up to bypass the established courts and eliminate political or religious undesirables. Global and home-grown terrorism would raise the problem of special laws and special measures all over again.

Even transparency, another ideal of 1789, seemed impossible to assure, and a poor guarantor of virtuous outcomes in the courts. The halo surrounding the notion had grown even brighter with time, and the courtroom became its proving ground. Secrecy, transparency's dark counterpart, was tolerable in matters of defense and security, but not in matters of guilt or innocence. In 1957 a Communist deputy declared simply that in judicial proceedings "le secret est inquiétant pour le citoyen" (secrecy is worrisome to the citizen): the *cahiers de doléances* and the members of the Third Estate had said no less. But successive Republics came to grant that prosecution and defense alike depended upon secrecy in the pretrial investigation, the rights of the defendant upon the confidentiality of the lawyer-client relationship, and publicity in the courtroom upon media that now and again insisted on withholding the identity of their sources. Where now was the panacea of transparency? Another principle of republican justice required another compromise.

The most Anglo-Saxon of solutions to the problem of the place of justice—total independence, assured by the separation of powers—proved to be the most difficult of all. The magistrates themselves often seemed to demand it, whenever the powers in place outraged their sense of propriety. In 1880, when the government issued decrees dissolving Catholic congregations and expelling some of their members, the Ministry of Justice requested the enthusiastic participation of the prosecutors. Many resigned instead, forced, as one of them wrote, to choose between "justice and arbitrariness." During the Fifth Republic the Syndicat de la Magistrature that sprang forth in the aftermath of 1968 made the independence of the judiciary its raison d'être and seemed by the 1980s and 1990s at moments to have succeeded. Magistrates boldly inquired into the occult ways of electoral finance and launched serial scandals in their wake—"les affaires"—that deeply embarrassed Presidents Mitterrand and Chirac and sent some of their closest collaborators into political oblivion or worse. "The year of the judges," a journalist called 1995, as some of them hailed the advent of the rule of law for all. Meanwhile the Conseil Constitutionnel, founded in 1958 to rule on the constitutionality of laws that the Assembly enacted, slowly expanded its jurisdiction and its accessibility. Unlike the U.S. Supreme Court, it crowned no judicial hierarchy and enjoyed no status as an ultimate court of appeal. Yet the power to declare a law or an election invalid suggested a measure of independence that other tribunals might now invoke or even emulate.

But what of Rousseau, what of the sovereignty of the people? Old fears still surfaced, and old resentments still rankled, expressed in cautionary predictions of an incipient "République des juges." Presidents and their governments had ways of arresting the unwanted, and neither Chirac nor Mitterrand—himself a lawyer, and a former minister of justice—held back when the reach of the agents of justice exceeded, in their eyes, their grasp. The police answered to the Ministry of the Interior, the prosecutors to the Ministry of Justice, and no case could go forward without either. A majority in Parliament might refuse to pass laws ceding too much independence to the magistrates as a corporate body. In 1999 only a small minority, perhaps ten out of six hundred magistrates, was actively pursuing politically poisoned dossiers. In the end the Constitution of the Fifth Republic still held sway, and it had emphatically declined to speak of a judicial "power," only a judicial "authority," whose ultimate guarantor was none other than the President of the Republic. The obligation to protect carried the opportunity to intrude. "Was Montesquieu French?" Valérie Turcey, an investigating magistrate, asked in 1997. "One might doubt it, considering the meager success his theory of the separation of the powers has enjoyed in France."

To scan the media in 2008, the uneasy marriage between the Republic and justice, mixing devotion with distrust, has lost none of its power to provoke the parties, even if passions are more contained and ideologies less consuming than in the Third and Fourth Republics. Magistrates still resent the omnipotence of the legislature, in an age when no expectation, however petty, is too mundane to demand its own law. "Even today, we live largely on our inheritance from Rousseau," the jurist Guy de Carcassonne declared, "and aside from the Conseil Constitutionnel, there is no limit to the powers of the majority."

Judges and ministers still feared each other. Every day Renaud Van Ruymbeke, the investigating magistrate in the Clearstream affair, which sent a former prime minister, Dominique de Villepin, before a correctional tribunal, feared the breath of political vengeance. In the eyes of skeptics, members of the Conseil Constitutionnel, appointed by the President and the heads of the National Assembly and the Senate, appeared infinitely docile to their benefactors. Transparency seemed more elusive than ever, as secret databases, invited by science and allowed by technology, proliferated in the hands of the police: 45 databases in 2008 against 34 two years earlier, containing the profiles of a million citizens. Accusations of the resurrection of political crime flew freely. During 2008 President Sarkozy brought six lawsuits against organizations or individuals who had violated his privacy or his dignity in some way, and at once provoked accusations that he had reestablished the crime of lèse-majesté. Defenders of civil liberties discerned such regressions away from the Élysée Palace as well. The police arrested nine individuals suspected on shaky grounds of forming a terrorist group and disrupting the high-speed rail network. *Le Point* published the *carnets noirs,* the notebooks that Yves Bertrand, head of the Renseignements Généraux, had kept for ten years on the private lives of politicians high and low. For anyone old enough to remember, they recalled the infamous "notes Jean" of the interwar years that assured the embarrassment of public figures then and the delight of historians since. And was France not the only country in the European Union to operate—and acknowledge a—political police of this sort?

Yet, taken together, such episodes tell a tale of progress. Apostles of *l'état de droit* can recall the Conseil Constitutionnel bearding the government's wrath on occasion and prevailing. Sarkozy, far from indulging his resentments in the invention of a secret police force like Mitterrand's, has pursued his detractors in the public arena of the courts—and lost, at least on one occasion. Nowhere is the progress of rights in France more apparent than in the single most daunting challenge faced by the justice system in the past decade, the threat of terrorism. If the police arrested suspected terrorists in the TGV affair, intellectuals mobilized at once on their behalf. It had taken six years for their forebears do so against the use of torture by the military tribunals during the Algerian War.

Eight times between 1997 and 2007, the French government increased its legal arsenal of antiterrorist weapons, determined on each occasion to prosecute with the utmost vigor a "war" against "global jihadism," as one minister of the interior called it. Not for the first time in its long history, the French state has taken up arms against a deracinated enemy, one who frequents the national soil but is no longer of it. And not for the first time, resistance against the new measures, mounted in defense of civil liberties, has forced the state onto the defensive. "The greatest victory of the terrorists," one of the doubters exclaimed, "would be to have us renounce the state of laws." The rival claimants, civil liberty and public safety, are warily circling each other as they long have, in evolutions set in motion whenever political violence has struck.

How is the state to assure its own security and simultaneously respect the privacy of its citizens? The increase in wiretaps and intercepted telecommunications messages of all kinds pits the cause of national security against two fundamental human rights, that to privacy and to freedom of expression, both assured by French law as well as the European Convention on Human Rights, which has repeatedly called for limits to state acts of this sort.

Since the mid-1980s, faced with Basque, Corsican, and radical Islamist terrorism, the French state has steadily extended its range of legal and administrative options. It began by defining the crime of terrorism and continued by expanding its powers of arrest, detention, surveillance, and prevention. More recently it increased the limit on detention without charge from four to six days for terrorism suspects, gave investigators broader access to Internet and telephone data, and empowered local authorities to set up video surveillance of public places. The number of Muslim men arrested for "association with wrongdoers involved in a terrorist enterprise" climbed annually, from 58 in 2002 to 170 in 2005. A minister of the interior invoked a "permanent adjustment of the law to the realities of the day," suggesting a permanent pas de deux between terrorist cunning and official ingenuity. In the summer of 2005, after the London bombings, counterterrorist specialists in France as well as Britain worried aloud at the apparent inadequacy of their preventive efforts. A new generation of terrorists, home-grown and decentered, appeared to challenge their most sophisticated electronic surveillance, credited until then with having kept the public safe, at least for a while. More legislative measures, more police powers, followed before the end of the year, true to the promise of the minister of the interior.

Would they work? was one question. Are they compatible with our liberties? was another. That summer, the summer of the London bombings, an article in *Commentaire* warned of a spiraling dialectic between the bourgeois and the barbarous. "If modernity has consisted of an immense enterprise to make the barbarian bourgeois," its author wrote, "it can also produce the inverse movement, the barbarization of the bourgeois" by the reaction to terrorism. That summer, as well, journalists raised the alarm, accepting the urgency of offensives against global terrorism, on all fronts—police, diplomacy, ideology—but insisting on the primacy of legality. "Nothing could be worse," one of them wrote, "in the battle against terrorism, than to renounce our values. That is, to restrict liberties, renounce habeas corpus, practice torture or internment without trial." In the French parliament, especially in the Senate, doubts sounded. "I am truly uncertain," Robert Badinter, a former minister of justice said, "when I contemplate the extraordinary cadence of legislative modifications in this domain."

After the wiretaps of the 1980s and 1990s, video surveillance, "Internet espionage," border controls, and other governmental measures have alarmed rather than reassured a political class already deeply troubled by its public standing. Not even the threat of transnational terrorism in the twenty-first century has interrupted the national will to redress the imbalance between *raison d'état* and civil liberties—an outcome that no contemporary of earlier national emergencies might have predicted.

Such doubts may express only skepticism about the gravity of the threat, or, more likely, a demand that the defense against terrorism respect the legal protections so laboriously built into French legal codes over a century and more of political and juridical struggles. But the measures in question, such as the wiretaps, are, by the admission of a former director of security services, child's play beside those of the Algerian War and its domestic sequels during the early Fifth Republic, little more than forty years ago. Then, against the terrorists of the Algerian National Liberation Front during the war, or of the French Organisation de l'Armée Secrète after it, any methods were good. Then the indignation was muted, almost inaudible. By contrast, our new millennium opened with a clamorous insistence that no official consideration could arbitrarily endanger the life or liberty of any citizen; that no one, not even a prime minister, could escape answering for the kind of negligence that had allowed the release of poisoned blood stocks to hospitals and transfusion centers; and that no one, not even a President of the Republic, could violate the privacy of citizens, notably journalists, in order to protect his own.

For centuries the French state had deployed repressive measures in the face of threats real or imagined, and for centuries even its excesses, contested in peace, had met with indulgence in war. But now, uniquely, the censors raise their voices in a moment of danger. The courts, the press, and occasional victims of cavalier treatment at the hands of the state seem newly audacious, newly stirred to pursue abuses of power of all kinds and pry open new chinks in the armor of *raison d'état*. Ironically enough, Draconian security measures in the United States and Britain—*les Anglo-Saxons*—provoked only selective indignation, while the specter of terrorist outrages in France has only redoubled the defense of rights and liberties against arbitrariness and unchecked caprice at the summit of the state, as though Montesquieu's alarms had sounded once again. "Under pretext of the vengeance of the Republic," he warned, "we would set up the tyranny of the avengers."

References

Baruch, Marc Olivier, and Vincent Duclert, eds. *Justice, politique et République.* Paris: Editions Complexe IHTP/CNRS, 2002.

Charvin, R. *Justice et politique: Évolution de leurs rapports.* Paris: Librairie générale de droit et de jurisprudence, 1968.

Georgel, Jacques, and Anne-Marie Thorel. *Le Brulot judiciaire: La justice sous la Ve République.* Rennes: Editions Apogée, 1997.

Royer, Jean-Paul. *Histoire de la justice en France.* Paris: Presses universitaires de France, 2001 [1995].

Royer, Jean-Paul, and Bernard Durand, eds. *Secret et justice: Le secret entre éthique et technique? Colloque international décembre 1998.* Lille: Centre d'histoire judiciaire, 2000.

Turcey, Valéry. *Le prince et ses juges: Vers un nouveau pouvoir judiciaire.* Paris: Plon, 1997.

18

THE STATE

Herrick Chapman

In 1970, two years after the upheavals of May 1968, President Georges Pompidou reminded an audience of public servants at the Conseil d'État: "For more than a thousand years...there has been a France only because there was a state...to keep it together, to organize it, to make it grow, to defend it not only against external threats but also against collective egotism, the rivalry of groups." A conventional French nostrum, perhaps, but such words carried weight in the halls of the Conseil both as history and as myth: history, insofar as the monarchs of France did indeed build a country outward from Paris to something close to its modern frontiers (in contrast to Germany, where, despite centuries of cultural integration, territorial unity under a single state came only in 1870); and myth, insofar as state authority in France depended on a widespread belief in the *idea* of the state as guarantor of order, justice, unity, and the common good. This French idea was a millennium in the making, and nowhere else in early modern Europe did the state—meaning here both a political form of governance and an administrative structure of agencies, laws, and procedures—play so large a role in constructing a national economy, culture, and language.

The rhetorical power of Pompidou's words also owed a great deal to a particularly *republican* conception of the state, the state as a rational actor giving direction to a conflict-ridden society in accord with the principles of liberty, equality, and fraternity. This conception harks back to the French Revolution, when revolutionaries from across a wide spectrum of opinion embraced the state as the chief instrument for forging "a one and indivisible Republic." Alongside this rationalist view, however, the Revolution also produced another republican idea of the state, a more democratic idea that elevated citizens' voice and political representation as defining features of the Republic. This tension—between a rationalist (often elite) view of the state's function, so evident in Pompidou's address, and a democratic (sometimes populist) view of how the state should be run and society governed—has remained unresolved since the French Revolution. Indeed, as the state expanded in its functions and authority, especially in the middle decades of the twentieth century, this tension even heightened.

Transformations of the state during the French Revolution and Napoleon's Empire set the stage for this later dynamic. At the beginning of the Revolution the new National Assembly swept away much of the social foundation of the Old Regime state—corporate privilege, venality of office, the church's quasi-statist authority in partnership with the monarchy—and replaced it with popular sovereignty, representative government, and constitutional accountability. These changes gave the French state sorely needed fresh legitimacy. The Declaration of the Rights of Man established the individual citizen, "free and equal in rights," as the fundamental unit in the polity and the ultimate source of the state's authority. This principle made the citizen-state relationship primary, while delegitimizing intermediary bodies as potential bastions of privilege and threats to state autonomy.

The dramatic expansion of the state and centralization of its authority, which Alexis de Tocqueville so scorned a half-century later, came with the "second dose" of revolution in 1792, the founding of the First Republic, and its radicalization during the Terror. Faced with civil war in the Vendée and European war on the nation's borders, radical Jacobins in Paris instituted mass conscription and took steps to exercise direct, Paris-centered control. They used the state's authority to mold a new republican culture with its novel calendar, a uniform system of weights and measures, a Panthéon of republican heroes, and a secular liturgy of ceremony, festival, and commemoration. They understood the revolutionary potential of education, laying (unimplemented) plans for public schooling and successfully founding the École Normale Supérieure, new medical schools, and the École Polytechnique. All this required extraordinary authority and resources. By 1795 the state administration had expanded in personnel fivefold over what it had been in 1788. It also finally became a bureaucracy in the Weberian sense—more disciplined and accountable to a rationalized chain of command than to the patronage network of local notables or the king.

If the First Republic expanded the scope of state activity, it was Napoleon who more fully realized the potential for centralization and made rule by administration a reality. In some respects he completed the work of the Revolution, most notably in the codification of law. But he went further than his predecessors in establishing centralized institutions. He did so first by creating the prefectoral corps, the regime's chief administrative officers and political agents in the *départements*. Modeled on the *intendants* of the Old Regime, prefects were more numerous, more amply staffed, more tightly supervised, and more powerful locally than their monarchical predecessors. Having sidelined the legislature and eliminated most forms of democratic participation, save for plebiscites, Napoleon still needed advice on the law. To fill this role, he established the Conseil d'État and appointed its members. Under Napoleon, careers in the high civil service, especially in one of his new *grands corps* or elite professional units of the state bureaucracy (especially the Finance Inspectorate, the Conseil d'État, and the state auditors' Cours des Comptes), brought extraordinary salaries, titles, and prestige. To bind elites, especially in the military, more firmly to the state Napoleon also created the Legion of Honor. Finally, through foreign conquest Napoleon gave the state an imperial mantle and a messianic mission, ostensibly to spread the Revolution's principles of liberty and equality across Europe, but in practice to aggrandize power and resources. If the scale of Napoleon's ambition was unprecedented, even by Louis XIV's standard, its imperial character had ample roots in the Old Regime, as did its messianism in the universalizing aspirations of Revolution.

The tumultuous era of the French Revolution and Napoleonic Empire did a great deal to deepen the tension between the rationalist and democratic visions of the state. The Revolution had advanced both visions but failed to reconcile them—which would have required the nurturing of a more robust parliament and the growth of the kinds of intermediary groups Jacobins were hostile to in principle. Napoleon showed no such dualism; he embraced administrative governance to the exclusion of representative democracy. The terrible violence of the era, much of it pitting the state against its citizens, produced a country deeply divided over how to organize and use state power. From 1815 to the present day, the Left and Right would each remain divided among statists, antistatists, and ambivalent moderates in between.

Yet the Revolution and Empire also gave later republicans a remarkable institutional endowment, provided they could harness it to the Republic and tame its antirepublican elements. Those institutions grew slowly but inexorably over the course of the nineteenth century, as state engineers presided over the planning of canals, roads, and rails; officials tiptoed into the realm of social protection; and Louis-Napoleon's Second Empire (1852–70) adopted extravagant (and ruinous) debt-financing for Baron Haussmann's rebuilding projects and encouraged new investment banks like Crédit Mobilier to promote industry. But it was under the Third Republic (1870–1940) that the state changed most between 1815 and 1914. For one thing, colonial expansion and the conversion of Algeria into three full-fledged *départements* boldly expanded the state's juridical and territorial reach. For another, the Republic's founders "republicanized" important swathes of the state administration, most notably through purges in 1879 of nearly the entire prefectoral corps and the Conseil d'État. Republicans, moreover, extended the state's tentacular reach into society, most substantially via the Ferry laws of the 1880s that established free, universal, secular education. Public primary and secondary education mushroomed elsewhere in Western Europe in this period, but with less centralized control and without France's pedagogical zeal to create new republican citizens. With education, republicans recovered some of the utopianism of their Revolutionary forebears, a faith that the state could refashion society itself. That faith found further expression in the late nineteenth-century growth of the so-called hygienic state, the extension of state authority into public health, and efforts to remedy the social "ills" associated with poverty, prostitution, and crime. This extension of state activity had ample precedent in the Revolution but also in the 1830s, when asylums came under prefectoral oversight, and public officials struggled to contain the ravages of cholera. After the Franco-Prussian War (1870–71), anxiety over France's demographic disadvantages vis-à-vis Germany inspired government officials to intensify efforts to support natality and to tackle such scourges as tuberculosis, syphilis, and alcoholism. From here it was a direct road to the creation of a Ministry of Health in 1920. The road was even shorter to a new Ministry of Labor in 1906, reflecting the growing visibility of the labor movement and an expanding regulatory role for the state following legislation on work accidents (1898), work time (1900), and the creation of a labor inspectorate. If many of these new forms of state activity were hardly unique to France, their republican pedigree gave them a patriotic valence and made this expansion of central state authority more palatable to property owners, large and small, who served as the political bedrock of the Republic.

This state in the early Third Republic, however, had its limits. To a degree these limits derived from republicanism itself. The founders, from Gambetta to Thiers to Ferry, set great stock in civil society as well as the state, and they saw much of the work of creating an enlightened, sober, and patriotic citizenry arising from a fraternalist fabric of Masonic lodges, mutual aid societies, bar associations, agricultural societies, trade organizations, and chambers of commerce. Most republicans, moreover, were still economic liberals at the turn of the century: the state, in their view, could venture into the hygienic realm for the sake of national defense, social solidarity, and common decency, but its role in the marketplace should be kept in check.

Organizational capacity limited the state as well. True, the French state's policing capacity was legendary, built as it was over eight decades of revolutionary ferment and government repression. The professional quality of the state engineering corps and the rigor of its training at the École Polytechnique remained first-class by European standards. But by the mid-nineteenth century much of the rest of the state bureaucracy had fallen behind its British and German counterparts in professionalism and rational organization. Frequent regime change since 1815 and republican aversion to a strong executive after two bouts of Bonapartism had taken a toll. As a result, when the state's functions grew, so too did its incoherence. The agency responsible for the merchant marine, for example, though formally in the Commerce Ministry, found itself answering as well to the ministries of Finance, Interior, Public Works, and the Navy. Likewise, if on the eve of the First World War France lacked an adequate international telegraph network, it was mainly for lack of coordination between the ministries of the Army, Navy, Colonies, and the PTT (*postes, télégraphes et téléphones*).

As the Third Republic took hold at the local level, moreover, state officials in Paris found it harder to call the shots. The regime restored local elections and by the 1880s gave mayors, municipal councils, and the *département* legislatures (Conseils Généraux) greater authority and financial independence. Prefects became much more accountable to local officeholders, and many a ministerial initiative could founder on the shoals of the local. State and nation building, of course, was not just a product of the center. Innovations in government action often came from the periphery, as, for example, the development of factory inspection in the Nord and Pas de Calais, or the role of the "lost provinces" of Alsace and Lorraine in pushing the country to adopt a Bismarckian social insurance scheme after they returned to France in 1918. In the more democratic political culture of the Third Republic, inhabitants in the provinces, especially France's border regions, and Europeans in the settler colony of Algeria could play larger parts than before in defining the role of the state and the meaning of national belonging where they lived.

Take, for example, the Algerian city of Bône, a booming center of European settler colonialism with local power brokers who had tight connections to the powerful colonial lobby in Paris. As historian David Prochaska has shown, the republican mayor of Bône, like his counterparts in the metropole, built a classic, patronage-fueled political machine. After Governor-General Jules Cambon dismissed him in 1895 for alleged corruption and for standing in the way of state efforts to improve conditions for Muslims, Bône's citizens promptly reelected him. What's more, within a year the colonial lobby won Cambon's dismissal. Settlers also used the occasion to secure an unwritten promise from Paris to leave Muslim-settler relations alone, and in a state of sharp and fateful antagonism. Republican leaders in Paris, struggling with the Dreyfus affair, could scarcely afford to alienate the settlers. Though Algeria was unique in many respects, this episode reveals strengths and weaknesses of the state in empire and metropole alike at the end of the nineteenth century. The responsiveness of this parliament-centered regime to well-organized interests groups gave it stability, while encouraging civil society to build the associational life and advocacy groups democracy required. But this same quality blunted the state as an instrument for bold national initiatives and kept the less-organized (women, workers, indigenous colonial subjects) at the margins.

Two world wars and the Great Depression changed this picture profoundly. During the First World War the colossal demands of total war put the state at the center of a command economy, much as war and revolution had done to the

First Republic, only this time on a far greater scale. The state conscripted soldiers and workers in staggering numbers, including from the colonies. It enforced wage and price ceilings, rationed supplies, and made major changes in business organization and labor relations. For example, the minister of armaments, Albert Thomas, made a showcase of the munitions sector for such labor reforms as shop stewards, union recognition, and infant crèches for the legions of women hired for war work.

A similar story of state expansion and experimentation could be told about other belligerent countries in World War I. What is striking about France, however, is how far its leaders went after 1918 to dismantle wartime innovations. Victory seemed to have redeemed the Republic, and it confirmed the conviction of many politicians, especially the conservatives who prevailed in the elections of 1919, that the conventional political and economic arrangements of prewar France were sufficient for the postwar world.

The more lasting breakthroughs in state expansion had to await the Depression and Second World War. Though short-lived, Léon Blum's left-wing Popular Front government of 1936 broke especially fresh ground. Social conflict, economic crisis, and war (or its imminence) had been pivotal occasions for state expansion in the past. The Popular Front now faced all three. To boost rearmament Blum's government nationalized much of the arms industry and a great deal of aviation. To stabilize a troubled farm sector Blum created the Wheat Board. To quell industrial unrest he brokered a nationwide wage deal, a forty-hour week, union rights, and compulsory arbitration. From the Popular Front too came new government programs for the arts, leisure, sports, and youth, as well as direct state involvement in radio—the beginnings of the "culture state" later associated with the Fifth Republic cultural ministries of André Malraux and Jack Lang.

The interwar growth of the state, however, paled in scale and symbolic weight in comparison with the changes French leaders ushered in with the Liberation and de Gaulle's Provisional Government of 1944–45. A huge wave of nationalizations in banking and insurance; coal, gas, and electricity; aviation; the merchant marine; and the giant Renault works gave postwar France the biggest public sector in the capitalist world. Jean Monnet's new Planning Commissariat would become the most ambitious and enduring experiment in economic planning in Western Europe. French governments after the Liberation also took direct control of the broadcasting media, a public monopoly that lasted well into the 1970s. Long a relative laggard in developing a welfare state, France established a social security system in 1945 built on a Byzantine network of public, quasi-public, and private insurance funds. By the 1980s, France had become a European leader in this domain. If French elites delayed their Keynesian turn until after the war, years later than their American and British counterparts, they made it with special conviction. Government bureaus dove headlong into national income accounting and economic forecasting, the better to serve the planning apparatus, bolster private-sector productivity, and regulate consumer demand.

All nations that had mobilized for World War II turned to new forms of state intervention to manage the postwar recovery. But the French did so more thoroughly, and for several reasons. They had strong statist traditions to build on. But even more important, the 1940 defeat had brought to a head changes in French elite thinking about the state gathering force since 1914. Although Vichy and the Resistance pursued radically different futures for France, they shared a common faith in statist strategies for national recovery. Thinkers in both camps, blaming defeat on weaknesses of the Third Republic, sought remedies in a newly fortified state inspired by the experiences of gigantic wartime mobilizations in France and abroad and unshackled from liberal economic inhibitions of the past.

Yet the dirigiste revolution of 1945 drew on more than wartime precedent and a new statist consensus in the elite. It also reflected a seismic political shift: the collapse of the Right, discredited by its wartime collaboration with Germany, and an immense groundswell of popular support for the Communists, Socialists, and left Catholic activists who had led the Resistance movement in occupied France. This powerful left-wing coalition, allied with a Gaullist Resistance more conservative and military in character, gave the dirigiste state of 1945 a patriotic republican legitimacy that would last well after this unique political moment had passed.

At the same time, French ambitions after the Liberation heightened that underlying tension between the rationalist and democratic dimensions of republicanism. Most French leaders emerged from the war years convinced of two national imperatives: the urgent need both to "modernize" the economy after the shameful defeat of 1940 and to democratize the polity after Vichy's authoritarian rule. In principle these goals cohered, but in practice democratization and a state-led modernization drive often clashed. On the one hand, the Left-dominated governments of the immediate post-Liberation period restored parliamentary governance and created new democratizing institutions—joint works committees in business enterprise, elected local boards to help manage the new social security and child subsidy systems, and a place at the table for labor, business, and civic associations in the Planning commissariat and other government councils. As the state's role expanded, so too did the call for new venues of representation within it—such as a board to advise the national statistical service or a voice for the unions regarding immigration controls. State intervention tended to politicize more of the territory of everyday life, which in turn stirred advocacy groups to action. In many respects democratic politics—from the orderly sort around the green felt tables of the Paris establishment to the rowdier strikes and protests in the streets—flourished under the Fourth Republic (1944–58).

On the other hand, the state-led modernization drive of the postwar era also empowered the experts—the knowledgeable top civil servants and politicians who used centralized planning, the ministerial bureaucracy, nationalized enterprise, and the financial circuitry of the Treasury to channel resources. De Gaulle, bypassing Parliament, created several key postwar institutions by executive decree: Monnet's Planning Commissariat, the new École Nationale d'Administration (ENA) to train top civil servants, and a powerful new Conseil National du Crédit. As Cold War politics divided the Left after 1946 and as the fragmentation of political parties weakened Parliament in the 1950s, administrators and experts assumed even greater responsibility for policy continuity and long-term projects. All the big postwar initiatives—revamping sectors like electricity and transport, creating nuclear power, rebuilding vast stretches of the urban landscape destroyed by the war, expanding the new social security system, mechanizing and reorganizing agriculture—concentrated power in the state administration and its "technocrats." An elite core of intellectually agile and highly placed civil servants, such as François Bloch-Lainé, Louis Armand, Maurice Lauré, and Pierre Laroque, acquired a new kind of visibility as leading architects of the postwar recovery. "We were the small number," Simon Nora later wrote, "who knew better than the others what was good for the country—and this wasn't completely false." State expansion during the Fourth Republic, then, nurtured in often contradictory ways both a democratic renewal and the ascendancy of a state elite heavily endowed with expertise.

De Gaulle's new Fifth Republic accelerated the trend to concentrate power at the summit. The new constitution not only strengthened the executive authority of the President and prime minister; it also allowed them to appoint nonparliamentarians to run the ministries. Over the course of the 1960s about a third of all ministers were high civil servants. Ministerial staffs, moreover, grew rapidly in size and power, becoming a kind of superadministration, further empowering an unelected, technically trained elite, especially the "énarques," or graduates of ENA, who catapulted into the grands corps and the top jobs. By the mid-1960s it was possible to talk of a "Gaullist state," resting on the triple pillars of a strong presidency, an administrative elite, and a new Gaullist party that gave these leaders the political backing they needed. Not for nothing did de Gaulle's detractors call him a republican monarch.

Yet images of an imperious, autonomous Gaullist state fail to capture how intricately intertwined state and society remained in the Fifth Republic and how buffeted state officials could still be by forces beyond their control. As political scientist Ezra Suleiman has shown, centralization could often make a state more susceptible to private interest groups, which could thereby focus their leverage on a key bureau or minister in Paris. Private groups could also exploit the state's internal rivalries, which were as common to the Fifth Republic as they had been to the Third. Notaries, for example, a powerful occupational group in France with business monopolies going back to the Old Regime, were able to fend off Justice Ministry efforts in the 1980s to restructure their profession.

Likewise, the state's capacity to pursue strategies for economic development still varied enormously by sector. Dirigisme worked well in high-technology industries, where the government had savvy private actors to work with and where the state's procurement, ownership, or regulation still gave it the upper hand—nuclear power, for example, or high-speed rail, aerospace, telecommunications, or architectural "grands projets" in Paris. Not so in steel, shipbuilding, and computers, where the state had less leverage, and projects flagged. In agriculture, to take a mixed case, success with mechanization and land consolidation in the 1960s required close partnership between state elites and the Young Farmers movement, a postwar association that challenged the older farm lobby. State effectiveness, in short, depended not just on state autonomy but on able private partners and public-private collaborations, increasingly facilitated in the Fifth Republic by the growing practice of *pantouflage,* the parachuting of high civil servants from government posts to the private sector.

The continued centrality of the state also depended on another seeming paradox—its leadership in adapting the country to the Europeanization and globalization of the French economy, processes that to some extent diminished state sovereignty. Every President of the Fifth Republic and his economic experts played a big role in building the integrated European economy, not least Socialist President François Mitterrand, who championed the Single European Act, the Maastricht Treaty, and the euro. By the end of the century, these EU developments had reduced the French state's control over investment flows and shrunk the énarques' power and prestige. But France's state elites surrendered less of their preeminence than the logic of globalization might have implied. Their prominent role in adapting to Europe meant that of the big countries in Western Europe, France still possessed the largest public sector and the most state-centered approach to economic management.

If state elites in the Fifth Republic proved adept at working with business and adapting to Brussels, they showed only marginal success in incorporating less powerful groups into the polity. Exuberant protest has a long tradition in France. But the concentration of centralized administrative authority under the Fourth and Fifth Republics and the concomitant decline of Parliament as an effective arena of social bargaining had the effect of exacerbating a confrontational style of politics that often spilled into the streets. In this respect the massive protests and strikes of May 1968 were not so much the last gasp of a nineteenth-century insurrectionary tradition, as was said at the time, as the spectacular template for a continuing dynamic of state initiative and popular resistance that has often substituted for effective consensus-building in the Fifth Republic. More so than elsewhere in Europe, in France students, workers, public employees, immigrants, and other constituencies continue to use strikes, marches, and symbolic violence to win concessions from what seems to them a remote and overbearing state. Government initiatives regarding school funding (1984), pension reform (1995), and employment rules (2006) all sparked big enough protests to arouse the specter of '68 and to force jittery officials to retreat. Thus, when President Pompidou extolled the state as the source of progress, order, and unity, he was telling only half the story. The rise of a talented political and administrative elite since 1945 indeed lent a dynamism to France's undeniably successful postwar recovery. But it also widened the gulf between the state and much of the public, which wanted a greater voice in the polity. By consigning a large measure of democracy to the streets, the state in the Fifth Republic served as much to sow as to quell disorder.

References

Baruch, Marc Olivier, and Vincent Duclert, eds. *Serviteurs de l'État: Une histoire politique de l'administration française, 1875–1945.* Paris: La Découverte, 2000.

Grémion, Pierre. *Le pouvoir périphérique: Bureaucrates et notables dans le systéme politique français.* Paris: Seuil, 1976.

Hazareesingh, Sudir. *Political Traditions in Modern France.* Oxford: Oxford University Press, 1994.

Kuisel, Richard F. *Capitalism and the State in Modern France: Renovation and Economic Management in the Twentieth Century.* Cambridge: Cambridge University Press, 1981.

Margairaz, Michel. *L'État, les finances et l'économie: Histoire d'une conversion, 1932–1952.* 2 vols. Paris: Comité pour l'Histoire Économique et Financière de la France, 1991.

Nord, Philip. *The Republican Moment: Struggles for Democracy in Nineteenth-Century France.* Cambridge, MA: Harvard University Press, 1995.

Prochaska, David. *Making Algeria French: Colonialism in Bône, 1870–1920.* Cambridge: Cambridge University Press, 1990.

Rosanvallon, Pierre. *L'État en France de 1789 à nos jours.* Paris: Seuil, 1990.

Suleiman, Ezra N. *Politics, Power, and Bureaucracy in France: The Administrative Elite.* Princeton, NJ: Princeton University Press, 1974.

——. *Private Power and Centralization in France: The Notaires and the State.* Princeton, NJ: Princeton University Press, 1987.

19

The Civilizing Mission

Alice L. Conklin

The idea of a special republican mission to civilize the "primitive" people of the earth provided the ideological framework for France's colonial empire in the modern era. While its antecedents stretched back to the Enlightenment and Revolution, this claim reached its apogee under the secular Third Republic, when French colonization of parts of Southeast Asia; North, West, and Equatorial Africa; and Oceania began in earnest. Republican civilizing discourse in the age of empire was always shifting and unstable; certain recurrent themes nevertheless structured what officials meant by "civilization" and its opposite, "barbarism." When fears of national decline set in during the 1920s, the Third Republic embarked upon its greatest attempt ever to sell the idea of the *mission civilisatrice* to the larger French public. In the aftermath of Vichy's humiliating collaboration with Germany, the Fourth Republic reinvented the terms of imperial governance, and with it the notion of France's imperial mission to civilize. As for de Gaulle's Fifth Republic, it remains an open question whether or not the "civilizing mission" has survived the formal end of the French empire. The term has dropped out of official circulation, but its binary structures of thinking remain deeply engrained in a republican culture once again confronted with negotiating postcolonial difference—this time within the Hexagon.

For a long time, historians ignored the role of civilizing rhetoric in modern French imperialism. The *mission civilisatrice* obviously rang hollow to scholars living through decolonization and after, who saw in the wreckage of empire only aggressive European conquest and exploitation of less technologically advanced societies. More recently, a new appreciation of the power of language and images to produce and perpetuate inequalities between colonizer and colonized has led historians to take France's modern civilizing mission more seriously, and to analyze it from a variety of theoretical perspectives and in multiple contexts. World's fairs, national symbols and commemorations, the military, domesticity and the home, government circulars, law courts, legal codes, school textbooks, imperial propaganda, the new social sciences, marriage and paternity debates, missionary societies, health manuals—and the list goes on—are seen as so many sites for the constant reinvention and assertion of notions of French civilization and the colonial need for it. Such notions were critical to maintaining white privilege in a republican regime officially committed to the unity and equality of humankind.

The notion of a secular civilizing mission is a particularly French one; the French invented the very word "civilization" in the eighteenth century, and have celebrated the achievements of their own ever since. But the idea acquired a noticeably stronger resonance after the return of democratic institutions in 1870, as the new Third Republic struggled to reconcile its ambitious new imperialism with its universalistic ideals. The republican civilizing mission rested upon certain contradictory assumptions about the superiority of French culture and the universal perfectibility of humankind. It implied that France's colonial subjects were too primitive to rule themselves but capable of being uplifted. It intimated that French men and women (in different ways) were particularly suited, by virtue of their revolutionary heritage and their current industrial strength, to carry out the task of liberating all of humanity—beginning with the peoples they were colonizing. Last but not least, it assumed that republicans in particular had a duty and a right to remake conquered peoples along lines inspired by the recent cultural, political, and economic development of France.

Underlying these general convictions, one principle more than any other dominated republican ideology of civilization from the 1870s onward: mastery—mastery of nature, including one's own body, and mastery of what can be called social behavior. To be civilized was to be free of specific forms of tyranny: those of the elements over humankind, of disease over health, of instinct over reason, of ignorance over knowledge, of men over women, and perhaps most importantly, of despotism over liberty. Mastery in all of these realms was integral to the identity that the leaders of the Third Republic sought to forge for the French nation after 1870. It was because French science and technology had triumphed over geography, climate, and disease to create new internal and external markets, and because France's leaders, before those of all other nations, had overcome oppression and superstition to form a democratic and rational government of equal male citizens, that republican France deemed itself so civilized. By the same token, it was because the inhabitants of the non-European world were perceived to have failed on these same fronts—because they appeared to lack the crucial ability to achieve mastery—that they were obviously barbarians in need of the universal civilization first developed in the modern era by republicans in France.

If a conflation of civilization with mastery was a defining and permanent characteristic of republican imperialist rhetoric, the specific content of the *mission civilisatrice* nevertheless shifted depending on particular colonial situations and changing political and economic trends in France. From the early years of the Third Republic until World War I, when republican zeal reached its zenith, several tenets dominated civilization doctrine. First, the new governing elite believed that civilization required that they improve their subjects' standard of living through the rational development, or what republicans called the *mise en valeur,* of the colonies' natural and human resources. This objective, they thought, could best be achieved by building railroads—because railroads would link interiors to the coast and promote the exchange of peoples, currencies, commodities, and ideas—and by improving hygiene to eliminate the endemic diseases deadly to the colonizer and colonized alike. Second, and contrary to the myth that France wished to assimilate the colonized culturally by making them fully French, the republicans in power insisted that the different African, Asian, and Oceanic peoples had to evolve within their own cultures. The only exception was when aspects of these cultures conflicted with the republican principles of French civilization. In these instances, the offending institutions or traditions were to be suppressed and replaced by French ones. The targets of eradication varied from colony to colony: in sub-Saharan Africa and Oceania—considered the most backward territories—indigenous languages, "barbaric" customs, slavery, and "feudal" chieftancies were loudly proclaimed incompatible with progress; in Indochina and North Africa the emphasis fell more on "regenerating" the decadent political, social, and religious institutions in place when the French arrived. Everywhere, however, the universal virtues of the French language, modern social relations, and enlightened justice were expected to triumph.

When liberal values lost favor in France after World War I, this definition of the civilizing mission began to change in subtle ways. Interwar governments dwelt less on the themes of eradicating institutions antithetical to French civilization; instead they emphasized more than ever the need to associate new and traditional colonial elites in policymaking and to preserve precolonial societies and cultures while encouraging them to change slowly from within. Politically, association meant consulting these elites in decisions regarding them—a policy already in place in the more "advanced" protectorates in Indochina, Tunisia, and Morocco, and which was now to be applied across the empire. Culturally, association stipulated respecting the exotic cultures of the empire, and incorporating them symbolically into an ethnically diverse but unified Greater France.

Also in the 1920s and 1930s, French imperial authorities rejected the formerly held opinion that railroads alone would trigger the desired increase in African standards of living. The key to tapping the economic potential of the different colonies was the *mise en valeur* of its human resources. Human *mise en valeur* meant a more intensive focus on improving the colonial producer's health, fertility, and farming methods compared to conditions and practices in the prewar era. It also included the conviction—implicit before but now clearly articulated—that it was necessary forcibly to inculcate a work ethic in colonized peoples, which they supposedly lacked. To be civilized, according to this definition, was to exchange "laziness" for wage labor under European supervision in a capitalist system of agricultural production for export. Coerced labor would gradually yield to free labor, as the local populations internalized the lesson that wage labor alone held the key to progress and prosperity.

As this brief summary suggests, the language of the civilizing mission in France was always both republican and racist. Or to put it another way, French civilizing discourse simultaneously manufactured ideas of sameness and difference in ways that twisted and turned according to circumstances of time and place. On the one hand, contrasting concepts of "civilization" and "barbarism" encouraged the French to view Africans and Asians as different and inferior "others," who needed a helping hand from the nation of the "rights of man"—at gunpoint if necessary. On the other hand, this same binary nevertheless held out the promise that these "others" were capable of improvement in France's own image; in this sense the colonized were viewed as fellow humans, with the same potential capacities as the inhabitants of France. Moreover, as colonizers, the French constantly claimed to take new reforming measures on behalf of the colonized as they evolved: first the abolition of slavery, then the eradication of ignorance, disease, and sloth. In due course forced labor, too, would be phased out, as further proof of French generosity; and after 1944 a diluted form of citizenship for all colonial subjects was introduced. Thanks to the endless recycling and recalibrating of these civilizing claims, which humanized colonial peoples and naturalized their inferiority in equal measure, republicans of good faith could more easily accept the perversion of democracy that their colonialism always represented.

As a concept structured around malleable notions of similarity and difference, republican civilization discourse incorporated gender and class assumptions as well as those of race. In France, the qualities of reason and rationality deemed necessary to democratic governance were understood to be the exclusive possession of men. Women, tied as they ostensibly were to the particularity of their sex, fell short of the abstract status of the individual necessary for full citizenship. Yet the same feminine qualities that dictated French women's exclusion from the vote made them ideal helpmeets in the republican civilizing project, in the metropole and overseas. Leading male politicians—and indeed many female reformers—insisted that due to their "natural" generosity of spirit and roles as *mères au foyer,* bourgeois women were particularly suited for bettering the lower classes and the lower "races" culturally and morally. Female social workers could penetrate within working-class families and instruct poor women how to fight the social diseases of alcoholism, tuberculosis, and infant mortality—thereby promoting class reconciliation and civilization. What was true in the slums of French cities was even truer in colonies like Algeria and Tunisia, where colonialists believed that Muslim men confined local women to harems, imprisoned them in the veil, and refused to educate them. White women alone could hope to enter these private and mysterious domestic spaces, uplift their Muslim sisters, and build trust—or so it was imagined—across the racial or religious divide. French wives in the colonies could also perform the important task of keeping their husbands from becoming decivilized in the "sensuous" and "decadent" tropics—by maintaining proper middle-class homes that would reduce the temptation of destabilizing sexual traffic across the color line.

Historians have just begun to examine the extent to which the ideas and language of the civilizing mission affected policymaking overseas, and the picture that is emerging is both incomplete and complex. During the crusading years of the early Third Republic, the regime's core values influenced high-level officials' actions on the ground more than later. In West Africa, for example, the governors-general from 1895 onward issued a series of edicts ending the legal status of slavery in their territories, liberating ethnic groups from African "oppressors," establishing courts to enforce civilized standards of justice, and requiring administrators to set up health services and build schools. Governors-general also sought to finance the port and railroad construction deemed essential—as the administration put it—to stimulating the economic development from which French and Africans alike would ostensibly benefit. They passed naturalization laws that would allow a select handful of the most "evolved" of their subjects to become citizens, and set official limits to the degree of coercion that could ever be used against the colonized. These measures convinced contemporaries that the civilizing mission was no mere window dressing designed to mask exploitation—but a guarantee of good administration for people deemed incapable of evolving on their own, and whose guardianship France had generously accepted.

Despite its close association with republican ideology and governance, France's civilizing mission was not an exclusively republican idea in the period between 1870 and 1914. Nor do ideas inherited from 1789 alone explain the timing and content of many of the civilizing measures adopted overseas. The Third Republic was in fact home to two competing missions: the secular one of its new governing elite, and a religious one espoused by the regime's greatest enemy, at least until World War I—the Catholic Church, which insisted on its own universal mission to civilize by bringing the heathen of France's new empire to Christ. In theory, the two missions were not hostile to each other; one of the most popular dictums of the early Third Republic—uttered by none other than Gambetta himself—was that anticlericalism was "not an item for export." Hardheaded pragmatism underlay this official decision to bury the hatchet with the church when it came to the empire. Having invoked the *mission civilisatrice* to help reconcile an ambivalent nation to imperialism, the leaders of the Third Republic had little interest in paying for programs to reform, educate, and improve the livelihoods of their newly acquired colonial populations—some sixty million people. After 1900 all colonies were made self-financing and thrown back on their own usually limited resources. Colonial officials, who numbered around four thousand, responded to this parsimony not by ignoring the Third Republic's official civilizing promises, but by turning to the most convenient and inexpensive alternative available for carrying them out: the fifty-eight thousand Catholic missionaries living abroad, most of them in the colonies.

Far from getting along together, however, missionaries and republican administrators routinely fought each other for "the hearts and minds" of their colonial subjects. Their conflicts mirrored the deep divide in late nineteenth-century France between Catholics devoted to their faith and republican anticlericals determined to cleanse the nation—and particularly its public schools—of the church's influence. These conflicts took a number of different forms. Some administrators and colonists resented the disruptive impact conversion had on the colonial populations, since conversion could turn neighbors against one another and split whole villages into feuding clans. They argued that the church's divisive presence prevented the colony from developing economically. In Paris, republican deputies excoriated missionaries in Indochina for teaching Latin in their schools rather than French and questioned whether any Catholic priest could be a good patriot. This bickering crescendoed in the wake of the Dreyfus affair, when the intensification of the Republic's war against the church ricocheted in the empire. The liquidation of the affair, however, opened a genuine era of reconciliation that endured until World War I and beyond. Secular republicans and Catholic missionaries set aside their disagreements and found common civilizing goals in pursuit of which they could and did cooperate. As J. P Daughton has argued, this deep pattern of interaction between France's two missions between 1870 and 1914 ultimately changed both of them, confirming that the secular civilizing mission in these years was shaped as much by the encounter with Catholics as it was by the Enlightenment and revolutionary principles of the Third Republic.

If the idea of the civilizing mission structured how colonial officials approached their duties overseas, over the life of the Third Republic this same idea became more firmly entrenched in the collective minds of metropolitan French. Recent work has revealed the many ways republican officials sold the idea of the civilizing mission to a country initially ambivalent—and poorly informed—about a faraway empire that most would never see. In the 1920s and 1930s, the government attached more importance than ever to France's colonies, seeing in them a reservoir of manpower and raw materials and a guarantor of grandeur for a depleted nation. As part of this reinvestment in empire the regime launched its first-ever mass propaganda campaign to educate public opinion about the *mission civilisatrice*. This campaign culminated in the monumental Colonial Exposition in Paris in 1931, attended by eight million French. The point of the Exposition, according to Commissioner Marcel Olivier, was to place "before the eyes of its visitors an impressive summary of the results of colonization, its present realities, its future." It projected a vision of a Greater France, in which the metropole and colonies were united in such a way as to promote a more secure sense of national identity. The Exposition took the form of a tour, in miniature, around the empire; a separate pavilion represented each colony, and inside the pavilions native craftsmen as well as their crafts were put on display. The central attraction was a full-scale reconstruction of the Khmer temple of Angkor Wat, the original of which the French claimed they had saved from ruin. The overall image was that of a grand imperial nation-state, centralized under the selfless guidance of the French. Onlookers were supposed to leave the fairgrounds persuaded that the Africans, Indochinese, and Pacific Islanders of the French empire were on their way to becoming as "French" as the peoples of the different provinces that had historically made up the nation.

The Colonial Exposition offers one example of how representational systems such as architecture could also serve as key sites for articulating France's mission to civilize, particularly in the 1920s and 1930s. By then, the first nationalist movements overseas were mobilizing against French rule. Leaders of these movements often belonged to a new group of French-educated elites determined to use the language of the civilizing mission to press for some form of power sharing, if not outright independence. The Third Republic, these nationalists insisted—in the impeccable French that they had mastered in schools provided by the colonizer—had conquered their homelands in the name of the universal principles of 1789. These same principles dictated the right of the colonized to a voice in their own government, if not self-rule. The Colonial Exposition turned these claims on their head by conveying aesthetically the message that native peoples had made some progress under French tutelage, but not yet enough to warrant the rights bestowed by civilization. Each pavilion ostensibly reproduced the "authentic" culture of a particular colony, while also mixing in French stylistic elements. Togo and Cameroon, for instance, built replicas of huts from coastal Africa, enlarged, however, to the monumental proportions of buildings in Paris. Such hybridization subtly underscored how different and exotic the inhabitants of France's overseas possessions remained—but also reminded the metropolitan viewer that French men and women together were quite literally lifting these evolutionary laggards up to new heights, which the latter could never hope to reach on their own. Compared to the early Third Republic, the superiority of French civilization over the cultures of indigenous peoples was now shown to be relative, rather than absolute—but the gap still legitimated colonization.

The fate of the ideology of the civilizing mission after World War II—colonialism's late period—has not been closely investigated, although studies of decolonization have suggested directions for future research. As anticolonial resistance escalated in Madagascar, Cameroon, Indochina, and North Africa, France showed no signs of preparing to leave; to the contrary, much as after World War I, it reinvested ideologically in empire while also reforming it, albeit on significantly different terms than in the 1920s. In Algeria and Vietnam, the Fourth Republic used civilizing rhetoric to justify nasty colonial wars designed to preserve these territories as part of France. And in many parts of sub-Saharan Africa—always a privileged site of civilizing claims, because colonizers considered its inhabitants the most primitive of the entire empire—the metropolitan government for the first time invested massively in the programs that had always been deemed central to the civilizing mission: education, infrastructure, and health care. French officials did so in a belated bid to win the allegiance of those seeking independence.

Yet in the wake of the Holocaust, when UNESCO officially condemned (1950) the notion that there were biological differences between the so-called races that justified their domination, the very term "civilizing mission" and its moralistic overtones became increasingly outmoded. If empires were to survive in the liberal postwar order, European hegemony would have to be justified and understood in different ways. As part of reconstruction in the 1940s and 1950s, European states increasingly emphasized production and welfare for all citizens. These metropolitan themes once again reverberated overseas, although—as in "early" and "middle" colonialism—in highly contingent ways, depending on the individual personalities involved, the local forces of accommodation and resistance that developed, and the kind of economic resources coveted. In official Fourth Republic discourse, Africans, Asians, and Oceanians were no longer cast as barbarians en route to civilization, but rather as members of backward societies that had not yet achieved full economic, political, and social modernization. Only Europeans, it was argued, possessed the expert scientific knowledge that could lead underdeveloped peoples to social progress. The latter were nevertheless granted citizenship in a French Union, albeit on more restricted terms than their metropolitan French counterparts.

And yet old habits died hard. In 1944 René Pleven, a leading colonial spokesman for the Free French, applauded "colonizing action, that is freeing people of the grand scourges which ravage primitive society, whether they be called superstition, ignorance, tyranny, corruption, exploitation or cruelty." To colonize, he added, "is in the final analysis to project in space one's civilization." Throughout the postwar decades, republican references to "civilization" became scarcer, but the same contradictory images, if subtler in form, that had always structured the *mission civilisatrice* remained in force. An ethnocentric one construed colonized peoples as refractory to progress thanks to their tribal pasts (if not their skin color), while a universalistic one insisted that such pasts could and should be overcome to make the colonized more like the French.

References

Clancy-Smith, Julia, and Frances Gouda. *Domesticating the Empire: Race, Gender, and Family Life in French and Dutch Colonialism.* Charlottesville: University of Virginia Press, 1998.

Cooper, Frederick. *Decolonization in Africa: The Labor Question in French and British Africa.* Cambridge: Cambridge University Press, 1996.

Daughton, J. P. *An Empire Divided: Religion, Republicanism, and the Making of French Colonialism, 1880–1914.* Oxford and New York: Oxford University Press, 2006.

Edwards, Penny. *Cambodge: The Cultivation of a Nation, 1860–1945.* Honolulu: University of Hawaii Press, 2008.

Lebovics, Herman. *True France: The Wars over Cultural Identity, 1900–1945.* Ithaca, NY: Cornell University Press, 1992.

Mann, Gregory. *Native Sons: West African Veterans in the Twentieth Century.* Durham, NC: Duke University Press, 2006.

Morton, Patricia. *Hybrid Modernities: Architecture and Representation at the 1931 Colonial Exposition, Paris.* Cambridge, MA: MIT Press, 2000.

Peabody, Sue, and Tyler Stovall. *The Color of Liberty: Histories of Race in France.* Durham, NC: Duke University Press, 2003.

Surkis, Judith. *Sexing the Citizen: Morality and Masculinity in France, 1870–1920.* Ithaca, NY: Cornell University Press, 2006.

White, Owen. *Children of the French Empire: Miscegenation and Colonial Society in French West Africa, 1900–1960.* Oxford: Oxford University Press, 2000.

20

Parité

Joan Wallach Scott

On June 6, 2000, French legislators enacted a law popularly known as the "parity" law. Aimed at increasing the representation of women in political office, the law required equal numbers of male and female candidates for most elections. Although government rhetoric heralded it as evidence of France's unique approach to gender equality ("this law will accelerate the modernization of political life and reinforce democracy"), in fact it has not yet led to the revolution in representation that its early proponents predicted.

The law followed the amendment of two articles of the Constitution in 1999. Article 3 now reads that the law "favors equal access of men and women to elective office"; Article 4 stipulates that political parties should "contribute to the realization of this principle." The law applies to different kinds of elections in different ways. France has two systems of election: proportional representation (*scrutin de liste*) and majority selection of single candidates (*scrutin uninominal* or *scrutin majoritaire*). Proportionality applies in municipal elections and regional assemblies. In 2000, it applied as well to those departments with three or more Senate seats; since 2003, it refers to those with four or more Senate seats. Proportionality also is used for the selection of French delegates to the European Parliament. In this system, parties submit lists and gain a number of seats in proportion to the votes they receive. The place assigned a candidate on the list thus determines who will actually hold office. Customarily, the person in the top spot (the *tête de liste*) of the winning list becomes the mayor in municipal elections, the president of the council in regional elections. Since 2003, voting in the regions is conducted along departmental lines, thereby multiplying the number of lists; for the European elections, a single set of national lists has been replaced by regionally based lists. Municipal and regional elections are decided in two rounds of voting; there is only one round for the Senate seats chosen proportionally and for the European Parliament. The remainder of the

Senate and all seats in the National Assembly are chosen by *scrutin uninominal;* in these contests there are individual candidates competing for each seat, and there are two rounds of voting before a final outcome is declared.

Under the law of June 6, lists are acceptable only when the candidates for the Senate and the European Parliament are alternated by sex. Since 2003, it has been the same for regional assemblies. And in 2007, this requirement was extended to municipalities (of more than thirty-five hundred inhabitants). Strict gender alternation made it impossible to place all the women at the bottom of a list, below the anticipated cutoff for gaining a seat, but it said nothing about the need to place women at the very top of the list (thereby putting them in line for leadership positions). This inequity has been somewhat addressed by the 2007 law that required parity in the executive councils of regions and municipalities, but it said nothing about those with most power, regional council presidents and mayors.

Regarding single candidacies (for the National Assembly and part of the Senate), the law was less forceful. It denied a portion of government stipends to those parties in which the difference for all of the nation between the total numbers of male and female candidates was more than 2 percent in the first round. A 2007 law increased the penalties, but since the large parties could easily afford them, they could continue to resist enforcement. In addition (as critics pointed out), since there was no penalty for the final outcome of the elections, parties could fulfill the parity requirement simply by designating female candidates for seats they knew were not winnable. In this way, they appeared to be in conformity with the law even as they undermined it. The 2000 law did not apply at all to cantonal elections, which are considered "the breeding ground for all the big national elections," and where women are notoriously scarce. (Cantons are departmental administrative units—like states in the United States—responsible for the maintenance of roads, transport, and other infrastructures, as well as certain allocations for schools.) In 2007, candidates in the cantonal elections were required to run with a substitute of the opposite sex, which did have the effect of bringing more women into the process, albeit for the most part in secondary positions. The implementation of the law was to be overseen by a kind of watchdog agency created in 1995 and charged with gathering data and making recommendations, l'Observatoire de la Parité entre les Femmes et les Hommes.

The parity law was the outcome of a decade of campaigning by feminists who thought that the attainment of greater political representation for women was a crucial dimension of the struggle for equality. Inspired by discussions in the Council of Europe and the European Union, by the examples of Green Party activists in Germany and France, and by several decades of feminist agitation within the French Socialist Party, *le mouvement pour la parité* took shape in the early 1990s. The movement was loosely organized as a network. It consisted of a few dedicated activists who mobilized the leadership of preexisting women's associations (with combined memberships of some two million) to address themselves to a simple goal: the need to improve women's access to political office. Actions were coordinated to achieve maximum impact; events that would draw publicity mattered. The point was to generate widespread support and to open national debate on the issue. Manifestos were issued, and petitions circulated; demonstrations were timed to coincide with electoral campaigns. The *paritaristes* gained widespread media coverage. After four years of intensive effort, the outcome began to seem inevitable in June 1996, when ten of the most prominent female politicians in France (representing all the major political parties) published a manifesto in the newsweekly *L'Exprès* calling upon their parties to commit voluntarily to *parité*. After the legislative elections of 1997, when the Socialist Party–which had gestured to parity by running increased numbers of women candidates—regained its majority, it seemed only a matter of time until a law was passed. Indeed, the new prime minister, Lionel Jospin, proposed a revision of the Constitution "in order to inscribe in it the goal of *parité* between women and men." After the usual debating and compromise, the Constitution was finally amended, and the law passed in 2000.

Although it built on earlier feminist strategies, *parité* was the articulation of a new conceptualization in which women's rights were assumed to be the same as men's. This was not a matter of simply ending discrimination by eventually extending men's rights to women (a compensatory move at best), but of recognizing the equality of the sexes as foundational, a constitutive principle upon which democratic social and political structures must be built. As Françoise Gaspard commented, "No real democracy is possible...if the question of equality between men and women is not posed as a political precondition, pertaining to the constitutive principles of the regime, in exactly the same way as universal suffrage and the separation of powers."

In France, the goals of the movement were articulated in a 1992 book, *Au pouvoir citoyennes: Liberté, égalité, parité*, by Françoise Gaspard, Claude Servan-Schreiber, and Anne Le Gall. They took their cue from a network of feminists working within the Council of Europe and the European Union (Gaspard was a member of this network) and boldly rewrote the French national motto, significantly replacing *fraternité* (the brotherhood of men) with *parité* (power shared by women and men) and explicitly calling for a law to implement it. The abstract notion of equal rights was no guarantee of real equality, they argued; *parité* was an attempt to bridge the divide between principle and practice, abstract and concrete, to bring about the compliance of male politicians with the power of law.

In contrast to earlier generations of feminists, who found themselves caught in the contradictions of a French republicanism that assumed that sameness was ground for equality and that the difference of their sex precluded equality for women, those who first developed the theoretical grounds for *parité* addressed the problem of sexual difference from the start. Their argument was ingenious and unique. Instead of saying either that women were the same as men (and therefore entitled to equal participation in politics) or that they were different (and therefore would provide something that was lacking in the political sphere), the *paritaristes* refused to deal in gender stereotypes. At the same time, they insisted that sex had to be included in any conception of abstract individualism for genuine equality to prevail. If women were to be acceptable as representatives of the people, then the abstract individual, that supposedly neutral figure— without religion, occupation, social position, race, or ethnicity—upon whom universalism depended had to be reconceived of as sexed. Anatomical dualism was a reality; sexual difference the attribution of social and cultural meaning to it. The one could be figured abstractly as the dual mode that the human form took, the other concretely as the historically specific set of definitions accorded to these physiological forms. Here was the innovation: unlike previous feminisms, women were no longer being made to fit a neutral figure (historically imagined as male), nor were they reaching for a separate incarnation of femininity; instead the abstract individual itself was being refigured to accommodate women. If the human individual were understood to come in one of two sexes, the theorists of *parité* reasoned, then the difference of sex could no longer be taken as the antithesis of universalism, and universalism's reach would be extended to women. The argument for *parité* was, in its initial formulation, neither essentialist nor separatist; it was not about the particular qualities women would bring to politics nor about the need to represent a special women's interest. Only by insisting on the necessary duality of the human species could a truly inclusive individualism (one in which sex no longer mattered) exist. "It is paradoxical, but interesting to argue," commented philosopher Françoise Collin, "that it was universalism that best maintained the sexualization of power, and that *parité* attempts, by contrast, to desexualize power by extending it to both sexes. *Parité* would thus be the real universalism."

This vision of equality created great debate among feminists, even as it gained support from the general population. As adherents were mobilized through existing women's organizations and as approval of the idea of gender equality in politics grew in the polls, some feminists attacked the movement from the left and the republican center. Those on the left objected to what they called the reification of women's identity, which they found to be essentialist because ultimately based in biology. Ignoring the *paritaristes'* attempt to distinguish between the abstract and the concrete, they argued—only in terms of the concrete—that it was more important to address social and economic differences among women; a law granting access to politics would benefit only some women and would not eliminate the economic causes of the oppression of others. The criticisms from feminists who identified as republicans also saw *parité* as a form of biological determinism and thus a threat to the meaning of universalism. Elisabeth Badinter maintained that "the greatness of the concept of humanity is that it is common to all of us despite all of our differences." Treating women as a group apart would create a contagion of communalism: special pleading for every identity group that felt itself to be a victim of discrimination. Badinter continued: "You have to be deaf and blind not to see that the rise of communal pressure in France is enormous. And what can the *paritaristes* say to the North African 'community,' which includes millions of people who can look at the National Assembly and say indignantly: 'And what about us? Aren't we excluded from the universalist Republic?'" In effect, the debate among feminists about *parité* exposed one of the contradictions at the heart of republican universalism: the insistence on sameness as the ground for equality at once creates and ignores exclusions based on difference. While leftist critics carried on the argument on the grounds of material causality (economic, not physiological), the republicans held to the singular abstract individual as the only possible unit of citizenship and representation. The fiction that individuals are without sex (and that sex is the equivalent of any other social characteristic) had to be maintained in politics, even if sex (conceived as more fundamental than any other social characteristic) was the basis for discrimination against women, disqualifying them as legitimate representatives of the nation.

The original formulation of *parité* did not, in the end, become the premise on which the law of June 6, 2000, was based. The theoretical distinction between abstract anatomy and the traits of sexual difference attributed to it was lost as lawmakers debated feminist demands for political equality at the same time that they considered the question of rights for gay and lesbian couples (in 1998 and 1999). When the constraints of nature and culture were evoked as arguments against homosexual adoption and procreation, the heterosexual couple became a critical figure for some proponents of *parité*. Sylviane Agacinski, philosopher and wife of the then Socialist prime minister, Lionel Jospin, wrote a book called *Politique des sexes,* which defined political equality as the complementarity of male and female. If the "natural" organization of society was a family based on a couple, then, she insisted, the organization of parliaments should follow suit. "To think of complementarity is to consider that there are two versions of man and to represent humanity as a couple." Agacinski's version of *parité* was the one that came to justify the law enacted in its name. "*Parité* ought to be the complementarity of the 'national representation' in its entirety," she wrote, "in order to represent the humanity of the nation in its entirety." In the hands of Agacinski, abstraction was entirely abandoned, and the heterosexual couple was substituted for the abstract individual as the universal unit of political representation.

It ought not to be surprising then that, even as the numbers of women elected increased, the law did not alter the terms on which gender inequalities are based: the attribution of different characteristics and roles to women and men. The proportion of women on municipal councils in towns of over thirty-five hundred inhabitants grew between 1995 and 2001 from 25.7 percent to 48.5 percent, and on regional councils from 27.5 percent in 1998 to 47.6 percent in 2004. But the prestigious and powerful positions of mayor and president for these bodies remain overwhelmingly in male hands. Women accounted for 4.4 percent of mayors in 1995 and 9.6 percent in 2008, and there was only one female president of a regional council in 2004. Women's assignments on these councils, moreover, tend to correspond to gender stereotypes—they were put in charge of more "domestic" concerns: education, the aged, public health, and cultural affairs, while men dealt with such matters as finances, sports, construction, and roads. The presence of large numbers of newly elected women was undoubtedly an achievement, but the division of labor resembled that of a couple; men still monopolized the direction of "serious business" and let women take care of the rest.

The impact of the law on the most powerful elective bodies has been less impressive. Women hold a few more Senate seats than in the past, and their presence in the National Assembly has increased from about 10 percent before the law to around 18.5 percent in 2007. Although it seems evident that national consciousness about gender equality has been raised by the decade of agitation for the law and by passage of the law itself, the discrimination it aimed to correct continues—and not only in the arena of politics and political parties, but in the economy and society more generally, where glass ceilings and wage differentials demonstrate continuing discrimination. Perhaps the ambiguous legacy of the law was most sharply evident in the 2007 presidential campaign of Ségolène Royal, who struggled unsuccessfully to find an appropriate way of representing herself as at once seriously political and female.

Still, it would be a mistake to underestimate the importance of having a law on the books that commits the polity to gender equity and that, at least in principle, accepts the idea that women are as qualified as men to represent the nation. It is there to be used by the women who choose to enter the terrain of politics and whose growing presence will alter the demography of parties and elective bodies with results that could well challenge prevailing stereotypes. It is there for future generations of feminists who seek to challenge those stereotypes upon which systems of inequality are built. Such feminists are already evident, most strikingly in the group called "les barbes"—a collective of young women who show up at meetings of corporate boards, political assemblies, and other associations that have little or no female representation. Like the Situationists of old or those 60s activists who created "happenings," the bearded ladies deploy irony to draw attention to the continuing absence of women in positions of power.

The *parité* movement believed in the power of law to change social relationships. "By *parité* in the political sphere, we mean the recognition, by law, of the equal representation of women and men." The rallying cry of *Au pouvoir citoyennes* was unambiguous: "Passing a law is essential." The *paritaristes* had a sophisticated conception of the way law worked to effect change. Of course, they expected some immediate results; in much the way that suffrage extended the vote to women, they assumed a law would quickly bring more women into the political world. But they were also pragmatists, aware that it might take time to achieve the kind of complete equality that they envisioned. The immediate goal was to make discrimination visible. "The demand for *parité*," warned Françoise Gaspard on the eve of the passage of the constitutional revision, "will be without immediate effect. It will have raised the question of the inequality of women and men. Undoubtedly the most difficult of the so-called social questions." Gaspard's prediction proved right. In the short term, the law that became known as the *parité* law challenged, but did not overturn, men's control of political power. At the same time, it drew increased attention to discrimination against women, and not only in the realm of politics. If law alone does not alter political culture and its practices, it serves nonetheless as a resource for those who work to bring about change.

References

Achin, Catherine, et al., eds. *Sexes, genre et politique.* Paris: Economica, 2007.

Agacinski, Sylviane. *Politique des sexes.* Paris: Seuil 1998.

Amar, Micheline, ed. *Le piège de la parité: Arguments pour un débat.* Paris: Hachette Littérateurs, 1999.

Fassin, Éric, and Christine Guionnet, eds. "La parité en pratiques." Special issue of *Politix: Revue des Sciences Sociales du Politique* 60 (2002).

Gaspard, Françoise, Claude Servan-Schreiber, and Anne Le Gall. *Au pouvoir citoyennes: Liberté, égalité, parité.* Paris: Seuil, 1992.

Gaspard, Françoise, and Philippe Bataille. *Comment les femmes changent la politique et comment les hommes resistent.* Paris: La Découverte, 1999.

Lépinard, Éléonore. *L'égalité introuvable: La parité, les féministes et la République.* Paris: Presses de la Fondation Nationale des Sciences Politiques, 2007.

Observatoire de la parité. www.observatoire-parite.gouv.fr.

Scott, Joan Wallach. *Parité! Sexual Equality and the Crisis of French Universalism.* Chicago: University of Chicago Press, 2005.

21

THE PRESS

Dominique Kalifa

Translated by Renée Champion and Edward Berenson

The monarchy invented newspapers, and the Republic granted them free-dom. This, in a nutshell, is the main axis around which the history of the French press has been told. Two major events support this idea: first, the revolutionary rupture of 1789–99, which initially sparked development of the media; second, the law of July 29, 1881, a veritable cornerstone of the Republic that sealed the definitive alliance between a newly liberated press and the new regime. The idea that there existed a special link between the Republic and the press emerged from a historiography of the press that had long focused on politics; historians promoted newspapers to the status of decisive player in the new re-publican "synthesis." This interpretation drew sustenance from evidence of the republicans' commitment to liberty of the press, from the significant role news-papers played in France's nineteenth-century revolutions, and from French de-mocracy's need for public information, civic education, and a diversity of ideas. In contrast to such political histories, recent economic and cultural analyses, which focus on the internal operations of newspapers, advance a more nuanced point of view. This newer historiography has shown that the huge professional and commercial transformation that newspapers underwent in the middle of the nineteenth century gave rise to a new press that was far less political than its predecessors. The new press catered more to market demands than to partisan positions. "The press is an industry before becoming a vocation," Albert Thibaudet lucidly remarked during the interwar period. Even though these developments never made the press generally hostile to the regime, com-mercialization did impose new constraints on newspapers and reshaped their priorities.

The ties between the press and the Republic become most evident in an ex-amination of the long fight for freedom of expression. France's earliest newspa-pers were created to celebrate the monarchy and as instruments of royal power.

The first paper, *La Gazette* (1631), was Cardinal Richelieu's idea; he chose Théophraste Renaudot as the paper's first editor, a man charged with furthering Richelieu's absolutist designs. If such constraints eased after 1750, allowing the progressive emergence of a "court of opinion," it was only with the Revolution that newspapers truly became emancipated. The "free communication of thoughts and opinions," enacted during the preparation of the Estates General in July 1788 and enshrined in the Declaration of the Rights of Man in August 1789 (Article 11), stood out as one of the major gains of the revolutionary event. That event unleashed an extraordinary profusion of newspapers, whose energy and ambitions escalated rapidly and whose momentum owed more to revolutionary euphoria than to the Republic, which, once established, revived restrictions on the press. A return to censorship was already perceptible in July 1791, following the *Journée du Champ-de-Mars,* and after August 10, 1792, when the royalist journalist Suleau was assassinated after the Commune condemned "poisoners of public opinion." Censorship finally became generalized in November 1792. Although the press still constituted an indispensable instrument for political debate, political repression gradually reduced the number of newspapers until the Consulate and then the Empire effectively muzzled the press, now reduced to obediently serving as the government's tool of communication.

Once Napoleon's Empire fell, the subsequent history of the nineteenth century witnessed the convergence of the fight for the Republic and the fight for freedom of the press. Under the Restoration (1815–30), newspapers led the attack on the monarchy (which was synonymous with hierarchy and control). *Le Globe, Le National,* and *La Tribune* were instrumental in organizing opposition to King Charles X (1824–30), and the famous *Protestation des journalistes* proved a major impetus for the Revolution of 1830. "In the situation in which we find ourselves," the *Protestation* declared, "obedience ceases to be a duty, and newspaper journalists must be the first to provide an example of resistance." Despite their central revolutionary role, newspapers quickly endorsed the idea of making Louis-Philippe their country's constitutional king, a move that gave the new monarch more republican credit than he deserved. "The Republic, which is so appealing to noble minds, did not suit us thirty years ago," wrote *Le National* on July 31, 1830. "We need this Republic, disguised as a monarchy, as a vehicle to a representative government." But the transformation in 1835 to a more repressive regime revealed its true nature and remobilized most of the newspapers and satirical revues. After the demise of *La Tribune* in 1835, it was up to *La Réforme,* launched in July 1843 by the Arago brothers, Ledru-Rollin, and Félix Pyat, to keep the republican idea alive. And it was in the headquarters of *La Réforme* and *Le National* that a new provisional government took shape in the wake of the Revolution of 1848. The editors of the two newspapers, Ferdinand Flocon and Armand Marrast, became charter members of the new republican government.

The following months, a time of intense and rich freedom, witnessed the burgeoning of more than three hundred newspapers in Paris (the first of which, published on February 26, was entitled *La République*) and nearly as many in the provinces. It was a true "newspaper frenzy," as Henri Wallon wrote. The turnabout was therefore brutal following the June Days, when the laws of August 1848 strictly limited freedom of the press by restoring *cautionnement,* a kind of escrow account for future fines to which all newspapers had to contribute. The purpose of *cautionnement* was to put small papers out of business and deter journalists from criticizing the government. This return to censorship, which intensified under the Second Empire, united the press and republicans more than ever in a common fight for liberty. It was essentially journalists from the opposition newspapers who furnished most of the personnel for the future Third Republic, whose victory also heralded that of the newspapers. The law of July 29, 1881, proved a signal achievement in this respect: by eliminating virtually all restrictions on what journalists could write, it officially celebrated the marriage between the press and the Republic.

Beyond the fight for liberty, definitively won in 1881, newspapers played a cardinal role in encouraging democratic debate. Once again, the Revolution figures as a founding moment. The roughly fifteen hundred periodicals published between May 1789 and December 1799 decisively contributed to the advent of political speech. It was through these papers, whose columns created a permanent effervescence in the Palais-Royal and other public places, that the individual became a citizen. Guaranteeing pluralism of opinion, newspapers incarnated the democratic system, understood as the reign of "publicity," and constantly encouraged involvement and action. From Mirabeau to Marat, including Desmoulins, Brissot, and Hébert, all of the preeminent revolutionary orators were or became journalists. They were joined by hundreds of "patriotic writers" or "sentinels of the people," who count among the great figures of France's democratic experience. This is why the First Republic, despite the censorship it imposed, constituted an important moment in the organization of public oratory and spirit.

Revived briefly in 1848 and then suppressed for the next twenty years, freedom of the press became central to the debates of the early Third Republic. If the 1881 law's liberalism partially stemmed from Tocqueville's famous principle ("The only way to neutralize newspapers is to increase their number"), it also resulted from a profound political conviction. As many parliamentary deputies noted, the press, as the expression of the plurality of opinions and sentiments, was essential to the Republic. "It is the instrument, the image, and the organ of all interests that exist in a democratic society," declared Allain-Targé, a fervent supporter of Léon Gambetta, the political leader who seemed to embody the new republican regime. It is "this speech that is available everywhere and at the same time" that "alone can keep France united in the public arena, keeping it, man by man, and day by day, abreast of all current events," declared Camille Pel-letan, *rapporteur* of the 1881 law in the Senate. "It is not enough," he continued, "for each citizen to have the right to vote; he must be conscious of the meaning of his vote. But how can he be unless we have a press available to all, wealthy as well as poor, a press committed to reaching voters in even the most remote villages?" To this civic mission republicans added a pedagogical function, mak-ing the newspaper—understood within the context of their positivist faith—an instrument of consciousness raising and republican education.

Is it surprising that under these circumstances the years following the enact-ment of the July 1881 law are considered the golden age of the French press? Between 1881 and 1900, the number of titles increased considerably (2,685 peri-odicals in Paris in 1899; more than 3,600 titles in the provinces), but it is especially through their expanding print runs and political influence that the newspapers demonstrated their power. The rapid rise of a hugely popular penny press, especially *Le Petit Parisien, Le Petit Journal, Le Matin,* and *Le Journal,* made newspapers a colossal force. By 1914, they were some ten million copies strong, invested with an undeniable authority and pampered by the Republic's leaders as the "Fourth Estate." Not only did the Republic leave the legislation of 1881 resolutely in place, even though politicians denounced it as a system of impunity and irresponsibility, but the regime enacted new measures even more favorable to the press. In addition to secret government funds periodically distributed to editors, republican leaders favored the press in a variety of other ways. Begin-ning in 1885, journalists benefited from a retirement system financed, without the least contribution from the interested parties, through a loan from the state. The status of ex-journalists as "retirees of the Republic" describes fairly well the immense symbolic importance they enjoyed.

Was this generosity then rewarded by a press firmly engaged in the defense of the regime and its institutions? The answer is ambiguous, for although the press in general strongly supported the Republic, its rapid commercialization put it at odds with some of the regime's core values. Aside from the militant antirepubli-can papers of the Far Left and Right, most newspapers expressed a profound loy-alty to the Republic until its twilight years. It was not until the crisis of the 1930s that a paper like *Le Petit Journal* joined the nationalist side (in 1937 it became the organ of the Far Right Parti Social Français), or that weeklies close to the anti-parliamentary right began to prosper (e.g., *Candide, Gringoire, Je Suis Partout*).

If the main papers supported the President, the army, and the 14th of July, if they praised parliamentarism and meritocracy and thus played an important role in republican acculturation, their endorsement of the republic stemmed not only from shared political commitments, but also from developments internal to the press itself. Some of these developments proved troublesome. The Re-public's stabilization occurred simultaneously with two significant changes in the orientation and nature of the French press. The first was the substitution of traditional "opinion journalism," a mixture of politics and literature, with a newer "American" style, oriented toward quick information, the spectacular, and the quest for the largest possible readership. This evolution, under way since the early 1860s, when the *Petit Journal* registered its extraordinary commercial success, and nourished by the growing popularity of feature articles and the *fait divers* (miscellaneous, often sensational, stories), caught most newspapers in its wake. The result was a progressive depoliticization of the press. A second change saw the gradual transformation of the newspaper into a commercial commodity, the product of a cultural industry whose ties with the world of money were increasingly important. The signs of this evolution first appeared during the July Monarchy, when Émile de Girardin's *La Presse* (1836) inaugurated a kind of journalism less political and more commercial than what had existed to date. His initiatives, such as halving the long-standard subscription price, aroused the hostility of republicans. In July 1836, Girardin fought a duel with *Le National*'s editor, Armand Carrel, who thought it undignified for the profession to sell newspapers for the price Girardin had set. Another great republican figure, Louis Blanc, recognized that *La Presse*'s initiative "called a great number of citizens to public life that had been for too long put off by the high price of newspapers," but he nonetheless condemned Girardin for transforming "what was a public office, nearly a vocation, into vulgar trafficking." Journalism, he concluded, "would become a megaphone for speculation." The confidence that the Second Empire granted to Moses Millaud's *Petit Journal* accentuated the republicans' mistrust of the mass-circulation press, synonymous for them with the abandonment of politics and critical perspectives. They were obliged, however, to adapt to this new, highly potent force. As a result, Girardin, an Orléanist who rallied first to the Empire and then to the moderate Republic, becoming director of the *Petit Journal* in 1873, came to incarnate a marriage of convenience between the Republic and the popular press. As such, he was named president of the commission in charge of preparing what would become the ultraliberal press law of 1881, though he did not live quite long enough to see it pass.

In fact, what Girardin had predicted already in 1836 was fully realized by the end of the 1880s: a press oriented more toward news than opinion, openly commercial, the pure product of an ascendant culture industry. Since the new press's objective was to reach the greatest number of readers, its editors avoided entrenched opinions in favor of consensus, promoting the shared ideas and causes that affirmed loudly and clearly the "independent" nature of the newspaper—independent, that is, of particular political parties or programs. These same virtues of conformism explain the "governmental" line defended by the main daily newspapers during the periodic crises that plagued the Republic: Boulangism (1886–89), the Dreyfus affair (1894–99), and the law of separation (1905).

Even so, from the Panama scandal to the Stavisky affair (1934), the press of the Third Republic was also notable for its venality and moral failings. During the interwar period, as financiers took a growing measure of control, the temptations of blackmail and corruption raised widespread doubts about journalism's mission. Beginning in 1928, Léon Blum questioned, in the Socialist Party's *Le Populaire,* whether the French press could be liberated from the tyranny of money. In any case, none of the era's reform efforts succeeded, not even the one undertaken by Blum's own leftist Popular Front government in November 1936, following the suicide of Roger Salengro, a cabinet minister driven to despair by a scurrilous press campaign against him. Economic factors, commercial constraints, and ideological antagonism seemed to have overwhelmed the republican ideal.

This was especially true during the crucial weeks of June and July 1940. It is an understatement to say that the defense of the Republic did not constitute a priority for the press. In the occupied zone, where *Le Matin* resurfaced as early as June 17, 1940, most of the papers played the continuity card, to the satisfaction of the German authorities, who hoped that the country would quickly resume its habits. Spurred by the henchmen of collaboration, newspapers soon became servile vehicles for Nazi ideology. Meanwhile, in the free zone, the principal newspapers endorsed the liquidation of the Republic with few second thoughts. "The newspaper directors have been fully won over to the Maréchal's politics," observed the editor in chief of the news agency Inter-France in 1941. Out of the three hundred titles published in Vichy France, not one protested the regime's laws of exclusion, and very few followed the example of *Le Figaro,* the *Le Progrès,* and the *Le Temps* by choosing to cease publication in November 1942, when the Germans occupied the entire country. Passivity, opportunism, and the profit motive seem to have reigned over a subjugated press. And if wartime journalists had a particular vocation, it was "to serve the pilot—meaning the Maréchal," as Paul Marion declared in Lyon in April 1941. As for the Republic, it was now little more than a scapegoat, accused by the newspapers of every evil under the sun.

Only a couple hundred mainstream journalists (approximately 7 percent of the profession) contributed to the Resistance. It was therefore up to the clandestine press to represent the republican ideal. However, these combative papers, whose political and moral role was obviously decisive, maintained only a very distant relationship with the world of the press. This sad failure of the Third Republic's newspapers explains both the sharp sanctions (suspension and judicial sequestration) imposed after the war on papers published during the Occupation and the Liberation government's profound desire to begin anew. Of the various ideas circulating among the postwar commissions charged with reorganizing the press, two appear essential: punishing the guilty papers in order "to reestablish a press in France worthy of its mission"; and stripping journalism of its preoccupation with sales and audience. "Less blood on the front page," recommended the Cuvier-Clerval report in 1943. "Get rid of astrologers and other fortune-tellers; less room for celebrities and stars." A year later, Albert Camus explained in *Combat* the deeper reasons for the newspapers' earlier betrayal of republican values: "The appetite for money and the indifference toward things of grandeur had simultaneously worked to give France a press that, with rare exceptions, had no other goal than to increase the power of the few and no other effect than to sully the morality of all. It was therefore not difficult for this press to become what it was from 1940 to 1944: the shame of the country." From *Franc-Tireur* to *Combat,* including *Liberation, Défense de la France,* and of course *Le Monde,* launched in December 1945 to tacitly express the restored Republic's point of view, a new national press promised a revivified journalism that was more moral, more critical, and more committed to democratic debate. The new journalism would be liberated from the grip of money, once again becoming a "journalism of ideas" true to the spirit of the reestablished Republic.

The effort to return the press to its republican origins was, however, quickly thwarted by the imperious demands of the market. Despite the judicial and professional purges that struck more than a quarter of the profession, most purged journalists found themselves quickly called back to work. "I know large regional newspapers where three-quarters of the staff are journalists who wrote during the four years of the Occupation," affirmed Pierre-Henri Teitgen in 1945. The erosion of readership and mounting financial difficulties accelerated the progressive return to prewar news journalism and commercial formulas. Politics lost favor, causing the majority of papers that had emerged from the Resistance to disappear. Those that remained turned to the routines of the past, featuring crime stories, factual news items, celebrities, and the like—all symptoms of journalism's submission to the market. Emblematic of these developments was *Défense de la France,* which in November 1945 changed its title to *France-Soir* and gradually but inexorably resorted to sensationalism. In 1948, the paper lost its independence to the publishing conglomerate Hachette. *Combat* followed the same trajectory, as did *Franc-Tireur,* sold in November 1957 to the Italian businessman Cino Del Duca. As head of Mondial Press and king of sentimental journalism, Duca transformed the former Resistance paper into *Paris-Journal* and then *Paris-Jour.* Although these developments did little to slow the decline of national dailies, they nonetheless signaled the dashed hopes for an independent and moral journalism that the Liberation had wrought. Between the Republic and the market, the newspapers chose sides.

La République française! was the title of the daily newspaper founded by Gambetta on November 7, 1871. Despite his expression of resolve and the unmitigated support republicans contributed to the cause of newspapers, the regime did not benefit from a media system in conformity with its ideals. Like bookstores and leisure activities, the press had become an industry in the mid-nineteenth century, an industry that could be fruitful, yield profits, and attract capital. Such possibilities guided or justified many choices—and not always the noblest ones. This did not mean, however, that newspapers lost all republican import. In fact, they never ceased to be "instruments of reflection and pluralism in the service of democracy," as Minister of Information Alain Carignon observed in May 1993. But to appreciate what the press has actually become requires us to abandon nostalgic visions and anachronistic expectations so we can think clearly about the links between mass culture and democracy.

References

Ajchenbaum, Y.-M. *À la vie, à la mort: Histoire du journal "Combat," 1941–1974*. Paris: Le Monde Éditions, 1996.

Bellanger, C., J. Godechot, P. Guiral, and F. Terrou, eds. *Histoire générale de la presse française*. Paris: PUF, 1969–76.

Bellet, R. *Presse et journalisme sous le Second Empire*. Paris: Armand Colin, 1967.

Delports, C. *Les journalistes en France, 1880–1950: Naissance et construction d'une profession*. Paris: Seuil, 1999.

Eveno, P. *"Le Monde," 1944–1985: Histoire d'une enterprise de press*. Paris: Le Monde Éditions, 1996.

Kalifa, D. *La culture de masse en France*. Vol. 1, *1860–1930*. Paris: La Découverte, 2001.

Ledré, C. *La presse à l'assaut de la monarchie*. Paris: Armand Colin, 1964.

Martin, M. *Médias et journalistes de la Republique*. Paris: Éditions Odile Jacob, 1997.

Popkin, J. D. *Revolutionary News: The Press in France, 1789–1799*. Durham, NC: Duke University Press, 1940–49.

Wieviorka, O. *Une certaine idée de la Résistance: "Défense de la France," 1949*. Paris: Seuil, 1995.

22

Times of Exile and Immigration

Lloyd Kramer

The Republics of France have always had complex connections to the history and experience of exile. Beginning with the First Republic in 1792 and continuing through the collapse of the Third Republic in 1940, the rise and fall of French Republics have produced streams of French exiles who condemned or defended the influence of republicanism in French society, politics, and culture. Since the late eighteenth century, however, France has also constantly attracted exiles from other countries who viewed France as the enlightened advocate of republican political and cultural traditions. For both the French exiles who settled abroad and the foreigners who settled in France, the Republic has evoked intense political, intellectual, and emotional responses. The contested meaning of French republicanism has therefore often evolved through the political debates and polemics that have connected even the most alienated exiles with the critics or advocates of republicanism in French political culture.

Although most of the first exiles from republican France (the Emigration of 1792–94) were hostile to republicanism and to the revolutionary upheaval that had brought republicans to power, the French exiles who fled from later political upheavals (1849–1851, 1871, 1940) generally supported republicanism and claimed to defend its political ideals against groups accused of distorting or destroying republican principles and institutions. The following summary of the interactions between exile and republicanism therefore focuses on specific moments in the history of the First, Second, and Third French Republics and then concludes with a brief reference to the foreign exiles who have gone to France because they supported republicanism as an alternative to the political systems in their own countries. Each of France's early Republics provoked migrations out of France, but each Republic also enhanced France's international reputation as the center for modern republican culture. Exiles have thus left or entered France because they held strong opinions about French republicanism, which suggests that the history of French Republics must also include the history of exile migrations, exile writers, and exile anger.

✆

The first exiles to leave France during the French Revolution departed in 1789, long before the Republic was established in September 1792. Members of the royal family, most notably the king's brothers, the comte d'Artois and the comte de Provence, led this first wave of noble exiles; they began a long royalist campaign to restore the political and social system of the Old Regime. Moving from city to city in continental Europe and settling finally in Great Britain, this most conservative faction of the exile community sent diplomats to various European governments, created an army of émigré soldiers during the 1790s, called for military invasions of France, described the French Revolution as an irrational, godless explosion in the midst of European civilization, and expressed unbending hostility to every aspect of republican political culture.

Yet this first wave of noble exiles was by no means the most important faction of the great emigration from France in the 1790s. Most exiles left France after the establishment of the Republic in September 1792, thereby creating an antirepublican exile population of roughly 130,000 people during the most radical phase of the Revolution. Many of these second-wave exiles belonged to the clergy or the Third Estate, and many had supported earlier phases of the Revolution. The largest number of exiles settled in Britain, initiating a geographical pattern that would reappear in all later exile migrations. At the peak of the Emigration, in 1792–94, there may have been twenty or twenty-five thousand émigrés in Britain, but there were also thousands in the United States, the Caribbean islands, and European countries from Portugal to Russia. This flight of exiles was the largest political migration in the history of France's revolutionary Republics, and it expressed an influential, hostile view of republican politics and culture. Although this migration came in direct response to the revolutionary upheavals in France, it can be placed in a wider, transatlantic context by noting that a greater percentage of the population fled from America's emerging republic after 1776 (about twenty-four émigrés per thousand people) than left France in the 1790s (about five émigrés per thousand people).

The intellectual center of the French antirepublican movement was located in London, where thirteen different émigré newspapers were published between 1792 and 1814. This exile press developed antirepublican arguments that would reappear throughout the following century. Historians now view the émigré press as an important component of the international history of the Revolution, because exiled journalists became an influential source of political information for European elites and governments. The most prominent antirepublican, exile writers—Jean-Gabriel Peltier, the comte de Montlosier, Jacques Mallet du

Pan, and Jacques Regnier—all advocated a restoration of the French monarchy, but they often differed on specific questions of politics and historical analysis. In general, the more moderate *monarchiens* (for example, Mallet du Pan) believed that the Old Regime political system needed to be reformed and that a restored monarchy would have to accept constitutional limits on its power and prerogatives. The more conservative *purs* (for example, Peltier) believed that the monarchy could be restored in a more or less absolutist form, that most French people would welcome such a regime as a stable alternative to republican oppression, and that the Catholic Church should provide an essential cultural bulwark against the dangerous legacy of the Enlightenment's *philosophes.*

Despite their political differences, exiles in all factions of the Emigration argued that the Republic had destroyed the deepest values of French social and political life. It rejected religion, overturned traditional social order, confiscated property, and shattered the long-established unity of the monarchical state. The Republic, as its exiled opponents described it, opened the way for greedy, immoral people to manipulate the masses and pursue their own selfish desire for power and wealth. In contrast to the popular republican references to ancient Rome, Enlightenment political theory, and political virtue, exile writers typically portrayed the Republic as a conspiracy of corrupt political thieves who had stolen France from both its legitimate ruling class and its own people. In this intellectual framework, the Terror was interpreted as the logical outcome of a criminal usurpation that could be sustained only through violence and bloodshed.

This view of the Republic's inherent violence, irreligion, and political oppression gained wide influence among antirepublican and antirevolutionary Europeans, in part because the French exiles seemed to confirm the ideas of English and German writers such as Edmund Burke and Friedrich von Gentz. Although European governments often resisted émigré demands for military action, the exiles' narrative of the French Republic enjoyed wide acceptance—even in Britain and the United States, where many intellectuals and workers had welcomed the Republic as the political embodiment of a new freedom and democracy. Exile writers' vivid reports of bloody scaffolds in French cities gave them dramatic evidence to support their arguments, and for a long time in Europe and America, the very idea of a "French Republic" would evoke images of bloodshed, violence, and brutal de-Christianization.

The antirepublican exiles thus used the violence of the Republic to justify their claims for the legitimacy of a strong monarchy, a powerful church, and deference to social traditions, but this counterrevolutionary program had only limited support in France, even among those who opposed the Republic's repressive policies. Most exiles misjudged the level of support for a restored monarchy in France, and they could not readily understand the failure of the émigré military expedition at Quiberon in 1795 or the later emergence of Napoleon (who first gained political attention by opposing royalists). As often happens in exile communities, many émigrés lost contact with the actual conditions in France; others decided that the rise of Napoleon effectively destroyed the likelihood of a Bourbon restoration and that it was time to accept the new regime. For these "realists," exile became both futile and unnecessary. Napoleon's Concordat with the Catholic Church in 1801 and his offer of amnesty for émigrés the following year brought 90 percent of them back to France. By the end of 1802, only the die-hard, monarchist *purs* remained in exile.

The French exile community of the 1790s thus mostly disappeared, but its leading writers and political critics had contributed to a negative historical image of the Republic that survived long after they had returned home or died. It was thus dangerous to advocate republicanism in France and most of Europe after 1815, and republicans went into exile more often than monarchists throughout the nineteenth century.

The Revolution of 1848 and the establishment of the Second French Republic generated a resurgent political optimism among republicans, many of whom had become profoundly alienated from French politics during the previous twenty-five years. The barricades in Paris, the crowds in the streets, the flight of Louis-Philippe into exile in London, the creation of a provisional republican government, and the proliferation of new republican and socialist publications all suggested that France was entering a new era of democratic republicanism. But these expectations soon turned to disillusionment, especially within the republican Left. The violent repression of Parisian workers in June 1848 showed that a democratic, socialist republic was not going to emerge from the new Revolution, and some republican radicals soon began to leave France. Meanwhile, the government moved quickly to deport almost fifteen thousand political prisoners to Algeria, thus producing a forced exile of republican sympathizers that altered Parisian political culture almost as dramatically as the emigration of antirepublicans had changed Paris in 1792.

The election of Louis-Napoleon Bonaparte as President of the Republic (December 1848) and the subsequent French military intervention on behalf of the pope in Rome confirmed the fears of left-wing republicans, whose political aspirations were expressed through their self-defined identities as *montagnards* and *démocrates-socialistes* (*démoc-socs*). The suppression of new antigovernment demonstrations in June 1849 forced another wave of republicans to flee the country (including prominent leaders such as Alexandre Ledru-Rollin, Étienne Arago, and Victor Considerant), but the stream of exiles did not become a flood until Louis-Napoleon's coup d'état in December 1851. At least ten thousand new political prisoners found themselves exiled to Algeria or Cayenne, and thousands of others fled the country before they could be arrested or detained. This new wave of exiles included some of the best-known writers of the day—for example, Victor Hugo and Edgar Quinet—as well as many of the *démoc-soc* activists who had led republican groups in the countryside. After 1851, the leading representatives of French republicanism lived in Belgium, Switzerland, and England.

The republican exiles who fled from the Second Republic and from Louis-Napoleon's authoritarian consolidation of power thus settled into émigré communities that both resembled and differed from the emigration of the 1790s. The similarity was that most exiles went to the same countries in which émigrés had sought refuge after leaving the First Republic. At least 1,000 exiles settled in England and 1,500 in Switzerland, but some 7,000 had first fled to Brussels. Like their antirepublican predecessors, the new republican exiles produced pamphlets and newspapers describing the crimes of the government in Paris and calling for a new political order that would more accurately express the public opinion and political values of the French nation. The new exiles also assumed that they would soon return to France because the French people would rally to their ideas and reject the usurpers who had seized power from a legitimate French government.

Beneath these surface similarities, however, there were of course crucial differences between the French exile communities of 1792 and 1852. The new exiles did not come from the Catholic Church, the old noble families, or the army. They came instead mainly from the lower and middle classes, from intellectual and educational circles, and from socialist groups or labor associations. Their ideology represented an optimistic, utopian blend of Romantic, republican ideas that stressed the need for "social democracy," universal suffrage, the fraternity of all European peoples, and adherence to constitutional institutions. Most of the *démoc-soc* exiles believed that the French public had moved steadily toward their vision of the social republic in the period between 1848 and 1851, and they maintained that an unpopular President and "party of order" had stolen power to protect the interests of property-holding elites and the Catholic Church.

Exiles such as Ledru-Rollin and Victor Hugo contrasted this Napoleonic "theft" with their own uncompromising defense of the French republican tradition. Hugo spent his first months in exile writing a series of angry attacks on the new political order and corrupt political leadership. All of these works— *Napoléon le petit* (1852), *Les châtiments* (1853), and *Histoire d'un crime* (unpublished until 1877–78)—mocked Louis-Napoleon's personal flaws and pointed more generally to the "crime" of usurpation that had destroyed both the Republic and French liberties. Settling into a long exile on the British islands of Jersey and Guernsey, Hugo began to transform himself into a symbol of the Republic that had been forcibly evicted from French society. Like Hugo, the Republic was stranded in exile, but republican ideals could never be destroyed or imprisoned or sacrificed to the "amnesty" that Napoleon III offered to all political exiles in 1859. Although most exiles accepted this amnesty and returned to France by the early 1860s, Hugo viewed the offer as a new strategy to hide Napoleon's political crimes and a new opportunity to affirm his own republican principles. "I shall share the exile of freedom to the end," he wrote in a brief rejection of the amnesty. "When freedom returns, so shall I."

Exile thus became the most honorable badge of republicanism, and it offered a privileged position from which French republicans could define the meaning of the true republican tradition. In this respect, exile served the "pure" republicans of the Second Empire in much the same way that it had served the "pure" monarchists during the First Empire: it was a sign of uncompromising devotion to the highest political ideals. Exiles once again claimed to define the meaning of the Republic, but after 1851 (in contrast to the 1790s) exiles described republicanism as the most authentic and free expression of French political culture. When the Empire finally collapsed in 1870, the returning exiles brought exceptional political credibility into the campaign to establish the Third Republic. Hugo would soon emerge as the cultural symbol of the new republican order, and yet the social vision of left-wing republicanism could never quite move from the realm of exile to the realm of political reality.

The declaration of a new French Republic in September 1870 produced a new republican political mobilization and the reappearance of a familiar republican optimism about the future influence of the popular classes in French political life. Following the traditional route of French exiles, Napoleon III fled to England—just as the last republican exiles returned to France. The Third Republic would survive much longer than its two predecessors, but the most radical, left-wing republicans soon faced the kind of repression and exile that had disrupted the republican Left in 1849–51. The radical Paris Commune of March to May 1871 terrified and angered the new Republic's "party of order," and the communal, Parisian experiment in left-wing republicanism was soon destroyed. Its defeat marked a crucial turning point in the history of French republicanism, in part because the national government's suppression of the most radical republicans ensured the survival of a more conservative Third Republic. In the context of the history of French political exile, however, the fall of the Commune represents yet another episode in a recurring left-wing republican pattern of flight and emigration.

Government troops killed at least ten thousand people as they retook Paris in May 1871 and arrested almost forty thousand others. Although many of these prisoners were eventually released, thousands were sentenced to prison terms or deported to New Caledonia. More than four thousand people thus went off to forced exile in the South Pacific, where they found themselves effectively re-moved from all contact with French political culture. Hundreds of other Com-munards escaped arrest or deportation by fleeing to Switzerland and England. A new exile community of ex-Communards and radical republicans began pub-lishing narratives of the recent events, defending the Commune as the true ex-pression of the French revolutionary and republican tradition, and attacking the conservative "Versailles republicans" as the enemies of France. This new politi-cal emigration, like all the others, included numerous authors and journalists. Exiled writers such as Jules Vallés, Pierre Vésnier, Félix Pyat, Benoît Malon, and Prosper-Olivier Lissagaray undertook the now-habitual exile work of analyzing their political failures and debating tactics for future political action. Like their predecessors, they claimed to represent the future direction of the French re-publican movement, which they often linked with socialism. Many of the exiles in London came into contact with Marx and other European socialists (two of Marx's daughters married ex-Communards), but their personal or political in-terests kept most French exiles looking toward France. As Lissagaray explained in a widely read history of the Commune, the exiles steadfastly defended the "democratic republic" and never "sullied the honor of the cause." Throughout the early years of the Third Republic, left-wing republicans within France de-manded a political amnesty that would allow the exiles and deportees to return home. This comprehensive amnesty was finally granted in 1880, thus ending the long history of nineteenth-century republican exile.

The hundreds of thousands of right- and left-wing exiles who left the vari-ous French Republics from the 1790s to the 1870s held very different social and political ideas, but the exiles in all political factions claimed that their accounts of republican theories, actions, and traditions provided the most accurate descrip-tions of French republicanism. Although this pattern of exile political commen-tary gradually came to an end as the Third Republic established a more stable government in the late nineteenth century, specific political crises could still cause people to flee the country. General Boulanger, for example, fled to Brussels after the collapse of plans for a coup d'état in 1889, and Émile Zola took refuge in England after his vehement critique of the government during the Dreyfus af-fair in 1898. But it was the collapse of the Third Republic in 1940 that provoked the final, large-scale political emigration from modern France.

A new generation of exiles claimed once again to represent the true spirit of France and French republicanism against the reactionary, antirepublican poli-cies of the Vichy government. Thousands of French soldiers escaped to form "Free French" military units, while intellectuals, writers, teachers, political activ-ists, workers, economic leaders, and endangered Jews settled in England or the United States. This new emigration followed its predecessors in stressing that the authentic France would emerge from the latest national crisis, and that the exiles would in the meantime represent or defend the true essence of France. There were of course debates about what had gone wrong and why the Republic had fallen in defeat, but the political message was as defiant as the messages of all previous émigré generations. "Must we abandon all hope?" Charles de Gaulle asked in his famous radio address to the French people on June 18, 1940. "Is our defeat final and irremediable? To those questions I answer—No!...Whatever happens, the flame of the French resistance must not and shall not die."

The French Republic was once again a Republic in exile, and its most prominent defenders were again forced to issue their political pronouncements from England. This new struggle to reestablish France's republican institutions would require massive military assistance from other nations, but de Gaulle's predictions eventually became reality. The Fourth French Republic emerged after de Gaulle and thousands of other exiles finally returned to reclaim the republican tradition from the Vichy collaborators. As so often in the past, exiles had used the relative safety of England or the United States to describe the meaning of the French Republic to foreigners as well as to compatriots in France. The exiles who fled in 1940 likely represented the broad currents of French public opinion more accurately than the exiles of previous generations, and yet the strategies for spreading their political message, the struggle to survive amid alien conditions, the claim to represent the true history and future of France, the use of London as a base of operations, and the expectation of eventual triumph all replicated patterns of exile life that had reappeared in almost every era of modern French history.

The complex relation between exile and republicanism, as this brief survey suggests, has influenced French history for more than two centuries. Yet a comprehensive analysis of this aspect of French republicanism must also note the history of foreign exiles within France. The ancient experience of exile took on new political and cultural meanings at the time of the French Revolution. Foreigners began moving to France because they viewed the Republic as an alternative to the monarchical regimes in their own countries, and exile became a personal political strategy for supporting republican ideas about human rights and national liberation. Foreign-born activists such as Thomas Paine and Anacharsis Cloots participated in the political life of the revolutionary Republic and were even elected to the republican Convention of 1792. Paine was eventually imprisoned, and Cloots was executed during the Terror, but foreigners continued to identify with the First Republic long after it had disappeared. This political identification was especially important after the Revolution of 1830, when thousands of Poles, Germans, Italians, Russians, and others became exiles in July Monarchy Paris because they opposed regimes that controlled most of central and eastern Europe.

People who left their home countries for political or cultural reasons in the early nineteenth century were among the first to become national exiles of the modern type, and the history of the French Republic explains why so many radical foreigners chose Paris as their destination. "Exile in France" conveyed specific political and intellectual meanings, particularly for central or eastern Europeans who wanted to express allegiance to the French Revolution, democratic government, Enlightenment tolerance, nationalist or internationalist political movements, and various strands of republicanism. The history of the Revolution and republicanism gave the French capital a quasi-mythic quality for persons who felt constrained by social inequalities and repressive political systems in their own societies. Many of the most creative European writers and theorists of the 1830s and 1840s were therefore drawn to Paris and to the thriving exile communities in which they could promote their ideas. This exile migration included Germans, Poles, Russians, and Italians destined for fame: Heinrich Heine, Karl Marx, Adam Mickiewicz, Alexander Herzen, Mikhail Bakunin, and Giuseppe Mazzini.

The German exile Arnold Ruge, who in the 1840s collaborated with Marx on the short-lived *Deutsch-Französische Jahrbücher,* summarized a common political assumption when he claimed: "Alone in Europe, France represents the pure and unalterable principle of human liberty." He added: "One can judge the intelligence and independence of a man in Germany by his appreciation for France." Although this was the most optimistic view of what the French republican tradition meant to European radicals in the nineteenth century (a view that lost credibility after 1848), it was by no means an isolated sentiment. It evokes the revolutionary, republican, and almost mythic meanings that French history carried for generations of foreign exiles.

The creation of the Second Republic in 1848 briefly attracted a new wave of migrants, but many more exiles, seeking refuge from upheaval and authoritarian regimes, would flow into the twentieth-century French Republics. They fled the Russian Revolution, Nazism, the Spanish Civil War, and (during the Fourth and Fifth Republics) the communist repression in Eastern Europe. More recently, exiles from Iran, Algeria, Vietnam, Cambodia, and sub-Saharan Africa have all settled in France—drawn in part by the republican tradition and the conception of human rights that Ruge and many others had described in the nineteenth century. The social and political reality for exiles in France often differed from the republican ideals of liberty, equality, and fraternity, but new exiles always continued to arrive. Every modern revolution, nationalist movement, and political cause seems to have had exiled advocates (or opponents) who settled for a time in republican France to formulate their ideas, condemn the ruling powers in their home societies, and plan their strategies for future action. Much like the French writers and political activists who opposed or supported republicanism in France from exile positions abroad, the foreign exiles in France used the history of French republicanism and republican political theories to define their own identities, aspirations, and fears.

References

Atkin, Nicholas. "France in Exile: The French Community in Exile." In Martin Conway and José Gotovitch, eds., *Europe in Exile: European Exile Communities in Britain, 1940–45,* 213–28. New York: Berghahn Books, 2001.

Baldensperger, Fernand. *Le movement des idées dans l'émigration française (1789–1815).* 2 vols. Paris: Plon-Nourrit et cie, 1924.

Barrows, Simon. *French Exile Journalism and European Politics, 1792–1814.* Woodbridge, Suffolk, UK: Royal Historical Society, 2000.

Carpenter, Kirsty. *Refugees of the French Revolution: Émigrés in London, 1789–1802.* London and New York: Macmillan and St. Martin's Press, 1999.

Carpenter, Kirsty, and Philip Mansel, eds. *The French Émigrés in Europe and the Struggle against Revolution, 1789–1814.* New York: St. Martin's Press, 1999.

Godechot, Jacques. *The Counter-Revolution: Doctrine and Action, 1789–1804.* Translated by Salvator Attanasio. New York: H. Fertig, 1971.

Greer, Donald. *The Incidence of the Emigration during the French Revolution.* Cambridge, MA: Harvard University Press, 1951.

Harsanyi, Doina Pasca. *Lessons from America: Liberal French Nobles in Exile, 1793–1798.* State College, PA: Pennsylvania State University Press, 2010.

Johnston, Robert H. *"New Mecca, New Babylon": Paris and the Russian Exiles, 1920–1945.* Kingston and Montreal: McGill-Queens University Press, 1988.

Kramer, Lloyd S. *Threshold of a New World: Intellectuals and the Exile Experience in Paris, 1830–1848.* Ithaca, NY: Cornell University Press, 1988.

Mehlman, Jeffrey. *Émigré New York: French Intellectuals in Wartime Manhattan, 1940–1944.* Baltimore: Johns Hopkins University Press, 2000.

Payne, Howard C., and Henry Grosshans. "The Exiled Revolutionaries and the French Political Police in the 1850s." *American Historical Review* 68 (1963): 954–73.

23

The USA, Sister Republic

François Weil

Translated by Arthur Goldhammer

republicanism *n* (1689) 1: adherence to or sympathy for a republican form of government 2: the principles or theory of republican government 3: *cap* a: the principles, policy, or practices of the Republican party of the U.S. b: the Republican party or its members

"There is no word in the English language less intelligible than republicanism," wrote former president John Adams in 1807. To begin our exploration of the fluctuating meanings of the term since the birth of the American Republic, one can refer to the definitions above, from *Merriam-Webster's Collegiate Dictionary,* eleventh edition. The history of American adherence to or sympathy for a republican form of government begins with the choice of a government without a king or hereditary nobility. But that is not the end of the story.

In the British colonies of North America, adherence to republican government was not common, because republicanism and its associated ideals were widely disparaged. The word evoked the city-states of antiquity; European republics such as Venice and the United Provinces, which were not very attractive to eighteenth-century observers; and above all the dictatorship of Cromwell, which followed the fall of Charles I and the establishment of the English Commonwealth. Many Americans were fascinated with antiquity, but prior to 1776 American political rhetoric, with few exceptions, emphasized the decline of the ancient city-states and the Roman Republic. For most commentators, the ideal regime was the constitutional monarchy that England established after the Glorious Revolution of 1688, which Montesquieu had described as achieving the perfect balance among Aristotle's three forms of government: aristocratic, monarchic, and democratic.

The colonial critique of republicanism, which was shared even by future revolutionaries such as John Adams, did not stand in the way of either criticism of the English monarchy or, in practice, colonial political independence from the mother country. Indeed, we can assume that the pragmatism of the colonists was such that the future Americans were in many respects republican in practice, even if they criticized republicanism in theory and did not recognize it as their own. In other words, the British colonists in North America drew on an ideology that would subsequently be baptized republican in search of references, ideas, and modes of action that ultimately shaped their society. Thus the presence of an implicitly "republican" school of thought in colonial America should lay to rest the once widely accepted idea, due primarily to Louis Hartz, that America has been primarily a liberal society since colonial times.

Americans became aware of their republicanism early in 1776, thanks in large part to Thomas Paine's luminous pamphlet *Common Sense*. But this revelation did not resolve the question of what form the republican regime ought to take, what its limits ought to be, and what it should require of citizens. The Declaration of Independence laid down the principle that sovereignty should arise from the will of the people, but it did not proclaim a republic, and the only mention of a republican regime in the Constitution of 1787 occurs in Article 4, Section 4, which simply states that "the United States shall guarantee to every state in this Union a republican form of government."

Nevertheless, the first generation of Americans was conceptually well-armed to meet the challenge of the new era inaugurated by the rupture of colonial ties to Britain. Of course it was no simple matter to define the content of revolutionary and postrevolutionary republicanism. As Bernard Bailyn and Gordon Wood have shown, the republican project drew on various traditions, including that of English radicalism, which it adapted to its own political goals. Before 1776, the critics of republicanism, who knew their Machiavelli and Montesquieu, pointed out that a republican regime required a virtuous citizenry. Since the success of the American colonies depended on their commercial spirit, they were scarcely in a position to demand the frugality that republican virtue seemed to require.

But the revolutionaries stood this argument on its head. From the classic republican tradition of civic humanism, which had been transmitted to the colonies by way of France and Britain, the new Americans took a certain moral severity and utopian vision of the world. At the heart of this worldview was the idea of virtue, that is, the supremacy of the common interest over special interests. This virile idea of virtue became the cornerstone of the new Republic, whose citizens, independent and equal before the law, were joined together in one organic community based on the delegation of authority.

What republicans proclaimed was the necessity of virtue, not its universality. They saw no fundamental contradiction between the republican project and the exclusion of slaves or the subjection of women. What counted most was the translation of republican principles into law, which the Constitution of 1787 achieved thanks to James Madison and the solutions he offered to the problems of sovereignty and the separation and balance of powers.

But if republicanism was to endure, it had to be passed on and taught to future generations. From this need came the ideal of the republican mother, whose home became the primary institution for instilling virtue in future citizens. This ideal also resolved the question of how women were to be integrated into the republican project (in a subaltern position): the ideology of domesticity confined woman to the home, but there she was assigned a patriotic mission whose political significance was obvious to all.

In addition to receiving civic instruction at home from republican mothers, the question of how young Americans should be brought up and educated was one of the central issues of the early decades of the Republic. Benjamin Rush, one of the most fervent proponents of improved American education, put it this way: "We have our forms of government, but we still need to revolutionize ideas, opinions, and manners so as to adapt them to the forms of government we have chosen." Rush's wish became a reality with the gradual increase in the number of elementary schools, the pace of which was still accelerating in the Northeast and Midwest in the 1830s and 1840s. Along with the home, the schools became a crucible of republicanism. Textbooks such as Noah Webster's *American Spelling Book* (1783) helped to create a common culture and a republican mythology. In this mythology the figure of George Washington loomed large, the first president having experienced a veritable civic apotheosis after his death.

More surprising, perhaps, is the civic role played by political parties in the early nineteenth century. Many American revolutionaries, including John Adams, Thomas Jefferson, and George Washington, had seen parties as a threat to the republican ideal, yet they soon came to be viewed as schools of citizenship and political engagement that helped Americans to maintain their ties to the community.

The republican aspirations of revolutionary-era Americans were a source of anxiety because they felt compelled to live up to their lofty ideals of morality and civic virtue. They feared the emergence of an aristocracy and vowed to prevent it. That is why Jefferson and Franklin fought so hard against the Society of the Cincinnati, an organization of former officers that was created at the end of the Revolutionary War. Even Washington, though not hostile to the organization at first, quickly turned against it as many people came to believe that the Cincinnati saw themselves as the nucleus of a hereditary American nobility. But the nascent Republic seemed to hold appeal for many, which encouraged people to believe in its future. One reason for its success, which was by no means assured, was that the Tories, the Republic's most zealous opponents, fled after Britain's defeat. In their absence, republican ideology was free to develop without challenge to its basic principles. The successful integration of women as "republican mothers" and the exclusion of slaves and Indians from the political sphere also contributed to this success.

※

American republicanism was not a straightforward copy of classic republicanism. It was distinguished in particular by its relation to commerce, to which civic humanism was antipathetic. American republicans were generally much more nuanced: they advocated virtuous commercial growth, defined by hostility to excess of all sorts but not to necessary production. In other words, they favored economic development controlled in such a way as to ensure that commercial activity would not endanger the independence of citizens and thus, potentially, the survival of the Republic. Commercial growth and territorial expansion were not ends in themselves for Madison and Jefferson but rather means to preserve the republican project.

Hence republicanism was not incompatible with a certain liberalism, although historians carefully distinguish between the two for analytical reasons. As Jean Heffer has noted, republicanism and liberalism "were not distinct in eighteenth-century minds. As contradictory as it might seem, Americans were to varying degrees both republicans and liberals." They embraced the Lockean version of liberalism, combining self-interest with moral judgment. The Jeffersonian coalition that formed in the 1790s and struggled to win the presidential election of 1800 attracted those Lance Banning calls "liberal republicans," individuals who combined Locke's liberalism with civic humanism by adapting both traditions to the American environment. Jeffersonian republicans rejected the Federalist ideal of deference in favor of a republican ideal that laid the groundwork for later democratization. Robert Shalhope summed up the result as follows: "In many ways, republicanism—a familiar ideology that informed all aspects of life—shaped American thinking. It gave Americans meaning and identity. Liberalism—which at the time was more an unarticulated behavioral model than a well-defined mode of thought—unconsciously shaped their daily activity. Most Americans subscribed to a harmonious and organic conception of themselves and of American society, while conducting their daily lives in a materialist and utilitarian manner."

In the nineteenth century, a period of economic growth and territorial expansion, liberal republicanism triumphed. Yet it was subject to major changes and challenges over the course of the nineteenth and twentieth centuries as contemporaries reevaluated the liberal republican synthesis. Republicanism was first pushed in a democratic direction during the Jacksonian era, as the public sphere was expanded to accommodate some who had previously been excluded. The democratic dynamic was slow and incomplete, to be sure, but non-propertied white men were included in the 1820s and white women in the 1920s. Many of the struggles to which these changes gave rise did not draw directly on republican ideology, however. Rather, they pointed up republicanism's shortcomings with respect to egalitarian and democratic principles. The situation of African Americans was even more complex. Indeed, the Southern states invoked the republicanism of the revolutionary era against what they perceived as a conspiracy led by a party that called itself Republican. The ensuing Civil War, which represented the most important frontal attack on the political regime in place since the 1780s, led to the abolition of slavery and thus marked the beginning of a long process of integrating African Americans into the civic community. With the failure of Reconstruction, however, it was not until the 1950s that the process really began to bear fruit.

The liberal republican synthesis of the early nineteenth century also became the object of two contradictory assaults in the decades that followed. The first attack drew on classical economics and social Darwinism, which enjoyed immense success after the Civil War. Both of these ideologies advocated a version of liberalism that was individualistic and profit-oriented, the exact opposite of classical republicanism. Lockean liberalism was abandoned in favor of the Hobbesian version of the doctrine.

Instead of criticizing republicanism in the name of individualism, other Americans felt that the liberal component of the dominant ideology was receiving undue emphasis at the expense of the republican component. Thus, between 1820 and 1860, the American working class, from the textile mills of Lowell, Massachusetts, to the artisans and shop workers of New York City, borrowed the political and moral vocabulary of republicanism to restore what many saw as a lost balance.

Similarly, the populists of the late nineteenth century rejected not so much capitalism as its excesses. They did so, once again, in the name of republicanism (and not because they were marginal, irrational elements or the vanguard of a mass democratic movement). They accused industrial capitalism of creating monopolies that distorted competition, and proposed instead a "democratic capitalism," in which small producers would be able to compete against large corporations. Similarly, the Progressives of the late nineteenth and early twentieth century drew on the vocabulary of republicanism and adapted it to the demands of the moment. They refurbished the idea of public interest and developed new ideas about social cohesion in forging a critique of what they saw as the liberal and individualistic turn of the late nineteenth century. Similarly, the reformist liberalism that dominated the American political landscape from the New Deal until the end of the 1970s rejected classic economic liberalism in favor of an ideal of solidarity and a vision of community ultimately derived from republicanism.

The many avatars that republicanism has known in the course of what Daniel Rodgers has called its "career" have given it a certain protean character, which can be disconcerting. Its semantic range extends from classical republicanism to liberal republicanism and on to republican liberalism. Furthermore, the party that called itself Republican captured the word in the 1850s and ultimately diluted its meaning until it became little more than a term for patriotism expressing a certain collective aspiration and what Abraham Lincoln called the "emotional bonds" that joined the citizens of the American Republic in a single Union. Republicanism was not so much a coherent ideology as a catalog of references, ideals, and aspirations on which Americans have drawn for more than two centuries.

References

Appleby, J. *Liberalism and Republicanism in the Historical Imagination.* Cambridge, MA: Harvard University Press, 1992.

Bailyn, B. *The Ideological Origins of the American Revolution.* Cambridge, MA: Harvard University Press, 1967.

Banning, L. "Jeffersonian Ideology Revisited: Liberal and Classical Ideas in the New American Republic." *William and Mary Quarterly* 43, no. 1 (1986): 3–19.

Gerstle, G. "The Protean Character of American Liberalism." *American Historical Review* 99, no. 4 (1994): 1043–73.

Hartz, L. *The Liberal Tradition in America: An Interpretation of American Political Thought since the Revolution.* New York: Harcourt, Brace, 1955.

Pocock, J. G. A. *The Machiavellian Moment: Florentine Political Thought and the Atlantic Republican Tradition.* Princeton, NJ: Princeton University Press, 1975.

Rodgers, D. T. "Republicanism: The Career of a Concept." *Journal of American History* 79, no. 1 (1992): 11–38.

Shalhope, R. E. "Republicanism and Early American Historiography." *William and Mary Quarterly* 39, no. 2 (1982): 334–56.

———. "Toward a Republican Synthesis: The Emergence of an Understanding of Republicanism in American Historiography." *William and Mary Quarterly* 29, no. 1 (1972): 49–80.

Wood, G. *The Creation of the American Republic, 1776–1787.* Chapel Hill: University of North Carolina Press, 1969.

24

The Local

Stéphane Gerson

The local as jetsam of the Republic: such was until recently the orthodox view about modern France. The story held that the one and indivisible Republic, committed as it was to equality and unity, tolerated neither local prerogatives nor internal diversity. "France must not be a collection of small nations. She is a unique whole," declared the abbé Sieyès. Camille Desmoulins echoed this view: "We are no longer from Aix or Arras. We are all French, we are all brothers." The Revolution stifled expressions of local autonomy, association, and individuality. So did the regimes that followed. Republicans were not the only protagonists, but they seemed more offended than others by claims made on behalf of the commune and the municipality, the parish and the *pays*. Traveling across the provinces in the 1830s, historian Jules Michelet dismissed the local spirit as an "internal dissidence" that reeked of privilege and social inequality. Excessive attachment to a specific territory could redirect loyalty away from the nation. Intemperate affection for the locality could likewise cloak the necessary communion, fraternity, and solidarity that underlay a true republic. And exclusive concern with local interests could lapse into egoism, corporatism, intolerance, and social fragmentation. This *esprit de clocher* threatened the public good and refuted the Republic's Kantian universalism—whose abstraction negated individual differences—by narrowing intellects, closing off horizons, and rooting individuals in their milieu. At the turn of the twentieth century, republicans could thus lambaste the local as the preserve of rural superstitions, aristocratic nostalgia, and the New Right's cult of immemorial traditions. Moribund and retrograde, it slowed the formation of a modern, republican France.

This story of disquiet and rejection endured by appealing to both the Republic's defenders and its critics. It also coincided with accounts of modernization in which a centralized (republican) state, expanding markets, improved communications, and literacy did away with local, backward ways of thinking. There is plenty of evidence to support all of this, and yet the story is incomplete. Recent scholarship, much of it skeptical of modernization theory and partial to cross-pollination between center and peripheries, unveils a more complex state of affairs. Here, antagonism and apprehension mingle with collusion and attraction before a local that, as both a whole and part of a whole, could seduce and mystify at the same time. The Republic's misgivings are real, but no more so than its turn to the local as a frame of reference and a locus of self-definition, a framework for action and a set of practices. The local is where the Republic has sought to renew its own foundations. It is where its twin inclinations toward change and conservatism have come into full view. And it is where it has confronted its own tendencies toward uniformity and central control.

Doctrine is the necessary starting point, and it rapidly leads to the history of the state, institutions, and cultural practices. It is common knowledge that French Jacobins entrusted the central state with the tasks of defending the general interest, promulgating equality, and enlightening the citizenry. But republicanism comprises other strands besides Jacobinism, most notably municipalism. Convinced that democracy hinged upon vibrant local political life and that an overbearing state harmed civic activity, nineteenth-century moderates such as Jules Barni and Jules Simon called for municipal emancipation within a national political framework. As a space of political participation and local government, the commune gave expression to an ideal of citizenship that fused liberty and order, suffrage and the leadership of local elites, rights and responsibilities, law and education. It was the linchpin of republican democracy—a means of grappling with the contours of collective life, the limits and organization of governmental authority, and the social distribution of power. The Parisian writer Aristide Guilbert hence argued that republican democracy and national renewal required administrative decentralization, expanded attributions for municipal councils, and a truly national history. His six-volume *Histoire des villes de France* (1844–48) left the capital for the provinces, where the communes had gloriously sought "guarantees for the protection, the prosperity, the rights, and the liberties of all in the republican forms of election, justice, taxation, and administration." Decades later, the young Third Republic combined parliamentary democracy, central regulation of local interests, and expanded attributions for mayors and municipalities. The communes, said politician Pierre-Étienne Flandrin, would continue to govern in the name of the collective interests they embodied. If politics entailed participation, initiative, free expression, debate, and negotiation, then the local became a daily civics class.

Granted responsibility and measured autonomy within a republican institutional framework, the commune came into its own as the birthplace of national opinion, a counterpart to autocracy and bureaucratic centralization, and a place of social experimentation. Everything did not percolate from the top down.

Instead, much reform began at the local level. Municipal life generated what one historian calls "mini-welfare states," as local reformers built public housing complexes and retirement homes, stadiums and public pools, medical clinics and insurance systems to promote public health. This was true in the late nineteenth century and during the interwar period too, in the wake of a conflict that displayed all too clearly the need for government aid.

Sometimes, the central state generated local initiatives. At other times, local initiatives provided blueprints for governmental action. This dual dynamic comes into full view in the realm of pedagogy. By the end of the nineteenth century, republican (and some liberal) circles had·thought through the relationship between the local and the national. First, the local was a small, often-neglected, but indispensable building block of a stronger national edifice. Second, the local provided an obligatory conduit toward national self-understanding. Localities learned about themselves; they learned about one another; and France grew aware of its identity as a diverse yet united nation. Third and most important, the local was the familiar setting in which citizens learned to love a place and abstract values. Founded on sentiments and solidarity, this local sense of place taught people to look beyond their personal circumstances, toward larger, abstract communities that were not always visible. By fusing affective and familial referents with a civic rhetoric, this pedagogical model promised to recompose the *grande patrie* through the *petite patrie*. The local yielded "true national love" and revitalized the French public spirit.

Such ideas circulated in philanthropic associations, learned societies, provincial newspapers, religious gatherings, and city halls. In the small town of Montargis in the 1840s, the radical deputy Louis-Marie de Cormenin and other residents turned their city hall's great room into a permanent commemoration of great men and virtuous actions born in the local soil. Directed toward children and adults of all classes, the venture would inspire emulation and instill those values—service, utility, merit, patriotism—that underlay good citizenship. At century's end, the republican lawyer Edmond Groult founded more than seventy *musées cantonaux* to extol all aspects of local life, from natural history to great men. Coupled with conferences, guided tours, and festivals, these museums deepened affection for one's place of residence and developed patriotic sentiments among the local citizenry.

This cult of the *petite patrie* benefited from more direct state support as well. In 1848, the minister of public instruction asked prefects to follow the example of Montargis and encourage the creation of local pantheons. It is in the locality, said the minister, that one had to praise illustrious figures, modest citizens, and those public and private virtues that made the *pays* proud and the Republic strong. But it fell upon the Third Republic to turn this idea into a national policy, define the local in terms of its affective relationship with the national polity, and make the *petite patrie* a keystone of civil participation and national identification. Far from imposing an indivisible vision of France on their pupils, republican schools adapted their programs to local circumstances and inculcated a local sense of belonging. A loose but widespread pedagogy took form, with concrete *leçons de choses* (lessons of things) in a local milieu instead of abstract teachings and irrational utopias. The *petite patrie* was a miniature nation and the launching pad for a cognitive and affective progression from the locality to the nation.

The young Republic thus predicated French grandeur and its own long-term prospects not only on an imperial civilizing mission, but also on internal diversity and a local sense of belonging. Gambetta's well-known quip that "the Republic will be won in the town halls" did not only mean that the new regime would conquer a rural electorate that had supported the Second Empire. It also expressed a pragmatic desire to convert various constituencies to its political project by addressing communal matters and displaying the regime's concern with the local. It furthermore reflected the conviction that the education of virtuous citizens had to begin in the locality. "The child's soul," said Jules Ferry, "moves effortlessly from knowledge of the *petite patrie* to knowledge and love of the *grande.*"

Such was the path of renewal for a wounded, divided nation, still recovering from the dual trauma of military defeat against Prussia and the Communard uprising. These unfortunate events seemed to show all too clearly that the French did not know or love their country with as much depth and passion as the Prussians. The latter had mastered topography and formulated a *Heimatkunde* that progressed incrementally from the family to the locality, the region, the nation. In France, this republican pedagogy persisted after the First World War, whose terrible casualties softened French nationalism while exacerbating rural nostalgia—the locality as refuge for the nation. The Popular Front likewise embraced a local diversity that countered doctrines of racial unity, turned the countryside into a reservoir of popular values, and promoted the study of one's locality as a critical posture.

This local pedagogy long focused on the countryside because that is where most Frenchmen lived and because new modes of transportation, new paths of mobility, and new social and political claims made many republicans anxious about rapid, disruptive change. The nefarious consequences of such changes were clear enough: rabid ambition, moral dissolution, and political unrest. Rural depopulation proved especially alarming, even if the number of migrants jumped less dramatically than many believed. The Republic's pedagogical ventures hence captured its contradictory impulses. Alongside civic education and new opportunities for social promotion would come social harmony, organic community, and a mythical rural France whose residents accepted social hierarchy. Groult spoke of "a concert of thankful voices" in which all classes forgot their mutual mistrust and the living conversed with the dead. The regime likewise sought both to moralize French citizens (without resorting to Catholic doctrine) and to root them in their locality, where they would occupy their allotted place within the social order. Schoolteachers inculcated modesty of behavior and aspirations.

Modesty had long had its place among classical republican values, alongside austerity and subordination of the self before the public good. Rousseau asserted that the citizens of Geneva, all of them equally devoted to their laws, displayed the modesty, gravity, and respectful resolve of individuals secure in their rights and duties. During the Revolution, the Jacobin backlash against individuation made modesty the order of the day. "Education in France must teach modesty, politics, and war," declared Saint-Just. Jacobin modesty was a moral quality, part of a simplicity of mores that tapped Roman stoicism and eschewed suspect honors. This virtue overlapped with the sociological modesty of ordinary citizens who devoted themselves to the public with greater purity than exceptional but self-centered individuals. The cult of modesty thus fed social change, but it could prove more cautious as well. In ensuing decades, modesty and the local came together as responses to Paris-centered ambition and delusional aspirations that weakened the social order. By downgrading personal expectations, modesty became the cornerstore of a social world in which heroic resilience constituted an acceptable alternative to stirring victory and, more commonly, public failure. Reconciliation with one's modest fate would avert the sorrow of punctured aspirations and ensure that individuals with adequate skills occupied all social functions. Cormenin told schoolchildren to emulate not Parisian celebrities but those ordinary yet virtuous individuals who had led a peaceful life in and for their locality. Renown in the *pays* trumped fame in the capital; renown of the *pays* trumped recognition of any one individual.

The republican marriage of localism and modesty comes into full view in the President's journeys across the provinces. Plenty of kings and emperors had embarked on such tours over the centuries, but the Republic turned them into permanent tools of governance. Sadi Carnot launched the practice. The seventeen journeys he took in the 1880s and 1890s reflect the fragility and resourcefulness of a regime that faced inventive opponents. The Assumptionists' modern-day pilgrimages drew hundreds of thousands of traditionalist Catholics to Lourdes and elsewhere. Likewise, the populist General Boulanger traveled from one city to the next by train, depicting himself before huge crowds as a true man of the people. The President's journey was thus several things at once: a response to such challenges, a mode of legitimation for the new regime, and a civics lesson. Rather than drawing citizens to the capital, the President came to them. Everything was carefully planned as he traveled from province to province, locality to locality, *petite patrie* to *petite patrie*. At each stop, there were folkloric ceremonies, paeans to local celebrities, and episodes from the town's history. Like Michelet's tour of France, the President's journeys embodied and bolstered the unity of a country that was diverse yet unified through its political ideals, its representative institutions, and its communications networks.

Beyond this familiar synthesis, the local became a means of legitimating new national institutions. From the Third Republic to the Fifth, the President has periodically left his Parisian abode in order to personify the regime in situ and renew his direct connection with the electorate. "Vive Lons-le-Saunier, Vive la République, Vive la France!" declared de Gaulle in 1962...in Lons-le-Saunier. In town after town, the Republic and the media have manufactured enthusiasm and acclamations that appear spontaneous and unanimous. The local population, the landscape, and elected officials capture the revivifying virtues of *la France profonde* (or, more recently, *la France d'en bas*). This local France is grounded and apolitical, authentic and harmonious. It is a place of heartfelt relationships, where things are real, and people tell it like it is. Towns are modest, people are modestly virtuous, and the Republic too can express its inherent modesty. The President has left the capital to celebrate people and places and institutions rather than his own person. In Paris and abroad, he cannot escape the rituals of power and the necessities of political self-glorification. In these localities, by contrast, he can claim to recover the natural simplicity of a head of state who, unlike monarchs or emperors, eschews personal glory. The local revitalizes and counterbalances the Republic's tendencies toward pomp and formal symbolism, its latent cult of the leader, and its central, distant rule.

In some cases, however, the state's cult of the *petite patrie* merely provided a conceptual framework. When governmental efforts met natural limitations, due to diffidence or indifference, municipal or private ventures took over. Tourism illustrates the point. An incipient industry took form during the Belle Époque, in a context of growing leisure time and motorized travel. Day travelers and hikers set out to explore bucolic villages. Local tourism then benefited from the reconstruction impetus and the heightened concerns about rural depopulation that followed the First World War. The Touring Club de France and other associations advocated a cultural tourism that would create jobs in the countryside, improve local living conditions, and push residents to invest themselves in the locality's past and future. Eager to entertain, they instructed the country's new tourist offices to transport visitors into a picturesque Old France by maintaining traditions, preserving monuments, and staging festivals and processions. After the war, dozens of cities from Brittany to Provence launched tourism campaigns around the local past, folklore, and cuisine.

The local remained a resource during the second half of the century, especially after the economic crisis of the 1970s. The central state played a secondary role. The recession weakened schemes of planning and partnership between this state and cities. As municipal autonomy became the new modus operandi, mayors sought to forge new coalitions and find local (even private), rather than governmental, sources of revenue and municipal notoriety. The local acquired a new resonance as a place of experimentation, solidarity, and cultural affirmation against a backdrop of global uniformity, anxieties about immigration, and a crisis of political representation. Open-air markets and historical pageants have accordingly flourished since the 1980s. These stagings of the local promise economic dividends to municipalities that have seen other revenue streams dry up. They also constitute cultural resources: troves of memories and collective activities around which municipalities can undertake the symbolic reconquest of forlorn city centers, unite old and new residents, and define local solidarity against American-led materialism.

Since the Second World War, municipal welfare states have lost most of their prerogatives to the central authorities. But municipalities can still take matters into their own hands if these authorities seem overly timid. When Le Kremlin-Bicêtre celebrated its centennial with historical pageants and a monograph in 1996, it was both building on the Republic's cult of the *petite patrie* and palliating its shortcomings. This venture countered social dislocation and sought to integrate recent immigrants by turning residents old and new into vested citizens of a town that they now knew intimately. A similar yearning for local intimacy and solidarity transpired during the bicentennial of the French Revolution in 1989. The organizers staged elaborate festivities in Paris and encouraged communes to commemorate the Revolution in their own way. While Jean-Paul Goude's televised parade celebrated universalism on the Champs-Élysées, countless towns excavated inherently local memories and honored local communities. Revolutionary history became a synecdoche for a broader local past. Nostalgia and fear of change came into play, but so did a quest for meaning and coherence, for community and sacred ideals. As a historical horizon and a mode of voluntary association, the local proved more concrete than abstract universal referents and more tangible than a Republic and a nation that seemed distant, incapable perhaps of unifying the social body.

Some of these provincial commemorations reacted, to be sure, against the Republic's preoccupation with the center, its affection for Paris, and its reservations about particularism. The regime's commitment to local diversity and development has not always met the expectations of French citizens. Michelet's vision of the local as internal dissidence still imprints the Republic's DNA. But so does a conception of the local as alter ego of the Republic's penchants for abstraction, centralization, bureaucracy, and homogeneity. Here as elsewhere, to speak of a stark opposition between the local and the Republic simplifies a far more complex situation. Whether their organizers and participants knew it or not, the local commemorations of 1989 built upon what had been accomplished in provincial classrooms around 1889.

The republican conception of the local as place of initiative and renewal, of integration and edification, of pacification and legitimation, has sometimes faded from view or grown blurry. Still, the local has repeatedly promised and sometimes delivered what the central state, the capital, and national frameworks could not provide on their own. Sometimes, it is a new blueprint for collective life. Sometimes, it is a refuge from history. And sometimes it is a clear-eyed understanding of the Republic's conceptual tensions and limitations.

References

Bensa, Alban, and Daniel Fabre, eds. *Une histoire à soi: Figurations du passé et localité*. Paris: Éditions de la Maison des Sciences de l'Homme, 2001.

Chanet, Jean-François. *L'école républicaine et les petites patries*. Paris: Aubier, 1996.

Dumons, Bruno, and Gilles Pollet. "Espaces politiques et gouvernements municipaux dans la France de la IIIe République: Essai sur la sociogenèse de l'Etat contemporain." *Politix* 15, no. 53 (2001): 15–32.

Garcia, Patrick. *Le bicentenaire de la Révolution française: Pratiques sociales d'une commémoration*. Paris: CNRS Éditions, 2000.

Gerson, Stéphane. *The Pride of Place: Local Memories and Political Culture in Nineteenth-Century France*. Ithaca: Cornell University Press, 2003.

Mariot, Nicolas. *Bains de foule: Les voyages présidentiels en province, 1888–2002*. Paris: Belin, 2006.

Ploux, François. "Une mémoire de papier: La monographie de commune, expression et vecteur du culte des petites patries villageoises des années 1840 à l'entre-deux-guerres." Mémoire pour l'habilitation à diriger des recherches, Université Paris I-Sorbonne, 2008.

Smith, Timothy B. *Creating the Welfare State in France, 1880–1940*. Montreal: McGill-Queen's University Press, 2003.

Thiesse, Anne-Marie. *Ils apprenaient la France: L'exaltation des régions dans le discours patriotique*. Paris: Éditions de la Maison des Sciences de l'Homme, 1997.

Young, Patrick. "La vieille France as Object of Bourgeois Desire: The Touring Club de France and the French Regions, 1890–1918." In Rudy Koshar, ed., *Histories of Leisure*, 169–89. New York: Berg, 2002.

Part III

DILEMMAS AND DEBATES

25

The Republic and the *Indigènes*

Emmanuelle Saada

Translated by Renée Champion and Edward Berenson

At first glance, the fate of France's *indigènes* could be interpreted as one of the Republic's major internal contradictions. By denying indigenous peoples full citizenship and the benefits of the Declaration of the Rights of Man, the Republic seemed to overlook the universality of its own values, or to deny the humanity of the *indigènes*. It was to restore a semblance of consistency with their definition of the social contract that republicans outlined a means by which the "worthiest" *indigènes* could be integrated into the national community. And, in a vast corpus of doctrine concerning colonized subjects, Republicans also felt compelled to justify the exclusion of all others.

Yet, a closer look at the situation of the *indigènes* reveals not a set of contradictions, but rather a powerful way to understand two essential features of the republican regime: how it dealt with "otherness," and precisely what it meant to belong to the body of French citizens.

Before the notion of *indigène* appeared in the middle of the nineteenth century, much of the drama destined to unfold in the colonial period was already in place. It was in the founding moments of the French Revolution, in connection with "people of color," whether free or slaves, that the first breach of republican principles appeared. Despite pressure from the Société des Amis des Noirs (Society of Friends of the Blacks), the antislavery positions of Enlightenment philosophers, and the impassioned speeches by the abolitionists abbé Grégoire and the marquis de Condorcet, free "men of color" did not gain civil and political equality until 1792, and the emancipation of slaves was promised but put off. Their ultimate emancipation resulted less from the triumph of Enlightenment principles than from facts on the ground. Slave revolts in Saint Domingue forced the Convention (the French revolutionary parliament) to free the island's slaves in August 1793. Elsewhere in the French Caribbean, slaves rose to demand a Republic true to its name, one that would grant them freedom and equality and universalize the French Revolution. As a result of their intervention, abolition was extended throughout the colonies in February 1794.

It lasted just eight short years. In 1802, Napoleon Bonaparte reinstituted slavery and then revoked the civil and political rights that the Revolution had granted "people of color." They were now forbidden to enter metropolitan France and to legally register interracial marriages. During the July Monarchy, the debates of the Revolution flared up again with new priority given to equality. A law of 1833 ruled out any distinction among French nationals, guaranteeing to "each person born free or having legally acquired freedom" the benefit of civil rights and "political rights under the conditions prescribed by law." This text did not apply to Algeria, the conquest of which began with the taking of Algiers in 1830, followed by full annexation four years later. As for the debate over liberty and the abolition of slavery, it was postponed until the 1840s, when it began to engage an educated public. The debate was resolved after the Revolution of 1848, when the Provisional Government decreed on April 27, 1848, "the immediate abolition of slavery."

This decision freed some 250,000 men, women and children, and it immutably linked liberty and equality in the exercise of citizenship. The antislavery advocate Victor Schoelcher, president of the commission created to prepare the abolition decree, was instrumental in granting citizenship rights to former slaves. He refused to transform former slaves, in his words, into "half-citizens, quarter citizens, political hermaphrodites." France, the commission affirmed,

> has just provided the nations of the world an example for all eternity. It has reestablished the form of republican government that had once extended civilization far and wide, and it has rejected slavery. The Republic no longer intends to make distinctions within the human family. She does not believe that it suffices to boast of being a free people, while remaining silent about an entire class of men excluded from humanity's common rights. She has taken her principle seriously. She intends to make amends for the crime that took these unfortunate souls from their parents and from their native countries, by giving them France as their motherland and allowing them to inherit all the rights of French citizens; she has thus clearly demonstrated that she does not exclude anyone from her immortal motto: "Liberty, equality, fraternity."

The message was heard: slaves from the four "old colonies"—Guadalupe, Martinique, Guiana, and Réunion—abandoned their shackles to become citizens. This transformation took place without the lag time that would later characterize the North American experience. Starting in 1848, the colonies sent deputies to Paris, some of whom, like the representative from Guadalupe, were men of color. Despite these unprecedented gains, Schoelcher's commission re-introduced a "distinction in the human family" by agreeing "not to pre-judge the situation of native populations" in Algeria, that is, not to give them full citizen-ship rights. Thus, in freeing slaves and having them join the community of citi-zens, the Republic paradoxically turned all native residents of the newest French colonies into *indigènes*, "subjects" of the colonial empire bearing a particular per-sonal status that excluded them from political rights. Schoelcher had justified the attribution of political rights to former slaves by evoking "the moral effect" that "participation in the creation of laws" could have. He suggested, in effect, that more than two hundred years of bondage had prepared slaves for citizenship by inculcating them with their masters' customs. In the second half of the century, colonial officials would commonly make this oddly paradoxical argument.

The inhabitants of colonies without a slaveholding past benefited from no such "moral" preparation. Their status remained to be defined. In 1848, male residents from nonslaveholding territories conquered before the nineteenth century—what became the "four mixed communes" of coastal Senegal and French possessions in India—gained the right to vote, but without having the nature of their citizenship defined. This ambiguity would be the source of fierce debates in the years to come. As for Algerian natives, leaders of the Second Re-public deliberately avoided any effort to clarify their fate; they would remain in legal limbo for nearly two decades. A simmering controversy over their nation-ality was resolved by the court of Algiers, which in February 1862, decided that France's annexation of Algeria gave its inhabitants the status of "French nation-als" but did not make them French citizens. They were to remain different from the "French from France," as "French subjects" deprived of citizenship rights. The dissociation between nationhood and citizenship was consecrated by the *sénatus-consulte* of 1865, which declared the Algerian "Muslim *indigènes*" and "Jewish *indigènes*" to be French nationals without the benefit of "civil and political rights."

The Third Republic remained within the broad outlines of these earlier de-velopments. Its treatment of the *indigènes* has long been neglected by historians who have emphasized the process of nationalization of French society between 1870 and 1900. They have described how the French state traced a sharp divid-ing line between "French" and "foreigner" by mobilizing an expanding legal and administrative apparatus and through new legislation, most notably the na-tionality law of 1889. What historians have mostly overlooked is the Republic's analogous effort to categorize people in the colonies, which led to the crystalliza-tion of another system of oppositions, this time between "citizen" and "subject."

In this regard, the Second Empire would, in retrospect, appear more liberal than the Republic that followed it. The *sénatus-consulte* of 1865 introduced in Al-geria the possibility for "Muslim *indigènes*," "Jewish *indigènes*," and "foreigners" to acquire citizenship on an individual basis. In October 1870, France's wartime government of the National Defense went even further with its Crémieux decree, granting citizenship collectively to the Jews of Algeria. The Third Republic would not revoke this decree, though it would limit its application to Jews who resided in the territory of Algeria in 1830 and their descendants.

More generally—and paradoxically—it was the Third Republic that defined the legal status of the "subject," which until then had been poorly distinguished from that of the foreigner. In a burgeoning body of texts on colonial law, the subject's status was defined simultaneously by its submission to France's sovereignty and by its nonparticipation in this same sovereignty: the subject was a French national who was not a citizen. Subjection constituted a major breach of the Rousseauian social contract by reintroducing a gap between nationality and citizenship that French metropolitan law had tended to erase, at least for male adults. The act of defining certain French nationals as subjects possessing fewer rights than other French nationals (i.e., citizens) violated the principle inherited from the French Revolution that each individual enjoys a single, unified legal status and that all individuals are equal. As a specialist in colonial law put it, "[There] exists in the colonies, and in the protectorates, several kinds of French. They can be divided into three categories: the French strictly speaking, having the full rights granted by this title; French subjects; and French *protégés* [the population of the French protectorates: Tonkin, Annam, Laos, Cambodia, Tunisia, and Morocco]."

But there is more at work here than a contradiction between the principle of equality and the reality of colonial exclusion. In fact, the distinction exposes an essential dimension of republican citizenship: its anchorage in culture, civilization, and even race. In effect, France's entire colonial doctrine conspires to link the deprivation of political rights to the enjoyment of a specific personal status defined by a set of local customs, incompatible with the norms of France's Civil Code. As Pierre Dareste, the eminent specialist in colonial law, observed in 1916, "no one ever accepted" that an *indigène* would follow "rules diametrically opposed to the Civil Code" and "nonetheless (potentially) receive a voting card, influencing through his vote the choice of deputies, general and municipal counselors, even running for election and holding office in French assemblies where the making of laws inapplicable to him are discussed on a daily basis"(Dareste 1916, 8).

This observation leads us back to the initial concepts of citizenship defined during the Revolution by Emmanuel-Joseph Sieyès among others, in which civil equality stood out above all else. Sieyès "imagined law at the center of an immense globe; all citizens, without exception would be located at the same distance on the circumference and occupy equal places." But as the Revolution played out, civil participation became a function of an individual's social condition rather than a right. After the fall of Napoleon, a revived republicanism restored Sieyès's original conception of civil equality, creating a new understanding of suffrage defined as a fundamental right. To exclude colonial natives from exercising this right, jurists introduced a new, more rigid way of articulating morality, civilization, and citizenship. In explaining why natives could not be citizens, French jurists focused on mores and religion, especially in discussing Muslim natives. Legal writers argued that since Muslim codes of behavior stemmed from the Qur'an, their judicial system could never accept the secularism fundamental to the principles of French public law. Muslims would stand outside the law, and thus outside citizenship as well.

But the situation of French converts to Islam living in Algeria demonstrated that religion was more than a matter of faith. French citizens could not be demoted to subjects or permitted to follow the precepts of the Qur'an rather than the standards of the Civil Code. Polygamy, in particular, remained a crime for them. Conversely, Algerians who converted to Christianity would not automatically become citizens. Instead, they acquired the status of "Christian Muslim *indigènes,*" as a 1903 judgment by the court of Algiers called them. In jurists' minds, it was not religion but rather origins or, in the vocabulary of the late nineteenth century, "race" that determined personal status and, therefore, justified the denial of citizenship. This conception was inspired both by the conservative republicans' philosophy of history, a philosophy that, following Taine and Renan, made race a central element in the formation of civilizations, and by more recent theories of evolutionism and social Darwinism.

Unto each race, its civilization; unto each civilization, its law. As a colonial administrator affirmed, "personal status is the law that governs each individual according to his race" (Asmis 1910, 23). This argument, often cast positively as "respect for native customs," was intended to be "realistic." The republican doctrine of the late nineteenth century rejected the supposed idealism of 1848, characterized by the "theory of assimilation" and blindness to "differences between races." The new and more rigid conception of the late nineteenth century maintained that, but for rare exceptions, citizenship in the Third Republic's colonies was limited to Europeans. These late-century ideas moved jurists to dismiss the 1848-era ideas that had given citizenship, en masse, to former slaves. Insufficiently "evolved," inhabitants of the Caribbean and Réunion were considered to fit poorly in the French political community.

Colonial domination, therefore, led to an inversion of revolutionary logic according to which equality between men forms the foundation for equality of rights. By the early twentieth century the prevailing doctrine now held that the difference of legal systems and civilizational norms justified the hierarchy of status. Thus, in 1918, Marius Moutet, future president of the League of the Rights of Man and the Front Populaire's future minister of colonies, opposed a parliamentary bill designed to standardize accession to citizenship in the different colonies. "If we want to be practical," he declared, "we must definitely give up the idea of a mystical unity of human beings all equally capable of accepting and adapting themselves to the same laws."

By linking citizenship to "civilization," French officials permanently postponed all projects designed to grant citizenship rights to natives, even the most educated and French-acculturated among them, who retained their particular personal status in private matters. Although colonial reformers repeatedly proposed to grant the right to vote to Algerian *évolués* (estimated to be twenty-four thousand in 1936), doing so first in the Second Empire, then in 1911 in the *Revue Indigène,* during the First World War, and finally in the Popular Front's Blum-Violette bill of 1936, the *colons* and their supporters rejected even such a compromise measure out of hand. Within this framework, the situation in the French possessions in India and the Four Communes of Senegal appears to be the exception that proves the rule. If the interim government in 1848 had granted the right to vote to the inhabitants of these territories, it "had not anticipated...the great difficulty of treating a Muslim or a Hindu exactly like a French person from France." But even in these exceptional cases, although Africans and Indians received voting rights, their citizenship, strictly speaking, remained an object of debate. Over time, the distinction between the Four Communes and the French settlements in India on the one hand and the rest of the empire on the other became even more pronounced. In India, in 1881, French officials gave natives the ability to "renounce their particular personal status" and thus become part of French citizenry by simply affirming their desire to live under the exclusive jurisdiction of French law. This possibility, however, was quickly withdrawn three years later when the colonial government reestablished two separate electoral colleges, one reserved for "European French citizens," the other for "natives, whether citizens or not." In the midst of the First World War, Blaise Diagne, Senegal's representative to the French parliament, succeeded in enacting a bill giving full citizenship rights to all *originaires* of the Four Communes (those who ancestors already lived there in 1848). This law was immediately qualified an aberration, and jurists would interpret it narrowly and limit its application. In the colonies, the horizon of citizenship would remain out of reach for most people.

The dissociation of nationality and citizenship would cease only with the Constitution of 1946, which conferred the title of "citizens of the French Union" on all inhabitants of the colonies. But by creating separate electoral colleges, the Republic reproduced its long-standing distinction between "French strictly speaking" and subjects of France. The "Loi-Cadre" (Overseas Reform Act) of 1956 proposed full universal suffrage with no distinctions between Europeans and *indigènes,* but it came too late to have much political significance.

Throughout its history, the imperial Republic not only excluded natives from the ranks of French citizens by defining them in terms of their customary legal status; it also violated some of its most fundamental principles by imposing on its subjects a set of repressive measures alien to the traditions of republican law. These measures were embodied in the *Code de l'indigénat,* voted by Parliament in 1881 for Algeria, and then extended to all colonies populated by "subjects." This code established a distinct colonial order by creating a list of special legal infractions that, by definition, only natives could commit. These infractions were peculiar to the colonial realm; they existed nowhere in France's Penal Code. For example, *indigènes* could be punished for expressing "disrespect to the administration and its civil servants." Because the *Code de l'indigénat* violated bedrock republican principles such as the separation of powers and the equality of punishments, it faced opposition in France and thus had to be presented as "temporary"—even though French parliaments regularly renewed it until 1944, when these special colonial laws were abolished altogether.

The colonial period was thus characterized by a differential treatment of the *indigènes.* "The mystical unity of human beings" gave way to a human hierarchy that placed Europeans at the top. Asians came next, followed, in order, by North Africans, Madagascans, sub-Saharan Africans, and, on the lowest rung of this evolutionary ladder, New Caledonians. All but Europeans found themselves excluded from citizenship, although, in theory, the non-European peoples were believed capable of evolving toward civilization and thus citizenship, if at different rates. This colonial hierarchy led to variable applications of the *Code de l'indigénat* and different procedures for acquiring citizenship, as well as unequal educational opportunities, public health policies, and approaches to the management of labor. It is unsurprising, therefore, that a prominent textbook on constitutional law affirmed that in the colonies "the ideology we inherited from the French Revolution has suffered one setback after the other: (1) the metropole is organized along liberal lines, our colonies along authoritarian ones; (2) our law assumes the inherent equality of men; our imperial system presupposes the inequality of races; (3) we unceasingly proclaim the people's right to self-determination, but we do not extend that right to our colonies, which we forbid to secede" (Barthélemy and Duez 1985 [1933], 288–89).

For a time, several accommodations allowed this system of contradictions to be acceptable in metropolitan France and the colonies. Throughout the empire, officials envisaged procedures to permit the most "worthy" (*dignes*) natives to attain the status of citizen. But even repudiating one's local status—the legal and cultural norms governing indigenous social life—proved a necessary but insufficient condition for the acquisition of citizenship rights. Candidates were therefore few in number, and those chosen for the "highest distinction to which *indigènes* can aspire" even rarer. The conditions were Draconian, and very few met them. The rare ones who did held diplomas of higher education or had pro-vided "exceptional services" to wartime France or to the country's economic life. But even the most exceptional often found themselves refused citizenship by a colonial administration loath to judge candidates "worthy" enough. In the 1920s, only a few dozen natives achieved French citizenship each year in an empire with some sixty million inhabitants.

Despite these restrictions, a colonial bourgeoisie developed thanks to the growth of positions for native people as intermediaries between the dominant power and the *indigènes*. Beginning in the early twentieth century, a sizable group of *évolués* broke with the earlier generation's strategy of pure anticolonial resis-tance by applying for French citizenship. The Republic would mostly reject them out of hand. Refusing to create the status of "evolved citizen" or to allow part of this elite to enter collectively into the French citizenry, the Republic would not open the door to citizenship even slightly until the 1930s. Taking this refusal as a given, the following generation borrowed from the repertoire of both national-ism and internationalism to oppose a republican France untrue, in the colonial sphere, to its own principles. This generation would not hesitate to turn France's values against it, as demonstrated, for example, in the letter that the FLN (Alge-rian National Liberation Front) addressed to the French people on May 20, 1956: "The prestige of France lies in its principles of liberty, equality, and fraternity, principles that we have learned to cherish as a tradition that today is denied by those who hold in their hands the destinies of your country."

This understanding of French republicanism, which distinguishes two con-tradictory faces of the Republic—the rights of man and the *Code de l'indigénat*—was instrumentalized as a general nationalist strategy. It has also been adopted by all those who consider the dissociation between nationality and citizenship a "judicial monstrosity," in contradiction to "true" republican values. But far from an aberration localized in colonial time and space, the split between na-tionality and citizenship also characterizes the situation of those who have been denied political rights—women, the insane, children, criminals—based on the putative limits on their participation in civil society. Beyond this mirroring ef-fect, the colonial situation must also be analyzed as a phenomenon in itself, as a rupture in the universalist conception of citizenship, which in the colonies was solidly anchored in civil status and strongly linked to the notions of civilization and race. Just as the *indigène* was a subject by virtue of a personal legal stand-ing incompatible with French civilization, so the French individual living in the colonies was a citizen by virtue of his allegiance to the Civil Code, which became, within this context, nothing less than the customary law of the *indigènes* of France. In the colonies, the French nation revealed itself as having racial traits, and this understanding of French identity would leave its mark on the postcolonial Republics to come.

References

Anonymous. "La nationalité aux colonies." *Recueil de legislation, de doctrine et de jurisprudence coloniales,* II (1911): 9–18.

Asmis, Dr. "La condition juridique des indigènes dans l'Afrique Occidentale française." *Recueil de legislation, de doctrine et de jurisprudence coloniales,* II (1910): 17–48.

Barthélemy, J., and P. Duez. *Traité de droit constitutionnel.* 1933; Paris: Dalloz, 1985.

Bonnichon, A. *La conversion au christianisme de l'indigène musulman algérien et ses effets juridiques (un cas de conflit colonial).* Paris: Recueil Sirey, 1931.

Burbank, J., and F. Cooper. "Empire, droits et citoyenneté." *Annales, Histoire, Sciences Sociales* 3, no. 63 (2008): 495–531.

Dareste, P. "Les nouveaux citoyens français (loi du 29 septembre 1916)." *Recueil de legislation, de doctrine et de jurisprudence coloniales,* II (1916): 1–16.

Dubois, L. *A Colony of Citizens: Revolution and Slave Emancipation in the French Caribbean, 1787–1804.* Chapel Hill: University of North Carolina Press, 2004.

"La naturalisation des musulmans dans leur statut." *La Revue Indigène* 63–64 (July–August 1911) and 66 (October 1911).

Shepard, T. *The Invention of Decolonization: The Algerian War and the Remaking of France.* Ithaca, NY: Cornell University Press, 2006.

Solus, H. *Traité de la condition des indigènes en droit privé: Colonies et pays de protectorat et pays sous mandat.* Paris: Recueil Sirey, 1927.

Weil, P. *How to Be French: Nationality in the Making since 1789.* Translated by Catherine Porter. Durham, NC: Duke University Press, 2008.

Werner, A.-R. *Essai sur la réglementation de la nationalité dans le droit colonial français.* Toulouse: Imprimerie F. Boisseau, 1936.

Wilder, G. *The French Imperial Nation-State: Negritude and Colonial Humanism between the Two World Wars.* Chicago: University of Chicago Press, 2005.

26

Immigration

Mary Dewhurst Lewis

Immigration has raised fundamental questions about the very nature of French civic life, as the arrival and settlement of immigrants have repeatedly amplified the tension between the pluralism inherent in democracy and the unitary thrust of French republican ideology. This dilemma now spans most of modern French history. While much of Europe witnessed emigration in the nineteenth century, France received an influx of foreigners: the country's immigrant population nearly doubled from 1870 to 1890 and increased another third by 1921. As of 1931, France's rate of foreign population growth was the highest in the world, surpassing that of the United States. By the time its continental neighbors became net recipients of immigrants, after the Second World War, France had been an immigrant society for nearly a century. Yet ever-shifting social and economic circumstances continue to inject the immigration issue into public life in new ways.

Crucially, the onset of mass immigration to France accompanied the consolidation of democratic rule under the Third Republic. Since that time, with the Vichy years from 1940 to 1944 a notable exception, France has encountered immigration as a republic. Thus issues pertaining to immigration have been filtered through the lens of a republican conception of citizenship whose origins lay in a revolutionary Jacobinism that eschewed difference in the name of radical equality and uniformity. This often has meant a certain intolerance toward the distinctiveness of immigrant culture, whether the Catholic piety of Italians and Poles at the turn of the twentieth century or Muslim expressions of faith in the twenty-first. But the Republic has also promoted the universal rights of man, making France an apparent haven for workers and refugees and a country where the children of foreigners acquire citizenship with relative ease. Even so, the promise that republican egalitarianism holds for immigrants and their families has been forestalled repeatedly by reactionary political movements, labor protectionism, deportation drives, and discrimination. The social unrest visible in France in recent years shows the extent to which this is true. Indeed, there has been no single "republican" stance toward immigration; over time, French leaders have repeatedly implemented new policies in response to rapidly changing economic conditions or social transformations, only to find that the complexities of modern society defy uniform legislative or administrative solutions. For all the country's vaunted centralization and organization, the story of immigration in France reveals not only the extent but also the limitations of state power.

The coincidence of mass immigration and a return to republican rule in 1870 served simultaneously to limit and expand the rights of the country's new immigrant workforce. The effort to placate recently enfranchised working-class voters led to social legislation that, according to historian Gérard Noiriel, helped native workers identify themselves as "French" by distinguishing their rights from those of the non-French. Legislation from this era barred foreigners from holding union office or participating in employee councils—restrictions that mostly remained in place until the early 1980s. Unlike in the United States, where a working-class foreign-language press flourished, France's immigrant press had to contend with an 1881 law that barred foreigners from directing any periodical. Moreover, the state retained the right, based on an 1849 law aimed at political militants, to deport any foreigner without cause and without appeal. The integration of the working class into the Republic thus came with a price: the bifurcation of French and foreign rights, which both built on and bred popular xenophobia. But other legislation from the same era produced opposite effects. Among the young men living on French soil, only those with French citizenship faced military conscription. To prevent employers from preferring foreigners, whose work would not be interrupted by military service, Parliament liberalized the country's citizenship laws. In 1889, a major reform of the nationality code adopted the principle of double *jus soli,* which granted citizenship from birth to third-generation descendants of immigrants. By the same legislation, children born in France to foreigners born abroad could acquire citizenship at adulthood, provided they remained domiciled in France at that time.

If these reforms incorporated the children of foreigners into the French nation by making them eligible for military service, they also served to shore up white privilege in colonial Algeria, where a majority of "settlers" hailed from southern Europe and Mediterranean islands. By allowing these settlers to gain French citizenship, the 1889 law increased the number of white Frenchmen in the colony, while continuing to relegate Muslims to a separate status. Thus, even as lawmakers limited the rights of adult foreigners living in the Hexagon, they integrated their children—and their counterparts in Algeria—permanently into the Republic and its empire. Today's citizenship law is a liberalized version of the 1889 code, but this liberalism has its limits. Unlike U.S. law, which automatically confers nationality on anyone born in the United States, French law usually grants citizenship to the French-born descendants of immigrants only at adulthood, thus building in a lengthy socialization period.

From the beginning, socialization occurred primarily at work and in working-class communities, since it was France's rapid industrialization in the latter part of the nineteenth century that brought immigrants to the country en masse. Initially arriving from as close as Belgium or Italy, immigrants answered the call of employers in every imaginable economic sector—coal mines, steel mills and textile plants, farms and quarries, docks and sugar refineries, among others. Often an outgrowth of regional and seasonal migration, international migration mirrored these patterns at first: Belgians were prevalent in northern France's mining, metallurgy, and farming sectors, while Italians flocked to manual labor and factory jobs in the farms and cities of the south. While economic opportunity was the primary lure of immigrants, it was not the only one. Eastern European and Russian Jews fled to France after religious persecution drove them from their homes, only to arrive in the 1890s at the height of France's own anti-Semitic movement, epitomized by the Dreyfus affair. Jewish migrants played an important role in manufacturing and small business, becoming especially prevalent in a number of commercial and craft trades. Before long, clusters of immigrants had emerged in every industrial region and most major cities of France.

During the First World War, France's immigrant population diversified further as state officials recruited migrants to serve in war industries and as farm laborers. Numbering well over four hundred thousand, they came from as nearby as Italy, Spain, and Portugal, and as far away as Greece, North Africa, sub-Saharan Africa, Indochina, and China. Unlike laissez-faire nineteenth-century migration, wartime migration was heavily regulated, as heightened security concerns led to more state scrutiny of those who entered. Police activity was also expanded and modernized to monitor the whereabouts and behavior of the migrants once admitted.

After the war, even as they retreated from their intensive involvement in the economy, state authorities crafted migration policy in response to the war's consequences, which had increased the need for migrants all the more. Western-front fighting not only had killed a million and a half men and permanently disabled as many more, it also had devastated much of northeastern France, which could not be rebuilt without imported labor. Elsewhere, weapons manufacture had advanced France's industrialization, spawning enormous round-the-clock factories and a voracious need for workers. These developments also heightened a technocratic obsession with France's population size and anemic birthrate, already worrisome to officials before the war. Migrants became both the solution to and a constant reminder of this problem.

Once it was clear that the need for migrant labor had not ceased with the armistice, the question became who should enter and on what terms. France's answer to this question was to establish what amounted to Europe's first guest-worker system (though it was never given that name). The idea had originated with the labor unions, which, expecting the peace settlement to yield uniform labor laws across Europe, called for foreign labor and "workers of color" (by which they meant colonial subjects) to arrive on temporary contracts, receive the same salary and benefits as native workers, and return home upon the contract's expiration. All of this would be guaranteed by states in consultation with organized labor.

But for several reasons the harmonious give-and-take of workers across borders never came to pass. First, the war had unleashed the twentieth century's first refugee crisis, sending large numbers of Russians and Armenians to France for reasons other than the quest for work (although of course many wanted and needed jobs). Although these people had no obvious way to return home when they encountered unemployment, it took several years for this reality to penetrate official thinking. Until it did, refugees who lacked work often faced expulsion and, when they refused to leave, incarceration. Second, the guest-worker program was a product of diplomacy and, as such, mirrored postwar Europe's divisions. Preference in recruitment went to allies, which meant Italians before the neutral Spanish, and the Spanish before enemy Germans. Although French nationals from the colonies had aided the war effort by fighting in French regiments or working in munitions plants, colonial subjects received no official standing in this new regime. Indeed, at the war's end, colonial workers frequently found themselves "repatriated" even as new European workers were recruited.

The Depression of the 1930s engendered a backlash against immigrants, not least from the very unions that once had planned their recruitment. Quotas were placed on the number of foreigners allowed employment in many industries, and repatriation drives were especially successful in the company towns of the heavily industrial north and northeast, where employer paternalism facilitated round-ups. To make matters worse, growing xenophobic and anti-Semitic movements exploited the coincidence of the Depression with the arrival of new refugees, especially from Germany, and pressured the government to adopt tougher policies. In this hostile climate, expulsions of immigrants increased, often for minor infractions of the law. Overall, however, the Depression put the guest-worker system to the test. Guest workers had made lives for themselves in the communities where they worked and often resisted being forced to return home. Expulsions often proved impossible to enforce, and the increased incarceration of refractory expellees did little to change this situation. Over time, the guest-worker model was gradually replaced in practice, albeit not in policy, by the selective incorporation of families as more permanent settlers. Yet this new inclusiveness had an underside: in making decisions about residency, local officials were encouraged to "discriminate" between "worthy" and "unworthy" immigrants, though even the "worthy" often found their status insecure in the lead-up to the Second World War. In those years, immigrants of all kinds were viewed as potential threats to national security. Arrests, expulsions, and incarcerations increased—in prisons and in newly formed internment camps—only to be reversed in cases where officials deemed immigrants useful to the war effort. On the eve of war, the Republic's treatment of immigrants reached new levels of incoherence as its officials frantically struggled to distinguish friend from foe. Still, this difficult situation grew markedly worse after the fall of the Republic, when the authoritarian Vichy regime extended internments and made foreign Jews the first targets for deportation to certain death in Nazi camps.

It was in part to avoid the haphazard measures of the interwar era that immigration policy was systematized in the aftermath of the Second World War. Unlike any previous time in its immigration history, France now also had to compete for immigrant workers with other European countries, which also had lost huge numbers of working-age people. Even before the end of the war, General Charles de Gaulle identified the population problem as the "principal obstacle to our recovery." Accordingly, the postwar government abandoned the idea that all migrants should be temporary guest workers. Instead, it codified the experimental practices of the interwar years by authorizing three types of residency: "temporary," "ordinary," and "privileged." The three categories referred to the length of time for which the immigrants were initially admitted—one year, three years, and ten years, respectively—and to differences in the rights each type of immigrant would have. Both temporary and ordinary immigrants would be limited in where they could work and live, while permanent immigrants were free to move about the country at will. To coordinate recruitment and settlement policy, the government created the National Immigration Office (ONI).

Despite an unprecedented degree of planning, immigrant recruitment fell short of employer demand throughout the 1950s. The extraordinary economic boom of those years, marked in particular by a rapid expansion in the consumer market, created a huge need for labor. Spontaneous foreign immigration, subject to ad-hoc "regularization" after entry, made up some of the gap between the demand and supply, but industry became increasingly dependent on France's colonies for its personnel. Ironically, this dependence on colonial labor emerged precisely as the empire's days appeared numbered. In an effort to weaken the appeal of nationalist movements, the French government granted a form of commonwealth citizenship to colonial peoples, which allowed individuals from the newly christened "French Union" (and later "French Community") to circulate freely between colony and metropole, thereby sidestepping the controls of the ONI, which organized migration from foreign countries exclusively. As a result, Algerian immigration to the metropole increased nearly tenfold between 1946 and 1954, and while the Algerian war of independence (1954–62) stemmed this tide, it did not halt it. By the war's end, Algerian immigration to the metropole had again increased by more than 150 percent. After independence, the two governments negotiated agreements maintaining the right of their citizens to free circulation between Algeria and France, and similar agreements were signed with the new governments of France's former colonies in sub-Saharan Africa. In 1961, the government also established an agency to encourage internal migration of French citizens from overseas departments, notably the Antilles islands of Martinique and Guadeloupe.

De Gaulle had hardly imagined such diversity when setting postwar immigration policy, having explicitly advocated "Nordics" over "Mediterraneans." The prospect of migration from colonies or overseas departments seems barely to have occurred to him. Although some members of the High Committee on Population shared de Gaulle's views, the committee's negotiations led to a more open-ended policy. Unlike the United States, France never systematically adopted country-specific quotas, and French immigration policy has always remained officially color-blind. At various moments following Algeria's independence, however, numerical limits on immigration were negotiated into bilateral agreements between the two countries, and the ONI also worked to offset the arrival of nonwhites through such means as establishing recruitment offices in select European countries.

As long as full employment continued, immigration remained mostly invisible to much of the larger population, especially since migrants' workplaces and housing tended to be concentrated on the periphery of urban centers. Poor living conditions in these periurban areas garnered little attention until the Algerian War, when it was feared that they might provide fodder to the National Liberation Front. In response, social services targeted Algerian families to teach them homemaking *à la française* in a real, if paternalistic and cynical, effort to "assimilate" Algerians as part of the larger struggle to keep Algeria French. But these same social-welfare programs also subjected Algerians to increased surveillance and raised barriers to their integration into vast newly constructed low- and middle-income apartment compounds, where they might have come into contact with their metropolitan French counterparts. Today these "*cités*" have fallen into disrepair and are known for unemployment rates many times that of the national average. By the measures of the day, however, the apartment complexes symbolized upward mobility and offered state-of-the-art amenities, making them popular among metropolitan French residents whose own households, according to a government poll conducted in 1954, often lacked running water or appliances such as washing machines and refrigerators. Over time, unprecedented postwar affluence—French GDP per capita grew 150 percent between 1950 and 1973—allowed many of the original residents of suburban projects to move into better housing. Only then did immigrants and their children become the *cités*' main inhabitants. In the meantime, immigrants often lived in a variety of marginal spaces: self-constructed *bidonvilles* (shantytowns) with no electricity or running water, built on muddy lots in the shadow of the new housing complexes; condemned buildings within cities; or purpose-built dormitories for men unaccompanied by family, where several crowded into a single room and endured the paternalistic oversight of the dormitory management. If the years of economic expansion after the Second World War were "glorious years," as Jean Fourastié called them, the state of immigrant housing made them glorious only for some.

As the era of active immigrant recruitment ended in the 1970s with the economic downturn of those years, immigrants paradoxically became more visible. In 1974, the government terminated foreign labor recruitment and canceled bilateral agreements assuring the free movement of former colonial subjects in and out of France, prompting workers to calculate that they could not afford to go home, even temporarily, out of fear that they would not be readmitted. Instead, more and more workers brought their families to France, permitted under provisions for family reunification, and the influx of wives and children increased immigrants' visibility at precisely the time the government had decreed immigration's end. So did the transition away from an industrial economy, as immigrants increasingly worked in the service sector, where citizens encountered them in their everyday lives. Immigrants' new prominence helped foster the erroneous notion that immigration was a "novel" phenomenon, a perception that Jean-Marie Le Pen ably exploited to build his xenophobic National Front (FN) into a potent political force.

It was to counter this misperception and the extreme right-wing politics facilitated by it that studies of immigration first began to proliferate in the early 1980s. Gérard Noiriel gave immigration a central role in his 1984 study of industrialization in Longwy and expanded this thesis into the groundbreaking *Le creuset français* (The French Melting Pot), published in 1988, the same year that Yves Lequin published an essay collection entitled *La mosaïque France*. Noiriel's book began with a stinging indictment of historians for leaving immigration out of standard accounts of French history. But by the time *Creuset* appeared, many other historians were already working to remedy this problem; as a result, the 1980s also saw the publication of numerous works on the different ethnic groups and nationalities that constituted the "melting pot" or "mosaic" of France. The implication of much of this work was not only that France had long been a diverse society but also that the present xenophobic moment eventually would pass. The sociologist Abdelmalek Sayad was one of the few scholars to dissent from this latter view, pointing to the structural disadvantages facing Algerians and certain other immigrant groups. Sayad was careful to place Algerian immigration in a larger context, but much other early work tended to focus narrowly on particular groups or places of settlement. In the 1990s, a spate of policy analyses examining immigration writ large remedied this narrowness of focus, but often at the expense of the human dimension to the story. It was not until the following decade that work on immigration examined both the everyday lives of migrants and the larger question of immigration policy, or considered these questions alongside the legacies of colonialism. Scholarship on immigration proliferated as political developments continually thrust the subject into public view.

As governments shifted between right and left throughout the 1980s, 1990s, and into the first decade of the twenty-first century, immigration policy vacillated between crackdown and liberalization, ensuring that immigration remained a hotly contested subject. The Right tended to adopt a hard-line approach, advocating immigrants' repatriation and limiting the renewal of their residency permits, measures apparently calculated to undercut the increasing appeal of the FN. Left-wing governments reversed some of the Right's harsher policies, allowing large numbers of illegal aliens to "regularize" their status in 1981 and again in 1997–98. The Left also restored the automatic ascription of citizenship at adulthood to French-born children of foreigners, which the Pasqua law of 1993 had modified. Since the 1980s, republican rhetoric has undergone a renaissance, as the Left and parts of the mainstream Right have sought to counter the FN's message by offering visions of a unitary and unified Republic allergic to the extremists' racist and xenophobic line. As during the 1930s, these efforts have produced uneven results. Anticipating the formal European Union accords of the 1990s, the French government waived the new restrictions on labor migration instituted in the early 1970s for nationals from countries in the European Community as well as those slated to enter, such as Spain and Portugal (which joined in 1986). These exemptions, combined with family reunification policies and a higher expulsion rate among former colonials, resulted in an astounding growth of the Portuguese immigrant community. Between 1968 and 1982, this population increased by over 250 percent, and in 1975 it represented almost a quarter of France's foreigners—more than the Algerians' share at the same date.

As politicians and pundits touted the republican model's supposed genius in integrating foreigners, activists took to the streets to demand that real life conform better to republican rhetoric. In 1983, following violent unrest in the Lyon suburbs, a group of second-generation descendants of immigrants, mostly of North African background, launched a "march for equality and against racism" that traversed France and grew to be a hundred thousand strong. The following year, the antiracism organization SOS-Racisme was founded. More recently, in 2005, a petition signed "Nous, les indigènes de la république" created an uproar by likening today's Republic to a colonial regime and the descendants of immigrants of color to colonial subjects or "natives." These movements and others like them have focused primarily on the rights of full-fledged citizens whose parents or grandparents were immigrants. But the plight of recent immigrants has also fostered new organizations, such as the Sans-Papiers movement, which emerged to defend undocumented aliens in the wake of the center-right government's crackdown on them in the early and mid-1990s. Composed primarily of Malians, the Sans-Papiers movement has contested the arbitrariness of expulsion practices with visible strategies such as the occupation of churches.

Despite activism on behalf of immigrants and their descendants, discrimination has proved difficult to combat, in part because France's republican tradition makes any official recognition of race or ethnic origin illegitimate. Nonetheless, French social life abounds with evidence of ethnic identification. The sobriquet "Beur," for instance, derived from the *verlan* (reverse-language slang invented in France's underprivileged suburbs) for "Arab," turned a derogatory use of the word "Arab" into a label denoting second- and third-generation descendants of North African immigrants. First popularized in the 1980s, when this generation aggressively asserted its right for recognition as at once French and "Beur," the word has since entered the general French lexicon. More recently, the development of a "black" politics in France—bringing together the concerns of individuals, whether French or foreign, of Antillean or sub-Saharan African heritage—has provided further confirmation of the nationality law's limited ability to structure experience. Indeed, the very insistence that the Republic knows no differences within its citizenry has contributed to the frustration of citizens from minority populations whose everyday experiences tell them otherwise. Police profiling, educational tracking, and poor housing have all contributed to a growing sense of disillusionment on the part of some descendants of immigrants. From time to time, such frustrations have erupted into riots, first in the early 1980s and, most dramatically, in the fall of 2005, when residents of France's ethnic suburbs reacted violently to the electrocution of two young men who took refuge in a power station as they fled police pursuit. The deaths triggered three weeks of unrest as rioters set fire to cars and public buildings.

If the 2005 uprising exhibited the frustrations of young French men of immigrant origin, the controversy surrounding headscarves in school has been a lightening-rod issue for teenage Muslim girls. In 2004, the French parliament banned the headscarf and other "ostentatious religious signs" from public schools. The headscarf ban stood out as an especially dramatic example of the recent policy shifts that have signaled a weakening confidence in the ability of France's republican institutions to forge a unified citizenry. When the republican school was founded in the 1880s, it was with the expectation that cultural conformity would be education's end result, not a litmus test for entering school in the first place. In our own time, new immigration policies have made a potential immigrant's French-language ability and acceptance of the "values of the Republic" a prerequisite for family reunification. If the early Third Republic expected immigrants to integrate after living in France for some years, the Fifth Republic's law of 2007 asks some of them to do so before even setting foot there. Of course, "integration" is an utterly subjective term, which is why the historian Pap Ndiaye has called the 2007 law a veritable "invitation" for arbitrary administrative treatment.

Indeed, it is the very lack of confidence in the power of "republican values" to unify present-day France that explains why immigration and the "integration" of immigrants' children have garnered so much attention lately. But this is nothing new. Debates over immigration have always been about so much more than meets the eye, for they reveal the contradictions of the republican project since the late nineteenth century: the impossible effort to reconcile democracy and imperialism, together with empire's lingering aftershocks, and the tensions between national unity and pluralism, freedom of religious expression and laicity, the principle of equality and the reality of social distinctions. In this sense, the question of whether immigrants share "republican values" somewhat misses the point: the notion of "republican values" itself has developed alongside the advent of immigration. The very definition of what it means to be French, as enshrined by the 1889 law and subsequent modifications, is a response to immigration. In the era of imperialism, the presence of colonial migrants in the metropole exposed the hollowness of the republican promise for some, and throughout France's immigration history, the treatment of immigrants and their children has repeatedly tested the Republic's claims to universalism and egalitarianism, while at the same time helping to define and put flesh on these concepts. In short, the story of the modern French Republic is inseparable from the human saga of immigration, present since the Republic's birth and a defining issue ever since.

References

Lequin, Yves, ed. *La mosaïque France: Histoire des étrangers et de l'immigration.* Preface by Pierre Goubert. Paris: Larousse, 1988.

Lewis, Mary Dewhurst. *The Boundaries of the Republic: Migrant Rights and the Limits of Universalism in France, 1918–1940.* Stanford, CA: Stanford University Press, 2007.

Lyons, Amelia. "The Civilizing Mission in the Metropole: Algerian Immigrants in France and the Politics of Adaptation during Decolonization." *Geschichte und Gesellschaft* 23 (2006): 489–516.

Ndiaye, Pap. *La condition noire: Essai sur une minorité française.* Paris: Calmann-Lévy, 2008.

Noiriel, Gérard. *The French Melting Pot: Immigration, Citizenship, and National Identity.* Translated by Geoffroy de Laforcade. Minneapolis: University of Minnesota Press, 1996.

Ponty, Janine. *Polonais méconnus: Histoire des travailleurs immigrés en France dans l'entre-deux-guerres.* Paris: Publications de la Sorbonne, 1988.

Sayad, Abdelmalek. *The Suffering of the Immigrant.* Preface by Pierre Bourdieu. Translated by David Macey. Cambridge, UK; Malden, MA: Polity Press, 2004.

Viet, Vincent. *La France immigrée: Construction d'une politique 1914–1997.* Paris: Librairie Arthème Fayard, 1998.

Weil, Patrick. *How to Be French: Nationality in the Making since 1789.* Translated by Catherine Porter. Durham, NC: Duke University Press, 2008.

27

The Immigration History Museum

Nancy L. Green

The opening of the Cité Nationale de l'Histoire de l'Immigration (CNHI) on October 10, 2007, clarified the distinction between two terms: opening and inauguration. The new museum opened its doors to great media attention, but it did so without any champagne or petits fours. Neither the President of the Republic nor the new minister of immigration, integration, national identity and codevelopment appeared, and no formal inauguration was ever held. This opening without an inauguration serves as a double reminder of how museums can be both a product of and a challenge to the French republican ideal: a product thanks to public funding, a challenge due to the politics surrounding both the institution and its subject matter.

From its origins, the "republican" museum has been a paradox. The contents of classical beaux-arts museums in France have most often been regalian if not imperial. The Louvre opened as a museum in 1793 to show artists and the public (on weekends) the royal collections and the art seized from émigrés. That later additions came from Napoleonic foreign pillaging tarnished the image of early nineteenth-century museum-making, and after Napoleon's defeat, many objects were returned. As Dominique Poulot has pointed out, the French museum is fundamentally republican: it represents the "culmination of the Enlightenment in that it is consecrated for the purpose of public enjoyment and national interest." The idea of museums open to all became a tenet of republican museum ideology. Under the Third Republic the debate over the role of museums expanded beyond the nonetheless recurrent question of where they should be located—Paris versus the provinces, that is, the Louvre versus local museums—to question their very purpose. Under Jules Ferry, the museum was conceptualized as an important accessory to civic education, thanks to its rigorous methods of historical classification and the pedagogy of class field trips.

While the content and object of the museum, classically defined, have remained those of the beaux arts, two concomitant trends expanded the very nature of museums in the second half of the twentieth century. Calls for the democratization of museum attendance (Bourdieu and Darbel) went hand in hand with expanded ideas of what museums should house and display. Ecomuseums and history and societal museums have turned mine shafts and textile mills into settings for displays. Just as Old Regime royal and noble finery entered museums as objects to be seen rather than worn in the nineteenth century, so nineteenth-century industrialization became an object of "museification" in the late twentieth century. Furthermore, the monarchical role of museum-makers would take on yet new life under the Fifth Republic as Presidents Georges Pompidou, François Mitterrand, and Jacques Chirac successively sought to leave their mark on national cultural institutions.

The history of creating a museum dedicated to immigration must thus be placed in a quadruple context, combining old and new: the continuing educational imperative; the resumed political impetus to museum-making; a break with the beaux-arts tradition of museums; and a new desire to reflect social issues such as immigration. It is the politicized conjuncture surrounding this last point that led to the opened but not inaugurated CNHI.

In October 2006, Minister of Culture Renaud Donnedieu de Vabres announced the coming museum by emphasizing its "premier role—that of maintaining and furthering the social pact which unites all of our people in the country [*concitoyens*] among themselves." A year earlier, in November 2005, the poor neighborhoods of the French *banlieues,* peopled by immigrants and their (French-born, French-citizen) children, had erupted in riots. The prolonged violence evoked sharp debates over history and memory and France's colonial past and made clear that significant numbers of immigrants and their descendants felt alienated from French society. In this context, the immediate political agenda behind the project seemed evident: perhaps a museum could save the suburbs by solidifying the social contract in giving due credit to the rioters' immigrant past. But beyond the immediate situation, the idea for the museum had a much longer history. The real question is, Why, after two centuries of immigration to France, three decades of historiography on the subject, and two decades of proposals for such a museum, had the project finally taken shape?

In deciding to recognize the foreign origins of much of France's population, the French Republic did not stand alone. During the second half of the twentieth century, renewed immigration, combined with a new historical sense of migrations past, moved cities from Adelaide to New York to Buenos Aires to begin planning history museums dedicated to this theme. New York's Ellis Island Immigration Museum was the one most often invoked in the planning for the CNHI, not least because of the common French trope of Franco-American comparison and because it symbolized what the French have often seen as an uninterrupted history of immigration to the United States since the Pilgrims. That the Ellis Island museum presents but a partial history of U.S. immigration, largely based on the experience of those European immigrants who passed through the island during its 1900–1914 heyday, is lost on most French (and many American) observers. But because Ellis Island is an important, high-profile museum symbolizing a long history of immigration, the CNHI understandably wanted to emulate its success.

The French project was a national one, and the museum's historical purpose was, from the outset, much broader than that of its New York counterpart: the CNHI intended to represent a vast panorama of all of French immigration history over the last two centuries. (The Ellis Island museum itself plans to expand in this sense.) Moreover, unlike Ellis Island, the CNHI was not built around a site where immigration had actually occurred; the project came first, the choice of the building later. Indeed, the edifice has been more a hindrance than a help. An early debate about where to place an immigration museum confronted the long-standing question of Paris versus the provinces. Suggested sites included Marseille, a historically major port of immigrant entry; Saint-Denis, on the northern outskirts of Paris, a heavily immigrant suburb today; and the abandoned Renault auto works in Boulogne-Billancourt, just southwest of Paris, where many immigrants had worked. In the end, Paris won out (as usual), with the idea that such a museum should be centrally located. Several buildings currently "available" within Paris were then examined, with the Palais de la Porte Dorée chosen because of its impressive character as a historic monument. But because the Palais had long been associated with French colonialism, the museum had to construct itself *against* the building in which it is housed, rather than thanks to it, as at Ellis Island. As a result, the CNHI project faced repeated criticisms over its location.

Built as the entrance hall for the Paris Colonial Exposition of 1931, the Palais de la Porte Dorée was one of the few buildings to remain standing after the Exposition closed its doors. Commonly referred to as the Musée des Colonies from 1932 on, the museum's plotline fell into disrepute along with colonization itself in the 1950s. With decolonization, the museum was saved only by Culture Minister André Malraux, who transformed it into the Musée des Arts Africains et Océaniens in 1960. In 2003, this museum closed its doors, its collections transferred to the new Musée du Quai Branly, inaugurated by President Jacques Chirac in 2006. The Porte Dorée building was now available for the CNHI, but using it for that purpose meant that a museum celebrating two centuries of immigration to France would be housed in a colonial-period relic.

Criticism came from three directions: first, that the immigration project would prevent use of the building for a critical look at the history of colonization (an alternative idea that had never taken shape); second, that the bas-reliefs on the outer wall and the elaborate murals in the main hall, however aesthetically striking, were nonetheless offensive for their stereotypical representations of the colonial "other" and unabashed hubris of France's old "civilizing mission" at the height of its imperial empire; and third, that the building's colonial background would overpower the long history of immigration to France that the museum was supposed to represent. Against these criticisms, the project's directors and historical advisory board argued (optimistically? too academically?) that housing a museum of immigration history in a former museum of the colonies could function as a clever, reverse symbolism, a veritable taunt to France's colonial past. Patrick Bouchain, the architect chosen to transform the building, reminded everyone that many buildings go through use changes, and argued that the transformation of a "palace of the colonies" into a "palace of immigration" could be a way of settling a score with history.

If Ellis Island's museification can be correlated with the renewal of the historiography and memory of immigration in the United States in the last third of the twentieth century, the new immigration history museum in Paris likewise arose out of the relatively recent rise in French interest in those phenomena. While the history of immigration to France itself is "old," historical knowledge and historiography have lagged behind historical fact. An article by Michelle Perrot in 1960 took an important step toward a new history of immigration by showing that immigrants had long been a significant part of the French working class. In 1972, the CNRS (Centre National de la Recherche Scientifique, France's major research-funding organization) took another crucial step by organizing a major conference on immigration and labor history. Conference participants, along with other historians, such as Serge Bonnet, Jean-Charles Bonnet, Philippe Dewitte, René Gallissot, Pierre Milza, Janine Ponty, Ralph Schor, Benjamin Stora, and Émile Témime, became interested in the history of immigration to France early on. A center for research on Italian immigration history, the CEDEI (Centre d'Études et de Documentation de l'Émigration Italienne), created in 1987, was the first of its kind. And then, in 1988, two books, both widely reviewed—*Le creuset français,* by Gérard Noiriel, and *La mosaïque France,* edited by Yves Lequin—marked and abetted a more general renewal of interest in the foreign origins of the French.

In 1990, an Association pour un Musée de l'Immigration was created to encourage the establishment of an immigration history museum, and a fact-finding mission went to visit the just-opened Ellis Island museum the following year. Largely for political reasons, nothing came of these initiatives. Museums are state-funded in France, and with the rise in the 1980s of a virulently xenophobic extreme Right, the Socialist government in power apparently did not want to be associated with a history museum devoted to such a high-profile, contested topic. The Republic's own history was thus seen as politically dangerous, given the politics of the late twentieth century.

At the same time, however, two private museum initiatives emerged, Génériques and Toute la France. Founded in late 1987, Génériques is a voluntary association devoted to "engaging and supporting all scientific and cultural activities that would further an increase in the knowledge of migration in France and in the world." With modest means but great determination, it began identifying and cataloging public and private archives in France, created a prize for the best dissertation on the subject, and founded a magazine, *Migrance* (in 1992). By 2005 it had completed a four-volume guide to archival sources on foreigners in France, coedited with the Archives de France. Génériques also set up one of the first temporary exhibits on the topic in 1989, entitled "France des étrangers, France des libertés" (France of Foreigners, France of Freedoms) and charting the history of immigration to France through the myriad of newspapers created by different immigrant groups.

The second important initiative, Toute la France (All of France), was an exhibit curated by the Bibliothèque de Documentation Internationale Contemporaine in 1998. Organized around groups (Russians, Poles, Algerians, etc.) and themes (e.g., education, sports, art, cuisine, the world wars), the highly successful exhibit suffered only from having too small a space. The need for a permanent museum dedicated to the history of immigration in France became more and more evident.

In 2001, as interest in a museum continued to grow, the Socialist prime minister, Lionel Jospin, commissioned a report on a museum project from Driss El Yazami (delegate-general of Génériques) and Rémy Schwartz (maître des requêtes of the Conseil d'État). Submitted in November 2001, it argued strongly in favor of the creation of a Centre National de l'Histoire et des Cultures de l'Immigration. Then nothing happened. Different reasons have been suggested to account for this: interagency governmental squabbling (jealousies, who was to pay?); political cold feet (again). The presidential elections of 2002 were approaching, and the Socialists apparently did not want to identify themselves too closely with a topic—immigrants—that the increasingly popular Far Right abhorred. The project was tabled. Jospin lost his bid for the presidency nonetheless, and Chirac was reelected.

In a surprising move (from the perspective of most immigration historians), Chirac's center-right government resuscitated the museum project. It may be that his crushing second-round victory over the right-wing extremist Jean-Marie Le Pen (85 percent to 15 percent) gave him the political capital to act. Some have mused that it was a demagogic ploy by a politician concerned with the ultimate historical verdict on his presidency. In any case, Chirac named a close political ally, Jacques Toubon, to head yet another committee: the Commission de Préfiguration du Centre de Ressources et de Mémoire de l'Immigration. Working closely with Luc Gruson, director of the Agence pour

le Développement des Relations Interculturelles, and Philippe Dewitte, director of the journal *Hommes et Migrations,* Toubon met with the commission for a
year. A museum project was officially approved in July 2004, with a scheduled
opening for April 2007. It is unheard of to open a museum within such a short
period of time, particularly one that does not have a preexisting collection, but
the French political calendar dictated the timing. Chirac wanted to inaugurate
the immigration museum before he left office in May 2007.

The creation of an immigration history museum in France was thus partly
due to the evolution of memory and historiography, as in the United States, but
also to French party politics. Many historians had expected a Socialist government to create it, and they were initially wary of the Chirac government's plans.
Historians' participation remained conditional on keeping the museum's content
free of politics. Toubon turned out to be an open, enthusiastic supporter of both
the museum and the historians involved, and because he imposed no overt political line on the exhibits, the project moved ahead.

However, the long delay from the initial idea of an immigration museum
in 1990 to its opening nearly twenty years later enmeshed the project in a set of
new and unprecedented political contexts unimagined decades before. Whereas
twenty years previously, such a museum might not have generated widespread
debate, by late 2005, race relations in France had deteriorated and become more
openly contested. Major events had pitted historians against lawmakers, and immigrants' children against the police. A law of February 23, 2005, that included
an article stipulating that school programs should teach the "positive role" of
French colonization angered a great many historians. They rejected the government's attempt to impose a particular historical analysis. (After a year of tergi-
versation, Chirac finally abolished the article.) Shortly after the Palais de la Porte
Dorée was chosen as the site for the museum, a group of *sans papiers* (undocumented immigrants) briefly occupied the grounds, arguing that money should
be allocated to living immigrants, not dead ones. And then came the riots of
November 2005, to which hard-line members of Toubon's and Chirac's party, the
UMP (L'Union pour un Mouvement Populaire, notably, then Interior Minister
Nicolas Sarkozy) responded with demeaning and xenophobic statements criticizing the second-generation youth. These developments produced a vigorous
public response on the part of immigration historians involved in the museum
project. In any event, it was materially impossible to open the museum before the
end of Chirac's term.

When Sarkozy was elected President of the Republic in May 2007, new problems arose. His creation of a Ministry of Immigration, Integration, National
Identity and Codevelopment moved eight historians on the museum's consulting board (including the author of this article) to resign. They did so not to protest the yet-to-open museum (which they continued to support) but to reject the

notion implicit in the naming of the new ministry, namely, that there is only one national identity possible in France. This idea contradicts one of the central premises of the museum. Neither the President nor any minister came to inaugurate the new museum when it opened in October 2007. Presumably, the new administration wanted to signal its disinterest, even hostility, to a Chirac-inspired project on a politically sensitive topic.

Since the CNHI, unlike the Ellis Island museum, was not initially defined by a historical period or (on the contrary) a building, the question of what exactly to represent shaped the initial discussions surrounding the scope of the future museum. While the French government sought, at least in the museum, to include immigrants in France's official history, there was considerable debate over who should be included. The Ellis Island museum was originally conceived to depict the "old" European immigration; only recently have its directors decided to include the post-1965 Asian and Hispanic immigrations as well. The French CNHI sought to present an all-inclusive history of immigration, representing the "old" nineteenth- and early twentieth-century European immigrations along with the post–World War II Portuguese, Spanish, North African, sub-Saharan African, Turkish, Chinese, and other mass immigrations. But CNHI directors made their plans in a contemporary political context in which colonial and postcolonial immigration dominate the late twentieth-century conceptualization of immigration to such an extent as to render earlier immigrations almost invisible.

Thus, not only did the CNHI have to negotiate the question of old and new immigration, it had to define the scope and meaning of "immigration" itself. One of the first choices had to do with the chronological range of the museum. Arguably, the history of immigration into France reaches back to Burgondes and Visigoths and includes, later on, itinerant clerics, artisans, the wandering poor, and the mobile nobility from the Middle Ages to the early modern period. Another viewpoint limits the history of immigration to the past two centuries on the grounds that it was the formation of the nation-state in 1789 that created immigration, henceforth defined as the act of crossing political boundaries with the intention to remain on the other side. This state-centered determination of who is an immigrant—as opposed to one based on immigrant experience—ultimately prevailed. Although a prologue to the main exhibit was to have reminded visitors of the longer history of movement into France, it disappeared in the final plans (but remains on the museum website), which limited the permanent exhibit to the last two centuries, with a far heavier emphasis on the twentieth than the nineteenth.

The question of state-determined identification papers versus experience in defining immigration was not just a matter of chronology. Another unresolved issue in the debates prior to the opening of the CNHI had to do with the place of French citizens who hail from abroad. Before Algerian independence, Algerians who lived in metropolitan France possessed French citizenship: were they "immigrants" or not? And what about "internal" movement to the Hexagon from France's overseas departments—Martinique, Guadeloupe, Guiana, and Réunion? Even though those coming from these departments possess French citizenship, they may experience movement as immigration, both through their own understanding and in the eyes of others. Historians are beginning to include Pieds-Noirs (the European, as opposed to Arab/Berber, residents of pre-independence Algeria) and French West Indians in the definition of immigration. The groups/individuals themselves can be divided between those who emphasize their citizenship and do not want to be melded into the category of immigrants and those affronted by the idea of being excluded from a museum of immigration. Memory and historical consciousness can furthermore change over time, complicating the question of who should be included in an immigration museum.

Beyond questions of chronology and inclusion there were also debates over the structure of the permanent exhibit. Three organizational principles were possible: sections devoted to different groups, a chronological presentation, or a thematic layout. One early version of the permanent exhibit had highlighted different groups whose presence marked the great waves of immigration to France since the nineteenth century. Ultimately this approach was abandoned, in keeping with the "republican" model of French immigration, which most French historians and sociologists have argued is distinct from an "Anglo-Saxon" multicultural one. That is, they have argued in keeping with the "republican" model, which insists on the equality of the unmediated individual in relation to the state, in contrast to a "multicultural" model, in which communities represent groups in social life and vis-à-vis the government. To make chronology explicit, the historians proposed, among other things, a time line spanning the exhibit. But the head curator and exhibit designer rejected this idea, preferring contemporary art, not historical pedagogy, for the walls, and seeking to keep textual displays to a minimum. The permanent exhibit was thus ultimately organized around neither groups nor time periods but around three major themes (not immediately apparent to the casual visitor): emigration, immigration and settlement (called, somewhat cryptically, Ici et là-bas, "Here and There"), and diversity (represented by film and music, the latter being mostly French songs referring to migration).

The very name of the new institution, Cité Nationale de l'Histoire de l'Immigration, so dubbed by the ministry, was also debated, each word reflecting discussions over the content of the museum. "Cité" was chosen instead of "musée" to the dismay of most of the commission's members. There had been heated discussion over the use of the word "museum." Officials from the Direction des Musées de France argued that the term was not applicable, since the project had no preexisting collection (of famous paintings?). The Commission de Préfiguration, however, felt strongly that the term both ennobled the project and recognized that museums were no longer the dusty dark places of yesteryear. To a non-native French speaker, the word "cité" also had the disadvantage of being frequently used to describe the lower-class housing projects in which poor immigrants and their offspring live. Native speakers countered that "cité" simply means "city," in the Greek sense of the term. Other recent museum projects in Paris have used the word to name their multifaceted activities: Cité de la Musique, Cité des Sciences et de l'Industrie at La Villette.

Also in question was the use of "nationale" for a museum devoted to immigration, a fundamentally transnational activity, especially since not all immigrants become naturalized. Did the term "nationale" represent an effort to impose an assimilationist republican project onto the site or simply to link the Paris museum to a national network of immigrant associations, which is one of the pillars of the project? Some argued that the term "nationale" showed the importance of the project to the centralized French state. For others, it was "un mot de trop." As for the word "histoire," it came to replace both "culture" and "memory," suggested in previous proposals. French historians, increasingly outspoken against identity politics, which they consider to be based on nostalgia for past identities, and adamant about the professional nature of academic history, were anxious to distance their work from that of memory, but many felt that culture at least could have been recognized in the museum title. In meeting after meeting, the term "immigration" also raised the question of emigration. To what extent would the countries of origin also be included in the story? Finally, an audience participant at one of the public conferences presenting the project even questioned the word "the" ("l'") preceding "history" in the institution's name. Wouldn't the plural, "histories," be more appropriate?

The Republic's use of museums as part of its civic educational mission does not obviate the problem of determining the content of that mission. Museum-making more generally is a matter of choices, all the more so in those museums dedicated to history or social themes. The problems of defining immigration in France are multiple and freighted by the term's often-derogatory connotations in popular parlance, especially as used in a rightist political discourse, which has long stigmatized Algerian and African immigration in particular, making these groups seem to represent immigration overall. (This is the opposite of Ellis Island, whose mostly positive story of European immigration has stood for the whole.) Immigration historians have argued that a view of the long history of immigration to France is necessary in order to understand both the specificity and the similarity of postcolonial migrations while at the same time widening the geographic scope to other parts of the empire (the Indochinese, often forgotten even in the recent postcolonial debates about immigration) and to those who have and continue to come from beyond the ex-empire (e.g., Turks, Chinese). Jacques Toubon, imbued with the very republican purpose of the project, repeatedly emphasized that the museum's aim was to change the very meaning of the word "immigration" in France, to shed its negative connotations.

Debate over the museum has continued after the opening, with some feeling it was too republican/assimilationist in perspective; others complaining that their group had been left out; still others considering that social problems had been slighted or that the main exhibit was simply a pedagogical jumble. But overall the museum's very existence has made it seem a considerable success. Within the first year, more than a hundred thousand people, many of whom did not usually frequent museums, had visited the new Cité Nationale. It remains to be seen whether a state-directed project snubbed by the President and his minister can change the image of immigrants' place within the French Republic.

References

Association Génériques. *Les étrangers en France: Guide des sources d'archives publiques et privées, XIXe-XXe siècles.* 4 vols. Paris: Génériques, Direction des Archives de France, 1999, 2005.

Bancel, Nicolas, and Pascal Blanchard. "Incompatibilité: La CNHI dans le sanctuaire du colonialisme français." *Hommes et Migrations* 1267 (May–June 2007): 112–27.

Blanc-Chaléard, Marie-Claude. "Du non-'lieu de mémoire' à la CNHI." *Diasporas* 6 (June 2005): 12–22.

———. "Une Cité Nationale pour l'Histoire de l'Immigration: Genèse, enjeux, obstacles." *Vingtième siècle, Revue d'Histoire* 92 (Oct.–Dec. 2006): 131–40.

Bourdieu, Pierre, and Alain Darbel. *L'amour de l'art: Les musées et leur public.* Paris: Éditions de Minuit, 1966.

Commission Internationale d'Histoire des Mouvements Sociaux et des Structures Sociales. *Les migrations internationales de la fin du XVIIIe siècle à nos jours.* Paris: Éditions du CNRS, 1980. [1972 conference proceedings]

Gervereau, Laurent, Pierre Milza, and Émile Témime, eds. *Toute la France: Histoire de l'immigration en France au XXe siècle.* Paris: Somogy Éditions d'Art, 1998. [BDIC exhibit catalogue]

Green, Nancy L. *Repenser les migrations.* Paris: Presses Universitaires de France, 2002.

Lequin, Yves, ed. *La mosaïque France: Histoire des étrangers et de l'immigration.* Paris: Larousse, 1988.

Noiriel, Gérard. *The French Melting Pot: Immigration, Citizenship, and National Identity.* [1988]. Translated by Geoffroy de Laforcade. Minneapolis: University of Minnesota Press, 1996.

Perrot, Michelle. "Les rapports des ouvriers français et des étrangers (1871–1893)." *Bulletin de la Société d'Histoire Moderne* 12, no. 12 (1960): 4–9. [supplement to the *Revue d'Histoire Moderne et Contemporaine* 1 (1960)]

Poulot, Dominique. "Le musée." In Vincent Duclert and Christophe Prochasson, eds., *Dictionnaire critique de la République,* 923–28. Paris: Flammarion, 2002.

"Vers un lieu de mémoire de l'immigration." Special issue of *Hommes et Migrations* 1247 (Jan.–Feb. 2004).

28

DECOLONIZATION AND THE REPUBLIC

Todd Shepard

The end of direct French suzerainty over almost all of the overseas territories that various governments had conquered since 1789 began in 1942, when Free France recognized Lebanese independence. It continued after World War II, when men and women in Hanoi, Damascus, and Sétif (Algeria) urgently demanded freedom from French domination, and was largely completed by 1962 (with New Caledonia, Polynesia, Wallis and Futuna, and Mayotte notable exceptions). Decolonization, many argue, marked the end of the Republic's imperial "detour," of practices and arguments that flagrantly violated republican values, comforted the Republic's enemies, and thus sapped its institutions. This vision echoes some of the small number of French voices that, before 1959, struggled to have France recognize that the time for empire was over. It also rehearses the claims of President Charles de Gaulle, who worked tirelessly after 1959 to pretend that he and France had chosen decolonization, in Africa and then Algeria, rather than having been forced out by circumstances beyond their control. A quite different interpretation presents the history of decolonization as key to understanding how the pursuit and government of empire were, rather than a diversion, an inextricable part of the French history of Republics and republicanism since 1792. Every French Republic, after all, was also an empire; historically, the overwhelming majority of republicans had accepted empire, some had ardently called for it, and many anticolonialists relied on non-, even anti-, republican arguments. More specifically, the histories of both the Fourth and the Fifth Republic, notably their institutions, were tied to often forgotten but substantive efforts to redefine republican principles and state structure in order, first, to keep the colonies and, then, to get out of Algeria. These histories have taken on new importance since 2000, as discussions of the Algerian War and the imperial past have become embroiled in political debates about immigrants in France, notably those with ties to former colonies.

In 1945, the defeat of Nazism and fascism seemed to promise an end as well to the age of European empires. The Allies, after all, fought in the name of democracy and in opposition to the Axis powers' blatant and brutal celebration of both racial hierarchies and imperialism. Yet among French politicians, intellectuals, and officials—notably those who most loudly trumpeted the Republic's triumph—such views were seldom heard. Rather, leaders who had fought to defeat Vichy drew very different lessons from recent French history.

The French government's capitulation to Germany, on June 22, 1940, and the July 10 vote at Vichy to transform the Republic into the French State magnified the bond between Republic and empire. Symbolically, on June 21, 1940, some thirty French politicians embarked on the ship *Massilia* for French Morocco, where they planned to reestablish a republican government that could continue the fight against Germany (they were arrested on arrival). Less well-known at the time, but more successfully, on June 18, Charles de Gaulle proclaimed from London that the empire meant that the Republic could and would fight on. It was in French colonies that his claim to embody a still-existing Republic, which rendered the Vichy State's exercise of sovereignty illegitimate, gradually gained strength. In autumn 1940, Félix Éboué, governor-general of Chad, recognized de Gaulle's authority, buttressing it with French (African) territories and troops. Eventually, the hundreds of thousands of French soldiers raised overseas allowed Free France to participate in the liberation of Europe and, as the battle song of the Algerian-based Army of Africa proclaimed, "to come from the colonies/to save *la Patrie*." This did not stop French officials from excluding Arab, Berber, and African troops from the victorious march down the liberated Champs-Élysées in August 1944.

The dark days of World War II proved to many that France needed its overseas colonies more than ever. In the words of Socialist deputy Paul Ramadier, "The problem of empire is now the problem of our country's life and existence." The empire's gift of both troops and evidence that the Republic had soldiered on after June 1940 anchored the efforts of de Gaulle and others to deny U.S. supremacy over France: as the Guianese politician Gaston Monnerville proclaimed on May 12, 1945, "without its Empire, France would be nothing but a liberated country. Thanks to its Empire, France is one of the victors." Such interpretations gave added urgency to efforts to counter calls, from among the colonized and on the world stage, for quick independence for all colonies. With similar convictions, British officials, most vocally Winston Churchill, who had authored the 1941 Atlantic Charter alongside President Franklin D. Roosevelt, worked to sidestep its anticolonial summons "to see sovereign rights and self-government restored to those who have been forcibly deprived of them." Both before and after their return to Paris, de Gaulle and other French leaders forthrightly contested the Atlantic Charter's road map. The 1944 Brazzaville Conference, which brought together colonial administrators to map out the new principles and structures that were supposed to redefine the empire, formally declared that neither "autonomy" nor "self-determination" was among the options. In perhaps the most brazen repudiation of Roosevelt's wartime promise that European empires would end, the French version of the United Nations' Charter of 1946 starkly differed from its English-language "twin": whereas the latter committed signatories "to develop self-government" in their colonies, the former enjoined them merely "to develop the ability of colonized peoples to administer themselves."

In 1947, the newspaper *Le Monde* interpreted the "end of the British Empire" in India as resulting from Britain's historical incapacity to respond to popular demands for liberation. France's revolutionary heritage, by contrast, made it possible for the Republic to maintain the shape of the empire yet wholly alter its content. To show how much would change, French officials began with new names. Speaking at Brazzaville, Charles de Gaulle had invoked the "Bloc France-Colonies," and commentators had many other suggestions for renaming the French empire; one article, for example, called for a "Global France" ("La France mondiale"), while a book coauthored by the Senegalese poet-politician Léopold Sédar Senghor proposed the "French Imperial Community." It was the term "the French Union," first advanced by the Provisional Government of the French Republic's minister of the colonies, that quickly gained popularity. By 1945, it also had become de rigueur to refer to colonial territories as "Overseas France." The new Constitution of October 1946 ensconced both names in law. More was promised than a change of terms. In a series of laws, including the Constitutions of 1946 and 1958, definitions of "republic" and "citizen" were repeatedly stretched and reworked. While they threatened to render these dual leitmotifs of modern French history meaningless, such maneuvers suggested that the right institutional frame would allow anticolonial challenges to be overcome.

The Constitution of 1946 declared that the Republic encompassed the metropole as well as "Overseas France," itself divided into "overseas departments" and "overseas territories." The former title was given in 1947 to the so-called old colonies (Guadeloupe, Martinique, Guiana, Réunion), which had been French before 1789; these had the same governmental institutions as the metropole. The latter category encompassed the former colonies. Legally, it was unclear whether the three departments of Algeria were part of the metropole or had the status of "overseas departments"; unlike either, but like "overseas territories," they shared a local assembly. Such confusion typified this era of indecision, which resulted from the unresolved conflict between federalists and those committed to the (Jacobin) traditions of French republicanism.

Beginning at the Brazzaville conference, there were repeated proposals to transform the empire into a federation, "despite the objections it may raise." René Capitant, minister of education in the Provisional Government of the French Republic (GPRF) and a close ally of de Gaulle, argued during the first Constitutive Assembly: "The French Union will be federal, or it will not be"; fellow Gaullist Jacques Soustelle, the minister for the colonies in 1946, also ardently pushed for a federal solution. Christian Democrats, Socialists, and Communists as well gave strong support to federalist schemes, which received vocal backing from "indigenous" deputies representing the colonies. The Socialist Senghor, speaking in the second Constitutive Assembly, called for a "real federation—that is to say a union of equal Socialist French Republics." His fellow deputy, the Algerian nationalist Ferhat Abbas, urged support "for autonomy within the framework of French federalism; for a local Parliament, a local government, and an Algerian citizenship." The French Union, however, was not a federation; final decisions remained in the hands of what one speaker termed the "federating organ" and what another called "the locomotive": France.

While reticent to embrace federalism, it was only during two relatively short periods between 1945 and 1962 that a French government clearly marked its preference for the Republic, over and against any supranational structure. In early 1955, in response to the November 1, 1954, attacks that announced the start of the Algerian revolution, Prime Minister Pierre Mendès-France named Soustelle to take over as governor-general of Algeria. Soustelle told legislators in both Paris and Algiers that he no longer supported a federal solution: with a new policy termed "integration," he and the government would both move beyond colonial-era debates over assimilation versus association and focus their efforts on building what he called a Franco-Muslim (or Franco-Algerian) Republic, which would be dealt with as a unit distinct from the French Union. He argued that figuring out how to synthesize the diverse populations of Algeria with the people of France would revitalize the nation as well as the Republic.

The left-wing Republican Front won elections in January 1956 on a platform that rejected integrationism and supported peace in Algeria. Some integrationist social reforms were, in fact, adopted, but between 1956 and 1958, French governments renewed with federalism. In Europe, the 1957 Treaty of Rome established the European Community; in French sub-Saharan Africa, the Deferre law of June

1956 territorialized the budget and most government responsibilities; in Algeria, the Loi-Cadre of January 1958 established an explicitly federal form of government: the existing twelve departments, which a 1957 reform had mapped out, and the southern territories of the Sahara would be transformed into eight to ten regions. That the latter reform was never applied highlights the extent to which May 1958 marked another sharp rejection of federalism and a turn back to the Republic.

In May 1958, a massive demonstration in Algiers demanding that the French government guarantee Algeria's place in the Republic led to the collapse of the Fourth Republic. Even some observers who wanted Algerian independence, or accepted it as inevitable, were surprised at the enthusiastic crowds, made up of both "Europeans" and "Muslims"; many came to believe that, as in other "revolutionary" moments, fraternity had emerged to open new possibilities and reestablish the Republic. Decisions taken in 1958, notably the October Constitution, aimed to manage the separation of most of the remaining former colonies while staving off any autonomy for the Algerian departments; they did so by resolving the constant post-1945 indecision concerning the connections between France and its overseas possessions. The new Fifth Republic distinguished Algeria from the others, affirming that it was one with the metropole—a republican center—while leaving the status of overseas departments untouched and redefining the Union as a community (a much looser relationship that soon led to formal independence for all the territories of West and Equatorial Africa). Officially, distinctions between the continental and Algerian shores of the "metropole" now were based on exceptional laws—notably a series of social-welfare provisions to address the results of discrimination and extravagant restrictions on civil liberties to crush nationalist activity—rather than being the norm. (De Gaulle's government also drew back from the European Community; it was not until June 1962, right before Algerian voters approved complete independence, that France would reengage with the EEC.)

The year 1958 also saw the resolution of the enormous uncertainty around the institution of citizenship. During the Second World War, the National Council of the Resistance had made "the extension of political, social, and economic rights to the indigenous and colonial populations" a key principle in its 1944 platform. The recommendations from the Brazzaville conference declared a "concern to push aside anything that leads to subordination and, to the contrary, take account of the consent of colonial populations"; while Monnerville and others linked the need to extend new liberties to the "blood debt" that France owed its colonial subjects. Between 1944 and 1947, France abolished the status of "colonial subject"; extended French citizenship to all former French subjects from the overseas territories (colonies) and Algeria; and created a new French Union citizenship, which included all French citizens (newly minted as well as the others) and the peoples of the "associated states" and protectorates who had their own (non-French) nationality—Morocco, Tunisia, and the new Indochinese Federation. What Parisian decision-makers failed to do was define what rights accompanied either status. Some were clear: forced labor and the infamous "native codes" were abolished; "French citizenship" guaranteed free circulation throughout the Union, including France; all "citizens" were eligible for civil service posts. Most were unclear: the double college system divided all elected posts between those with "French status" and those with "local" status, yet some "qualified" men with "local" status were given "French status"; Algerians with "local status," who had restricted political rights in Algeria, enjoyed full political rights if they moved to the metropole; laws proclaimed that "local status" women would have the vote, which French women had won in 1944, yet many places, such as Algeria, did not extend this right. Tens of millions of people from outside the metropole now carried a title sacralized by the French Revolution, but accompanied by multiple, radically different, and wholly unequal sets of rights.

These inequalities and ambiguities resulted from the decision of the second Constitutive Assembly, elected in June 1946, not to resolve the uncertainties. The immediate goal was to avoid extending the vote to the majority of non-European "French citizens." In the words of former prime minister and Radical Party stalwart Édouard Hérriot, this might give "overseas citizens" more votes than "citizens of the metropole," in which case "France would become the colony of its former colonies." Hérriot's speech led, within days, to the project being sidelined. Plans for territorial assemblies to be elected via universal suffrage were shelved, replaced with a double college system, which guaranteed that "Europeans" in Algeria and colonists elsewhere would be disproportionately represented. All references to the consent of colonial peoples, notably to their right to leave the Union, disappeared. The disappointment of "indigenous" representatives was palpable, particularly that of West African deputies, such as Senghor and Amadou Lamine Guèye of Senegal and Félix Houphouët-Boigny of Côte d'Ivoire, who had privileged quick reforms within the French space over efforts to move toward national independence. Even the meager hopes of Ferhat Abbas, who had worked since the 1930s to refocus Algerian nationalism around the goal of establishing meaningful autonomy, were dashed.

The immediate recognition given to the political rights of "overseas citizens" was small: a new French Union Assembly theoretically represented France's "new citizens," those from what used to known as colonies, but the body contained as many metropolitan representatives as overseas ones. In any event, the new Assembly was a legislature with essentially no legislative authority. It was not until 1956 that Houphouët-Boigny became the first African minister in a French government. There were, however, more gains in terms of social rights.

Across West Africa, notably, labor unions invoked citizenship in their successful efforts to gain the same social rights as other French people, including a minimum wage, unemployment insurance, and family allowances.

As with uncertainties about the shape of the Republic, the Algerian War also brought some clarity to what citizenship meant. In 1958, the double college system was abolished, giving all Algerians (including women) equal political rights. Elections that year led to dozens of so-called Muslims from Algeria entering Parliament; they made up just under 10 percent of French deputies and senators. The "Muslim" Nafissa Sid-Cara, named secretary of state for Muslim social affairs in January 1959, became the first woman appointed to a French government since 1937. A new legal definition of "Muslims from Algeria," based on origins (and not religion), allowed the extension of "exceptional" political and social rights to this group of French citizens. A new electoral law guaranteed a minimum number of seats for "Muslims" in all elections held in Algeria, from the National Assembly to municipal councils. The extension of social rights went further than formal equality. Officials began to refer to the concept of "discrimination" in order to explain why it was necessary to take exceptional measures to create the possibility for real equality. Interestingly, the first official French document to refer to "discrimination" appears to be a 1954 report on the situation of "Algerian Muslim" workers in the metropole. Subsequent plans for integrationist policies explained the cause of the problem as economic inequality accentuated by anti-Algerian racism in France as well as Algeria. While these policies had some real effects on the lives of Algerians, it is also significant that the Fifth Republic used the policies, which targeted anti-Algerian racism and its effects, as models for the "social promotion" policies it inaugurated across France in 1959. Taking a "social citizenship" approach, these policies sidelined questions of class to address handicaps of specific groups (e.g., the illiterate, disaster victims, drought-stricken farmers).

The government presented these policies on the world stage as emblematic of the Fifth Republic. In 1959, Prime Minister Michel Debré pushed the French army to name a "Muslim" general "before the next session of the UN General Assembly." Integrationism, French ambassadors and officials repeated, showed that the French Republic, once again, was pioneering efforts to create "liberty, equality, [and] fraternity" and to extend the "rights of man," this time in a context of stark ethnic differences. Algeria, they reminded listeners, was not a colony; the situation there should be compared, instead, to the far less aggressive efforts to fight the effects of racism in countries like the Soviet Union or the United States of America.

From World War II onward, French leaders preferred to contrast their plans to transform the colonial situation with the "hypocritical" anticolonialism of the United States and the USSR. In fact, the most direct challenges to French colonialism came not from the two superpowers but from colonized peoples themselves. Many demonstrations were met with a heavy hand, notably against nationalists. In early May 1945, reacting to news that the war in Europe was over, anticolonial demonstrators took to the street in Damascus and in Sétif, Algeria. The former demonstration was largely peaceful until May 29, when French forces bombed the parliament building and "modern quarters," killing at least four hundred Syrians; during the latter protest, violent attacks targeted local "Europeans," murdering about one hundred. The French response was brutal, resulting in the massacre of (perhaps tens of) thousands and the roundup of nationalists across Algeria. In March 1947, a violent revolt broke out in Madagascar, driven jointly by recent elections and rural discontent; French repression over the next year killed upwards of one hundred thousand Malagasy.

The two most significant French wars of decolonization—in Indochina, and then Algeria—involved even greater violence. In 1946, French troops sought to crush the Democratic Republic of Vietnam, which had proclaimed its independence on September 2, 1945. By 1954, when the Treaty of Geneva led to the departure of the French from Indochina, some 75,000 French soldiers (over two-thirds from the French Union) and 18,000 allied Vietnamese troops had died; the number of North Vietnamese killed is unknown, although estimates commonly begin at 400,000. Between late 1954 and early 1962, 17,000 French troops died in combat in the Algerian War, with some 2,500 "European" civilians and over 16,000 "Muslims" killed by nationalist organizations and at least 150,000 Algerians killed directly by French actions. Estimates for the total number of Algerian dead range much higher.

These episodes forced responses from many French politicians and intellectuals, revealing much about how they envisioned the Republic's role in its overseas possessions. On the left, there was no unified response, with events in Algeria producing the greatest divergences and uncertainty. The French Communist Party (PCF), most notably, responded to developments in Algeria very differently than it did to events elsewhere. Whereas Communists vigorously criticized the crackdown in Madagascar, they offered strong support for the official response to Sétif, which they blamed on "Nazi agitators." With Indochina, as in Madagascar, the Communist ties of the local leaders targeted by French actions and the peripheral connection to the Republic facilitated PCF anticolonialism: French Communist opposition included defending the enemy leader, Ho Chi Minh (who had helped found the PCF while a student in Paris). In the case of Algeria, although willing to call for more "liberty," the PCF argued against "divorce." In 1956, after campaigning to end the conflict, PCF deputies voted for imposing a state of emergency and against negotiations. For the French Communists, Algeria was France, and France, party theorists like Laurent Casanova and Paul Faurisson explained in the mid-1950s, was a "proletarian" republic, which would soon complete the revolutionary process begun in 1789. Why would Algerian workers want out? Beyond small groups on the Far Left, intellectuals such as Simone de Beauvoir and Francis Jeanson, who rejected republicanism, and a minority of Communist dissidents, very few could bring themselves to support the Islamically inflected Algerian nationalists—particularly after the National Liberation Front announced its use of terrorism as a tactic.

᪇

It was the use of terrorism in 1961 and 1962 by the pro-French Algeria Secret Army Organization (OAS)—which targeted random "Muslims," Gaullists, and leftists in Algeria, and intellectuals and anticolonialists in the metropole—that finally catalyzed a formidable left-wing movement for the "defense of the Republic." Earlier critics of French forces' systematic use of torture on "suspect" Algerians had castigated the violation of republican principles—above all, justice, the rule of law, and the rights of man. The protests that developed in early 1962 moved beyond arguments that a colonial "gangrene" was damaging the Republic to insist that the delayed decolonization of Algeria threatened to let "fascists" abolish the Republic altogether.

Over the following months, the French government agreed to a cease-fire and then withdrew from a now-independent Algeria. The government took advantage of this process to redefine key aspects of the Republic. During the fight to keep Algerian French, exceptional laws had temporarily authorized the violation of civil liberties (e.g., press censorship, exceptional tribunals, police searches after sunset, mandatory I.D. cards); the need to leave Algeria (and fight the OAS) legitimated making these measures part of French law. Executive power to interfere in court decisions was extended. The marginalization of legislative power, and the affirmation of executive primacy, which most jurists and politicians had understood to be exceptional—linked, that is, to the Algerian emergency—became standard practice. This redefinition of the Republic was accompanied by a reframing of the nation, as the French government, in violation of the accords that led to Algerian independence, stripped almost all Algerians of their French citizenship, with the exception of the "European" minority. As citizens, the latter enjoyed the right to "repatriate" to France. Another executive decision authorized government efforts to treat "Muslims" who had worked to keep Algeria French—the so-called harkis—as potential refugees, rather than repatriating citizens. In the fall of 1962, a referendum, widely seen as violating the Constitution, authorized the direct election of the President of the Republic. Former Prime Minister Michel Debré, explaining why he had not included this proposal in the 1958 text, which he had largely authored, closed the circle that Edouard Hérriot had opened in 1946. In 1958, "the body of electors was the body of electors of the French Union, with all the African peoples and the Muslims of

Algeria. This was stated explicitly." Under those conditions, Debré continued, "election by universal suffrage was impossible."

The government's response to Algerian independence made the Fifth Republic more "European" than any regime since 1789—and established government institutions that broke with republican orthodoxy. That response also served to exclude from French history the central role that overseas lands and peoples had played. Such a move was possible because French voters were eager to clear away the confusion that post-1944 efforts to maintain French positions around the globe had entailed. Ambiguities surrounding the French Union and "overseas citizenship" had created widespread public bewilderment over which parts of the world were France, what kind of people were French, what a republic was, and what citizenship meant. That the government of the early Fifth Republic defined these phenomena in less than universalistic terms suggests that Algerian independence occurred at a time when "republicanism" was a less compelling catchphrase than it had been in other eras—or would be again after 1989. Most interesting, perhaps, was how decolonization—and Algerian independence most emblematically—came to be seen as a victory for "the Republic," a Republic defined primarily in reference to abstract values (liberty, equality, and fraternity; the rights of man), rather than as a failure of efforts by actual Republics (above all the Fourth and Fifth) to transform the colonies into France.

References

Aldrich, Robert. *Greater France: A History of French Overseas Expansion*. New York: St. Martin's Press, 1996.

Cole, Joshua. "Intimate Acts and Unspeakable Relations: Remembering Torture and the War for Algerian Independence." In Alec G. Hargreaves, ed., *Memory, Empire, and Postcolonialism: Legacies of French Colonialism,* 125–41. Lanham, MD: Lexington Books, 2005.

Connelly, Matthew. *A Diplomatic Revolution: Algeria's Fight for Independence and the Origins of the Post–Cold War Era*. New York: Oxford University Press, 2002.

Cooper, Frederick. *Decolonization and African Society: The Labor Question in French and British Africa*. Cambridge: Cambridge University Press, 1996.

Cooper, Frederick, and Ann Laura Stoler. "Between Metropole and Colony." In Frederick Cooper and Ann Laura Stoler, eds., *Tensions of Empire: Colonial Cultures in a Bourgeois World,* 1–56. Berkeley: University of California Press, 1997.

Girardet, Raoul. *L'idée coloniale en France de 1871 à 1962*. Paris: La Table Ronde, 1972.

Lebovics, Herman. *Bringing the Empire Back Home: France in the Global Age*. Durham, NC: Duke University Press, 2004.

Shepard, Todd. *The Invention of Decolonization: The Algerian War and the Remaking of France*. 2nd ed. Ithaca, NY: Cornell University Press, 2008.

Spire, Alexis. *Étrangers à la carte: L'administration de l'immigration en France (1945–1975)*. Paris: Grasset, 2005.

Thénault, Sylvie. *Histoire de la guerre d'indépendance algérienne*. Paris: Flammarion, 2005.

29

The Suburbs

Frédéric Viguier

After a century and a half of industrialization and deindustrialization, *la banlieue* (suburb), in the singular, no longer evokes pleasurable luncheons on the grass or popular dances by the Marne River or affluent neighborhoods to the west of Paris, as it did for Manet's contemporaries; nor does it recall the French capital's Red Belt, long the geographic center of French communism. Rather, over the last twenty-five years, the term *banlieues* has been mostly used as a synonym for *cités,* as the housing projects in working-class suburbs are known, or for *grands-ensembles,* a term representing the high-rise towers and low-rise blocks that constitute the projects' material and architectural form. All three terms now refer to the persistent social and economic problems of France's impoverished neighborhoods. The suburb has become a metaphor of social isolation and distress and the primary symptom of postindustrial France's sluggish economic growth and rising social inequalities. *Banlieues, cités,* and *grands-ensembles* have fueled an inflating discourse of panic, which, in its different guises, presents these territories as a threat to the social and political fabric of the French Republic. Because these political and intellectual representations so powerfully shroud the reality of the *cités,* it is then necessary to examine first the discourse surrounding the *cités* and, second, the actual social experience in these places.

Even if they have different views about the *banlieues,* most political parties in France frame the economic and social problems experienced in the blue-collar suburbs as questioning the terms of the French Republic, as if the vocabulary of the Republic has become the only intellectual resource to politically articulate social problems in France. From President Jacques Chirac, first elected in 1995, to President Nicolas Sarkozy, elected in 2007, the right-wing party, the Union pour un Mouvement Populaire (UMP), has gradually toughened its discourse about the poor suburbs, portraying them as secessionist territories, bristling with forces hostile to the French nation and to the republican general interest. Enough with "excuses" they say; unemployment alone does not account for the hostility to the Republic in these neighborhoods, but *communautarisme* does. *Communautarisme,* a social pathology seemingly perceived more acutely in France than other countries, refers to a supposed tendency among some ethnoracial groups to live by the standards of their separate communities rather than by the values of the national republican society.

In the UMP view, regular clashes between the police and the youths in *cités* around Paris and other urban areas, culminating in the large-scale riots of November 2005, confirm the harmful consequences of distinct identities nurtured in the housing projects of working-class suburbs. In these places, conservative officials claim, violence soars, perpetrated by youths ever younger, because these youths have no desire to live with the rest of the nation. Their hostility to the Republic is said to pervade poor public middle and high schools in poverty-stricken suburbs, where teachers are supposedly confronted with their students' refusal to learn about Voltaire and Rousseau in the name of the Qur'an. According to conservative politicians, the republican rule of law no longer exerts its authority in the projects, which are now subjected to trafficking of all sorts. Such views have made the UMP readily martial in its political platform, and its current agenda offers a heavy-handed authoritarian surge: slashed social-welfare budgets but increased surveillance and punishment; decreased tolerance for second offenses; and hardened penalties for minors.

France's other major political force, the center-left Parti Socialiste (PS), whose electoral base consists largely of civil servants viscerally attached to the public service, uses a different variant of republican discourse. It presents the material and moral misery of the working-class suburbs as an insult to the republican ideal of equality. To remedy it, Socialists have worked to improve social welfare, rehabilitate dilapidated neighborhoods, subsidize neighborhood associations, and enhance public services, especially transportation, schools, post offices, unemployment services, and the justice system. Since the early 1980s, social-welfare budgets have always risen under Socialist governments and decreased when the Right holds power. While Socialists are less inclined than conservatives to blame young residents of the *cités* for their supposed secessionist aspirations, the PS nonetheless shares the belief that the Republic needs to win the hearts of the *cités'* youth. To do so, the Socialists promote civic education in public schools and seek to restore the emotional value of republican symbols such as the French flag and the national anthem. If these efforts resemble those of the Right, so does the Socialist approach to public safety. The center-left has grown increasingly worried about being perceived as weak on crime, and it now emphasizes the need for reinforced policing, especially at the community level.

As for the new radical Left, it has left aside the critique of socioeconomic inequalities to focus on the critique of the Republic. Radicals reject what they view as the domineering and imperial Republic promoted by the UMP and the paternalistic Republic advocated by the Socialist Party. They blame the republican rhetoric of the UMP and the PS for hypocritically lecturing about civic virtues while accepting the daily reality of social injustice and racial discrimination. Against idealized visions of the republican past, the radical Left points to the colonial subjection of native peoples, arguing that the French Republic has always violated its own noble and universalistic principles. "We are the new *indigènes* of the Republic," they claim, meaning that residents of the *cités* suffer much the same treatment as did the subaltern peoples of the Republic's former colonial empire. Rather than demand that republican promises of equality be upheld, following the civil rights movement in the United States, they reject the Republic as intrinsically hypocritical, as forever promoting hollow ideals. According to them, it is no coincidence that Prime Minister Dominique de Villepin declared a "state of emergency" to curb the November 2005 riots, a measure used during the war of independence in Algeria and the 1980s anticolonial surge in New Caledonia. This measure, which granted the government extraordinary rights to restore public order, revealed the true postcolonial nature of republican domination over the *banlieues*. The repression of protest in the *cités* mirrored the repression of nationalist and proindependence energies abroad.

Like the debates in the political sphere, arguments among intellectuals frame all issues relating to the suburbs in terms of the lack of efficiency of the so-called republican model of social policy. Conservative intellectuals, increasingly vocal over the past twenty years, see the social problems that unfold in working-class neighborhoods as evidence of moral failures on the part of the youths and their permissive teachers. A best-selling book of 2002, strikingly titled *The Republic's Lost Territories* (ed. Brenner), explained violence in public schools as the by-product of antirepublican and antimodern sentiments among youths of the impoverished suburbs. According to its authors, teachers daily encounter religious fundamentalism, anti-Semitism, and sexism in the classroom. The phenomenon, the authors maintain, calls for renewed republican vigilance in combating evils everybody thought were long gone in secular France, sixty years after the Holocaust and with women's emancipation supposedly secure.

Left-wing writers, who still dominate the intellectual field, are divided into two camps. Their debates, especially in light of the riots of November 2005, focus on the "republican model's" relevance in ensuring social integration. According to the first camp, which includes radical postcolonial critics and center-left economists, the time has come to do away altogether with the republican model of public policy. The universalist Republic's indifference to individual distinctions, whether social, religious, or racial, has proven incapable of alleviating the racism and discrimination that afflict the young residents of the *cités* and stoke their anger. Policymakers, they argue, must address racial discrimination directly through affirmative action. The second camp, which includes center-left republicans and anticapitalist radicals, is reluctant to develop race-sensitive social policies. They argue that the main problem is social inequality and an ingrained hierarchy of social class. The remedy is economic: a fairer allocation of the value workers add to the marketplace and a system of fiscal redistribution that allows increased spending on public schools and an expansion of the welfare state. Such classic recipes of reform, they argue, may have lost currency in our neoliberal society, but they remain relevant today.

In short, in both the political and intellectual spheres, the French tend to understand their current socioeconomic problems as a challenge to their political system (the Republic) in specific territories (the poor suburbs). Yet this intellectual and discursive frame obscures the real situation by reducing complex problems to overly simple dichotomous oppositions: the city vs. its periphery, race vs. class, the republican model or not. All too often, French social scientists, who should know better, appear to endorse such oppositions when asked to comment in the media. In the current social and political context, the supply of analysis is overdetermined by the demand for heavy-handed solutions. Yet the scholarly works of French social scientists over the last fifteen years provide in-depth perspectives that correct the binary debates over the Republic. They help us understand how the current republican narrative completely overlooks the specific changes in the political ecosystem of a Red Belt that once integrated its residents into the Republic. Instead of exoticizing the *cités'* youth, social scientists allow them to speak directly, revealing their powerful aspirations for social integration. Sociologists and anthropologists also demonstrate how class-based discrimination and race-based discrimination intersect in the experience of these youths. Finally, by exploring the various forms of national and local governments in these neighborhoods, they show how the "republican model" of public intervention has shifted since the mid-1980s from providing equal public services across the entire French territory to targeting specific territories and populations. In doing so, they expose the limits of public intervention, caught between social prevention and policing in a context of deindustrialization fostered by the state.

In their scholarly work, if not always in their public interventions, social scientists have demonstrated particularly well the extent to which the false dichotomy between the cities and their suburbs misrepresents a more nuanced social landscape. First, suburbs are not uniformly poor; the suburban growth in the last twenty years has actually increased the number of middle-class residents—in part through new housing developments designed for schoolteachers, clerical employees, and skilled industrial workers. In the process, towns already suburban have increased their density, now resembling small cities, and rural communes have become suburban. Second, while the outer rings of cities have turned into suburbs, the inner rings have gentrified, as have working-class neighborhoods within cities. In Lille, Lyons, Marseille, Toulouse, and especially in the former Red Belt of Paris, the active cultural policy of the remaining Communist municipalities, as well as programs of urban rehabilitation of old town centers like Saint-Denis, have attracted new residents from the middle class. These new inhabitants are richer in cultural capital than economic capital and more often employed in the public sector than the private sector; they have replaced the former blue-collar elite (Bacqué and Fol). Third, the landscape of the *cités,* while bland and bleak, is certainly misrepresented by the word "ghetto," which journalists, politicians, and experts have increasingly used since the mid-1990s.

Borrowing from the American experience, those who use the term "ghetto" seek to dramatize the French situation by emphasizing some obvious commonalities with poor urban neighborhoods of the United States. The term primarily suggests France's worsened spatial segregation and its rising racial dimension. Indeed, even if the suburbs as a whole have not seen heightened racial segregation, the *cités* have experienced an exodus of white middle- and upper working-class residents. As these groups purchased houses or rented in better neighborhoods during the 1970s and the 1980s, the share of nonnationals in the *cités* increased from 10 percent in the 1960s to 20 to 40 percent in the 1990s, depending on the region in question. Both in the United States and in France, these neighborhoods have been depressed, losing population and economic activity. And in both countries, residents experience the powerful stigma associated with living in housing projects abandoned to those at the bottom of the income scale.

Despite these convergences, the situations of American ghettos and French *cités* remain very different, and the term "ghetto" elicits misrepresentations when applied to the French as well as to the U.S. case. While Chicago's ghetto spreads over hundreds of square miles and harbors three hundred thousand inhabitants, no *cité* in the urban periphery of Paris, Lyons, Lille, or Marseille reaches even one-tenth the size of the typical American ghetto (Wacquant). Unlike the French *cités,* which are residential clusters scattered in the urban peripheries, the American ghetto is not solely residential. Racially and socially, the French *cités* remain more diverse than the "black" ghettos, which still reflect a long history of racial dualism, although many poor American neighborhoods have increasingly harbored immigrants from everywhere. Foreign families in the French *cités* are diverse in their ethnoracial makeup, and they still constitute a minority, mostly because public-housing agencies have carefully organized the dispersion of immigrant families across and within the housing projects. Poverty rates and living conditions are also worse in the American ghetto than in the *cités,* where destitution is mitigated by a stronger welfare system. If crime in the poor *banlieues* is higher than in the central cities of France, it mostly comprises confrontational behaviors and petty thefts—nothing like the endemic armed violence of the 1970s and 1980s that emptied all public spaces in American ghettos, where crime rates have now dropped significantly. Finally, the American ghettos receive little public money, whereas the bland and bleak *cités* are maintained and rehabilitated, because the local and national governments, which own significant portions of the projects, have kept a direct interest in managing these neighborhoods.

Not only does the panic-stricken notion of French suburbs as territories excluded from the Republic misrepresent the nuanced social landscape of urban peripheries, it fails to situate them within the larger global social context of "postindustrial" France. First, the entire social composition of French society has changed, not just that of the *cités*. As middle- and upper-middle-class white-collar workers make up a larger proportion of French society, these groups also occupy a larger proportion of the French territory. In a society that, globally, has become more affluent, industrial spaces appear poorer by comparison than when they were more common. Similarly, the gentrification of city centers gives a grimmer appearance to the *cités*. In addition, the social exclusion experienced by residents of dilapidated neighborhoods does not result from their hostility to republican integration. On the contrary, social exclusion finds its origin in a general tendency in postindustrial France for social groups to settle in neighborhoods that are socially more and more homogeneous. Rich neighborhoods are the most segregated, and poor suburbs owe their concentration of poverty to the out-migration of the middle classes (Maurin). Finally, the focus on impoverished *cités* diverts attention from the neighboring *banlieues pavillonnaires,* as the modest single-family suburban housing developments are known in France. Yet the lower middle-class people who live there are also economically and socially unstable. Trapped by their mortgages, these homeowners often have no choice but to stay put, a situation that makes them eager to distinguish themselves from residents of the projects, even when they are themselves children of immigrants raised in a *cité* (Cartier et al.). To maintain their social mobility, they invest significant energy in the education of their offspring and often choose private schools over public schools. The blend of social distance and spatial proximity to the *cités,* especially among inhabitants of the *banlieues pavillonnaires,* accounts for much of the panic that surrounds the French *banlieues.*

For all these reasons, the republican conceptual framework cannot accurately portray the nuanced social situation of contemporary France, especially with respect to its complex suburban landscape. It also overlooks a crucial political transformation underlying suburban social life, namely, the demise of the so-called Red Belt, whose Communist municipalities once served as crucial intermediaries between the Republic and the suburban working class. Historians of the Paris Red Belt in the interwar period have shown how the working-class movement and its newly elected Communist officials helped integrate blue-collar workers into the Republic. Unlike the individualist model of middle-class integration, which occurs without the mediation of intermediary bodies such as churches, political parties, and trade unions, the integration of urban workers owed a great deal to such bodies, and especially to Communist-led towns. By weaving special links with working-class families and offering welfare benefits such as emergency relief, health centers, child care, and leisure facilities decades before the central state, Communist administrations developed great legitimacy in the eyes of working-class citizens and contributed to their collective social promotion. This legitimacy moved blue-collar citizens to vote regularly for Communist mayors and council members, thus ensuring blue-collar workers' massive participation in electoral politics.

In the 1950s and 1960s, state-sponsored construction of large-scale housing projects initially allowed the Parti Communiste Français to strengthen its local presence among skilled industrial workers and clerical employees. But the influx of new immigrant proletarians in the 1960s and 1970s produced a white, working-class flight from long-standing Communist towns and gave officials there a stigmatized population to which they were unaccustomed. Long preoccupied with the advancement of working-class conditions, Red Belt municipalities have resisted incorporating children of the new migrants from the former colonies, who embodied proletarian destitution rather than betterment (Masclet). As the municipal Communists lost their base of industrial workers, they proved largely incapable of appealing to the population that replaced them. As a result, municipal communism suffered a sharp decline: the crisis in the poor suburbs is more a function of that decline than of inadequate or ineffective state intervention. Today's republican narrative neglects this history, obscuring the integrating role played by the French Communist movement—especially in the working-class suburbs. Antidemocratic as it may have been, communism was not just an ideology; it was a social movement that long helped working people play a key role in the republican regime.

Today, electoral participation in the *cités* stands in sharp contrast to what it was in the 1950s and 60s. Despite a modest surge in the 2007 presidential elections, electoral abstention has reached historic highs, particularly in the most deprived projects (Braconnier and Dormagen). In these places, whose names often evoke Cold War Communist sensibilities, electoral participation was, until the 1970s, even higher than in neighboring, non-Communist towns. Shaped by a century of working-class activism, these communities were intensely mobilized. In de Gaulle's losing referendum of 1969, electoral participation in housing projects was 10 percent higher than in the rest of the country: almost 90 percent compared to 80 percent nationwide. Abstention rates started rising in the mid-1970s, reaching nearly 50 percent in the mid-1990s. Failure to register to vote also rose—25 percent of the potential electoral body in the projects is not registered today. While some of these nonvoters claim to reject electoral and partisan politics, most are either indifferent or lack the necessary political skills—such as understanding the differences between various parties or knowing candidates. Viewed from the projects, election nights on television appear entirely irrelevant. Civic beliefs originally fostered by the Third Republic, which represented electoral abstention as immoral and backward, and which the Communist movement had once instilled in the working-class suburbs, today appear obsolete. In the *cités* of contemporary France, youths readily confess their lack of interest in electoral politics or their reluctance to go register at the city hall, where they feel out of place. By contrast, civic behavior has become a form of distinction for housing-project residents of French descent; they find in political participation a way to distance themselves from an environment they would escape if they could. In the former Red Belt of today, low-ranking public-service workers are virtually alone in constituting the nucleus of what remains of the local Left.

Indifference to mainstream national politics does not imply acceptance of one's position in the social order. The riots that set fire to nearly a hundred *cités* in November 2005, spreading from Clichy-sous-Bois outside Paris to almost every *banlieue* in France, were so unprecedented in scale that they assumed a quasi-revolutionary form, especially when they turned into full-fledged battles with riot police. What triggered these riots was the accidental death of two youths chased by the police; the unrest escalated when the then interior minister, Nicolas Sarkozy, promised on national television to rid the projects of their "scum" (*racaille*). Rather than sheer delinquency or gratuitous violence, this violence expressed moral indignation at state injustice in a context of social and spatial segregation, racial discrimination, and hopelessness on the job market. In the end, the riots had no revolutionary implications, because they remained outside the framework of legitimate collective action (Mauger). Despite their attention from the media, rioters have remained incapable of articulating political claims, short of connections with any political organization. Ultimately, the 2005 riots exposed the immense gap between suburban youths, who expressed a strong sense of injustice, and mainstream political parties, unable to translate this sentiment into political action.

Despite the violence and the depth of anger these events revealed, ethnographic surveys conducted in the *cités* demonstrate that most young people there long to feel included in mainstream French society (Beaud and Pialoux). But the obstacles are many. While unemployment and underemployment have afflicted the entire French economy for three decades, youths of the *cités* have borne the largest share of its weight, with unemployment rates commonly above 30 percent. Many young people are thus obliged to live with their parents much longer than they would like. The few recent periods of economic improvement amply demonstrate the ardent desire among these youths to lead a normal life. When the French economy picked up between 1998 and 2001, the grip of economic competition loosened, and the general atmosphere and environment in the *cités* improved tremendously. Unfortunately, because they were hired on short-term job contracts, young, unskilled workers were the first to be laid off when the economy deteriorated in 2001. They felt confirmed in their belief that they are French society's victims of choice.

Ethnographic accounts of the informal and illegal economy, known as "bizness" in the *cités,* also reveal that project residents who engage in it nevertheless aspire to normalcy. The *cité*'s illegal economy sometimes involves drug dealing but predominantly the selling of stolen and smuggled goods. It takes place in various social scenes, on street corners, in school—including at the university— and in the extended family (Tafferant). Dealers do not primarily seek easy money but rather the symbolic status of local merchants. Far from facile, their activity requires a durable commitment and accountability. They seldom and only reluctantly engage in activities that violate their values—overpricing, selling goods stolen from individuals, and forcefully collecting debt. In short, *bizness* activities break the law but are compatible with a sense of social respectability in a world shaped by economic survival and class skepticism. For this reason, the ethnography of deviance in the *cités* offers a different picture from the nightmarish representations put forth by advocates of a martial republican order. The latter see the *banlieues* as threats to the Republic's moral and social fabric, but their views overlook the essential sources of the problem, namely, three decades of deindustrialization in the Red Belt.

The decline of Communist municipalities has made the central state the lone safety net and sole recourse for marginalized residents of the *cités.* Contrary to widely circulating clichés, the so-called republican model of public policy has shifted its organization enormously since the mid-1980s. Whereas the Republic once provided the same public programs to all neighborhoods across the country, it now offers measures targeting the poor suburbs, such as incentives for home ownership, promotion of social diversity, tax-free zoning to foster private investment, schools with enhanced means, and subsidies to community associations. These programs have mitigated the weight of poverty in the *cités,* without, however, overcoming the effects of deindustrialization there. What residents want above all are steady jobs, something the state has been unable to provide (Maurin). Whether the failure to genuinely improve economic circumstances in the *banlieue* stems from policies that inefficiently target victims of the crisis or, on the contrary, from policies that emphasize "urban issues" rather than economic redistribution (Tissot) is the subject of recurring public controversies in France. If state institutions have taken a preeminent role in the *banlieues,* they have, perhaps inevitably, fueled complaints about the insufficiency of government intervention. The more it acts in the *banlieues* to mitigate poverty, the more the Republic reveals the persistence of economic problems and the more residents of the *cités* demand that it give them better lives.

References

Bacqué, Marie-Hélène, and Sylvie Fol. *Le devenir des banlieues rouges*. Paris: L'Harmattan, 1997.

Beaud, Stéphane, and Michel Pialoux. *Violences urbaines, violence sociale: Genèse des nouvelles classes dangereuses*. Paris: Fayard, 2003.

Braconnier, Céline, and Jean-Yves Dormagen. *La démocratie de l'abstention*. Paris: Gallimard, 2007.

Brenner, Emmanuel, ed. *Les territoires perdus de la République: Antisémitisme, racisme et sexisme en milieu scolaire*. Paris: Mille et une Nuits, 2002.

Cartier, Marie, Isabelle Coutant, Olivier Masclet, and Yasmine Siblot. *La France des "petits-moyens": Enquête sur la banlieue pavillonnaire*. Paris: La Découverte, 2008.

Masclet, Olivier. *La gauche et les cités: Enquête sur un rendez-vous manqué*. Paris: La Dispute, 2003.

Mauger, Gérard. *L'émeute de novembre 2005: Une révolte protopolitique*. Bellecombe-en-Bauges: Croquant, 2006.

Maurin, Eric. *Le ghetto français: Enquête sur le séparatisme social*. Paris: Seuil/La République des Idées, 2004.

Tafferant, Nasser. *Le bizness: Une économie souterraine*. Paris: Presses Universitaires de France, 2007.

Wacquant, Loïc J. D. *Urban Outcasts: A Comparative Sociology of Advanced Marginality*. Cambridge and Malden, MA: Polity, 2008.

30

The Republic and the Veil

John R. Bowen

Although French theories and anxieties about Islamic headscarves date back to colonial days, they took on added force in the late 1980s, when fears about international political Islam combined with the greater domestic visibility of Islam to produce new cries of alarm. Objections to public wearing of Islamic scarves were based on multiple claims: some expressed concern that boys would pressure girls to don scarves; others argued that the scarves had become signs of political Islam; still others claimed that the scarf stood for the oppression of women. The debate centered on the presence of such scarves in schools and produced a 2004 law banning conspicuous signs of religious affiliation from public schools. No longer were scarves (*foulards*) at issue, but rather the inexact term "the veil" (*le voile*).

"The veil" evokes memories and *imaginaires* of colonial rule and in particular the late period of Algerian colonization and the Algerian War (1954–62), when women's dress became a salient sign of affiliation to either indigenous or Western modes of life. In metropolitan France, however, for the first half of the twentieth century Islam was largely present in the form of North African male workers, cycling between their birthplaces and France to work in factories. But during the postwar recovery period, the Algerian War, and especially after the 1970s, Algerians and other Muslims from northern and western Africa increasingly settled in France with their wives and children. Labor migration as such ended and was replaced by immigration based on family reunification, which usually meant that a man or woman came to join his or her lawfully resident spouse in France. The presence of Islam now included settled women and men.

By the 1980s, the sons and daughters of those resident Muslim families began to come of age and to search for their identities. Many found it difficult to find acceptance as French, despite their status as French-born citizens. Prejudice against Muslims and against people of color, coupled with bitter memories of the recent Algerian conflict, would have made acceptance difficult in any case; the economic downturn of the 1970s exacerbated tensions all the more. But the new generation did not find themselves at ease "back home" either: they were French in some way, and not Algerian or Senegalese.

The search for identity led some of these young Muslims to study Islam as a formal religion rather than simply to inherit it as a tradition. They began to attend lectures by charismatic young preachers, read books that taught them "true Islam," and frequent mosques. Joined by new immigrants from Islamic countries, some younger Muslims, French- and foreign-born, began to "look Muslim." Some women wore scarves pulled tightly over their heads, concealing their hair and ears, and that contrasted with their mothers' scarves, which were worn more loosely and casually. They might wear a simple scarf or a combination of two head coverings, one covering the forehead and the other the top of the head and the shoulders, or a more unified garment including head covering, blouse, and skirt. Non-Muslim observers tended to reduce the many elements that make up markedly Islamic dress—head coverings, blouses and tunics, skirts and trousers, and perhaps gloves—to the matter of how, and how much of, the head was covered. Did the particular scarf cover the ears, leave the roots of the hair exposed or not, or come down over the forehead? For many non-Muslims in France, these differences in degree of covering came to signify differences in the degree of religiosity or of moral difference being signaled by a Muslim woman.

Eventually these new scarves assumed the general rubric of "the veil" (*le voile*), although often Muslims speak of wearing a *hijâb,* following the Qur'anic injunction to erect a "curtain" (*hijâb*) between women and men. The younger women drawn to wearing a scarf did so for a variety of reasons. Some did it to satisfy their parents that they were remaining good Muslims even as they moved into a French world of study and work. Many adopted the scarf during middle-school years and may or may not have taken up regular religious practice. Other girls began to wear a scarf in a conscious effort to create a new identity as they entered or left high school. For them, wearing a scarf was part of two simultaneous processes: defining themselves in Islamic terms and entering the world of postsecondary education and work. These women tended to be educated and successful, and to regularly pray, fast, and observe dietary rules.

It is unsurprising that the highly publicized debates over scarf wearing would center on schools. Since the mid-nineteenth century, the public school has been a major focus for debates about religion and the Republic. But when scarves first appeared in schools, they did not elicit public comment and violated no rule. By late 1989, however, teachers and principals began to react against the scarves; they did so because of events taking place in France and elsewhere in the world. Many in France saw Islam as a new threat and Muslim students as its carriers. They saw Islam this way because of two simultaneous developments:

the children of Muslim immigrants in France were proclaiming Islam as their identity, and political leaders in other countries were proclaiming Islam to be their guide. Since 1989, conjunctures of events at home and abroad—war in Algeria, the attacks of 2001 on New York and Washington, problems in the poor suburbs—have continued to shape the headscarf story as it has exploded into, or drifted out of, public awareness.

The first of several "affaires du foulard" began in September 1989, when three girls of North African background arrived at school wearing Islamic dress. This in itself was not new—the class photo from the school's previous year showed a girl in a scarf. For at least several years, girls had been coming to many schools with scarves and either attended with their scarves or agreed to remove them during class.

What had changed to make this event into an "affaire"? The late 1980s had been a dispiriting period for many on the right but especially many on the left: President Mitterrand's economic policies had proved disappointing; his government's celebration of the French Revolution bicentennial appeared to many as a betrayal of revolutionary tradition; and the fall of the Berlin Wall left some without a touchstone, and others without an enemy. A candidate for new enemy was political Islam. Stories on the three schoolgirls were accompanied by photos of Iranian women in dark Islamic dress, photos that recalled the Iranian Revolution, the brutal war in Lebanon, and allegations that Islamists had manipulated striking automobile workers in 1983.

This first "affaire du foulard" was settled legally when the Council of State (Conseil d'État) ruled that pupils in school were protected in expressing their religious beliefs through their clothing, as long they did not proselytize or disturb order and followed the school curriculum. The Council held to this ruling thereafter, endorsing school expulsions in just a few cases, and then only because some other reason was given: the girls had also refused to take gym class, proselytized, or evoked protests that disturbed order.

When a second peak of public interest occurred in 1993–94, it again resulted from a conjuncture of international and domestic anxieties. In Algeria, the cancellation of the 1992 elections had been followed by a cycle of violence between the Armed Islamic Group (GIA) and the army. Thousands died, and the violence eventually reached France. Attention returned to scarves in schools, and in 1994 the minister of education banned them, creating a spike in cases reaching school disciplinary councils and a new group of expelled high-school girls.

Matters quieted down in the late 1990s, but the 2001 attack on the World Trade Center and Pentagon in the United States turned the mass media toward possible internal threats attributable to Islam. Politicians and reporters linked scarves to political and social problems in three ways. First, a series of government reports described malfunctioning schools and a growing separation between those deemed ethnically French (*français de souche*) and the children of immigrants. As Prime Minister Raffarin later would say, "the major sign of communalism [ethnic and racial separation] in the schools, the most symbolic, is wearing religious signs." Second, some saw scarves as signs of political Islam or "Islamism" in France, represented notably by the Union of French Islamic Organizations (UOIF), an organization associated with the radical Muslim Brotherhood and with the lecturer Tariq Ramadan. Their advocacy of the right to wear headscarves cemented this association in the eyes of many. Finally, leading feminists and many other public figures charged that the scarf signaled the oppression of women. As Education Ministry mediator Hanifa Chérifi stated in 2001, "the intrinsic significance of the *voile* is to remind women, starting at puberty, that Islamic morality forbids mixing of the sexes in all public spaces, including the school." By 2003, others added the claim that the scarves were linked to violence against women in poor suburbs.

Throughout 2003, politicians on both the right and the left raced to denounce scarves. Future President (but then Interior Minister) Nicolas Sarkozy chose his April 2003 speech before the UOIF to denounce Muslims who refused to remove scarves for identity photos. The President and National Assembly each created commissions charged with producing reports ostensibly "on laicity" but motivated by the furor over scarves. The more important commission was chaired by Bernard Stasi, a former minister of state security, and its hearings were broadcast over the new C-SPAN-inspired Public Sénat Internet and cable station. The hearings served to heighten public concerns over communalism, Islamism, and the oppression of women. Commission members took testimony from educators, religious leaders, and a wide range of public figures (but they largely ignored the many sociologists who had studied young Muslim women and their choices of dress).

Most telling for the outcome were complaints by school heads that they could no longer cope with disorder in the schools, some of which they attributed to tensions between religious communities. Although educational personnel were divided on the issue—three of the four major confederations of teachers' unions asked President Chirac not to propose a new law—those heard by the Stasi Commission tended to favor a law. Several teachers and principals testified that families pressured girls: one teacher thought that a girl's knowledge of the State Council's ruling in favor of scarf-wearing meant that she had been coerced or manipulated. A Parisian high-school principal recounted a series of incidents he considered disturbing: students praying in the school, bringing in Islamic books, claiming that required lessons conflicted with their Islamic beliefs, and engaging in vocal debates over religion. She observed growing numbers of girls in headscarves, conflicts between mothers and daughters, troublemaking boys, fighting, voodoo ceremonies, proselytism, and anti-Semitic insults. Jewish students, meanwhile, often missed Friday late-afternoon or Saturday classes. Despite the wide range of troubles, the principal claimed that headscarves were for her the most visible sign of the crisis of secularity (laicity).

President Chirac urged the Stasi Commission to work quickly so that a law could be passed before the spring 2004 regional elections. The new law would be central to the government's effort to forestall a repetition of the Far Right's April 2002 victories. By the time the commission issued its report on December 11, 2003, public opinion had swung firmly behind a new law, from 49 percent favorable in April to 72 percent favorable in early December. Those who followed the news would have heard about other Islam-related threats to the Republic: separate hours for women at swimming pools, women patients refusing to be treated by male doctors, jurors wearing scarves while in court, and Muslims booing the interior minister. Some of the media reports concerned serious problems, such as anti-Semitism or attacks on women in the poor suburbs, albeit linked to scarf wearing only indirectly at best. Other reports were highly fanciful, such as the claim that Carla Bruni's CD contained secret Islamist messages. The overall effect of these reports was to move the public—and some on the Stasi Commission—toward the general sentiment that "something had to be done."

Passed by Parliament in March 2004, the law took effect the following September. Although the law was expected to produce a number of confrontations, none occurred, in no small part because militants in Iraq took two French journalists hostage, demanding that the law be abrogated. This event made it difficult for French Muslims to stand firm against the law and provided an opportunity for the new "Muslim notables" to prove their loyalty. Over the next three years very few cases arose that could not be resolved through discussion, although a number of girls moved to Belgium, took distance courses, or dropped out of school. What the law will bring in the longer term is unclear. Muslim groups undertook efforts to build private Islamic schools (where scarves would be allowed), opening four as of 2009, only one of which predated the 2004 law.

The law arguably had its greatest effect outside the schools, as, here and there, city officials and private citizens cited it in support of other efforts to ban headscarves from public places. In some cases, women were not allowed to enter city halls for marriages, refused service at university canteens, or denounced by fellow citizens for wearing scarves. In these and other cases, people inferred from the ban on religious signs in schools (which they correctly understood to target Muslims) that Islamic scarves were inappropriate in other state-run settings, or even in all "public space," playing on the ambiguities of that phrase. These inferences were "reasonable" in the sense that the politicians and writers arguing for a law in 2003–4 maintained that the scarves were intrinsically signs of the oppression of women, political Islam (as the prime minister stated), a refusal to integrate with rest of the society, or simply, as President Chirac said, "aggressive." If the nation's leaders said that scarves were intrinsically at odds with the Republic, then why not ban them everywhere? Why stop at the school door?

By 2008, some officials had moved from condemning scarves in public spaces to condemning certain putative values shared by some Muslims, sometimes signaled by their choice of dress. In June 2008, for example, the Council of State refused to grant French nationality to a woman from Morocco, citing her religious practices. Islam, the Council declared, had given her values that ran counter to the equality of men and women and prevented her from assimilating as a French citizen should: she had an "assimilation defect" (*défaut d'assimilation*). The woman had married a French convert to Islam who had requested that she wear a full face covering (called a burqa by the court). Though she had met the formal conditions for citizenship, having waited the required period of time after marriage before requesting naturalization, she was deemed to have insufficient knowledge of the right to vote and the basics of laicity. The couple had three children, and the woman in question was reported to stay at home during the day.

Public response to the case focused on the woman's dress. State Minister Fadela Amara declared: "The headscarf and the burqa are the same. I am against wearing the headscarf, which is not a religious sign but, like the burqa, a sign of women's oppression." The issue no longer was behavior in civic institutions or protecting the secular space of the public school; what counted now was the very decision to dress in a certain way, taken to be a sign of values and orientations incompatible with the French Republic.

References

Ahmed, Leila. *Women and Gender in Islam: Historical Roots of a Modern Debate.* New Haven, CT: Yale University Press, 1992.

Bowen, John R. *Can Islam Be French? Pluralism and Pragmatism in a Secular State.* Princeton, NJ: Princeton University Press, 2009.

———. *Why the French Don't Like Headscarves: Islam, the State, and Public Space.* Princeton, NJ: Princeton University Press, 2006.

Gaspard, Françoise, and Farhad Khosrokhavar. *Le foulard et la Republique.* Paris: La Découverte, 1995.

Guenif-Souilamas, Nacira. *Des beurettes aux descendants d'immigrants nord-africains.* Paris: Bernard Grasset, 2000.

Joppke, Christian. *Veil.* London: Polity, 2009.

Laborde, Cecile. *Critical Republicanism: The Hijab Controversy and Political Philosophy.* Oxford: Oxford University Press, 2008.

Roy, Olivier. *Secularism Confronts Islam.* New York: Columbia University Press, 2007.

Scott, Joan Wallach. *The Politics of the Veil.* Princeton, NJ: Princeton University Press, 2007.

Winter, Bronwyn. *Hijab and the Republic: Uncovering the French Headscarf Debate.* Syracuse, NY: Syracuse University Press, 2008.

31

ANTISEMITISM, JUDEOPHOBIA, AND THE REPUBLIC

Steven Englund

> One may have every vice in his inkwell, commit every sin with his pen.
> —Victor Hugo

Few topics have received the attention that French Antisemitism has, or given rise to as many misconceptions. It has long been common to see the Third Republic as saturated with Jew-hatred, as the "laboratory of fascism," in Zeev Sternhell's words. This will not be my approach. Rather, I shall apply to the field of Antisemitic studies the kinds of fundamental comparisons and distinctions commonly regarded as progress in studies of nationalism and imperialism for example, but which, for complex reasons that cannot be treated here, have been resisted in the study of Jew-hatred. I shall distinguish between *Judeophobia*—a generalized dislike of Jews in a given population—and *Antisemitism* (capital A)—a systematic public attitude incarnated in an organized political movement. Judeophobia encompasses greatly varying degrees of hatred, contempt, scorn, and fear vis-à-vis Jewish people; in one form or other, it was an unfortunate constant of all of pre-1945 European history, a social condition of virtually any era. Antisemitism, however, dates from 1879–80 and was a European phenomenon, arising all but simultaneously in several of the Continent's leading polities. To discuss it in the context of France alone would be like considering only the moves of the white pieces in analyzing a game of chess.

The consequence of telescoping Antisemitism with Judeophobia is to amass studies of generalized, banalized "Antisemitism" that impose a discursive identity on *any and all* instances of Jew-baiting, from Édouard Drumont's diatribes in the Dreyfus affair (he demanded the expulsion of French Jewry) to Charles de Gaulle's 1967 arch observation that Jews "are an elite people, self-confident and domineering." Common in the post-Shoah world, the general category of "Antisemitism" construes all of French history as "shot full" of the same sort of organized Jew-hatred that one customarily associates with the histories of Austria and Germany. If, however, we make the distinction between Judeophobia and Antisemitism (capital A), it will become clear that the French case is not well summarized by the word "fascist."

Obviously, the Judeophobia/Antisemitism distinction may be challenged for being artificial; and, to be sure, in the absence of popular Judeophobia, Antisemitism is less likely to appear. Still, it is strangely the case that Antisemitism initially surfaced in France when few Jews were present, and no noticeable eruption or alteration in popular attitudes toward them was visible. Whereas in central and eastern Europe, Jews numbered in the many hundreds of thousands and millions, in France before 1914 they attained perhaps ninety thousand in a population of nearly forty million. French Jewry was a small and highly assimilated community, which, unlike its German counterpart, produced few works that featured Jewish identity or accomplishment in distinction from the French. There was no Franco-Jewish equivalent of the historian Heinrich Graetz, whose seven-volume *History of the Jews* piqued German patriotic sensibility for its "impertinent" remarks about German achievements.

It was common in France of the early 1880s to hear the defensive claim that Antisemitism was a foreign import—from Germany. A decade later, such a claim would be easily refuted, for the Third Republic had by then developed its own version of this new politics of protest. Nevertheless, the thing itself—the word *Antisemitismus* and the organized entity—did indeed make their appearance in Germany before coming to France from across the Rhine. Beginning in 1879, the so-called Berlin Movement—a large, loose congeries of Antisemitic parties, leagues, leaders, doctrines, intellectuals, newspapers, and, not least, of riots and widespread violence—swept the German capital, to become the talk of Europe. Western countries, including the Third Republic, reacted with disgust, but in France the disapproval was also met by a few local imitative initiatives. A weekly newspaper, *L'Anti-Sémitique,* appeared in 1883–84, enjoying the collaboration of a few modestly well-known Jew-hating publicists like Auguste Chirac or the abbé Chabauty. There were even plans for a league and an international congress, which did not materialize. Their propaganda shows early French Antisemites to be positively responsive to the events taking place in central Europe. It flattered them that the "great names" of the new German movement (Marr, Stoecker, Duehring, etc.) occasionally cited polemical classics of French Judeophobia going back to Toussenel.

The first large and successful flourishing of Antisemitism in France occurred in 1886, characteristically not around a movement or a government manipulation, but in the publication of a large tome. *La France juive* (Jewified France) appeared in bookstores at a time when the Berlin Movement had passed away, but electoral Antisemitism was proving itself a political force in parts of Germany (and soon in Austria). The two-volume, apparently erudite opus was the brainchild of an obscure but gifted journalist, Édouard Drumont. Its twelve hundred pages are a sprawling pastiche of arcana, assertion, and artifice, attaining nothing like the levels of prose, learning, and originality that characterized the works of the era's German Antisemites—Richard Wagner, Eugen Duehring, and Julius Langbehn. Rather, Drumont's book commended itself to readers for being riddled with salacious political gossip and commentary. Then, too, from stem to stern, it emitted the scent of the sacristy. It was not so much a Catholic book, per se—its episcopal anticlericalism was too violent for that, and its Judeophobia contained some secular-racial elements—but it was unmistakably fashioned in and for a Catholic culture in palpable conflict with the republican regime. A key slogan of Drumont's was "Judaism is the enemy," which of course laid stress on religion. (Neither he nor anyone around him developed a Gallic equivalent of the powerful and polyvalent German concept, *Judenthum.*) Historians have vastly overestimated the reception of *La France juive.* At eighty thousand copies sold by the war, it was a respectable commercial success, but far from one of the great best sellers of the century. It fell well short of the sales of many similar German works (e.g., those of Rohling or Fritsch), not to mention their greater political influence.

Drumont's book failed to launch anything like the mass, clerically based political movement that France's long history of Catholic Judeophobia and formidable opposition to secularism (laicity) might have been expected to engender. No powerful Center Party—the pride of German Catholicism—emerged west of the Rhine. Specifically, French Antisemitism proved unable to profit significantly from the large and varied Boulangist movement (1886–93), the most serious and lasting political attack the Third Republic sustained before 1939. Since Boulangism's founders included a few Jews, the movement largely disapproved of Antisemitism. In later years, as Boulangism's huge initial base evaporated, a handful of second-line adepts—Vergoin, Laur, the young Barrès, and others—made fitful attempts to revive the movement around a catch-all ideology of Antisemitism, as they had seen Otto Boeckel successfully do in rural Hesse, or Lueger in Vienna. But their efforts proved futile, not least because the would-be leaders of such a party, many of them corrupt and intellectually challenged, squabbled hopelessly among themselves.

The Berlin—and presently, the Vienna—movements mobilized tens of thousands of strong backers and loyal voters and eventually gave rise to powerful countermovements like the twelve-thousand-member Union of Resistance to Antisemitism. Meanwhile, as Bertrand Joly shows, the French Antisemitic League of Jules Guérin had trouble assembling more than fifty activists and never remotely mounted a serious electoral organization. French Antisemitism evoked no lasting mobilization in the traditional right-wing or left-wing milieux where Jew-hatred was known to exist. French Royalists, Catholics, and Socialists had discrete traditions of Jew-hatred, but none of these social sectors responded to calls for active membership in the new political movement. Then, too, the Third Republic itself was hostile to the movement, while east of the Rhine, the Bismarckian Reich occasionally trucked with Antisemitism for political ends.

A word about so-called Socialist Antisemitism, a misnomer if used to designate an organized force on the left. No important Socialist party or sect in France (or *Mitteleuropa,* for that matter) embraced Antisemitism; on the contrary, after some initial ambivalence, Socialists often publicly opposed Drumont and the forces around him, for they understood that Antisemitism offered itself as an alternative to Marxism, as a form of anti-Socialism. What has confused the issue was the unrelenting Socialist critique of capitalism, which occasionally deployed Judeophobic language. Nota bene, however; it did not use Jew-baiting as an organizing or analytic principle of Socialist ideology or as a party political program but contented itself with hurling epithets like "Down with Jewish finance!" and "Down with Rothschild!"—commonplaces throughout European society in the pre-Shoah era.

Antisemitism in France, far more than in *Mitteleuropa,* remained an affair of language, a catchall discourse that casually deployed "Jew" to mean German, Freemason, Protestant, or republican, as well as actual Jews. As a language, it was all the more violent *precisely because* it was free-floating in a Republic that guaranteed rights (including to opinion), unanchored in any important party or institution and dissociated from reference to a vast social presence of ascertainable human subjects—as was the case in contemporaneous Berlin, Vienna, Budapest, Bucharest, and Warsaw. As the dissertation by Damien Guillaume will make clear, French Antisemitism was largely an *affaire de plume et de scandale* in its prewar manifestation.

By the early nineties, Drumont's ideology was moribund, but it received unexpected resuscitation from external events: first, the Panama scandal (1892–93), which sullied a large number of business and political reputations, including those of several Jews. The affair saw the birth of Drumont's Antisemitic daily, *La Libre Parole* (Free Speech), which, thanks to its editors' polemical talents and the intense topicality of the issues covered, became a notorious publication for the rest of the decade. Although its print runs occasionally soared to three hundred thousand, it typically sold fifty to eighty thousand copies a day.

Second, in 1894, a new scandal erupted when a Jewish officer on the General Staff, Captain Alfred Dreyfus, was condemned for espionage. The Dreyfus scandal immersed the Third Republic in near-universal opprobrium and became synonymous with the generic phrase "French Antisemitism." Not without some reason: Judeophobic sentiment (but not membership in Antisemitic organizations) was widespread among senior officers of the General Staff, who rapidly and automatically accused Dreyfus, the lone Jew among them. From the outset of the case, Drumont and a handful of editors at several newspapers raised a violent hue and cry against Jews—sometimes in an ethnic-racial sense, though their epithets were always underpinned by religious allusions and shared cultural understandings. Antisemitism in France, even more than in Austria and unlike in Germany, was first and last a matter of Catholic culture.

The scandal factor in the Dreyfus affair needs to be highlighted: Antisemitism, by the mere fact of its existence in a Republic that prided itself on direct descent from the French Revolution, was flagrant, a cudgel used by France's friends, rivals, and enemies, who constantly reported it as a betrayal of French achievements and pretensions, at the painfully visible cost of an innocent victim's mind, body, and family. It happened that German newspapers shamed "the French" for wrongly prosecuting Dreyfus, insisting, "It couldn't happen here." This was true enough: no Jew could get within a Pomeranian furlong of an officer's commission in even the reserve, let alone on the revered *Generalstab*.

The paroxysm of prewar French Antisemitism arrived in 1898, with the anti-Jewish riots of winter and spring, made famous by the work of sociologist Pierre Birnbaum. The perturbations affected as many as sixty-nine areas around the Hexagon; jeering throngs spewed epithets at many targets, including Jews. The crowds numbered in the hundreds, rarely the thousands, did modest material damage, shed no blood, and the turbulence stopped as swiftly as it arose, requiring only light repressive action from the police or army. Bertrand Joly's work makes it clear that the triggering event in the riots was the publication of Zola's *J'accuse,* which, although it was greeted by Zola haters with "Death to the Jews!" itself bore almost entirely on the clerical-anticlerical/conservative-republican divisions in French society. Zola had little to say about Antisemitism. Where there is evidence of real local Judeophobia, moreover, it appears to have arisen with no help from organized Antisemitism and often came in second to anti-anticlericalism and ambient xenophobia as a mobilizing force. (Mob violence in France in this era resulted in the deaths of Italian or Belgian "guest" workers, not Jews.) The Stettin riots in Germany and the pogroms in Russia, by contrast, focused only on the Jewish population and entailed violent assemblies of *many* thousands of people, recurring over weeks and months, doing great material damage and shedding blood. Moreover, in Russia and Germany, the violence elicited mixed political signals from the top, as was not the case in France or Austria-Hungary, where the governments sternly reproved these melees.

The Dreyfus case was a major public issue, but it was not the only cynosure of its era, as is often alleged, still less so in the provinces, as Michael Burns shows. Other issues—notably the Franco-British set-to in the Sudan, and other events in foreign affairs—also mesmerized or polarized the public but had nothing to do with the Jews. Still, Antisemitism was the newcomer political presence on the scene and as such garnered attention. Drumont and his small team tirelessly strove to make the affair seem to turn on the "Jewish question," but to their abiding frustration, the same old topics presently reemerged. Even Maurice Barrès and Henri Rochefort, the journalist, and the newcomer ideologue, Charles Maurras, founder of the *Action Française*—for all the abuse they periodically heaped on "the Jew"—ruthlessly subordinated this gambit to a supporting role in their multifaceted defenses of army and church and their attacks on the "Slut" (the Republic). Moreover, in the formal iterations made by judges, lawyers, officers, and politicians; in the founding statement of the League for the Rights of Man; or in the lengthy appraisals offered up by leading writers and intellectuals, the Jewish theme was muted, when not absent altogether. As Vincent Duclert's magisterial biography of Dreyfus makes clear, what the whole turned on—for Dreyfusard and Anti-Dreyfusard alike—was less "the Jew in French society" than the clash of individual rights and *raison d'État,* or of "la République laïque" and "la République nationale." By 1899, and down to 1906, the year the Cour de Cassation acquitted Dreyfus, the affair, to Drumont's dismay, assumed the familiar outlines of the ongoing Franco-French "civil war," which had seen far bloodier avatars, having nothing to do with Jews, in 1848 and 1871.

The elections of 1898 sent to Paris 23 deputies (out of a total of 565) whose political platforms contained Judeophobic or Antisemitic discourse, though almost never overtly. These men proved wholly inactive in the Chamber, and in the next elections, in 1902, were virtually all defeated and/or gave up any use of the "Antisémite" *étiquette.* By contrast, the numerous Austro-German Antisemitic political parties mobilized hundreds of thousands of voters over two decades, which, in the case of Vienna, led to the municipal administration of the capital falling into the Antisemitic party's hands for a generation.

French Jewry largely saw the acquittal of Dreyfus as a victory over Antisemitism, understood by then as, in the words of a leading Jewish editor, straightforward "antirepublicanism." The French Jewish population evolved even further from any sense of communitarianism toward ever-closer association with the Republic. The founder of Zionism, Theodor Herzl, said of the, in his opinion, overassimilated French Jews: "They're not really Jews in our sense." For its part, the government reacted against anti-Dreyfusism by developing a "republican" social model that simply ignored formal religious affiliation in assessing the civil population, focusing instead on issues of social equality. In 1895, 7 out of 260 members of L'Institut de France, five generals, numerous Paris municipal councilors, and national deputies, senators, and prefects were Jews. The most serious threat to Judaism, according to a leading Jewish organ, was the growth of religious indifference, not the Antisemitic campaign. Be that as it may, a great many French Jews saw the era after 1906—culminating in 1914 with the Jewish philosopher Henri Bergson's election to the French Academy—as a golden age.

Édouard Drumont died a bitter man in 1917, knowing he had failed to do more than pique interest in his doctrine. Antisemitism had indeed emerged as one political strain among many—and far from the most powerful—on the French right. "The French" could not by any stretch be said to have "become Antisemitic." The big nationalist battalions—the League of Patriots and the League of the French Fatherland—rejected Jew-hating as the grand *Integrationstheorie* that Antisemitism took itself to be. In this, they were largely (if not always) followed by royalists and Catholics who "rallied" to the Republic, as of course by mainline republican conservatives. Rather, the new "ism" offered itself as an occasional, barely viable form of political oppositionalism constantly criticized for being incendiary and divisive.

The Great War witnessed an apex in Franco-Jewish assimilation. A famous episode, widely praised by the Right as much as the Left, featured a Jewish rabbi killed under fire as he held up a crucifix for a dying Catholic soldier. The politics of the twenties did not alter this picture, despite the victory of the rightist "national" coalition; mainstream conservatives were no more Antisemitic than any other large political party.

Socially, however, things changed dramatically. The severe perturbations in eastern and central Europe hastened the flow of *Ostjuden* to France, as the Third Republic reluctantly admitted these new refugees. Eastern European Jews came by the impoverished and desperate tens of thousands, speaking no French and, in cultural background and income, clashing profoundly with the rest of society, including France's acculturated Jews. Paris's Jewish population climbed steeply from sixty thousand in 1905 to two hundred thousand in 1939, though the Jewish influx still represented only 15 percent of the country's total immigration, which reached three million during the interwar years. Press commentary characterized France's American community, not its Jewish one, as the foreigners most resistant to assimilation, tarring the Yankees as "financiers cosmopolites."

Still, Antisemitism did reawaken, and, in classic French fashion, remained narrowly political. The closest thing France had to a right-wing mass party— arguably a fascist one (though this is a highly disputed issue)—was the Croix de Feu (CDF), known after 1936 as the Parti Social Français (PSF). This organization had nothing good to say about Jews, yet, unlike that of its counterparts in Germany, Austria, and Hungary, the CDF/PSF's ideology or politics did not feature Antisemitism as a leitmotif; Jews were occasional targets of opportunity but were less important than many others, including Freemasons. (Indeed the CDF boasted of having a few Jewish members.) The backbone of the Jew-hating movement in the Hexagon was the Action Française. Though not a mass organization—it counted around ten thousand militants—the AF boasted a prestigious "think tank" of well-known publicists and intellectuals and published an influential daily newspaper with a readership of forty-five thousand to seventy thousand. The organization's attacks on Jews consisted mainly of verbal and editorial violence, though some of Maurras's *camelots* (rowdies) physically assaulted residents of Paris's Jewish quarter.

The government dissolved the AF after its thugs attacked Léon Blum, the leader of the Socialist Party and a Jew. Blum was dragged from his car and badly beaten, but he recovered, soon to become the premier of France's first Socialist-led government, the Popular Front (1936–37). At his behest, the National Assembly passed legislation criminalizing language deemed to incite hatred. Still, it is important to note: the AF never turned overtly racist, as Drumont had been or the Nazis now were. Laurent Joly's recent work demonstrates that Maurras believed the restoration of the monarchy would solve France's "Jewish Question," as well as the—to him, larger—problems of Protestants, foreigners, and anticlerical republicans.

Even so, Judeophobic discourse grew more commonplace in the 1930s, attaining a kind of legitimacy that comes with banality. That an important newspaper like *L'Ami du Peuple,* with several hundred thousand readers, could without flinching mount a campaign against "Jewish financiers" was unprecedented. Too, a few of the small handful of serious Antisemites, notably Xavier Vallat, the future Vichy commissioner for the Jewish Question, now amounted to figures of some intelligence and standing. But Vallat and his colleagues confronted a phenomenon largely new to France: an extraordinary Jewish mobilization against the Jew-haters. Unlike the Dreyfus era, when the assimilated Jewish community had let others do its fighting for it, the presence in the 1930s of many thousands of politicized young Jewish immigrants, more identified with the European Left than with the French Republic, spawned a movement intent on going toe to toe with its enemies. The International League against Antisemitism, with fifty thousand members, brought the battle against the Action Française to the streets.

The Jewish immigrants to France accomplished even more than mounting a battle royal with reaction and counterrevolution; they also inspired a renaissance of Yiddish and Hebraic identity to a degree that the assimilated Franco-Jewish community would not have dared to attempt on its own. The Jewish renaissance affected French society as influentially as—and far more positively and lastingly than—the Action Française did. As Paula Hyman shows, French (largely immigrant) Jewry in the interwar era proved to itself and the world that "the inertia and complacency of 'false' assimilation" were not the last word to be written in the story of modern French Jewry.

For the better part of a painful decade, France witnessed as vicious a political Donnybrook as the country had experienced since the Commune; compared to it, the Dreyfus era was "a glass of rosewater," said one noted Antisemite, who lived through both eras. Still, the issues involved do not begin to be adequately summarized in the phrase "the clash of Jew and Antisemitism"; the forces involved—revolution, counterrevolution, church, laicity, and so on—were far greater, older, and more complicated than that. Antisemitism, *pur et dur,* only somewhat integrated these issues and could easily be sacrificed or played down for public relations' sake.

The Antisemites, few in number but backed in part by Nazi money, put out a relentless attack on "the Jew as Bolshevik," but their cause was seen as "artificial" by more than one neutral observer. The novelist Céline published his ferociously Antisemitic *Bagatelles pour un massacre* (1937), while in the Chamber of Deputies, a number of extremist conservatives assailed "the Jew," meaning Blum. But the editor of *Gringoire* rejected the label of "Antisemite," insisting his quarrel with Blum and the Jews was purely political.

The Republic itself continued to have no truck with Antisemitism, but as Jewish emigration from Germany rose sharply after the violent attacks on Jewish individuals and property of Kristallnacht (November 9–10, 1938), discussions of the "Jewish Question"—entailing the whole issue of refugees and immigrants—were now heard in regions that had not mentioned these subjects in decades, if ever. As the country slid into war, thousands of foreigners, including Jews, were interned in camps. His Majesty's government would do the same to German nationals living in Great Britain; the matter had nothing to do with Antisemitism.

The tragedy that presently broke upon the hapless Jews of France in 1940 was unforeseeable, without example in modern French history. Vichy's legislation drew on the language and employed some of the personnel of France's own counterrevolutionary tradition, but its anti-Jewish policies, as Laurent Joly exhaustively shows, were carried out in the shadow and under the influence of the implacable Nazi presence. All states perforce have *some* measure of continuity with what directly preceded them, but in all meaningful senses, Vichy's État Français resulted from the destruction of the Third Republic and intentionally sought to be its antithesis. *Pace* Gérard Noiriel, there are no significant "republican origins of Vichy," at least where the Jews are concerned. It would make more sense (if be no more convincing) to speak of the Catholic, or even the Christian, "origins of Vichy." For French Jewry, the continuity between the regimes was the continuity between a rope and a hanged man.

French Antisemitism in the pre-Vichy era, as Bertrand Joly observes, is not well studied as a political entity unto itself; there was no "pure state" of it in France, as there was in *Mitteleuropa.* It was a free-for-all discourse of changing objects occasionally taken up in the Franco-French wars. To focus on cumulative instances of anti-Jewish rhetoric in the press or in books, without coldly appraising its quantity and typology in comparative terms, is to radically misconstrue the true extent and role of this new oppositional form on the crowded French public scene. Antisemitism was a public issue among many, *many* others: economic crisis, political scandal, colonial empire, immigration, class conflict and socioeconomic reform, strikes and unions, church-state relations, right-wing oppositionalism, and revanche (including a military reform law, armament, and diplomatic prestige and crisis)—*all of which dwarfed it in significance*. Moreover, the excessive attention to anti-Jewish rhetoric imposes too uniform an identity on France's Jewish community, whose members, particularly in the thirties, identified with one another mainly because they were forced to by Antisemitism—and indeed, even then, many did not. This is Jean-Paul Sartre's point in his brilliant book *Anti-Semite and Jew* (1946).

This is not to say that Judeophobia was not present in French society. It was rife by our standards—as, sadly, it was rife everywhere. In *Remembrance of Things Past,* Swann is regarded as "a Jew," even though his family had converted to Catholicism two generations before. Several of the most celebrated men of the Dreyfusard coalition—Romain Rolland, Émile Zola, and Charles Péguy—may all be read as "Antisemitic" if we judge some of their prose by post-Shoah standards. It is common to cite Theodor Herzl's revulsion at witnessing Captain Dreyfus's military degradation in the courtyard of the École Militare in January 1895. But what is rarely noted is the larger truth that Herzl never for a moment believed the French "case" to be as serious as the Antisemitic movement in his native Austria, let alone in Germany. It simply shocked Herzl, as it shocked many of his contemporaries, to see *any* of this in a Republic whose eighteenth-century Revolution had emancipated the Jews.

Since then, France as a society has rejected cultural pluralism as Americans practice it, but this is not simply another way of saying France is Antisemitic or xenophobic. Labeling the longest-lived French Republic (1870–1940) "Antisemitic" may provide a form of psychic satisfaction to contemporary guilty consciences, but it does not advance our understanding of what Antisemitism actually was.

References

Burns, Michael. *Rural Society and French Politics: Boulangism and the Dreyfus Affair, 1886–1900.* Cambridge, MA: Harvard University Press, 1984.

Byrnes, Robert F. *Antisemitism in Modern France: The Prologue to the Dreyfus Affair.* New Brunswick, NJ: Rutgers University Press, 1950.

Duclert, Vincent. *Alfred Dreyfus, l'honneur d'un patriote.* Paris: Fayard, 2006.

Hyman, Paula. *From Dreyfus to Vichy: The Remaking of French Jewry, 1906–1939.* New York: Columbia University Press, 1979.

Joly, Bertrand. *Nationalistes et conservateurs en France, 1885–1902.* Paris: Indes Savantes, 2008.

Joly, Laurent. *Vichy dans la "Solution finale": Histoire du commissariat général aux questions juives, 1941–1944.* Paris: Grasset, 2006.

Kauffmann, Grégoire. *Édouard Drumont.* Paris: Perrin, 2008.

Marrus, Michael, and Robert O. Paxton. *Vichy France and the Jews.* New ed., with a foreword by Stanley Hoffmann. Stanford, CA: Stanford University Press, 1995.

Sorlin, Pierre. *"La Croix" et les juifs.* Paris: Grasset, 1967.

Sternhell, Zeev. *La droite révolutionnaire.* Paris: Seuil, 1978.

Wilson, Stephen. *Ideology and Experience: Antisemitism in France at the Time of the Dreyfus Affair.* Rutherford, NJ: Fairleigh Dickinson University Press, 1982.

32

Feminism and the Republic

Karen Offen

At the dawn of the Third Republic, the word *féministe,* applied to advocates of women's rights and women's emancipation, began to circulate in French with Alexandre Dumas fils's diatribe *Homme-Femme* (1872). But neither *féministe* nor *féminisme* gained traction in French until the redoubtable suffrage advocate Hubertine Auclert appropriated them in her weekly publication, *La Citoyenne,* during the early 1880s. The eloquent anticlerical republican Maria Deraismes summed up the situation feminists confronted in 1882: "One must recognize that in France masculine supremacy is the last aristocracy." Toppling that aristocracy, that male privilege, was the ultimate goal, and feminist women and men became partners in that struggle.

In the 1890s the terms "feminist" and "feminism" took off, spreading far beyond the Francophone world and becoming the subject of much controversy. They offered a quick shorthand for referring to claims for women's rights and women's emancipation, and, more explicitly, to the overall project of challenging masculine domination—in the institutions, ideas, and practices that composed society and culture. Everyone then understood what feminism meant, even though many varieties of feminists could be identified.

Contrary to the claims of their fiercest opponents, the women who espoused feminist ideas had no interest in "becoming" men, or even "like men," but they did claim equal opportunities, equal voice, and autonomous control of and authority over their own lives. Feminists asserted their rights as fully embodied, rational women sharing the world with men, without being systematically dominated, legally, economically, physically, and intellectually by fathers, husbands, brothers, priests, or other male authority figures. Unlike so many feminists in English-speaking and Scandinavian countries, most French feminists understood individual autonomy in a relational way, emphasizing their unique public role as mothers—mothers of future French citizens and citizen-mothers active in civil society if not in government as such. This inflection of feminism was particularly evident during the later French Republics, from the Third into the early years of the Fifth, though it changed dramatically in the 1970s.

But feminism had deeper roots in French culture that extended back to the Valois monarchy. Since the early fifteenth century French women—and men— had been making claims for women's equality with men. These claims erupted amid discussions of specific pressing issues, such as men's slanders against women in print culture, claims for improvements in education for girls and women, and for justice in the civil laws governing the situation of wives in marriage. Feminist claims subsequently included the right to speak out, to read, write, publish, and meet together and to pursue equality before the law and equal pay for equal work.

Such challenges had emerged well before there was any possibility of a republican or democratic form of government in France. They gained momentum with the king's call to convene the Estates General in 1789 and continued through the abolition of the monarchy and the declaration of the Republic in September 1792. Initially, women and their advocates demanded representation in the assemblies, the right to vote, and the full application to them of the Declaration of the Rights of Man. Citizenship, they argued, must encompass both sexes. Some claimed that women should have their own assemblies and elect their own delegates; men could not represent them or their interests. The marquis de Condorcet insisted that women should vote and enjoy equal citizenship, while Olympe de Gouges proposed a "Declaration of the Rights of Woman and *Citoyenne.*" A century later, Alphonse Aulard, an eminent historian of the French Revolution, emphasized the "real historical importance" of the early feminist movement, because it had been so "involved with the origins of democracy and of the Republic." And, indeed, much of the discussion about women and the Republic could be equally well framed (as Christine Fauré, Éliane Viennot, and other French scholars have done) in terms of women's access to democracy.

From 1792 on, with the advent of a "republican" (i.e., constitutional and representative, and, following the arrest and execution of the king, antimonarchical) government in France, proponents of women's rights anticipated a favorable reception—and results—in the name of the republican principles of liberty, equality, and justice. The new regime had, after all, incarnated these principles symbolically in the form of female figures appropriated from Greco-Roman mythology. Aulard credited Louise Kéralio (Madame Robert), a republican journalist dedicated to promoting women writers, with being the true founder of the French republican (i.e., antimonarchical) party, as she had already proposed the idea in December 1790. And not long thereafter, in opposition to the "bourgeois" groupings of active, propertied (male) citizens, the idea of a republic took on a more inclusive, democratic form. Yet, with only a few notable exceptions, male adherents of even the most advanced republican ideas repeatedly attempted to exclude women from participation in political life—not on theoretical grounds, but on the grounds of "public utility." Already in 1791 Talleyrand promoted this argument, which he predicated on Article 2 of the Declaration of the Rights of Man, espousing a commitment to "separate spheres" of activity for each sex. Women we would now call feminists fired back. Olympe de Gouges published her "Declaration," and the Englishwoman Mary Wollstonecraft addressed Talleyrand directly in her "Vindication of the Rights of Woman," an essay quickly translated into French. She and others also made the case for the role of mother-educator as a public responsibility. Male revolutionaries such as the journalist Prudhomme, well versed in the writings of Rousseau, countered (in 1793) that women should "let men make the revolution," and abandon clubs and meetings to stay home to care for their children. Were "the people," then, de facto, a "fraternity" of brothers who also happened to be heads of households? Was women's "citizenship" inherently passive? By no means. From the outset, both under the constitutional monarchy and the budding Republic, feminists of both sexes denounced these restrictions as arbitrary sociopolitical constructions.

In the Year VII (1799), a certain Charles Theremin published a treatise, *De la condition des femmes dans les républiques,* that criticized those revolutionaries who had consigned women to domesticity by invoking the model of the early Roman Republic: "Are we in a Republic of men only, and should there be in France only *républicains* and not *républicaines?*" (54). The Roman model of old, Theremin declared, was not suited to revolutionary France's mixed economy of agriculture and industry. Theremin demanded equal opportunity for women to develop their talents and make their contributions to the larger society. He firmly believed that the position of women must improve with civilization and that under a republic, a more perfect form of government than monarchy, "women's situation [should] be sweeter" (11). Theremin maintained that the Declaration of the Rights of Man wholly encompassed women, though he did not think women needed the right to vote. "The husband and wife are only one person politically," he wrote (59), thus the man's vote counts for two. Wives are therefore represented; in Theremin's view, they could not possibly have political opinions different from those of their husbands. In making this argument, Theremin laid out a plan of complementary equality, but with separate spheres for each sex to make its respective contributions. This was effectively a "familial" or "relational" feminism—a version of "equality-in-difference" that transcended the status quo on some points, notably advancing education for girls and employment opportunities for single women, but drawing a sharp line on others. But Theremin added one idea that would be endlessly repeated throughout the course of the French Republics: "The republican regime must attach women intimately to the Republic" (63). How to do that remained a challenge, given French republicanism's project of secularizing Catholic society, in which the church turned to women as its principal pillars of support.

Though women's rights made only modest advances during the Revolution, proposals such as those of de Gouges and Theremin ultimately precipitated a strong antifeminist backlash. Napoleon's Civil Code (1804) greatly disadvantaged wives, while the rights of single, divorced, or widowed adult women, strengthened during the Revolution and untouched in principle afterward, were subject to constant police interference. In the face of these constraints, urban women of varying socioeconomic circumstances flocked to the Saint-Simonians, Fourierists, and Cabetistes, the so-called utopian socialists, who promised their sex a better future. These and other activists published numerous petitions, calling for the abolition of Article 231 of the Civil Code (which decreed wives' obedience to husbands in return for their protection), the reinstatement of civil divorce (abolished during the Restoration), public education for girls, and professional training and job opportunities for young women, among other reforms. A cluster of well-known women writers even developed a feminist version of republican principles, as Whitney Walton has demonstrated.

In 1848, with the establishment of the Second Republic, women protested the Provisional Government's idea of universal suffrage because it limited political citizenship to "every Frenchman [*Français*] of mature age [*en age viril*]." In French, "Français" could include men and women, but the qualification "en age viril"—virility—made it clear that political citizenship applied only to men. There was no "universal" suffrage, only *manhood* suffrage. A group of women promptly petitioned the new government, insisting on the complementarity of the sexes and that if the "revolution has been made for all," women were assuredly "half of everyone." The petition fell on deaf ears; as during the French Revolution, the republican leadership balked at granting women the right to vote.

Although women activists and writers continued to debate women's rights during the authoritarian Second Empire (1852–70), the Paris Commune (1871) placed the burning topic of women's citizenship "on hold." During the Commune a contingent of radical Parisian women claimed and briefly demonstrated their capabilities as *citoyennes*. But, afterward, the military trials of "*pétroleuses*," revolutionary women accused of setting Paris ablaze, and the conservative politics of "moral order" dissuaded leading partisans of women's emancipation from demanding a full menu of women's rights, including the vote, on the same terms as men. Instead, they chose to travel a more cautious road, arguing—once again—for dramatic modifications of the Civil Code, further educational opportunities for girls, the abolition of government-regulated prostitution, and better economic opportunities for women workers. In July 1878, the International Women's Rights Congress passed a capacious set of resolutions to this effect, even though women's suffrage had been taken off the table. Hubertine

Auclert, however, made sure that the vote, which she considered the keystone to all other reforms, did not slip from view. "I am astonished," she said, "that under a republic it is still necessary to cry out for such and such a right for one segment of humankind.... The weapon of the vote will be for us, just as it is for man, the only means of obtaining the reforms we desire."

In 1885, Auclert proposed a "women's electoral program" that demanded women's full inclusion in the French nation. It featured a series of measures designed to promote the equality of the sexes, including the vote, and to assure "security and work to able-bodied French citizens [and] assistance to children, old people, [and] the sick and the infirm." In conclusion, she insisted: "The human equality [this program] proposes is the goal of a Republic; for Republic and justice should be synonymous." In Auclert's view, and she was not alone, women had everything to gain under a republic.

Yet, as historian Florence Rochefort has pointed out, "the republicans in power" remained unwilling to acknowledge women as independent individuals outside the control of the male-headed family. Maria Deraismes, one of the most outspoken advocates for women's rights, put her finger on the problem, though conflating democracy and republic: "It is not Democracy, but the democrats who are against us." But who else might feminists form alliances with? The socialists were not yet the serious factor in French politics that they would become. And despite Auclert's best efforts, they largely refused to address sexual inequality head-on. The hierarchy of social classes had to be abolished first, after which the equality of men and women would follow naturally and inevitably. This position became crystal clear during the founding congress of the Second Socialist International, held in Paris in 1889, and remained in place through most of the twentieth century. Although many feminists in France continued to work across the lines with socialists and to concern themselves with the plight and problems of employed women workers, the women of the Second International, spearheaded by the German militant Clara Zetkin, continued to dig a trench between "bourgeois feminism" and "socialism." Although Madeleine Pelletier modified this position in 1907 by arguing that a "proletarian and socialist feminism" should be created in parallel to "bourgeois feminism," Auclert riposted: "There cannot be a bourgeois feminism and a socialist feminism because there are not two female sexes." Women, rich or poor, were all in the same boat.

Many republicans, committed as they were to building a secular society, continued to worry about the possibility that as electors, the greater mass of women would support the Catholic Church. This fear of clerical influence, best articulated in the 1840s by the renowned historian Jules Michelet, remained powerful throughout the entire Third Republic (1875–1940). During this period, competition between religious and secular groups for control of women's minds and bodies remained fierce, though republicans did not try to win women over by offering them political rights. If secularists rarely opposed women's citizenship on grounds of principle, they nonetheless framed a great many "utilitarian" arguments against women's equality. Women, they maintained, could not be reliable supporters of the Third Republic, because they were too Catholic and inadequately educated. Even granting suffrage at the municipal level seemed too extravagant, although England and a few other countries had done so in the second half of the nineteenth century. Subsequently, republican opponents of women's citizenship would argue demographics: women citizens and voters would or could or might outnumber men! Not only that, but the changes feminists proposed would disrupt men's privileges and pleasures—most notably their easy access to alcohol and government-licensed prostitution, but also their penchant for militarism and war. These arguments were fully in place by the early twentieth century, and they made a large number of men, including many republican men, fearful of women's rights.

Despite their refusal to grant political citizenship, leaders of the early Third Republic did make several important contributions to women's emancipation, especially the establishment of free and secular public schooling for girls as well as boys, the creation of lycées (secondary schools) for girls, and normal schools to prepare women instructors to teach girls at this level. Even though educators molded the curriculum deliberately to form good wives and mothers and resisted until 1924 the idea of preparing girls to pass the *baccalauréat* (which would have qualified them for university study), these opportunities for schooling signified a great step forward. Early on, some young women, eager to pursue professional careers in fields like law and medicine, studied privately for the *bac,* which they began to pass in growing numbers. Beyond these educational advances for women, republican legislators reinstituted civil divorce in 1884, which most feminists saw as crucial to women's emancipation. As for other legal reforms, only a small number of changes in civil law would be enacted by 1900. Even so, as historian Claire Goldberg Moses has observed, "for feminists, the nineteenth century ended on an optimistic note" (227).

Some scholars have been loath to admit that there was an intricate connection between secular feminism and the republic. But if the Third Republic was unrepentantly "gendered" male from the outset or hostile to women in its theoretical essence, as one historian has recently claimed, how does one explain the evidence of growing support among republicans for measures of women's emancipation? By the 1890s, a number of highly visible republican men, especially the Solidarists, advocated giving women the vote and several other substantive reforms. Was "feminism" inevitably marked by paradox, as Joan Wallach Scott has claimed, or was it actually gaining ground with respect to acknowledging women's claims to full citizenship? In fact, as contemporary evidence and recent historiography have demonstrated, leading feminists understood as early as the 1870s that because "the Republic" embodied liberal and democratic principles, despite its lapses in practice, it continued to offer women the greatest opportunities to become full and equal participants. The German feminist Käthe Schirmacher, who lived in France for several decades, claimed that "thanks to the republican and socialist movements, which for thirty years have controlled France, the woman's rights movement is for political reasons supported by the men to a degree not noticeable in any other country. The republican majority in the Chamber of Deputies, the republican press, and republican literature effectively promote the woman's rights movement." This is one of many observations by contemporaries that point to feminism's progress in France, not its paradoxes.

If by 1900 several varieties of feminism had emerged (often represented by competing publications and associations), the feminist congresses of 1900 made clear that there was increasing agreement on certain pressing issues. At those gatherings, secular republican feminists promoted a number of major legal changes, especially in the sections of the Civil Code that inscribed the subordinate status of wives before the law and outlawed paternity searches. Secular feminists also objected to the Third Republic's recent protective legislation, targeted exclusively at women workers (which would greatly disadvantage them in the labor market), and countered by advocating equal protection for workers of both sexes, or, alternatively, freedom in the workplace. Led by Mme Avril de Sainte-Croix of the Conseil National des Femmes Françaises, this group continued to condemn government-regulated prostitution and the double moral standard with regard to sexual activities. Meanwhile, the feminist journalist Marguerite Durand, founder of the daily paper *La Fronde* (1897–1903), helped advocate for women workers and voiced strong support for Alfred Dreyfus. From 1906, the weekly *La Française* underscored the patriotic intentions of French feminists, an effort that aided the cause of women's suffrage. By 1913 it looked as though the Third Republic might even accord women the vote, at least at the municipal level. The outbreak of war in 1914, however, dashed these hopes.

Though voting rights eluded French women, what the republican governments did deliver to women's benefit were social-welfare measures, from subsidies for mothers to payment to families to help with the costs of raising children. In this sense, France can be viewed as a leader in the process of welfare-state formation. This was due in great part to the republicans' fears of depopulation, their acknowledgement of the centrality of vigorous mothers in bearing and raising children for the state, and their concern about staving off class warfare. Most feminists used these concerns to press the republican state for beneficial reforms and to integrate themselves into it by serving on government commissions and lobbying for government jobs. In contrast, a minority of radical feminists such as Nelly Roussel and Madeleine Pelletier reclaimed a woman's right to control her own body, even calling for the legalization of contraception and abortion. Both feminists objected to the notion that women should merely provide "cannon fodder" for the state. Republican leaders rejected such demands.

France fell on hard times following the First World War, and the legislators of the Third Republic never delivered on women's suffrage, despite the best efforts of key advocates such as Maria Vérone, Cécile Brunschvicg, and Louise Weiss. The Chamber of Deputies overwhelmingly endorsed women's suffrage in 1919, only to have the Senate refuse to discuss it—four times running (1922, 1928, 1932, and 1933). Feminist-inspired reforms to the Civil Code suffered a similar fate, though some important changes were enacted in 1938. Finally, after France's liberation from Nazi occupation in 1944, Charles de Gaulle's Provisional Government gave women the "gift," as the general put it, of the vote. After the war, the Constitutions of the Fourth and Fifth Republics embraced the principle of equality of the sexes—at least in theory. In the meantime, Simone de Beauvoir's groundbreaking book, *Le deuxième sexe* (1949), turned public attention to the philosophical roots of the "woman question." Still, not until the 1960s and 1970s, did legislators break the logjam that had long blocked reform of the law codes concerning women. Once the break had occurred, change ensued at a rapid pace. As the political scientist Dorothy McBride Stetson observed, "between 1965 and 1985 every policy affecting women, from reproduction to retirement, was rewritten." These dramatic changes resulted in part from the efforts of the Mouvement pour la Libération des Femmes (MLF), founded in 1970, which reclaimed women's right to control their own bodies and exercise their autonomy. Thanks to MLF's efforts and to a major campaign in favor of family planning, the republican government finally legalized contraception and abortion. With the formation in 1974 of a Secrétariat d'État à la Condition Féminine, and through the heyday of the short-lived but well-funded, cabinet-level Ministry for Women's Rights (1985–86), "state feminism" developed in the Fifth French Republic, giving crucial institutional support to the effort to achieve equality of opportunity for women.

In 1992 President François Mitterrand chose his close associate Edith Cresson as prime minister—a major symbolic breakthrough for women's political participation under the Republic. Cresson at once enhanced the political visibility of women and highlighted just how few women candidates French political parties nominated for elective office. To remedy this problem, feminists led by the legislator Françoise Gaspard and the writer Claude Servan-Schreiber mounted a successful effort to amend the Constitution to require *parité,* or equal numbers of male and female candidates for most elections. Finally, in 2007, a leading politician and graduate of the prestigious École Nationale d'Administration (ENA, long closed to women), Ségolène Royal, ran for President of France, gaining an unprecedented 47 percent of the popular vote. Her campaign platform was openly feminist.

Since the French Revolution, the feminist struggle for women's rights and emancipation under the five French Republics has achieved many victories, while suffering some serious defeats. The struggle continues in an effort to integrate the history of women and the history of French feminist campaigns into the canon of republican historiography and to make a gendered analysis of French politics and political culture an integral part of the curriculum. In the mid-1980s, the Fifth Republic's educational leaders rediscovered civic education, but their rendition of French history largely ignored the extent to which women had been denied full citizenship rights, as well as their hard-fought efforts to win them. As the historian Siân Reynolds wrote in 1987, "the republican world remains remarkably male both in its points of reference and its vocabulary." The gender of French history, even under the Fifth Republic, remains startlingly androcentric. Maurice Agulhon's lengthy survey, *The French Republic, 1879–1992* (English ed., 1993), provides only a short four-page section—an "interlude" as he calls it—on women, which mentions a few women celebrities before returning "to the men, with the official universe of parliamentary, social, and diplomatic battles" (121). Agulhon's index contains no entry for either "feminism" or "women."

These historiographical failings stemmed in part from the relative paucity of works on French feminism published in French in the 1970s and 1980s. Except for Maïté Albistur and Daniel Armogathe's two-volume *Histoire du féminisme français* (1977), and their accompanying books of documents, the major articles and monographs on French feminism published were all written by Anglophone scholars who live outside France. This situation has changed dramatically since the late 1980s and 1990s as Francophone research and publication of French feminism have enjoyed exponential growth. Feminist scholars have established a new archive in Angers for twentieth-century materials, which has spawned its own association, an important publication (*Bulletin des Archives du Féminisme*), a website, and a prize-winning guide to sources for future work on the history of feminism in France. The broad field of women's history now has its own French-language journal (*Clio: Histoire, Femmes, et Sociétés*), and several other journals currently publish historical work concerning the gendering of history and feminism. Literary scholars, philosophers, art historians, and historians of science and economics have all made significant contributions to the field. The online museum Musea sponsors exhibits featuring the history of feminism in France.

Despite these major advances, old ways die hard, and the "politics" of knowledge can be both claustrophobic and brutal. France's academically trained *historiennes* who focus on women or feminism have had to struggle to establish themselves in the French university system and have yet to see their findings effectively challenge the canonical androcentrism of mainstream French historiography. A great many republican educators continue to insist that "universal" man encompasses woman. As a result, a republican regime that prides itself on the "universality" of its principles, on its commitment to liberty, equality, justice, and reason, demonstrates a stunning lack of attention to these principles when it comes to remembering and teaching the history of women's political struggles for full citizenship and inclusion in the French nation-state. Once French republican educators acknowledge the importance of these struggles and take pride in the worldwide influence French feminist ideas have enjoyed, they will give *les Françaises,* as well as *les Français* and many others throughout the Francophone world, a fresh and inclusive understanding of their past.

References

Fauré, Christine, ed. *Political and Historical Encyclopedia of Women.* London: Routledge, 2003.

Hause, Steven C., with Anne R. Kenney. *Women's Suffrage and Social Politics in the French Third Republic.* Princeton, NJ: Princeton University Press, 1984.

Lehning, James R. *To Be a Citizen: The Political Culture of the Early French Third Republic.* Ithaca, NY: Cornell University Press, 2001.

Moses, Claire Goldberg. *French Feminism in the 19th Century.* Albany: SUNY Press, 1984.

Offen, Karen. "Women, Citizenship, and Suffrage with a French Twist, 1789–1993." In Caroline Daley and Melanie Nolan, eds., *Suffrage and Beyond: International Feminist Perspectives,* 151–70. Auckland, NZ: Auckland University Press, 1994.

Reynolds, Siân. *France between the Wars: Gender and Politics.* London and New York: Routledge, 1996.

Rochefort, Florence. "The French Feminist Movement and Republicanism, 1868–1914." In Sylvia Paletschek and Bianka Pietrow-Ennker, eds., *Women's Emancipation Movements in the Nineteenth Century,* 77–101. Stanford, CA: Stanford University Press, 2000.

Scott, Joan Wallach. *Parité! Sexual Equality and the Crisis of French Universalism.* Chicago: University of Chicago Press, 2005.

Smith, Paul. *Feminism and the Third Republic: Women's Political and Civil Rights in France, 1918–1940.* 1996; reprint, Oxford: Clarendon Press, 1999.

Stetson, Dorothy McBride. *Women's Rights in France.* New York: Greenwood Press, 1987.

Thébaud, Françoise. *Écrire l'histoire des femmes et du genre.* 2nd ed. Fontenay/Saint-Cloud: ENS Editions, 2007.

Walton, Whitney. *Eve's Proud Descendants: Four Women Writers and Republican Politics in Nineteenth-Century France.* Stanford, CA: Stanford University Press, 2000.

33

Gender and the Republic

Bonnie G. Smith

As the result of legal, economic, political, and other gendered conditions, women had an ambivalent relationship to the Third Republic from its inception. As the Third Republic opened in 1870–71, women of the Commune participated in opposing the relatively poor social and political status quo offered by the new Thiers government. In Paris they set up nonprofit workshops, trained as soldiers, and generally proposed a revolution in the social order. The Communards, with women active among them, espoused a kind of antistate in an age of growing national power and centralization. As the Commune was violently put down in the spring of 1871, politicians interpreted it as the work of the *pétroleuse,* or "woman incendiary." It was a case of women run mad, crowding the streets in frenzy and fury. One founding myth of the Republic, then, held that the Commune-inspired burning of Paris was the work of women—"shameless slatterns, half-naked women, who kindled courage and breathed life into arson." Revolutionary men later became heroes in the history books, but women in political situations were characterized as "sinister females, sweating, their clothing undone, [who] passed from man to man." Theorists maintained that for the Republic to survive, the most basic kind of order was needed: a return to family values and the gender hierarchy resting on male privilege. The Commune had showed the results of collapsing the boundaries between the male political sphere and the female domestic sphere.

Most republics to that date had rested on gendered foundations that articulated male privilege and female inferiority. These foundations proved crucial to the way the Third Republic was experienced and understood, as women's equality on a number of fronts was specifically rejected down to the Republic's demise in World War II. Because the Code Napoléon remained in force, women's citizenship followed that of their husbands; male privilege in sexual matters remained the norm; and because the wages of married women legally belonged to their husbands, as under certain circumstances did other forms of property, French Republics enshrined the enrichment of men and impoverishment of women. Under the Code, women with children born out of wedlock or the children of unwed parents could not institute proceedings to certify paternity, nor consequently could they legally seek support. At the beginning of the Third Republic, women lacked other rights, such as the guardianship of their children in case of a husband's death, the right to divorce, the right to run a business without a husband's permission, the right to enter a number of professions, and numerous other human rights. It was this legal inferiority that formed the bedrock of gender in the Third Republic.

The conditions of everyday life mirrored the founding misogyny of French law. Within the family, working-class women not only earned a living but had the responsibility for all domestic arrangements and provisioning. In many cases, the idea was that a woman's wages (though they did not belong to her) would support the family, while a man's wages would support him. The privileges of masculinity resonated through the family down to young children. Girls did household chores, while their brothers played, although in urban households boys often had to help their sisters fetch water and scavenge the city for discarded clothes and food.

Work usually had similarly gendered characteristics. For the most part, women did the menial labor; the higher-paid jobs, whether machine operator in a factory or foreman, professional or factory owner, were closed to women either by custom or by law. Two of the lowest-paid jobs were predominantly female: domestic service and seamstress (or other outworker by the piece at home). Jeanne Bouvier, who would later become a well-known union official, began her life in the countryside multitasking as a girl by tending cows and knitting. Because her father started drinking while she was still young, she took on many different occupations, working in factories, tending children, and doing odd jobs for pay. Her mother then found them domestic-service positions in Paris, where she returned to factory work. To support herself independently, Bouvier ultimately took a position at a women's clothing shop, while also sewing privately for her own customers. Her goal was to have a small house in the country growing fowl she could eat. When asked if she wouldn't become bored away from the city, Bouvier answered: "No, my dears, I could never be bored knowing that I had enough to eat." Such was the condition of working women in the gendered Third Republic.

During the Third Republic several new work opportunities opened for women as the service sector expanded. These included department store clerk, telegraph and telephone operator, secretary, nurse, and teacher, to name a few. Although these jobs offered clean workplaces for women with skills learned in the Republic's new educational system, they did not change the gendered nature of the work. Still, the opportunity to teach in the public schools, even allowing married women to hold such jobs, connected women more closely to republican values and showed their young pupils that such values applied to girls as well as boys—even though this was not true. A few women became researchers studying the conditions of working women and their families and some found jobs in archives, museums, and institutes. In general, working conditions in the service sector were worse for women than for men. The female clerk experienced a closely monitored life in department store dormitories, low pay, and, like the domestic servant, sexual harassment on the job. Most service jobs were dead-end: women secretaries had no opportunity to advance to be head of a firm, for example, and nurses did not become doctors. Even though lower-middle-class women could now find "suitable" employment, the republican workplace, even its service component, was structured according to a gender hierarchy.

Worker activism accelerated during the Third Republic to protest conditions under industrialization. There were organizations and unions of many types, though politically most belonged to the Left. The mutualism of Proudhon, which remained attractive, was blatantly misogynist and had no room for women. Marxist socialism had a coherent ideology that acknowledged women's oppression and inequality but did little to combat them in the short run, believing that both would disappear once socialism had been achieved. In any case, working women under the Republic, though active politically, joined unions in far lower numbers than men, first because men hardly gave them a voice in the organizations, and second because union dues were steep for those earning far less than their male counterparts. When unions failed to stop increases in the price of food in 1910, working women took to the streets chanting:

> We've had enough of suffering,
> Without this increase in the price of butter and milk!
> Tomorrow all the women of France
> Will sell it at a discount!

The misogyny and male greed shaping the Third Republic sparked a movement of middle-class women subalterns to change the status quo and make the Republic live up to its rhetoric of rights and equality. Virtually at its origins, a number of activists assailed the gender inequities on which the Republic rested, establishing dozens of groups not only to dispense charity to impoverished women but to gain parity in the law, the economy, and legal and political spheres. Not infrequently, women reformers "sold" advances in gender equality as beneficial to men. They touted, for example, the advent of lycée education for girls in 1881 as a way to give men more interesting wives. The divorce reform of 1884 was supposed to increase the birthrate by allowing for more loving and fertile marriages. Although women battered open the doors of the professions, full equality proved difficult to achieve. Even after winning her second Nobel Prize in 1911, Marie Curie was refused the honor of membership in the Academy of Sciences; the supposed men of reason believed that, as a woman, Curie could not have done original work on her own. As for the much-vaunted equality in education, parents often denied it to their daughters. The father and grandmother of Marie Bonaparte, the future founder of the French Society for Psychoanalysis, forbid her to study any number of subjects, including Latin. They even excluded her from the *baccalauréat:* "The curse especially of my sex! Because if I were a boy, you couldn't have stopped me," she wrote her father bitterly.

Nonetheless, French "new women" who worked, lived apart from their families, and had sexual relations outside of marriage appeared to defy the Republic's founding ideology of male superiority. Their new behaviors faced widespread challenges, especially from those publicly opposing birth control and family limitation. As the French birthrate continued to decline throughout the nineteenth century and into the twentieth, men raised their voices against the "selfishness" of women in curtailing their fertility. Individual women countered by bringing suit against men who had impregnated them and walked away without acknowledging paternity or providing support for children. The conditions of motherhood under French law thus came under attack. Women like Nelly Roussel took to the stage, drawing hundreds of listeners to her talks on women's pain and sacrifice in childbirth and on their right to stop having children. Intellectuals and artists took up the cause, showing the effects of male abandonment in dramatic terms, while doctors pointed to high infant-mortality rates resulting from the Code's protection of male privilege. In 1912, a weak bill allowing some recourse for unwed mothers and their illegitimate children finally passed into law.

New women openly took lovers, and lesbians appeared in public, holding exclusive salons and publishing books about their sexuality apart from men. Renée Vivien's *A Woman Appeared to Me* (1904) celebrated lesbian life. Also outside the bounds of a hierarchized heterosexuality were the greater public presence of male homosexuality and more explicit and moving writing about men's love for one another. At the highest reaches of literature, Marcel Proust's *Remembrance of Things Past* (1922) described the intense passion of the narrator for Albertine—taken to be a male lover—as well as the more hidden but no less fervent passions of men in alleyways and male brothels. While many of these relationships featured men of the upper classes, erotic engagements existed among those of all social strata, offering up an array of autobiographical, fictional, and epistolary testimony to same-sex love. These relationships challenged the heterosexual foundations of the Third Republic, which rested on the brotherhood of citizens in public and the superiority of men over women in the heterosexual household.

Women posed another challenge to secular republicanism and its antiwoman stance in their religious and spiritual practices. In the nineteenth century, women's choice of religious vocations rose, while those of men fell away. Women such as Bernadette Soubirous, Sister Thérèse of Lisieux, and Claire Ferchaud achieved fame for their religious devotion and performance of miracles. Even as the Republic made secularism its political hallmark, a great many ordinary women intensified their religiosity, sending their daughters to religious schools and going on pilgrimages. Women's experience of the modernizing Republic included medical cures at Lourdes, where they stayed in hotels, bought religious objects from the town's many shops, spoke with religiously oriented doctors, and traveled on modern railways, all the while maintaining their traditional faith. By filming and novelizing these practices, republicans made them not only into an oddity but a danger. After the Dreyfus affair, both male and female members of religious orders were banished from the schools, while women barricaded themselves in threatened Catholic religious institutions to protect them from confiscation and secularization. Protestant and Jewish women commonly expressed more sympathy for the Republic, as it menaced their religions less than it did the traditional enemy, the Catholic Church.

The colonies also offered ways of articulating the gendered norms from which the Third Republic was constructed. From the beginnings of French trade with West Africa, for example, merchants from Bordeaux had set up second families with African women whose networks allowed the Bordelais better access to local traders. Across Southeast Asia, India, and indeed around the world, French men settled with local women, often in loving relationships but not in equal ones. Simultaneously, the colonies offered opportunities for same-sex relationships to flourish between gay French men and the colonized, often boys. Like other imperial countries, France took pains to prevent colonized peoples from enjoying republican rights, though the reasoning was tortuous and involved gender. One ploy was to say that Muslim men could not participate in republican citizenship because they had multiple wives and thus oppressed women. Muslims, it was said, did not value women's equality—an argument that overlooked rights over property and in marriage and the family that Muslim women often enjoyed, which French women under the Third Republic did not.

Opportunity nonetheless existed for French women in the colonies just as it did at home. Women traveled abroad to serve as missionaries and schoolteachers, some of them eager to escape oppressive conditions in the metropole. There they set up and staffed hospitals, clinics, orphanages, and other welfare institutions and trained local women in French domesticity. Some French women moved to the colonies as prostitutes, while others traveled with adventurous spouses engaged in shady as well as legitimate businesses. The colonies gave some women authors source material for novels, essays, and histories, some of which pointed to the advantages local women enjoyed in Muslim and other societies. But the exportation of a particularly French gender order to the colonies, including the right to plunder, rape, and otherwise exploit women, factored into the list of grievances against imperial domination, even as tensions arose among the European imperial powers themselves.

World War I, it was hoped, would right all disruptions to the Third Republic's gendered foundations that had come with modernity and a rising women's activism. Men on the battlefield would be men again, and women would return to their obsequiousness in the home. It was not to be. Although women were at first fired from certain occupations, many found employment in a range of men's jobs once it became clear in 1915 that the war would last longer than expected and that manufacturing would be crucial to victory in battle. Some aspects of gender privilege were fortified: for example, civilians on the home front were deprived of food and other necessities to provide for men on the front. Men's deaths were made into sacred sacrifices on behalf of the nation, and this sacralization of men in battle revivified male privilege as men became the nation's main heroes. Nonetheless, women gained new competencies and new freedoms in terms of job skills, income, and liberation from domestic confinement. These competencies came under attack in the post–World War I period as society as a whole worked to return to a "normal" gender order.

One major indication of the fragility of this order was the condition of men at war's end. Those men who returned from the front were often hysterical, maimed, or otherwise unfit for the vigorous civilian duties of husband or family head. State institutions housed some of these disabled veterans, while industries developed to make prostheses that would approximate a normal masculinity so that the body could once again do things such as hold a tool or work machines such as typewriters. But a great many men retained the psychic and physical scars of male vulnerability. To overcome or deny them, some joined paramilitary groups and right-wing organizations such as the Action Française. These groups aimed, among other things, to allow members to reclaim a vigorous, even militaristic identity and mark their superiority over women and immigrants of other races and ethnicities entering France in growing numbers after 1918. In this same postwar climate, when other countries approved women's suffrage, the French Senate defeated a bill (1922) that would have allowed French women to vote. Although men of all parties torpedoed the measure, republicans in the legislature disproportionately rejected it, showing clearly that male privilege was pivotal to the Republic.

Simultaneously, the tragic decimation of virtually an entire generation of young men made politicians and ordinary citizens alike see repopulation as even more of an imperative than it had been early in the twentieth century; as a result, the birthrate rose for a time in the 1920s. In this cause, public officials and intellectuals scolded "militantly emancipated women, the unbridled sports-women, the cosmopolitanites, and 'brains' " for not having enough children and demanded their return to maternity and feminine duty. The gender order in France, however, had always depended on legal and economic compulsion; mere words would not suffice. In 1920, the Chamber of Deputies outlawed birth-control information, contraceptive devices, and abortion. When the French Senate then made the Republic one of the very few major powers to deny women the voting rights of citizens, it in effect prevented them from ending these compulsory measures legally. At that point, for all the foreign idealization of Paris during the interwar years, there were many who came to see Third Republic France as among the most backward countries in Europe.

Many French people at the time, however, claimed to fear "a civilization without sexes," alleging that women had been transformed by the war. During the 1920s, the *garçonne,* the "new woman's" putative latest incarnation, blithely (and perversely, it was held) shunned marriage, discounting the demographic shortage of men caused by the war. Instead of seeing women-without-men as an inevitable result of the stubborn refusal to end the carnage and save lives by bringing the Great War to an early end, republican spokesmen invented a bland successor to the Paris Commune's *pétroleuse* on whose image all ills could be placed. That was the *garçonne,* whose negative influence supposedly dovetailed with the growing number of lesbians in Paris, said to be flocking there to live sexually free lives in all-female communities. In addition, women's slimmed-down, more unisex clothing, combined with a growing athleticism, seemed to confirm the masculinization of women and the shrinking difference between the sexes. Paris's attraction to highly accomplished women seemed to reinforce these trends: Marie Curie's international fame grew in the 1920s, while artists and writers such as Sonia Delaunay and Colette prospered.

Counteracting the fears of an ungendered world, where the blurring of sexual difference might spell the end of male privilege, was the world of popular culture. The popularity of Josephine Baker, a U.S. citizen embraced in France, highlighted the resexualization of women and the reracialization of colonial subjects after those subjects had helped rescue the Republic during the war. Music halls and film depended on exhibitions of women's nudity—more extreme than before—to stoke heterosexual desire and gain customers. Film, in particular, popularized the plight of the postwar man, showing him in such features as *A nous la liberté,* which depicted a down-and-out criminal inmate who nonetheless asserts his right to protest the injustices committed against masculinity. Thrillers also became popular, portraying cerebral but tough heroes who took on thugs, murderers, and other miscreants. Popular readership snapped up not only these books but biographies featuring male heroes of the French past and other male success stories from around the world.

In the 1920s and 1930s, German Nazism also offered an enhanced and re-worked model of gender hierarchy for the French to adopt. When the *Män-nerstaat* became enshrined in the Third Reich, some opinion leaders within the French Republic gravitated to it. This model of male rule was not so different from the gendered hierarchy of the Third Republic, but it was more extreme, violent, and more explicitly about male superiority. Some French men took up the call to employ violence as a way to restore manhood, leading to street riots, paramilitary training, and intellectual movements to overthrow the consensus politics of representative government and peaceful diplomacy. Writers on the French right valorized this militarization of masculinity, which for them im-plied the overthrow of republican values and their replacement by a politics of brute force. Others, however, protected republicanism and its more muted, civic-minded hierarchies, in such movements as the Popular Front. Scholars explain the appeal of right-wing movements as acting out wartime trauma and seeking to heal the battered male psyche.

When the Great Depression belatedly took hold in France, the gender order appeared to crumble as men lost their jobs and many women visibly kept theirs. It was not that there was no female unemployment, but that women kept their low-paid outwork such as sewing, making cutlery, and stone finishing at home while male artisans lost their livelihoods as mechanization continued. Moreover, before World War I, 344,000 women worked in white-collar jobs, while in 1936 more than a million were so employed, giving the impression of female pros-perity amid male immiseration. When paramilitary groups took to the streets, blaming the Republic for France's bleak economic situation, French parties of the center and Left responded by uniting the country's prorepublican forces into a left-leaning Popular Front government.

Although women still could not vote or stand for office, the new cabinet contained three women ministers: Suzanne Lacore, Irène Joliot-Curie, and Cécile Brunschvicq. Joliot-Curie had just won the Nobel Prize for chemistry in 1935, so appointing her undersecretary of state for scientific research might seem a natural choice. But Lacore had been a headmistress in the secular school system and was an even better, gendered fit for her post. Her assignment was to oversee the health of children threatened by the stresses of the Depression. The final choice, Cécile Brunschvicq, put an accomplished activist for women's suffrage and rights in an undersecretary's role in the Ministry of Education. Although Joliot-Curie soon resigned to return to research, Brunschvicq and Lacore were highly active in Léon Blum's short-lived Popular Front govern-ment (1936–37). They worked to achieve an end to women's civil disabilities in a number of areas; to improve health in schools, especially by expanding the sys-tem of school lunches; to prevent cruelty to children; and to help young women delinquents—to name a few of their efforts. As a young adult, Prime Minister

Blum had written a book calling for greater equality in morals between men and women; in selecting Lacore and Brunschvicq, his government took steps toward the social equality the Republic professed to uphold. Moreover, the public face of these ministers also made a huge impression: Lacore was known simply as a riveting public speaker on behalf of the government and the cause of reform. When Blum's cabinet fell the next year, its successor contained not a single woman.

Paul Valéry noted during the heyday of fascism that France would have a hard time defending its values and national integrity, since its gender order so closely resembled that of totalitarian countries. Valéry was proven correct with the outbreak of war in 1939 and the subsequent collapse of the Third Republic.

References

Accampo, Elinor. *Blessed Motherhood, Bitter Fruit: Nelly Roussel and the Politics of Female Pain in Third Republic France*. Baltimore: Johns Hopkins University Press, 2006.

Bard, Christine. *Les femmes dans la société française au 20e siècle*. Paris: Colin, 2001.

Childers, Kristen Stromberg. *Fathers, Families, and the State in France, 1914–1945*. Ithaca, NY: Cornell University Press, 2003.

Fuchs, Rachel. *Contested Paternity: Constructing Families in Modern France*. Baltimore: Johns Hopkins University Press, 2008.

Kaufman, Suzanne. *Consuming Visions: Mass Culture and the Lourdes Shrine*. Ithaca, NY: Cornell University Press, 2004.

Klejman, Laurent, and Florence Rochefort. *L'égalité en marche: Le féminisme sous la Troisième Répubiique*. Paris: Des Femmes, 1989.

Mossuz-Levau, Janine. *Les lois de l'amour: Les politiques de la sexualité en France de 1950 à nos jours*. Paris: Payot, 1991.

Peniston, William, and Nancy Erber, eds. *Queer Lives: Men's Autobiographies from Nineteenth-Century France*. Lincoln: University of Nebraska Press, 2008.

Sohn, Anne-Marie. *Chrysalides: Femmes dans la vie privée (XIX–XXe siècles)*. 2 vols. Paris: Publications de la Sorbonne, 1996.

Stora-Lamarre, Annie. *La République des faibles*. Paris: Armand Colin, 2005.

34

Order and Disorder in the Family

Éric Fassin

"Travail, famille, patrie." Vichy's motto does not borrow a single term from its republican countermodel "Liberté, égalité, fraternité." But while "work" and "country" belong equally to Right and Left, can it be argued that "family" has no place among republican ideals? "Family values" (to import an anachronistic phrase from the late twentieth-century American context) certainly carry counterrevolutionary connotations. Indeed, the family policies of the Vichy regime were defined in reaction to republican (alleged) disorder—although the image of the family they conveyed hardly coincided with the reality of a society in disarray, as evidenced by the contrast between the pro-natalist ideology expressed by the French state's propaganda and the actual declining birthrate under foreign occupation. In the wake of the Popular Front, the Vichy discourse opposing the "family mystique" to the "equality mystique" was meant as a restoration of the traditional sexual order. The "eternal feminine" studied by sociologist Francine Muel-Dreyfus was thus a French version of the first part of the Nazi slogan "Kinder, Küche, Kirche"—that is, children and kitchen (more than church). Under Vichy, "family" thus cast its gendered shadow on "work" and "country": while the former was apprehended (somewhat paradoxically, given the wartime depletion of the male workforce) as a prerogative of men, the latter was understood (not surprisingly, under the aging Marshal Pétain) as "fatherland."

In contrast to this sociological perspective grounded in political history, a genealogical approach insists not so much on specific ideologies of the family, but rather on "biopolitics," that is, a proliferation of political technologies controlling the modern body. In the wake of Michel Foucault's *Discipline and Punish,* Jacques Donzelot analyzed in 1977 what he called the "policing of families." Instead of opposing "liberation" ("liberals", "progressives," or "modernizers") to "repression" ("conservatives," "reactionaries," or "traditionalists"), Donzelot's book shows the normalizing process unfolding beyond ideological differences. This historical change amounts to a shift in governmentality: the idea is no longer to govern families, but to govern *through* them; families become not so much the goal as the instrument of control. Hence the radical difference between Donzelot's critique of psychoanalysis and the attacks that have been leveled against the so-called Jewish science by some partisans of "family values." Far from signifying the decline of the family, the rise of psychoanalysis can be read conversely, not as a symptom, but as a response to this "crisis"—underlining the dysfunctions of the family all the better to save its functions. The family itself thus becomes the central figure in the emergence of a sector, distinct from the "judiciary" and the "economical," that can be called "the social."

Is the family to be understood in terms of ideology, in an antirepublican tradition, or instead as part of a broader logic of normalization inherent in modern governmentality, thus transcending political oppositions? The history of family politics offers a way out of this alternative. While distinguishing the natalism of republican experts from the familialism of Catholic ideologues, one must still take into account the background they have in common. Sociologist Remi Lenoir's account thus emphasizes how the intersections of the two versions of family politics (church and state) in the first decades of the twentieth century indicate simultaneously an implicit consensus and an explicit dissensus. The family was then a shared battleground, as secular morality competed with its religious (counter)model under the authority of state science—in particular with the development of demographic knowledge solidified in bureaucratic institutions. Thus familialism is not to be understood merely as an ideology, but as the object of a political struggle relying on the same assumptions—that is, on similar categories of thought, often crystallized in state institutions. This is why the family that defines antirepublican rhetoric could also find its place, if not in the Republic's motto, at least in its politics and policies.

In this light, the family does not appear as a solution to the "crisis" of republican modernity—on the contrary, there is no resolution. This suggests another type of Foucauldian approach, in which the family is constructed as a problem. For the first time since Aristotle, the new political philosophy inaugurated by Rousseau in the eighteenth century dissociated the domestic and political spheres—the family and the city. Philosopher Geneviève Fraisse shows this disassociation clearly in her reading of the "two governments" that define the democratic polity: if the classical analogy between Prince and paterfamilias is revoked, then a space opens—the space of a problem. The articulation between the two spheres, public and private, thus becomes a central issue in liberal modernity—as the feminist critique has long pointed out. Hence the question: What happens to the government of the family, until then the patriarchal state writ small, and now independent of the government of the state? Or, to echo Carole Pateman's influential critique, once the "social contract" is perceived as such, what becomes of the "sexual contract"?

Instead of the family imposing its patriarchal rule on the polity, conversely, the democratic logic tends to unfold even within the family, between the generations. As Tocqueville makes clear in his discussion of the influence of democracy on social mores (*Democracy in America,* vol. 2), the rule of fathers over sons does not go unquestioned once the Revolution has introduced equality into the mix. This is true even in the use of the French language: the shift within the family from *vous* to *tu* is also a transition from hierarchical distance to democratic closeness. As a result, there is no longer any "natural" authority. This egalitarian revolution also takes place between the sexes—although the French political philosopher's reluctance to envisage the same logic within conjugal relationships makes him emphasize the complementary role of men and women in nineteenth-century America. In other words, difference (and not similarity) becomes the answer to the new logic of equality: according to Tocqueville, the relegation of American women to the domestic sphere is not a matter of political exclusion, but rather (somewhat paradoxically) of social recognition. Either way, the question of order (and disorder) in the family is thus integral to the republican experience inaugurated by the French Revolution.

The shift from political model to social problem is most obvious perhaps in the Third Republic's obsession with the family. Historian Judith Surkis underlines how universal male suffrage contributed to "sexing the citizen"—citizenship and masculinity mutually defining each other. Male sexuality thus became the foundation of the republican order. At the same time, however, that very same sexuality was also recognized as having the potential to jeopardize the established social order through disorderly conduct. Masculinity worked both ways—simultaneously normative and disruptive, equally regulatory and unstable. Hence the importance of the family: for Émile Durkheim, the founding father of French sociology, it is a controlling institution to be controlled. More precisely, marriage is crucial to Durkheim's argument about the "organic solidarity" that defines modern societies. His study of suicide, for example, claims to demonstrate that married men are less likely to kill themselves than unmarried ones, and thus that conjugal ties contribute to the preservation of men. For this reason, he vehemently opposed no-fault divorce: safeguarding the institution of marriage protected society as a whole. The institutionalizing function Durkheim attributes to matrimony thus translates into his opposition to an alternative, contractual conception. Again, one can see how the progressive argument partly overlaps with its conservative counterpart. What reactionaries call "disorder" may not sound so different from what the republican sociologist calls *anomie*. However, the latter's version of marriage appears not so much as the restoration of a sexual order ultimately founded in nature, but conversely as the civic foundation of a social order.

The crucial role of the family in republican discourse as part and parcel of modern (and not just traditional) sociality becomes even more apparent when approached in the broader colonial context, rather than the narrowly metropolitan one (as is generally the case, albeit implicitly). The historical anthropologist Ann Laura Stoler has powerfully demonstrated the importance of the politics of intimacy in the colonial order of things, while revealing the paradoxical absence of empire in Foucault's genealogy of Western bourgeois sexuality. (Foucault's *History of Sexuality* also does not include the reflections on race he developed in his seminar at the Collège de France.) The history of sexuality is not only a history of family: it is also (inseparably) a history of race—and in particular of racial boundaries drawn in the process of policing white families. In everyday colonial life, the normative control of cross-racial nursing and child-rearing as well as interracial sexuality locates the sexual boundaries of race within the family. While mixed-race children were far less numerous in French Indochina than in the Netherlands Indies, in both places officials expressed a similar anxiety over the potential threat métis offspring represented—and this despite their general absence, for example, from nationalist movements on either side. The colonial order of things is inseparably a familial order.

Métis children also figured prominently in discussions of citizenship in a colonial context. According to the historical sociologist Emmanuelle Saada, the problematization of *métissage* has to do with both race and family, as mixed-race children are understood both as hybrids and as bastards. The issue is not mixed marriages, since they are born out of wedlock; rather, it has to do with the legal recognition (and social recovery) of potential French citizens—the mixed-race sons of fathers of "French race." Métis men with French fathers could be eligible for French citizenship, Saada shows, if colonial authorities judged the young mixed-race males "culturally French." The ambiguities involved in such judgments led to political uncertainties concerning the boundaries of "filiation," uncertainties that revealed and heightened social anxieties about and around the colonial borders of the French Republic.

It is worth bearing in mind the double problematization of marriage (in Durkheim's reflections on the republican social order) and filiation (in colonial questions of identity and race) when pursuing the investigation into the present. It could be tempting to think that such issues belong only to the past; they clearly do not. Let us first consider marriage: in France, studies of the family have well documented its deinstitutionalization—what sociologist Irène Théry has called "démariage." Not that matrimony is gone, or undone; it has rather become a private choice, instead of a social and institutional norm. The legal revolution of 1972, which permitted the equal recognition of children, whether "legitimate" or "natural" (i.e., born in or out of wedlock, in the old terminology), has found its social confirmation in present-day statistics showing that over half of French children are born outside of marriage. Marriage is no longer the foundation of the family. Contrary to Durkheim, today's new generation of progressive sociologists welcomes this privatization of matrimony as a sign of individual freedom: no-fault divorce can now appear as the last frontier of family democracy.

However, the debates that prepared the 1999 law creating the Pacte Civil de Solidarité (PaCS—civil unions open indifferently to same-sex and different-sex couples) and that have followed since, by focusing on "homoparentalité" (i.e., gay and lesbian families), can be interpreted as an updated version of the "sacralization of heterosexuality" that defined Durkheim's thinking in Surkis's reading. Although, in theory, the PaCS referred only to conjugality, that is, to unions between two adults, its establishment provoked a violent debate over whether adoption and reproductive technologies should be reserved for different-sex couples. This debate revealed a "sacralization of (heterosexual) filiation," as most participants argued against the prospect of gay couples having children. This French controversy stands the American polemic over "gay marriage" on its head. In the United States, "sacralization" focuses on marriage itself, while gays and lesbians often encounter relative indifference when it comes to adoption and reproductive technologies.

The sacralization of filiation in today's France echoes Durkheim's preoccupations a century earlier, in that it emphasizes the importance of social cohesion in the face of rising individualism. Stability is still to be provided by heterosexuality—but "progress" means that today's progressives have shifted the ground upon which sociality is founded from marriage to filiation. If *couples* do not need to be heterosexual, *parents* do—whether married or not. It is precisely because contemporary intellectuals welcome the new family democracy that they want to balance conjugal freedom with the stability of filiation transcending history and politics to provide the bedrock of sociality.

But why should filiation play this role today? At this point, it is important to bear in mind the second part of the republican history evoked earlier—namely, the colonial context. The naturalization of filiation, founded on sexual difference and in return founding sexual difference, has been described by legal scholar Marcela Iacub as a new logic, partly inspired by feminism and resulting in a (rather counterintuitive, one may add...) supremacy of women, at least in matters of reproduction: after the 1972 law that erases the difference between "legitimate" and "illegitimate" children, marriage ceases to be the principle upon which filiation is founded. This opens the way for it to be founded instead in biology, as is clearly apparent today in the importance of DNA testing to establish filiation, in particular regarding paternity. But this naturalization first took legal shape with the so-called bioethics laws of 1994: access to reproductive technologies is limited to heterosexual couples, whether married or not, but only if they are of "reproductive age." Remarkably, the expectations are very different when it comes to adoption: age is not a legal criterion, nor is marriage, as individuals gained the right to adopt already in 1966. In a word, within a few decades, one can see a shift between a law that presupposes an "artificial" definition of filiation to one that implies a "biological" one.

This later starting point suggests a different logic as well as chronology. Filiation does not only belong to family law; it also defines citizenship in the Civil Code. This double role justifies investigating not only what happens in the family, but also in the nation; rather than assume that these are unrelated issues, their intersection helps us understand both. In the late 1980s, debates about citizenship, against the backdrop of anti-immigrant politics sparked by the National Front (although presented as the best way to resist the xenophobic party), resulted in a growing emphasis on *jus sanguinis* at the expense of *jus soli* (i.e., citizenship defined by blood rather than by birth), thus redefining the republican balance inherited from the times of Émile Durkheim. This naturalization of filiation, in terms of citizenship, clearly plays a role in the redefinition of family law.

Once again, the nation is defined inseparably in sexual and racial terms: the new family politics of immigration echo the old family politics of the colonial empire. As Saada points out, the Third Republic's anxious politicization of "fraudulent recognitions," which started in colonial Indochina in order to preserve a racial definition of the French nation, anticipated the renewal of this theme beginning with the first Sarkozy law on immigration in 2003—especially as applied to overseas territories and departments. The politics of suspicion that developed in the colonial world regarding filiation has gained new life in post-colonial France—as became apparent in the 2007 controversy over using DNA testing to prove filiation in the case of immigrants who apply for family reunification (the right to immigrate legally to France to join family members already there). More generally, the politics of "unwelcome" (in contrast to "chosen") immigration (*subie* vs. *choisie*), which inspired not only the immigration laws of 2006 and 2007, but also the 2006 law concerning the validity of marriages between French citizens and foreigners, helps identify binational unions as well as family reunifications as a "problem."

The consequence is an a priori suspicion of, along with systematic legal and bureaucratic obstacles against, immigration to France on grounds of marriage or family belonging. These obstacles appear to contradict the right to family life inscribed in the republican Constitution (as well as in European texts). Under President Sarkozy, the French government has persistently denounced "mariages blancs" (when partners falsely present themselves as a couple). In 2009, the minister of immigration even started speaking of another color—"grey" instead of "white"—with racial undertones. The new target is "mariages gris," in which a French citizen falsely claims to love a foreigner, being interested only in French residency or citizenship. Introducing immigration issues in the discussion of filiation thus makes visible that the sacralization of filiation applies only to "us," not to "them"; more profoundly, it contributes to defining "us" by opposition to "them." Of course, it can be argued that this racialization of the nation is anti-republican. But it is also worth pointing out that it is conducted in the name of republican values. Again, echoes from colonial times are revealing.

These echoes do not imply a simple repetition, from the colonial past to the postcolonial present. Nor should one assume, on the contrary, that past and present are radically unrelated. On the one hand, the logic of racialization is not radically new; but on the other, there is an important change. Today's crucial "problem" is no longer métis children; it has become the "mariages mixtes," the putatively fraudulent marriages between French citizens and foreigners. If from Durkheim to PaCS the grounds of sacralization have shifted from marriage to filiation, symmetrically, from colonial times to the immigration policies of today, the racial "problem" has been redefined from filiation to marriage. Under the Empire, the problem was "fraudulent" claims of French parentage; in the twenty-first century, it has become "fraudulent" claims of love for a French citizen. The real continuity between the Third Republic and today turns not on particular phenomena—these are constantly reformulated—but rather on the weaving together of the sexual and racial threads that define, today as much as yesterday, the politics of family life in the French Republic.

References

Borrillo, Daniel. "La vérité biologique contre l'homoparentalité: Le statut du beau-parent ou le 'PaCS de la filiation.'" *Droit et Société* 72 (Fall 2009).

Dorlin, Elsa. *La matrice de la race: Généalogie sexuelle et coloniale de la nation française.* Paris: La Découverte, 2006.

Fassin, Éric. "Same Sex, Different Politics: Comparing and Contrasting 'Gay Marriage' Debates in France and the United States." *Public Culture* 13, no. 2 (Spring 2001): 215–32.

Foucault, Michel. *Histoire de la sexualité.* Vol. 1, *La volonté de savoir.* Paris: Gallimard, 1976.

Fraisse, Geneviève. *Les deux gouvernements: La famille et la cité.* Paris: Gallimard, 2000.

Lenoir, Remi. *Généalogie de la morale familiale.* Paris: Le Seuil, 2003.

Muel-Dreyfus, Francine. *Vichy and the Eternal Feminine: A Contribution to a Political Sociology of Gender.* Translated by Kathleen A. Johnson. Durham, NC: Duke University Press, 2001.

Saada, Emmanuelle. *Les enfants de la colonie: Les métis de l'empire français entre sujétion et citoyenneté.* Paris: La Découverte, 2007.

Stoler, Ann Laura. *Race and the Education of Desire: Foucault's "History of Sexuality" and the Colonial Order of Things.* Durham, NC: Duke University Press, 1995.

Surkis, Judith. *Sexing the Citizen: Morality and Masculinity in France, 1870–1920.* Ithaca, NY, and London: Cornell University Press, 2006.

35

Children and the State

Ivan Jablonka

There is nothing straightforward in the meeting of child and state. Whether considered from a biological or legal point of view, the notion of child implies that of caretakers. The baby, the toddler, the adolescent, have one common attribute: their legal incapacity, commonly referred to as minority, which, within the household, makes them as dependent on the father-husband as the wife and the servants. Under the ancien régime the French state paid virtually no attention to children. An absolute monarch had every interest in preserving familial autonomy, since, according to a frequently used comparison, paternal authority was a scaled-down version of royal authority. As for foundlings, they grew up in church institutions. The state intervened only when public order was at stake. To avoid infanticide, for example, an edict of 1556 required from unmarried pregnant women a double notification, one for the pregnancy and one for the birth.

In the eighteenth century, the state gradually broadened its involvement by shouldering responsibilities families had refused. It funded homes for foundlings and interned troublesome youths using *lettres de cachet*. Still, state intervention into family life remained limited under the ancien régime, despite what Philippe Ariès calls the "sense of childhood" (developing since the end of the Middle Ages) and the call by Enlightenment doctors for active protection of the newborn. Not until the French Revolution did the state take an active interest in minors. In a democracy, the child is king: from the moment the national will replaced a single will, the people became sovereign and the child the sovereign of the future. To prepare him for his responsibilities, he had to be given every care—enlightened and guided as the dauphin had been under the care of Bossuet and Fénelon, two of the ancien régime's finest minds. The Revolution introduced the idea that the state could no longer afford to leave the child in the hands of his relations alone.

From the eighteenth century on, three interwoven functions fell to the state: the physical protection of minors, their preparation for the future through schools, and material assistance upon the death of their parents or other threats to their survival. But each of these missions posed a serious challenge. How was a child's upbringing to be supervised without trespassing on the father's rights (or on the freedom of employers, in the case of child labor)? How could authorities encourage autonomy in young people while also requiring them to conform to society's rules? How could the state and its allied institutions care for needy children at the taxpayers' expense? All these issues, more political than educational, can be summarized as a single, all-embracing challenge: How, within the framework of a democratic nation-state, could public authorities transform millions of children born in diverse conditions into good French citizens?

One might think that what is called the "French integration model" mainly concerns peasants in the nineteenth century or immigrants in the twentieth. Actually, children (and especially children in need of special care) are the core of this policy. Through the protection and the education of minors, the republican welfare state works toward national cohesion through the assimilation of both individuals and territories. As early as the end of the eighteenth century, the making of French citizens fell to the child-care institutions; and Jules Ferry's school belatedly implemented a much less thorough model.

In the eighteenth century, doctors and philosophers sought to protect babies' lives by promoting breast-feeding, increasing the number of midwives, and placing wet nurses under state control. But for all that doctors maintained, as Alphonse Leroy put it in 1772, "how important it is for the government to attend to children," positive results in this field would have to await technical progress to come. It was not until the second half of the nineteenth century that Pasteur's discoveries in microbiology, the fight against infectious diseases, and advances in obstetrics and child nutrition made it possible to protect the health of infants and young children. These developments led to the creation of pediatrics as a specialty, which in turn did much to improve infant mortality rates. The latter dropped from 25 percent in 1789 to 18 percent in 1860 and 7 percent in 1935.

France's defeat in the Franco-Prussian War of 1870–71, and the widespread fear of depopulation it caused, moved government officials and health professionals to attend all the more to the country's "precious little French folk" (Schnapper). In 1874, *sénateur* Théophile Roussel, a doctor's son and himself a country doctor, spearheaded legislation that required the "monitoring by public authorities" of all babies under age two entrusted to a wet nurse: once a month a supervising doctor had to visit the baby and give the wet nurse object lessons and advice. To protect infants and babies in other ways, the state accredited new medical specialties, imposed new standards on maternity hospitals, and created a Higher Committee for the Protection of Infants (Comité Supérieur de Protection des Enfants du Premier Âge). Since child mortality was particularly high among foundlings, the Assistance Publique (Public Child Welfare Agency) paid particular attention to wet nurses, encouraging breast-feeding and a Pasteurian vigilance against infection and disease. But inspectors from the Assistance Publique, most of them urban and male, often encountered resistance from wet nurses, who were suspicious of these city-dwelling men. In the 1920s, guidebooks for wet nurses still deemed it necessary to admonish against swaddling, the long-tube nursing bottle, and solid food in the first months of life.

The latter decades of the nineteenth century marked the turning point, when the state assumed parental roles, and soon others beside state authorities became involved. Mayors, journalists, scientists, and medical practitioners organized private structures such as the Œuvre de la Goutte de Lait de Belleville, which distributed pasteurized milk from 1892, and the Ligue contre la Mortalité Infantile, created in 1902 (Rollet, 1990). Still, it was the state that held the legal power over child protection, which by the late nineteenth century was no longer restricted to newborn babies or to physical care. Thirty years after the July Monarchy (1830–48) had enacted the first child-labor laws, legislation of 1874 banned factory work for children under twelve and night labor for the rest. The same year, the Loi Tallon protected children in itinerant jobs, and in 1889, the state extended public protection to abused and "morally abandoned" children. Now parents could be stripped of their rights, since, in the words of the *rapporteur* Gerville-Réache, "The child is a key element of society. Since the State personifies society as a whole, if a child lacks natural protectors, the State must intervene." The law was intended to protect abused children but also, by countering parental neglect, to fight juvenile delinquency in the lower classes. All these laws bore witness to an unprecedented interventionist approach: where the child is potentially a victim—a victim of malnutrition, disease, a drunken father or a greedy boss—the state is his recourse.

Throughout the first half of the twentieth century, the state progressively extended its apparatus of protection, especially after 1918, when the devastating toll of the Great War rekindled depopulation fears. A law of 1913 had already provided four weeks of leave for new mothers, and in 1922, Minister of Hygiene Paul Strauss tightened standards for day nurseries and required stricter training for those the nurseries employed. The government also created a new nursing degree and sent nurses into the homes of poor and sickly children, imitating the "health visitors" already in place in Britain and the United States. Although Strauss had attempted in 1918 to make medical record-keeping (vital statistics, vaccinations, physical examinations) mandatory for all children, opponents, citing family privacy, succeeded in delaying such a requirement until 1942. It would fall to the Vichy regime, concerned as it was with the "physical and moral preservation of the race," to enact this republican reform (Rollet, 2008).

State regulation of child welfare continued apace after the Second World War. An ordinance of November 2, 1945, created the Protection Maternelle et Infantile (PMI, Maternal and Child Welfare), charged with protecting pregnant women and children under six. School-age children would be seen by school doctors in the framework of the *médecine scolaire,* set up at the same time. (In the colonial empire, the PMI also attended to unschooled children up to the age of fourteen). In 1962 the PMI was integrated into the Directions Départementales de l'Action Sanitaire et Sociale (*DDASS*), the local branches of the Department of Health and Social Security. Although the general decentralization of government services initiated in the early 1980s shifted considerable responsibility for children's health to local authorities, a law of 1989 showed that there remained a national policy in this field. This legislation made the PMI responsible for the "promotion [rather than the protection, as in the past] of health, family, and the child." Several other developments are worthy of note. In 1950, the government required the vaccination of young children against tuberculosis, though here, too, the state encountered resistance. With tuberculosis almost wholly eradicated in metropolitan France by the twenty-first century, mass vaccination administered and funded by the state was replaced by a more tailored prevention policy. Still, refusal to submit to certain prescribed vaccinations remains punishable by law.

Since most child mortality occurs before the age of five, schoolchildren are the survivors. Partly for that reason, the modern state's primary interest in children has focused on education. During the French Revolution, two models contended for support: one sought to teach children to think freely; the other to venerate the fatherland, law, and virtue (Baczko). This debate turned less on educational content than on the kind of authority under which children would be placed. In their radicalization of Rousseau, who admired the city-states of classical Greece, the leftist Montagnards sought to place children under the authority of the revolutionary state and understood education as the means to create a patriotic citizenry committed to the fatherland. Educators would shape young minds through classes, pageants, readings, anthems, and prizes. In 1792–93, revolutionary leaders proposed legislation creating primary schools and making education mandatory for three years. Noncompliant parents would be punished. In the summer of 1793, on behalf of the murdered regicide Le Peletier, Robespierre unveiled a radical version of this project: all children between five and twelve would be raised and educated together in boarding schools/barracks operating as a "republican mold."

Robespierre and the Montagnards were overthrown before they could institute their educational plan; nearly a century later, the Third Republic would resurrect many of the Revolution's educational ambitions. In 1881–82, the National

Assembly enacted two crucial educational bills. They made primary education free and compulsory for all boys and girls aged six to thirteen. Though a great many French citizens greeted the "Ferry laws" as a radical departure from past practice, their goals were not in fact wholly new. Primary schools began to appear in rural regions in the sixteenth century; the Revolution, as we have seen, introduced the idea of compulsory education; and in 1833, the July Monarchy adopted legislation requiring municipalities to create a state primary school. Still, despite these premonitions, the schoolchild is clearly the Third Republic's creation; not until the Ferry laws was education freely available to all children six to thirteen years of age.

This regime, still the longest-lasting of France's five Republics, made several other crucial education innovations. In 1882, it created the preschool, or *école maternelle,* designed to emphasize the psychomotor, sensorial, and intellectual development of the young child. The towering figure in this realm was Pauline Kergomard, who served as general inspector of preschools for over forty years (Luc). In addition, the Republic addressed the problem of "abnormality," the children who could not be educated with the others, or so it appeared at the time. The 1882 law singled out mute, deaf, and blind children, acknowledging their right to an education. A law of 1909 created special classes for children deemed "backward."

The end of schooling was marked by an exam, the *certificat d'études primaires* (primary education certificate), created in 1874 and regulated by an 1880 decree. Through the "certif"—a "totem" institution for the French along with the *département,* the Civil Code, and gold-standard coins (*franc germinal*)—the state devised a rite of passage for young teenagers in direct competition with first communion (Cabanel). In the early years, the exam's official pass rate ranged between 75 and 90 percent, but since schoolteachers had only their brightest pupils take the exam, the actual proportion of primary-school graduates who passed the test hovered at 10 percent or below. The rate would remain at this low level until the interwar period.

Those who passed the test sometimes belonged to the lower social groups; but for the most part, children from peasant and working-class families left school at age thirteen. Even those who earned the *certificat d'études* were ineligible for France's prestigious lycées, since the exam in question did not qualify students for secondary school. The educational system thus largely reproduced the existing social hierarchy. From the 1880s until World War I, there was essentially no leakage between primary schools—in due course supplemented by intermediate schools such as the *écoles primaires supérieures*—and the lycées, whose students mostly came from well-off families. The system would not democratize until the 1930s, when the *sixième,* or first year of secondary education, became free and accessible through a limited entrance exam; the curricula in the intermediate schools paralleled those of the lycées. These mutations would lead in the 1970s to the *collège unique,* which merged intermediate schools and lycées for the pupils aged eleven to fourteen.

If the Third Republic's educational system made little effort to alter France's social hierarchy, it devoted considerable time and resources to building allegiance to the regime and wresting children away from the church. The education law of 1882 substituted "moral and civic instruction" for religious education. In 1886 the Goblet law secularized the state's educational personnel, forbidding clergymen to teach in public schools. To keep children away from the church after hours, officials created an array of youth clubs, associations, and libraries (Ozouf and Ozouf). Much of the schools' subject matter was designed in part to republicanize the students. Schoolmasters, those "black hussars" of the Republic (in Péguy's indelible words), taught generation after generation to read using books like *Le tour de la France par deux enfants: Devoir et patrie.* In the context of the humiliation of 1870, Mme Fouillée's best seller narrated the adventures of two orphans from Lorraine who discover the wonders of their fatherland. At the same time, this and other schoolbooks linked the new republican regime to a venerable French nation said to stretch back into the mists of time and to embody traditional values, behaviors, and practices. Schoolbooks also grounded patriotism in the very soil of the French countryside, regions, and local mores (Chanet). In metropolitan France and in its empire at large, children learned of their "ancestors the Gauls," and history education in general served to instill a politically inflected national saga that until recently ignored phenomena such as immigration, slavery, and the harsh side of colonialism.

Whenever the republican regime has felt threatened, educational content has been politicized all the more. After the defeat of 1870, "school battalions" helped prepare pupils for "revenge" against the German enemy. During World War I, the "children's war," fought with intensely patriotic school lessons and anti-German drawings, mirrored the wartime propaganda directed at adults (Audoin-Rouzeau). More recently, schools have battled against Islam, just as the educational institutions of the early Third Republic explicitly fought Catholicism and the church. In September 1989, three schoolgirls from Creil, a suburb north of Paris, were suspended for wearing Islamic headscarves. The incident gave rise to a violent controversy: many intellectuals and politicians thought these young women represented a danger to the Republic, seeing them as a Trojan Horse of religious fundamentalism and cultural separatism (*communautarisme*). Not until the Assembly adopted a law prohibiting "conspicuous" religious insignia (2004) did the controversy subside. At that time, it was clear that the majority of the French population welcomed the notion that public schools should foster cultural conformity and a sense of belonging to a Republic defined from above.

If the school system inherited from the Third Republic was designed in part to achieve these goals, so were a number of France's other institutions. But, as we have seen, policies as wide-ranging as vaccination, child-labor restrictions, and compulsory education met with resistance from families whose authority the policies were designed in part to supersede. In the case of abandoned or delinquent children, placed by law in the hands of the state, such opposition was easily overcome. For this reason, the republican project weighed especially heavily on them. The (supposed) failure of their parents gave the state free rein to shape youthful misfits into ideal citizens and integrate them into the democratic nation-state.

In the eighteenth century, the state did not feel implicated in the future of foundlings. Reformers suggested that they be used to clear wasteland, serve in the armed forces, colonize Louisiana, or repopulate the countryside. In the *Cahiers de doléances* compiled for the Estates General convened in 1789, the aristocratic First Estate proposed to enroll them in the French navy "under the heading of Children of the State." They would indeed become the state's children, but not until leaders of the French Revolution decided to care for them, protect them, and give them a place in society. A decree of June 28, 1793, supported orphans, foundlings, and children from destitute families, through allowances, apprenticeships, or both. "Bastards" were renamed "natural children of the fatherland." The nation, in effect, became their guardian; in return, political leaders presumed that these children, indebted to the Republic, would owe it unfailing loyalty. The Directory and the First Empire translated these revolutionary decrees into formal legislation, seeking to incorporate orphans and foundlings into familial and professional networks. A foundling's life was now regulated by law.

As for delinquent children, revolutionary and postrevolutionary legislation recognized that young people cannot always distinguish good from evil and thus that minors should enjoy certain legal dispensations until the age of sixteen. The 1791 Penal Code held that if a young criminal has acted "undiscerningly" (*sans discernement*), he would be formally "acquitted"—but not necessarily released. There were to be consequences, as the youthful offender could be sent "to a reformatory home there to be brought up and detained" until the age of twenty. The 1810 Penal Code would enlarge on this disposition in its famous Article 66, extending it to youths guilty of petty offenses. Under the July Monarchy, this disposition would make it possible to send thousands of vagrant children to the penal farming colonies that blossomed after Mettray, an agricultural reformatory founded in 1839 and destined for worldwide renown. Street urchins and first-degree murderers alike were removed from their family environments, deemed responsible for their bad habits. Such separation would be the first step toward the minor's rehabilitation. Until the law of 1889, it would be one of the lone infringements on paternal authority.

The Third Republic derived its social and family policies from French Revolution precedent, just as it had for primary education. The foundlings sector was structured into several clusters: the Direction of Public Welfare and Hygiene (created in 1886 in the Ministry of the Interior), the Higher Council of Public Welfare, and the District Inspectorate, which assumed the guardianship of children who had been in the care of religious hospices. Care models were diversified, albeit according to an unspoken hierarchy: while some children received assistance in their homes (in order to forestall their abandonment), little beggars and truants, dubbed "morally abandoned" under the 1889 law, were entrusted to youth organizations or to the Assistance Publique. During World War I, a law honored "wards of the nation" whose fathers had been killed or maimed at the front: this new status distinguished them from "wards of the state" consigned to a public-welfare category bereft of prestige. New legislation on adoptions (1923 and 1939) made it possible to integrate abandoned children into a family, although such an outcome was rare. During the interwar period, there were fewer than two thousand adoptions per year—this at a time when the Assistance Publique peaked at 120,000 children.

With these minors, the Third Republic conducted a real political project. Anxious about the harmful influence on children of the city, the factory, the asylum, and negligent parents, the Paris Assistance Publique shipped some 250,000 minors to the countryside. These "social rejects," as an 1908 inspector characterized them, were to become farmers, even though many had already begun industrial apprenticeships, and in many cases, their (urban) families wanted them back. Anchored in the land, cleansed of hereditary vices, the children would benefit from physical and mental regeneration; eventually they would be assimilated into the nation (Schafer; Jablonka, 2010). From the adoption of "the fatherland's natural children" to the rural resettlement of abandoned or delinquent youths (and today the "Frenchification" of immigrant children), the object remains to extract minors from their familial caves in order to purify them in the Republic's health-giving light.

Extended to the colonies, this policy would endure throughout the twentieth century. In Indochina, mixed-race children, born of a French father and an indigenous mother, became French if they were "presumed of the French race," on the strength of their name or their education. When sent to metropolitan France, they were directed to the farming or crafts sectors (Saada). Between 1963 and 1982, the DDASS sent sixteen hundred children on Réunion Island to the metropolitan countryside, mostly in the Massif Central and the southwest. The rationale, developed by Michel Debré, former prime minister and parliamentary representative for Réunion, was to replenish rural France's aging and increasingly sparse population. Debré claimed these "migrations" protected Réunion's youthful inhabitants from destitution and family violence, but mainly they served to thin the island's excess population and thereby relieve its strained economy. In 2002, associations representing these former "migrants" began to sue the French state for "abduction" and "deportation" (Jablonka, 2007).

Long before the League of Nations adopted the first Declaration of the Rights of the Child in 1924, the French Republic had become the main provider of care and assistance to children at risk in their own country through an increasingly tight control of child charities. But even as the Republic improved such children's chances of survival and integration, it increased their vulnerability by using them as means to its national ends. While the Republic has from the outset protected the child, no one seems to have thought, conversely, of protecting the child from the Republic.

References

Audoin-Rouzeau, Stéphane. *La guerre des enfants, 1914–1918: Essai d'histoire culturelle.* Paris: Armand Colin, 1993.

Baczko, Bronislaw. *Une éducation pour la démocratie: Textes et projets de l'époque révolutionnaire.* Paris: Garnier, 1982.

Cabanel, Patrick. *La République du certificat d'études: Histoire et anthropologie d'un examen (XIXe–XXe siècles).* Paris: Belin, 2002.

Chanet, Jean-François. *L'école républicaine et les petites patries.* Paris: Histoires Aubier, 1996.

Jablonka, Ivan. Les Enfants de la République. L'intégration des jeunes de 1789 à nos jours. Paris: Seuil, 2010.

——. *Enfants en exil. Transfert de pupilles réunionnais en métropole (1963–1982).* Paris: Seuil, 2007.

Luc, Jean-Noël. *L'invention du jeune enfant au XIXe siècle: De la salle d'asile à l'école maternelle.* Paris: Belin, 1997.

Ozouf, Jacques, and Mona Ozouf. *La République des instituteurs.* Paris: Gallimard, Seuil, 1992.

Rollet, Catherine. *La politique à l'égard de la petite enfance sous la Troisième République (1865–1939).* Paris: INED, 1990.

——. *Les carnets de santé des enfants.* Paris: La Dispute, 2008.

Saada, Emmanuelle. *Les enfants de la colonie: Les métis de l'empire français, entre sujétion et citoyenneté.* Paris: La Découverte, 2007.

Schafer, Sylvia. *Children in Moral Danger and the Problem of Government in Third Republic France.* Princeton, NJ: Princeton University Press, 1997.

Schnapper, Bernard. *Voies nouvelles en histoire du droit: La justice, la famille, la répression pénale (XVIème–XXème siècles).* Paris: PUF, 1991.

Scott, Joan Wallach. *The Politics of the Veil.* Princeton, NJ: Princeton University Press, 2007.

36

Commemoration

Daniel J. Sherman

The first French Republic began in September 1792 without an official proclamation and in a way that deliberately obscured the past, overturning the old
calendar and beginning time anew. "Memory" as such has never been a key word
for the Republic, and only within the past generation has it become the object
of historical research. But commemoration resembles the Republic—*res publica,* the public thing—in that both fundamentally concern politics, not memory.
Commemoration seeks to reinforce the solidarity of a community by fixing a
common version of events that have in some way disrupted it. The challenge
and dilemma of republican commemoration lies in the fact that the Republic's
claim on the community, the French nation, has long been contested, and the
events it tried to stabilize included those that repeatedly created and destroyed
it. If commemoration thus has difficulty representing the Republic as its object,
a republican *type* of commemoration gradually developed, emphasizing public
participation, pedagogy, and the values of secularism, progress, and the ideals of
the Republic's motto.

As a distinctively modern form of political praxis, commemoration has
evolved along with the Republic; it has roots in, or connections to, popular festivals, public art, and political symbolism, but its distinct role lies in seeking to
prompt affinity and allegiance in a number of registers. Four of these constitute
the core field of commemoration: the calendrical, the figurative, the genealogical, and the ritual; separately and together they make clear the difficulty of the
republican commemorative project. With regard to the calendar, Mona Ozouf
has cast the failure of the First Republic to establish a consistent commemorative
calendar as emblematic of its inability to stabilize the flux of history. The beginning of the Third Republic, the longest-lived to date, September 4, 1870, logi-
cally replaced the name of the street marking the inauguration of its predecessor
regime, the *rue du 2 décembre.* But the *4 septembre,* inextricably connected with

military defeat, did not suit the purposes of long-term commemoration. The *14 juillet,* made the national holiday in 1880, was a default date, commemorating a brief time of possibility and relative concord rather than any of the moments of violent upheaval that followed it; its success in defusing controversy ensured its survival.

The act of representing the Republic, whether in official documents, currency, or public art, is not solely commemorative, but it can take on commemorative overtones. Various attempts, from Hercules early in the Revolution to Daumier's nursing mother in the celebrated competition to depict the Second Republic, showed the difficulty of figuring the abstraction of a sovereign people. But in the decades from the Revolution to 1848 a popular resonance attached itself to one figure, Marianne. This popularity did not forestall controversy when republicans came to power in the 1870s, as different versions appealed to different constituencies: Radicals found a seated Republic by Jean-Baptiste Clésinger and commissioned for the 1878 Exposition Universelle too placid, prompting the Paris City Council to order more commanding figures by the Morice brothers for the Place de la République and by Jules Dalou for the Place de la Nation. As Olivier Ihl has shown, the Third Republic did not have an active program to distribute Marianne busts to the provinces, preferring to respond to local initiative rather than impose a symbol that might foster controversy.

The main genealogical impulse for republicans, particularly in the mid-nineteenth century, was to find prerevolutionary antecedents for the Republic, and the Enlightenment offered a promising source. The centennial of the deaths of Voltaire and Rousseau in 1878 provided an opportunity for republican commemoration, and like an 1867 public subscription for a statue of Voltaire, these commemorations attracted fierce opposition from clerical interests. Observances of the centennial of Jules Michelet's birth in 1898 depicted the historian as a model citizen, devoted to popular education, rather than a great man in an earlier mode largely discredited by its Bonapartist associations. During his lifetime Michelet had participated eagerly in republican political culture, which elaborated a host of commemorative rituals, from planting trees of liberty, popular in the Second and early Third Republics, to military parades and popular balls on the *14 juillet.* The state funerals and burials in the Pantheon initiated during the Revolution and revived during the Third Republic have become the most familiar of these rituals. Victor Hugo's funeral in 1885, which marked the definitive secularization of the Pantheon, lasted the better part of a day and, with its procession from the Arc de Triomphe to the Pantheon, elaborate decorations, and many orators, provided an enduring model. Over the course of the Third Republic the choice of those accorded the honor expanded to include scientists and artists as well as writers, politicians, and military leaders, staking the Republic's claim to embodiment in diverse fields and forms of achievement.

Like the Republic itself, commemoration underwent a significant shift after World War I, the event that to date has most marked the French commemorative landscape. Though postwar commemoration drew on existing forms and models, notably from the Franco-Prussian War, their fusion marked the emergence of a form of commemoration new in several respects. First, 1870 monuments were limited in the immediate aftermath of the war to regions most touched by combat, and their spread around 1900 was a political phenomenon, chiefly in larger towns or cities where the nationalist Right wished to broadcast revanchist sentiments. In contrast, the massive human loss of the Great War took commemoration to every corner of the country. The large number of unidentified and unrecovered remains made local monuments in effect substitute tombs, sometimes provoking controversy when families or veterans preferred to build a monument in the cemetery rather than in the town center. But whatever the sources of funding for the monument, and subscriptions led by veterans or family groups were common, the ultimate decision lay with the town council or its delegated committee, giving a public character to the monument's site, physical appearance, symbolic significance, and surrounding rituals. Second, only the existence of a monument industry, from local stone-carvers to major foundries offering a range of standardized products, made possible the proliferation of monuments to the dead. The state attempted to regulate both the industry and the appearance of monuments through departmental commissions of experts, but it had little power to enforce its standards. Often dismissed as futile, these efforts formed part of a larger critical attention that made aesthetic criteria—the idea that even the most modest monument must have a worthy appearance—an inescapable part of commemorative discourse.

The final shift in Great War commemoration came with the institution in 1922 of the *11 novembre* as the first truly secular holiday since the *14 juillet*. This national day of remembrance ensured the ritual repetition of the tribute to the war dead, their inscribed names the one universal feature of war memorials, and placed it at the heart of French commemoration. Yet frequent controversies engendered by monuments' iconography, location, and inscriptions, sometimes leading to demonstrations and vandalism, continued throughout the interwar period. Though historians have largely downplayed these controversies, as, for example in Antoine Prost's influential treatment of war memorials as primarily civic monuments and Annette Becker's work on the religious aspects of postwar commemoration, it was arguably the very contestation surrounding monuments' construction and initial use that made Great War commemoration profoundly republican. Monuments bore the traces of the Republic's complex imbrication of local and national: the ministers and members of Parliament attending dedication ceremonies and subsequent anniversaries intended through their presence to express the Republic's gratitude to its constitutive communities.

If these ceremonies often followed closely on religious observances, republican protocol required commemorative ceremonies to be secular. They were not, for all that, apolitical, as speakers ventured to speak in the name of the dead to promote policies deemed in the national interest. The conceit became so widespread, and so irritating to veterans, that the central device in the 1938 sound version of Abel Gance's *J'accuse* has the dead literally rising from the national cemetery at Douaumont, near Verdun, in order to prevent the outbreak of a new war. Édouard Daladier's stop at the tomb of the unknown soldier on his return from Munich in September 1938 offered a political counterpart to this cinematic trope, testifying to the inability of commemoration to knit together a badly frayed polity. The collapse of the Third Republic less than two years later further discredited the objects and rituals associated with its last two decades.

The monument boom of the interwar period thus had another lasting legacy. Artifacts of a disgraced political culture, local monuments became an embarrassment after World War II. Using aesthetic standards as a screen, the Provisional Government instituted and enforced strict regulations on the construction of any type of ambitious or figurative monument. As a surely unintended result, most towns guaranteed approval by simply adding names to the existing monument, thus preserving the Great War's dominance of the commemorative landscape. But the traumas of 1939–45—defeat, occupation, and civil war—made the prospects for a renewal of republican commemoration uncertain. On arriving in Paris in August 1944, Charles de Gaulle famously refused to repeat one of the most emblematic rituals of the Republic: its proclamation from the balcony of the Paris Hôtel de Ville. According to his *War Memoirs* he replied to calls that he do so: "'The Republic has never ceased. Free France, Fighting France, the French Committee of National Liberation have successively incorporated it. Vichy always was and still remains null and void. I myself am the President of the government of the Republic. Why should I proclaim it now?' Stepping to a window, I greeted the crowd that filled the square and proved by its cheers that it demanded nothing more." This was the type of gesture in which de Gaulle specialized, at once decisive and ambiguous, saying one thing but offering room for multiple interpretations. De Gaulle's questionable attachment to the Republic and its institutions, including those he himself founded in 1958, would haunt republican commemoration for decades, even as his insistence on republican continuity became a form of orthodoxy and a tool of selective forgetting.

The multiplicity of experiences of World War II—of veterans, prisoners of war, Resistance fighters, conscripted laborers, deportees—and their uncertain relationship to each other made fragmentation the predominant characteristic of commemoration after 1945. If republicanism played little part in this conflict of narratives, the proliferation of competing monuments still took place within a republican framework, albeit with messages more specific and sometimes more partisan than those on monuments to the Great War dead. Groups with connections and resources acted quickly, erecting a number of major monuments by the early 1950s: what is now known as the Shoah Memorial in the Marais in Paris began as the tomb of the unknown Jewish martyr, dedicated in 1956. Typically site-specific, Resistance memorials drew on earlier traditions of republican commemoration, notably in their reliance on the initiative of private associations, but also in their desire to instruct, made more urgent by the difficulty of reconciling the views of the main components of the Resistance. Heroic acts and martyrs found commemoration most readily in the early years. Thus a monument to the Resistance hero Pierre Brossolette overlooking the harbor of Narbonne was dedicated in 1952, and numerous plaques and two monuments (in Chartres and Béziers) honoring Jean Moulin were in place by 1951. French internment camps and sites of repression, on the other hand, like the deportation camp in the Paris suburb of Drancy, generally did not receive attention till the 1970s or 1980s. Two exceptions prove the rule. A national memorial at the Struthof concentration camp, dedicated in 1960, was in Alsace, juridically German territory during the war; the 1962 monument to the martyrs of the deportation on the Île de la Cité does not list the specific groups deported, and its site has no particular connection to the deportation.

But the larger effect of Gaullist orthodoxy lay in its refusal to acknowledge any connection between the Republic and Vichy, thus exonerating the Republic, and indeed France as a whole (as opposed to individuals subject to judicial penalties) of collaboration. The state and its constitutive entities could participate in memorial observances, grant space to associations seeking to build monuments, and rename streets in honor of Resistance heroes. But the position that the Resistance had incarnated the Republic, taken literally, meant that the Republic had nothing to commemorate other than the Resistance. Even this notion had its limits. The date chosen for commemorating World War II was VE Day, May 8, not June 18, the date of de Gaulle's appeal to resistance, or any date associated with the Liberation. The result of a prolonged campaign by veterans' groups, and not made official till 1953, the *8 mai* holiday associated France with the victors rather than with its own civil war.

After de Gaulle's return to power the state took a more active role in remembrance, though more in ritual than in monuments, and with the Republic itself largely absent as an object of commemoration. The Fifth Republic orchestrated a number of anniversaries of both world wars in ways that served its own narrative: observances in 1964 marked the fiftieth anniversary of the battle of the Marne and the twentieth of the liberation of the camps, both cast as French triumphs over Germany, but ignored D day as too American. The year 1966 saw the fiftieth anniversary of the battle of Verdun, though de Gaulle, who could never replace Pétain as the emblematic figure of that battlefield, skipped the 1967 dedication of a Verdun memorial museum built by veterans, a group in which, after his post-Algeria purge of the army, the President had remained highly unpopular.

After de Gaulle's departure from the political scene in 1969, the strains of a commemorative enterprise based on selective forgetting became increasingly apparent in calls for a fuller accounting of the Republic's failures and dark moments. As Henry Rousso observed, the debates unleashed by the cinematic release of Marcel Ophüls's *The Sorrow and the Pity* in 1971 and the French publication of Robert Paxton's *Vichy France* in 1973, beyond their impact on historical understandings of the war years, marked an important shift in the relationship between historians, commemoration, and the media. The centennial of the Revolution in 1889 had enlisted historians, under the leadership of Alphonse Aulard, to provide both scholarly publications, notably compilations of documents, and didactic works intended for popular audiences. Now the resonance of Paxton's work among French historians made clear that historical scholarship would no longer operate under the cover of apolitical scientificity. Historians and other scholars increasingly offered critique as well as knowledge and challenged the Republic to accept their contributions as consistent with its most profound values. In parallel, filmmakers and investigative journalists both responded to and helped reshape public interest in the war years by asking inconvenient questions and breaking unspoken taboos. Other factors also contributed to a new questioning of Gaullist memory narratives in the 1970s, notably de Gaulle's death in 1970, the ethical turn on the left after 1968, and the spread of media interest in the Holocaust.

Commemorative practice could not but respond, though with a notable time lag that reflected politicians' wary response to the changed media landscape and increased militancy of private associations in the 1980s and 1990s. After Valéry Giscard d'Estaing, seeking to distance himself from an old-style Gaullism rooted in the Resistance, caused an uproar among veterans by attempting to end national observance of the *8 mai* anniversary in 1975, François Mitterrand promised in his 1981 presidential campaign to restore its status as a national holiday. Acutely aware of the symbolic dimensions of commemoration, Mitterrand began his term with a televised visit to the Pantheon, presided over the lavish commemoration of the fortieth anniversary of D day in June 1984, and then, a few months later, used the seventieth anniversary of the outbreak of World War I to stage his celebrated hand clasp of reconciliation with German chancellor Helmut Kohl at Douaumont. During the bicentennial of the Revolution in 1988–89, which produced a raft of historical publications and no lack of debate, Mitterrand, while cautiously espousing the classic argument that revolutionary violence arose in response to external threats, chose to emphasize the symbolic character of commemoration, such as the planting of a tree of liberty in a village in the Vienne, as a way of defusing controversy. His few speeches on the bicentennial emphasized the values of liberty and solidarity and for the most part avoided both narrative precision and traditional republican protocol. All these actions served Mitterrand's larger political strategy of deradicalizing the French Left by moving his Socialists toward the center and claiming to incarnate not only the values of the Republic but those of the nation as well.

By the middle of his second term, however, some of Mitterrand's commemorative acts were attracting criticism, notably after the revelation in 1992 that he had had flowers placed on Marshal Pétain's tomb every Armistice Day since 1984. It began to seem as though the President's attention to large-scale anniversaries of the two world wars were serving as screen memories in the Freudian sense, displacing youthful memories too difficult to confront. In a televised response (July 14, 1992) to calls that he make a public declaration of responsibility for Vichy persecutions Mitterrand recited the Gaullist line: "Let us not ask the Republic for an accounting. In 1940, there was a 'French State,' the Vichy régime: it was not the Republic....I completely share the feelings of those who are interpolating me, but we must be clear: the Resistance, the de Gaulle government, the Fourth Republic and the rest, were founded on the rejection of this 'French State.'" Two days later, Mitterrand attended the ceremony marking the fiftieth anniversary of the 1942 roundup of Jews at the Vélodrome d'Hiver, but he limited his participation to a wreath laying and did not speak; his appearance prompted scattered jeers and whistles.

The commemorative calamity of 1992 led to the establishment the following year of July 16 as a day of national observance of Vichy racial and anti-Semitic persecution, and to the construction of a monument to the memory of the victims, near the site of Vel d'Hiv on the Quai de Grenelle. By the time Mitterrand presided over the dedication of this monument in 1994, with its inscription beginning "The French Republic in homage," revelations of his own Vichy past had tarnished his image and largely discredited the Gaullist discourse he had made his own. It was left to his successor, Jacques Chirac, the first Gaullist president since 1974, to make the long-sought avowal of responsibility. In his speech at the Quai de Grenelle monument in July 1995, Chirac declared: "These dark hours forever soil our history and wound our past and our traditions....Yes, the madness of the occupiers was seconded by Frenchmen, by the French State." Though he did not address the question of state responsibility directly, Chirac's speech paved the way for legislation on compensation, restitution for looted property, and new forms of memorialization. As philosophers and historians elaborated the concept of *devoir de mémoire,* a public and collective duty to remember, the recognition of responsibility and of the need to go beyond symbolism and ritual finally entered republican commemorative practice.

When the Socialist prime minister Lionel Jospin used the eightieth anniversary of the armistice in 1998 to urge the "reintegration" of executed mutineers in the memorialization of the Great War, he made clear that commemoration is never entirely fixed; new scholarship, media attention, and shifting political currents always have the potential to destabilize a fragile consensus. In the case of the Algerian War, no consensus has ever really existed. As Sylvie Thénault observed in the *Dictionnaire critique de la République,* the great obstacle to a nuanced historical understanding of the Algerian War, the prerequisite for responsible commemoration, lay in the failure to recognize the Republic's part in the atrocities and brutality of that conflict, and specifically of the continuity of torture and other forms of abuse from the Fourth to the Fifth Republic. The first monuments in the metropole, mostly the work of ex-colonists, went up mainly in southern cities with large *pied-noir* communities, as early as 1971 (Marseille); the Nice monument, completed in 1973, specifically mentions an Organisation de l'Armée Sécrète (OAS) officer executed by French military justice in 1962. Initial forms of recognition from the Republic, such as Giscard d'Estaing's attendance at the burial of the unknown soldier from Algeria in 1977, fell under the old paradigm of tribute to those who had died for the *patrie,* especially since it took place at the Great War cemetery of Notre Dame de Lorette. Successive governments of all stripes followed the same policies, which were designed more to repress than to come to terms with the past: a series of amnesties extended to members of the OAS, the award of combatant status to veterans (1974), and in both France and Algeria a refusal to resolve thorny issues of citizenship, military service, and immigration.

Public interest in the war had grown with the publication of Yves Courrière's four-volume history of the war (1968–71) and, fed by a steady stream of films, television series, and publications, has never ebbed. But only in the early 1990s, with new political turbulence in Algeria, demonstrations by the children of *harkis* (Algerians who had fought for France), and new books and films about war, including Benjamin Stora's strongly argued *La gangrène et l'oubli* (1991) on willed forgetting, did private associations begin to call for a fuller accounting of the war's effects on France. It took nearly another decade for Parliament to change the official designation of the conflict to "war" (1999), for the Jospin government to ease access to certain archives, and for official acknowledgment that the killing of Algerians peacefully demonstrating in Paris on October 17, 1961, amounted to a massacre. Yet the plaque memorializing that event in 2001 came from the new Socialist mayor of Paris, not the government, and referred only to a "bloody repression" causing the death of "numerous Algerians," without naming them or those responsible.

Even these tentative steps caused a backlash. In December 2002 Chirac dedicated a national monument on Paris's Quai Branly to French troops killed in the Algerian war; in the classic mode of a tribute to sacrifice, the monument acknowledged no responsibility other than to remember the dead. Most notably, a February 2005 law calling for greater recognition of the contributions of all who had suffered as a consequence of the Algerian War and subsequent population movements also granted state indemnities to members of the OAS. The law attracted notoriety for an amendment calling for school curricula to teach the "positive effects" of French colonialism, which prompted protests from historians, the Algerian government, and others. While this clause was later abrogated, the rest of the law remains in effect. In a sense it paved the way for the more truculent attitude of Nicolas Sarkozy, who in his 2007 presidential campaign called for an end to French "repentance." In his declarations as President, Sarkozy has acknowledged past abuses, including slavery and colonial massacres, while refusing to apologize for them and insisting on moving on. His absence from the 2007 opening of the Cité National de l'Histoire de l'Immigration, a still evolving project to include marginalized populations in the official narrative of French history, struck many as a symbolic repudiation of the *devoir de mémoire:* the center occupies the Palais de la Porte Dorée, built in 1931 as a didactic museum extolling French colonialism.

In 2007 and 2008, nearly a quarter century after the publication of *La République,* the first volume of Pierre Nora's immensely influential collection *Les lieux de mémoire,* two books appeared in France with titles that played on the phrase "guerres de mémoire," memory wars. In part, these books responded to Nora's 1992 afterword to *Les lieux de mémoire,* which notes the fragmentation of national memory, itself a recent invention, and, without predicting an end date, suggests that our own "era of commemoration" would be fleeting. Historians and philosophers uncomfortable with the omnipresence of memory in public debates may welcome Nora's prediction, but the pressure the discourse of memory puts on historical practice seems unlikely to diminish soon. If war is a continuation of politics by other means, memory wars make clear that the political stakes of commemoration remain as high as ever. And whatever its risks, by offering a place for multiple commemorations within a republican framework, the idea of memory as responsibility can play a part in constructing a new, more tolerant, and diverse republican community—or communities—in the twenty-first century.

References

Bacqué, Raphaelle. *La guerre d'Algérie: Une histoire apaisée?* Histoire en Débats. Paris: Seuil, 2007.

Barcellini, Serge, and Annette Wieviorka. *Passant, souviens-toi! Les lieux du souvenir de la Seconde Guerre mondiale en France.* Paris: Plon, 1995.

Becker, Annette. *La guerre et la foi: De la mort à la mémoire, 1914–1930.* Paris: Armand Colin, 1994.

Ben-Amos, Avner. *Funerals, Politics, and Memory in Modern France, 1789–1996.* Oxford: Oxford University Press, 2000.

Blanchard, Pascal, and Isabelle Veyrat-Masson, eds. *Les guerres de mémoire: La France et son histoire*. Paris: La Découverte, 2008.

Conan, Eric, and Henry Rousso. *Vichy: Un passé qui ne passe pas*. Paris: Fayard, 1994.

Garcia, Patrick. *Le bicentenaire de la Révolution française: Pratiques sociales d'une commémoration*. Paris: CNRS Editions, 2000.

Ihl, Olivier. *La fête républicaine*. Bibliothèque des Histoires. Paris: Gallimard, 1996.

Ozouf, Mona. *Festivals and the French Revolution*. Translated by Alan Sheridan. Cambridge, MA: Harvard University Press, 1988.

Prost, Antoine. *Les anciens combattants et la société française*. 3 vols. Paris: Presses de la Fondation Nationale des Sciences Politiques, 1977.

Sherman, Daniel J. *The Construction of Memory in Interwar France*. Chicago: University of Chicago Press, 1999.

37

Intellectuals and the Republic

Jerrold Seigel

In its most general sense, the term "intellectual" might refer to any person who somehow dwells in the world of thought. During the 1890s, however, the word took on a particular meaning in France, referring to those thinkers, writers, artists, and teachers who come forward to play a role in public debate. The crystallization of this meaning took place in connection with the fierce conflicts that divided the country over the conviction of Captain Alfred Dreyfus for treason, and it led to a new prominence for those it designated. The defining moment came with Émile Zola's famous 1898 article "J'accuse," asserting that high army officers had falsely prosecuted Dreyfus, both in order to shield others who had actually passed secrets to the Germans and to spread their conviction that Jews in high positions constituted a danger to the army and the state. Within a few days a declaration of support for Zola appeared, signed by several hundred writers, academics, and artists; it quickly came to be known as the "Manifesto of the Intellectuals." Among those who spoke out for Dreyfus were the novelist Marcel Proust and the philosopher and sociologist Émile Durkheim, countered on the other side by then equally prominent figures such as the writer and critic Maurice Barrès. From questions about justice and deceit in public life the debates quickly turned to fundamental issues of politics. Whether a Jew properly belonged in a high position was part of a broader argument about who belonged to the French nation and how it should constitute itself politically, questions that took on new dimensions and new weight with the rise of organized mass parties (where anti-Semitism would play a fateful role). By linking these questions to fundamental principles of ethics and identity, the people now dubbed intellectuals infused immediate political issues with high moral and historical significance, at once raising politics above petty everyday concerns and heating up the temperature of public discussion.

That France became the place where intellectuals earliest and most prominently assumed this role had to do with several distinguishing features of French
life. Sharp political conflicts were present in every country, but nowhere else
was the basic form of the nation and the state so open to question as in France.
England had been a parliamentary monarchy since the end of the seventeenth
century and no realistic alternative was in view at the end of the nineteenth;
neither the agitation for extending voting rights in the 1820s and 1830s nor the
rise of working-class political organization at the century's end led to fundamental constitutional challenges. Germany retained an inchoate and uncertain shape
through much of its history, but Bismarck's victory in 1871 and the establishment
of Prussian dominance gave a stable (even if deplored) form to national politics,
one that only defeat in World War I would have the power to alter. In Italy the
Piedmontese monarchy's success at the same point in unifying the country on
its terms effectively cast patriot visions of republicanism or greater regional autonomy into limbo until much later.

France was a case apart. Between the Middle Ages and the eighteenth century
the Bourbon kings established a state able to summon up great military power
and give the regionally diverse and divided nation many elements of a unified
culture, but on a basis that was riven with conflict, rightly derided as oppressive
and corrupt, and whose need to grant repeated tax privileges and exemptions to
both powerful regions and favored sections of the population sapped its ability to
survive financially. The monarchy's collapse in the Revolution of the 1790s and
the repeated changes in regime over the century that followed—from monarchy
to republic to empire and back again—at once reflected internal divisions and
kept them at a simmer, pitting Catholics against secularists, regionalists against
centralists, and Bourbon loyalists, Bonapartists, Orléanists, and republicans all
against each other. The result was a tissue of what Maurice Agulhon calls competing "legitimacies," all claiming to impose their shape on national life. That the
Revolution itself constituted one of these, signaling to some the nation's ability to
take its destiny in hand and throw off oppressors, and to others the potential for
collapse into anarchy inherent in the country's many divisions, contributed to the
persisting instability, providing more occasions than elsewhere for class tensions
to issue in violence, and leaving basic questions about the substance of the nation
and the form of the state unsettled. The enduring devotion to one or another
version of an overarching, ideal unity was the obverse of the recognition that the
country was sharply split between hostile groups and factions; overall this structure contributed to the slow development of political parties in France and to a
widespread view that the country was at once less able to reach the kinds of compromises the presence of Parliament encouraged in England and too wedded to
competing high principles to pursue a more prosaic politics of interests. Some of

these tensions appeared to find a resolution at the end of the 1870s, when moderate republicans triumphed over those who had hoped for a monarchical restoration after the fall of the Bonapartist Second Empire, and set up a parliamentary regime where issues could be publicly faced and compromises sought. But many Catholics and conservatives remained unreconciled to the secular Third Republic, and workers, alienated by the bloody repression of the Commune of 1871, kept their distance from it. Thus the struggle of "legitimacies" had not been resolved, leaving fundamental questions about political organization and social membership to become special objects of public debate.

This political framework helps to understand why the intervention of intellectuals in the Dreyfus affair, and in many later situations, had a character George Ross describes as "unmediated" making a direct appeal to the public as a whole, rather than by way of some organized group or party—and why abstraction itself became an explicit issue in French debates. The conservative politics that employed anti-Semitic rhetoric and heroic images (like that of General Boulanger) may have been no less literary and theoretical than the liberal Left's marshaling of universal principles, but the Right had much success in painting its enemies as peculiarly attached to abstract ideas, both because conservatives touted their loyalty to ancient national traditions, rather than to some as-yet unrealized vision, and because liberals themselves affirmed the importance of abstract ideas to their cause. The anti-Dreyfusard champion Maurice Barrès tarred liberals as hyperrationalists in his novels, portraying a typical republican of the 1880s and 1890s as barred from access to the nation's vital energies by the same a priori frame of mind that kept him from appreciating a natural landscape (Charles Maurras made a similar critique of the Dreyfusards, who were unable to make contact with what he called *le réel*). Partisan as these notions were, they accorded with the terms Émile Durkheim used in describing what made the Dreyfus affair the birth hour of the modern intellectual. Although a defender of modern social relations, Durkheim knew full well that they could often appear dull and cold, leaving people indifferent or alienated. Politics in particular often seemed to be about nothing more exalted than selfish ambitions and power struggles, goals that could not generate much emotional appeal. But he thought the situation created by Zola's intervention made the public stage the arena for "a great moral and social problem," opening up a wholly different prospect:

> Our political life was languishing miserably in questions of personalities. We were divided over who should have power. But there was no great impersonal cause to which to consecrate ourselves, no lofty goal to which our wills could cling…. But as soon as a grave question of principle was raised, the scholars were seen to leave their laboratories, the learned to leave their

libraries to draw nearer the masses, to involve themselves in life; and the experience has proved that they know how to make themselves heard.

Durkheim here depicted the emergence of the modern intellectual as requiring a situation in which everyday party politics yielded to the presence of some "grave question of principle," drawing the concerns of writers and scholars closer to those of ordinary citizens. The transformation he described had counterparts in other times and places (including a number of countries at the end of the 1960s), but its special relevance to France would long persist.

There are many reasons that Durkheim's contrast between ordinary political life and the intellectualized politics of high principle would retain its special power in France. One was the persisting fear that established politics was dangerously corrupt, a sentiment that became especially potent during the 1930s, just when the European-wide conflict between communism and fascism was in full cry. This mix of moral and political elements was bound to revive issues associated with the Revolution and its meaning, keeping alive the conflict of alternative "legitimacies" even after World War II, especially given that both Left and Right were able to support their claims to leadership by appealing to their participation in the anti-German Resistance, where Communists had been among the most active members inside the country and de Gaulle served as a rallying point outside it. In the postwar years de Gaulle's appeal to "a certain idea of France" testified that the old vision of the country as an integrated whole was still alive, but against his version of it (with its organic and nationalist overtones) figures on the left, refreshed by the Nazi defeat and the atmosphere of the Cold War, appealed to the heroic moment of 1789, and what many saw as its rightful offspring of 1917, as showing what form the nation should take.

While these developments worked to preserve the position intellectuals had assumed in the 1890s, however, others countered them. One was that party organization had taken on much greater importance, leading some writers to become party activists and others to deplore their doing so. A second was the marked expansion of secondary and higher education, which began in the fin-de-siècle period but mushroomed after 1945, bringing ever-larger numbers of people into occupations that required university degrees—in teaching, research, and the professions—and spreading them throughout the country. As a consequence, Paris now began to lose its near-total dominance over intellectual life, and its role as face-to-face meeting-ground for practically all those who mattered within it, a development also fostered by the rapid rise of new media of communication. Over time these changes would both alter the position intellectuals occupied in French life and reshape what it meant to be one. Signing manifestos and petitions would count for less; providing and diffusing knowledge and technical expertise, and participating in informal networks and groupings, more.

We can see this mix of continuity and change at work in the history of French intellectuals in the examples of particular figures. One such figure is Julien Benda, author of *La trahison des clercs* (The Betrayal of the Intellectuals), the best-selling critique of what his fellow intellectuals had become by 1927. Benda operated out of a passionate conviction that the only values deserving of loyalty from writers and thinkers were truth and justice, and that unless intellectuals devoted themselves wholeheartedly to defending them, accepting the mantle of the medieval *clercs,* these higher truths would lose their foothold in a world increasingly driven by base and destructive passions. The traitors, according to Benda, were the growing number—whether party activists or not—who devoted themselves to "the intellectual organization of political hatreds." Benda did not want intellectuals to steer clear of politics, but he thought they were right to join the fray solely when something like Durkheim's "grave question of principle" was at stake. Benda rallied to the Dreyfusards only after overcoming doubts that this was the case in the affair, and he remained at odds with those in the same camp who were using it, he thought, to further some faction or party. Like many others who believed that theirs was the politics of justice, however, Benda was a man of the Left; those intellectuals he found guilty of fomenting hatred were first of all and chiefly nationalists, some of whom later moved close to fascism. From the 1930s to the end of his life (in 1956) Benda exhibited a complex and sometimes tangled relationship to the Communists: although always at odds with Marxism and determined to retain his independence, he was so drawn to the clarity and consistency of its followers' opposition to fascism and their commitment to the poor and weak that he sometimes appeared as a fellow traveler. He knew that many of those with whom he joined in the antifascist cause were no more committed to putting truth above party than were those on the other side, but he justified his choice on the tortuous grounds that (as he wrote in 1938) "the Left honors justice and truth and does not practice them. The Right does not practice them and does not honor them." Would this have been enough to sustain him had he lived to confront the revelations about Soviet life that shook up the intellectual world (in ways we will consider below) in the 1970s, or would he have concluded, as others did, that the Dreyfusard model of commitment drew moralistic politicians into blind alleys? Whatever the answer, Benda's career reveals how the rise of organized mass parties was narrowing the ground of independence from which intellectuals could make an "unmediated" appeal. It suggests in addition that the fusion of moral commitment and political engagement effected by the Dreyfus affair may not have been so wholly beneficent as those who experienced it believed, since it left behind questionable expectations that a similar union could be sustained in the future.

Among those who had to confront these questions was Jean-Paul Sartre, more than anyone else the exemplary figure of the modern French intellectual.

As his friend and later critic Maurice Merleau-Ponty observed, Sartre was a man of stark oppositions. The chief of these polarities set consciousness against the external world—the first a realm of pure freedom where the imagination was not bound by anything outside itself, the second a sphere where everything was hemmed in by causal processes and dense, fleshy materiality. Consciousness was wholly free, by virtue of existing only "for itself"; since, however, it had always to be "consciousness of something," it was forever turned toward the world outside, the solid and substantial "in itself." Struck by the superior reality of this other form of existence, consciousness never ceased to yearn to be what it was not. On some level Sartre always feared the external world for the threat to freedom it harbored, but his career was a long series of attempts to join consciousness (and himself) to it, to find a formula that would infuse the "in itself" with the freedom of the "for itself." Philosophers had long dreamed of such a union, but Sartre made it new and vivid to his readers by creating fictional and dramatic situations that embodied the inner tensions and practical dilemmas it entailed (as in his novel *Nausea* and his play *Dirty Hands*), and his uncompromising insistence that a conscious being never ceases to be responsible for all that it does, regardless of its circumstances, made many regard him as a champion of pure truth and absolute moral accountability. As a young writer Sartre saw himself almost as a *clerc* in Benda's sense, keeping a protective distance from the world; yet the search for ways to enter into and alter the world, which became his abiding project, had already begun.

Literature and later Marxism were the main vehicles of Sartre's quest. In the 1940s he pictured the first as a means to join consciousness and the world, inasmuch as a literary work is always the free expression of its author's subjectivity, but its imaginative vision comes to life only when it is taken up by readers who encounter it inside the world. Such a relationship between a singular individual and the plurality of everyday existence provided an escape from the contrary and much darker vision of Sartre's play *No Exit,* which dramatized the view that because others always subject us to a consciousness that is not our own, relations with them deprive us of our essential freedom: "Hell is other people." Now, instead, the necessary dependence of authors on readers pointed toward a society where every individual's acknowledgment that others were necessary to fulfill his or her freedom would open the way to a world of mutual respect and justice. This perspective made literature akin to revolution, generating out of itself the vision of a communal and equitable society that many on the postwar French left pursued through communism, but it did so in a separate way that justified the independence Sartre still maintained. During the 1950s, however, Sartre began to perceive this separation (like his earlier one) as a source of isolation, and literature as too narrow a basis for changing the world; he moved much closer to the Party. In his *Critique of Dialectical Reason* he assigned to revolution the power to overcome the condition in which every individual is a threat to the freedom of every other, dramatically portraying the energizing fusion that hitherto dissociated people achieve in moments of common action, exemplified by the taking of the Bastille in July 1789. But as he himself acknowledged, there was no way to make the fugitive sense of unity such moments generated lasting. Both the ever-recurring opposition between free consciousness and the circumscribed world and the particular conditions of modern organized social life stood in the way. After 1956, when the Soviet Union repressed uprisings in Eastern Europe, Sartre moved away from the Communists and confessed to considerable disillusionment with politics. He would later seek to overcome the isolation into which this drew him (again) by supporting the young *gauchiste* activists of 1968. Behind each of these successive (and problematic) forms of engagement there lurked the painful yearning for reality and practical action that made Sartre in his own eyes exemplary of the conflicted man of consciousness.

Sartre's own understanding of what lay behind his trajectory focused on his persisting and tension-ridden devotion to intellectual abstraction. In his frank and probing autobiography, *Les mots* (Words), he used a spatial metaphor to convey the position in which his bookish devotion to writing and ideas placed him: "I lived on the roof of the world ... perched on the highest branch of the Central Tree." Despite every effort he made to come down, he never purged himself of the desire "to live in the ether among the aerial simulacra of Things." The special and sometimes desperate desire for involvement in the world that this sense of distance generated was visible in his own and many of his fellow intellectuals' attachment to Marxism, the paradigmatic modern endeavor to grasp the world in a way that promised to realize the philosophical dream of overcoming the split between consciousness and action.

It was this quality of Marxism that led Merleau-Ponty, who recognized in himself the same kind of penchant for intellectual abstraction as Sartre (he called it *la pensée de survol,* "overflight thinking"), to justify his devotion to Marxism even in face of its practical failures, on the grounds that no other perspective pointed the way to a society of "authentic intersubjectivity." Marxism was not just any historical hypothesis, but the last chance to find genuine meaning in history, he wrote in 1947: "After that there remain only dreams or adventures." By the mid-1950s, however, Merleau-Ponty had abandoned Marxism, citing the persisting abstractness even of its attempts to inspire concrete action as the weakness that opened it to totalitarian practice. But many others maintained the loyalty he had defended (this was just the moment when Sartre was undertaking his ill-fated *rapprochement* with the Communists), their confidence in the heirs of the Revolution of 1917 strengthened by a patriotic sense of its continuity with their own nation's heroic attempt to make politics philosophical in 1789. Their disillusionment would come soon enough.

The examples of Benda, Sartre, and Merleau-Ponty all testify to how much this disenchantment was already being prepared inside the forms of faith that held it at bay. The 1970s, in the aftermath of the failure of the heady events of May 1968 to issue in anything like a classic revolutionary transformation (we will come to their powerful but different kind of impact in a moment), and in response to Solzhenitsyn's wrenching testimony to the horrors of the Soviet gulag, would mark a watershed in the history of French intellectuals. The ground shifted in multiple ways. Even earlier, figures such as Michel Foucault and Jacques Derrida, seeking to preserve the radical spirit of the Left from drowning in the Communist shipwreck, turned from Marx to Nietzsche to inspire strategies of escape from modern social and cultural forms they found rigid and oppressive, exposing what they regarded as techniques of domination hidden inside the practices liberal societies represented as vehicles of freedom. As new social movements with more focused aims than the old revolutionary Left—feminism, gay liberation, prison reform, environmentalism—gained prominence in the aftermath of 1968, Foucault proclaimed the end of the "general" intellectual on the Sartrean model and the emergence of "specific" intellectuals oriented toward more concrete and practical goals. Utopian aspirations could still live on inside these more delimited programs, and Foucault in particular seems never to have rid himself of his transgressive dreams, despite a willingness sometimes to recognize the value of liberal principles (in particular human rights) of which he began as an acid critic. But for others disillusionment with the old Left and optimism about post-'68 society, based on the openings that hitherto-excluded minorities were finding in it, and the ability of Left parties to achieve electoral success (the Socialist François Mitterrand became President of the French Republic in 1981), all combined to make the figure of the "specific" intellectual represent a turn to a more moderate and practical politics. George Ross links this shift to the expansion of education and the "increasing numbers of practicing intellectuals of all kinds—academic, research, scientific, journalistic, artistic"—that it brought forth, suggesting that the "growing fragmentation of identities and…increasingly complex professional division of labor" entailed by the new situation encouraged a "retreat from the kinds of global, universalistic, and somewhat messianic self-assigned missions" assumed by earlier avatars of thought, notably on the left. The same reorientation was fostered by the evolving self-destruction of communism. François Furet, a former party member, drew many people to his reinterpretation of 1789 and its heritage, attributing the plunge into Terror to the abstract nature of the Revolution's principles, which stood in the way of political compromise, while analyzing its long-range effects as (in Sunil Khilnani's words) "centered on the construction and consolidation of stable democratic structures." Furet's project was both a sign and a vehicle of the turn prominent intellectuals were taking away from their own earlier forms of practice. His associates and followers have been at the center of a rediscovery and celebration of an indigenous and previously overlooked French tradition of liberal thinking, embodied in figures such as Benjamin Constant and François Guizot, who sought both liberty and stability inside representative regimes of whose limits and defects they were well aware.

By the end of the 1970s the long-standing centrality of questions about revolution and its meaning to French intellectual life had given way to a more splintered scene, at once more open and less confident than in Sartre's heyday. But certain features of the old style survived, even in some of the most insistent expressions of distance from it, notably the noisy emergence of the "new philosophers" in the same years. Led by André Glucksmann, Bernard-Henri Lévy, and others, the group's hallmark was antitotalitarianism, pursued together with a critique of the intellectual tradition that had disposed their predecessors to excuse tyranny and justify violence. "Never again," Lévy wrote, "will we be the counselors of rulers, never again will we hold or aim for power.... Never again will we be the guides and beacons of peoples, never again will we put ourselves at the service of rebels." Such a stance drew a determinedly apolitical conclusion from the basic commitment to truth and moral integrity that Benda had made the essence of the *clerc,* but it insistently reaffirmed that commitment, and with it the long-standing sense that the intellectual's value lay in providing an alternative to everyday politics. Lévy and others highlighted this alternative by modeling themselves partly on a type of intellectual sometimes demeaned by the politically engaged (including Durkheim and Benda), namely, the poet or artist, who, from the time of Romanticism, had manifested a willingness to accept suffering as the condition of separation from a debased and untrustworthy world.

This appeal to literary detachment, tied to the new philosophers' reluctance to take on specific political involvements, reveals that they preserved something of their predecessors' desire for an independent and "unmediated" relationship to the public. Such a connection may appear paradoxical, since as many observers have noted, the new philosophers (and especially Lévy) were very much "mediated" in a different sense, becoming TV personalities and often exhibiting little or no reluctance to write and speak in ways calculated to make a rapid appeal to mass audiences. From the start, critics, especially on the left, pointed to these features as evidence that the new philosophers were not genuine intellectuals and could not stand for independent values. The features of contemporary culture to which these critics point may well be regrettable, but we should not be too quick to take "mediatization" as incompatible with intellectual authenticity. Whatever its problems as a forum for serious discussion, television does provide the immediate and effective connection between speakers and audiences that an age of expanded (but less rigorous) education and decentralized interchange requires. Moreover, seeking a direct and emotional appeal to a wide public has been a practice of French (and other) intellectuals at least since the emergence of "public opinion" in the eighteenth century. Voltaire, in his famous defense of Jean Calas, the Toulouse Protestant executed for murdering his son in order—as rumor had it—to prevent his conversion to Catholicism, certainly employed rational argument against Calas's accusers, but his appeals to feeling and emotion were at least as prominent (affecting prints of Calas's tearful good-bye to his wife were widely reproduced, even on tobacco pouches). Durkheim expressed pride in the ability of Dreyfusard intellectuals to "make themselves heard," to address the public in effective terms as good communicators and rhetoricians, and Sartre was not above creating media events to publicize his views either. However critically we may regard the new philosophers' qualifications to assume the mantle of Durkheim and Sartre, the younger group's conviction that this heritage can be preserved only if it is subjected to the same kind of scrutiny their predecessors directed toward society and politics may be a necessary step toward its possible renewal.

References

Aronson, Ronald. *Jean-Paul Sartre: Philosophy in the World.* London: Verso, 1980.

Charle, Christophe. *Les intellectuels en Europe au XIXe siècle: Essai d'histoire comparée.* Paris: Seuil, 1996.

Gipper, Andreas. *Der Intellektuelle: Konzeption und Selbstverständnis schriftstellerischer Intelligenz in Frankreich und Italien, 1918–1930.* Stuttgart: M&P, 1992.

Hourmant, François. *Le désenchantement des clercs: Figures de l'intellectual dans l'après-Mai 68.* Rennes: Presses universitaires de Rennes, 1997.

Jennings, Jeremy, ed. *Intellectuals in Twentieth-Century France: Mandarins and Samurais.* New York: St. Martin's, 1993.

Judt, Tony. *Postwar: A History of Europe since 1945.* New York: Penguin, 2005.

Khilnani, Sunil. *Arguing Revolution: The Intellectual Left in Postwar France.* New Haven, CT: Yale University Press, 1993.

Lemert, Charles C., ed. *Intellectuals and Politics: Social Theory in a Changing World.* Newberry Park, CA: Sage, 1991.

Lemieux, Emmanuel. *Pouvoir intellectuel: Les nouveaux réseaux.* Paris: Denoël, 2003.

Racine, Nicole, and Michel Trebitsch, eds. *Intellectuels engagés d'une guerre à l'autre.* Les Cahiers de l'Institut d'Histoire du Temps Présent 26. Paris: CNRS, 1994.

38

Cultural Policy

Herman Lebovics

In France the idea that the state has a responsibility for aesthetic culture, as for national defense, the economy, and the highways, is old. But the term "cultural policy" dates only from the time when Charles de Gaulle, on assuming power in the new Fifth Republic, asked André Malraux to head a new Ministry of Cultural Affairs (1959). Despite a small budget, in a ten-year flurry of initiatives Malraux established "culture," rather than "civilization," as the proclaimed basis of French internal unity and international eminence. Like other democratizing ideas he championed as minister, Malraux adopted "culture," with its humanistic how-we-live connotations, from its usage during the heady years of the Popular Front, when democratic forces in France were rallying to the struggle to defend culture from growing European fascist "barbarism." By the 1960s Malraux, as well as other Gaullists, saw the threat of "barbarism" coming from the triumphant "way of life" waxing on the other side of the Atlantic. The word "civilization," with its elitist implications, did not fully express the national life that was in danger.

Malraux's work came apart in the heat of May 1968, when the future cultural elite went into the streets to reject the top-down culture that he had championed so forcefully. But after his resignation in 1969, a series of cultural ministers culminating with Jack Lang, President Mitterrand's choice for the post in 1981, built a praxis of cultural policy that confirmed the idea that saving, and directing, French culture was central to maintaining the integrity of the French state. Lang was the last great minister to guide national cultural policy. By the time he stepped down, the funding of culture had become primarily the task of regional councils and the cities. Much of the Ministry of Culture's budget thereafter has been spent sustaining existing establishments and simply maintaining and repairing the holdings of France's extensive built heritage. Increasingly, budgetary restrictions, the spread of market forces, and the growth of popular electronic media have called the idea of a state funded and guided cultural policy into question. Accordingly, the number of books by intellectuals and artists on some variation of the theme "the crisis of French culture" has grown exponentially.

As the French monarchy grew in power in the seventeenth century, rulers took upon themselves the sponsorship and guidance of institutions and activities as varied as learning and language (the Académie Française), art (the Académie des Beaux-Arts), theater (the Comédie Française), and even, with Louis XIV, a cuisine worthy of a grand state. As Roger Chartier has pointed out, Cardinal Richelieu's institutional establishments, especially his creation of the Academies, set a pattern that would mark the world of artistic culture in subsequent centuries: "All cultural production was to be judged on the basis of its conformity to, or its divergence from, the rules formulated by legitimating institutions" (Chartier 351).

For the sake of entertainment, prestige, and propaganda, other monarchies in Europe followed, to varying degrees, similar policies of directing cultural production and display. But the Revolution of 1789 connected French cultural institutions and the state in a singular way. The royal museum of the Louvre became a national museum that welcomed all citizens to view the treasures already there. The monarchy's holdings were greatly supplemented by works of art brought in to be protected from revolutionary vandalism, as well as art gathered as booty in the republican and Napoleonic wars. The new Louvre represented an instance of the revolutionaries' institutionalizing the idea of the French state as the keeper of a *patrimoine* (literally, an "inheritance") of the splendid treasures, both of France and of the great civilizations of the past. Seeking a way to consolidate revolutionary unity and inclusion, the Jacobins and their supporters took as their model the Catholicism the monarchy had used as ideological cement for its rule, fashioning a republican culture built around the aspiration to a common language and a unifying set of, now, secular beliefs. Moreover, as other nations forged ahead industrially in the nineteenth century, French commentators increasingly emphasized the superiority of the nation's cultural achievements. The scene was set for future Republics' *necessary* interest in culture and culture's dependence on the state. And with this notion of cultural unity came what, until near the end of the twentieth century, had been the self-evident corollary, that there could, and should, be but one culture uniting all the French.

In various ways the state's supervision of the aesthetic sphere continued during the Restoration (1815–30), the Orléanist monarchy (1830–48), and the reign of Louis-Napoleon/Napoleon III (1848–70). Under the Bonapartist regime in particular, government control served not necessarily to insure the highest artistic standards but to enforce the state's shibboleths, in particular on questions of religion and politics. Victor Hugo, perhaps France's greatest author, had to flee the country to escape the government's vengeance for his hostility to the dictatorial regime. And in the 1850s the nation's two greatest modern writers, Gustave Flaubert and Charles Baudelaire, found themselves prosecuted for offending public morality and for obscenity. Similarly, the painters Courbet and Manet angered imperial officials, the former because he painted what appeared to be drunken priests, and the latter because he did a large painting of the execution (by soldiers he dressed in French uniforms) of the French-sponsored Mexican Emperor, Maximilian von Hapsburg.

The Third Republic (1870–1940) was more benign but also less involved. Commentators like Jeanne Laurent have declared the new regime particularly lax in maintaining state interest in and encouragement of the arts. And it is true that in the last third of the nineteenth century France witnessed the golden age of aesthetic modernism in literature and art with little encouragement from republican authorities. In 1881, the new government canceled the annual salon of paintings so central to the official culture of Napoleon III's regime, and officials showed little interest, positive or negative, in the new art movements dubbed impressionism and postimpressionism. In general, the sphere of artistic creation was left largely to manage itself, guided increasingly by the market. Still, in recognition of contemporary trends, of which the "modernists" were but a small part, the Republic founded the Luxembourg museum to display the work of the living artists it had purchased. The republic, moreover, continued to fund and, to various degrees, supervise the major art and music schools, the museums, the state theaters, and the Academies it had inherited from the monarchies and empires of the past.

The relaxation of monarchical-style controls, and yet a sustained aesthetic fecundity, continued until the Republic dissolved itself in the wake of France's surrender to Germany in June 1940. Political power devolved to Marshal Pétain, whose authoritarian Vichy state took cultural institutions firmly in hand during the four years of its rule. Its actions included installing antirepublicans as heads of the beaux-arts administration, purging Jews and leftists from cultural life, and forcing private publishing houses to replace writers it considered undesirable with ones friendly to the new regime. The Vichy government also gave innovative fascist writers like Louis-Ferdinand Céline, Robert Brasillach, and Pierre Drieu la Rochelle special promotion and support. But, aside from interventions such as these, Vichy made no major alterations to the cultural institutions it had inherited and now controlled. The regime's conservatives did encourage folk art and visual propaganda celebrating religion, traditions, and the Marshal himself. But the main innovations of the period resulted not from official government policies, but from the interruption of national communications caused by Germany's wartime occupation of France. This otherwise traumatic experience allowed the blossoming of creative regional radio, music, and theater, giving, for example, Jean Vilar, the founder of the Avignon Festival, his start as a provincial theater director.

In terms of cultural policy, the Fourth Republic (1946–58) largely, but not entirely, reestablished the prewar relationship, or nonrelationship, between state and cultural production. The state's institution of an Avignon Festival was a notable innovation, as was the reestablishment of the annual film festival in Cannes. Several important new national theaters or troupes (in particular the Barrault-Renaud company) were also created. The Blum-Byrnes Agreement of 1946, which forced postwar France to accept the importation and showing of large numbers of American films, moved the government to subsidize a national film industry drowning in a sea of Hollywood production. The Fourth Republic's grants of compensatory financial aid to French filmmakers proved to be the regime's greatest contribution to postwar cultural life. This government-industry collaboration yielded both the renewal of older-style "French quality films" and the advent of the New Wave, which, ironically, took many of its stylistic cues from U.S. films, both old and new, showing everywhere. Still, the Fourth Republic's overall contribution to French cultural production remained modest at best. Not until its collapse over the war in Algeria, and the contemporaneous end of the colonial empire, which made the meaning of French national identity a pressing question, did the French state invent what came to be understood as a systematic "cultural policy." Henceforth, the Republic formally assumed responsibility for funding and administering what it defined as its citizens' cultural lives. As President de Gaulle's minister of culture, Malraux played the key role in this new arena of state power.

In the 1930s, Malraux became a celebrated writer in his own particular genre of adventure-military existentialism. He first aligned with the Left and then joined sides with de Gaulle during the Resistance. Malraux was largely self-educated, not even having attended high school, but he had made himself into a voracious autodidact. When de Gaulle returned to Paris to lead the new Fifth Republic, he brought the writer-adventurer with him. But what post could he assign Malraux, one of the few important French intellectuals to support the new regime? De Gaulle deemed Malraux too independent to serve as press spokesman but wanted to give him a highly visible and, he hoped, harmless place in his government. Ultimately, Malraux took the beaux arts and a few other minor cultural institutions and created a bureaucracy to administer *the* culture. The decree of July 24, 1959, creating a Ministry of Cultural Affairs (probably written by Malraux himself), assigned it the mission "to make accessible the great works of art of humanity, especially those of France, to the greatest possible number of French people; to foster the most extensive audience for our cultural heritage; and to encourage the creation of works of art and thought to enrich that heritage."

It is important to note that the ministry did not include oversight of youth matters, nor was Malraux entrusted with supervision of state radio or television.

More important, the Ministry of National Education remained totally uncon-
nected to Malraux's new organization. When we think of the culture of a modern industrial society, we think necessarily of the schooling of its members; de
Gaulle did not entrust the schools to this autodidact. According to republican
tradition, schools acculturated children and youths; other state agencies would
tend to the cultural competence of adults. Although Malraux endorsed this administrative division between education and culture, telling the Senate, "Knowledge is the task of the university; love [of art], perhaps, is ours," the imposed
barriers between the two did much to doom the efficacy of his efforts and those
of future culture ministers.

Although de Gaulle's initial intent was to place a faithful supporter at his side
and to endow his new government with the intellectual decor new French regimes have often needed, the value of his and Malraux's cultural initiative made
good social sense. At the outset of the Fifth Republic, the fissures in French society were especially marked and dangerous. The legacy of social conflicts stem-
ming from the Popular Front era (1936–38) and the Vichy regime's response to it
had not been fully laid to rest. And more important, the extraordinary economic
growth of the postwar years had transformed a relatively static society into one
of the most dynamic in the world. By 1958, France found itself in the middle
of perhaps the greatest economic, demographic, and social transformation in its
history. The roar of gasoline-fueled tractors and combines sounded the death
knell of the peasantry. Large urban industrial agglomerations grew—especially
the immense Paris region—populated by a new urban labor force lacking traditional social ties. A burgeoning professional and technical white-collar class
emerged in Paris and especially the provinces. The increasingly affordable automobile, high-speed trains, and especially the rapidly spreading electronic media,
television in particular, leveled differences between the city and "the provinces,"
the label for France-outside-of-Paris, a label Malraux claimed to hate.

What glue would hold this new French society together? Not necessarily
the formal educational system, created at another time for another world, and
which in any event had escaped Malraux's control. Embarking on a program
of "cultural action," Malraux decided to make culture the unifying force in this
moment of disunity, economic change, class conflict, and social fragmentation,
a moment characterized by what Émile Durkheim, France's great sociologist
of unity and fragmentation, would have called anomie. It must be recalled that,
in the postwar years, the arts world had been the special preserve of the French
Communists. Could a strong nationalist government of the Right continue to
suffer unopposed this cultural fifth column?

Malraux preferred to speak of "democratizing the culture." This usage of
the word "democracy" has caused some confusion in subsequent discussions
of the work of Malraux and his successors. Malraux had never run for elected

office; he openly scorned electoral politics as a way of governing. He regularly referred not to any popular will, but to the confidence of General de Gaulle as his mandate for office. Despite their shared goal of modernizing France, there was something quite feudal in the relationship of the two men. Democratizing culture for Malraux meant diffusing the high-art culture of Paris to the provinces and down the social ladder. It was about enhancing access to a precious heritage, not comanagement, nor even active participation. For him, high culture would replace the eclipsed religions of the twentieth century, folding the people of France into the bosom of this new transcendental aesthetic. The cathedrals of this new art-religion would be a series of Paris-inspired Maisons de la Culture with which he would dot the landscape of a once-provincial France.

The Soviet Union built the first houses of culture. These locales served as centers for the diffusion of socialist arts-propaganda and as Bolshevik mission stations for educating the masses. Malraux had learned something about them when he visited the USSR in the 1930s. In his hands, such institutions would become centers for inculcating a passive citizenry with a renewed national culture. Theater was the principal art form diffused in the Maisons de la Culture, which featured the classics and proven modern plays. Neither Beckett nor Genet, however, was considered suitable for audiences outside of Paris. Traveling art exhibitions, film showings, concerts—these were the other important activities. Émile Biasini, whom Malraux had put in charge of the Maisons de la Culture, made it very clear that their doors were closed to amateur theater groups, Sunday painters, local folklore groups, and indeed anything locally generated and lacking the Ministry of Culture's approval.

Only eight of a projected twenty Maisons had opened before the student rebellion of May 1968; all the heads of these state-sponsored arts centers, mostly theater directors, took a stand with the students. When the uprising subsided, and Gaullists strengthened their hold on power, officials in Paris began the process of closing, disbanding, and erasing the memory of institutions that had proven disloyal to Malraux's top-down plans. In later decades, some municipalities, especially in the suburbs of Paris, founded their own Maisons de la Culture, but these were different in both intent and control. In many ways, Malraux's houses of culture, his major institutional innovation, had failed.

Malraux did his work with a slim allocation that, at its maximum, represented only 0.42 percent of the total state budget. Perhaps his time in office was too short for the great tasks he set himself. Still, there is little evidence that his efforts made a long-term difference in the cultural lives of many French people. In a famous study, *The Love of Art,* published just before the May '68 events, the sociologist Pierre Bourdieu and his colleagues declared Malraux's entire project of expanding access to the arts a failure. Like the ministry itself, the Maisons de la Culture were made for the successful artists, some living, but most long dead, and the already-cultured. Workers, farmers, and others deemed to need cultural enlightenment showed no more interest in Malraux's cultural oases than in the traditional art museums he encouraged them to visit.

May '68, which marked the deliberate rejection of Malraux's projects for cultural renewal, put an end to de Gaulle's presidency and to Malraux's work. In step with his chief, Malraux resigned his post in March 1969. But his ministry remained, and with it the idea that the French state bore the principal responsibility for funding, managing, and protecting the nation's culture against decline, market forces, and foreign corruption. During the long, infertile period between Malraux and Lang, President Georges Pompidou (1969–74), a discriminating collector of avant-garde art, used his office to help correct the state's relative neglect of modern art as part of France's glorious cultural heritage. He left as the monument to his time in office the stunning and much-visited modernist structure, the Centre Pompidou (inaugurated in 1977).

In 1981, when the Socialists swept both the presidency and the legislature for the first time in the Fifth Republic, the new President, François Mitterrand, gave the Ministry of Culture the same status as the ministries of Defense, Finance, and National Education, a status it had not enjoyed under Malraux. Mitterrand appointed at its head the onetime professor of international law, but also man of the theater, Jack Lang, who occupied the post for nearly a decade—1981–86 and again, 1988–93, briefly exiting when the conservative Jacques Chirac served as prime minister (1986–88). Cultural policy now took a new turn and adopted an enlarged scope. In addition to culture, Lang's responsibilities included oversight of the media, the President's ambitious building of cultural institutions (*grands travaux*), and planning for the bicentennial celebration of the French Revolution (the Bicentenaire). In his last year, Lang added the Education Ministry and the office dedicated to promoting the French language worldwide (Francophonie).

On taking office, Lang saw his budget double and then continue to climb in subsequent years until it reached the symbolically important 1 percent of the state's total expenditures. With significant resources at his command, Lang launched energetic and far-reaching new projects. Unlike his predecessors, especially Malraux, Lang started from the premise that culture was everywhere and everything. It touched every area of public and personal life, and in particular the social realm. In the words of Antoine de Baecque, "Culture was no longer just a ministry's area of responsibility, but rather a center of gravity around which everything should rotate" (de Baecque 140–41). Influenced by the ideas of Pierre Bourdieu and Michel de Certeau, Lang changed the ministry's goal from diffusing the culture from on high to encouraging participation and creativity throughout society. To be sure, he continued to budget the "old" elite culture of museums, orchestras, and state theaters, in some cases even increasing their support, as with the founding of the Grand Louvre, the Opéra Bastille, and

Pierre Boulez's institute of musical experimentation, IRCAM. But now popular culture—comics, jazz, and photography—was encouraged and prized. So was youth culture: at one point the ministry was subsidizing three French rock groups. Lang introduced a U.S.-style tax deduction that unburdened benefactors who gave money to cultural institutions or events. And then there was the day of the summer solstice, La Fête de la Musique, launched in 1982, when everyone was encouraged to go out into the streets and play a musical instrument.

This so-called anthropological turn in the meaning of "culture" met with strong resistance among old-style intellectuals, who relished the privileges accompanying their status as the high priests of culture. In prestigious journals like Gallimard's *Le Débat* and a polemically titled book, *La défaite de la pensée* (1987), the *nouveau philosophe* Alain Finkielkraut argued for the superiority and priority of France's great intellectual heritage against what he considered the relativism and genre confusion of Lang's anthropological turn. Meanwhile, Marc Fumaroli's essay *L'État culturel: Essai sur une religion moderne* (1991) gave him the role of the inquisitional Torquemada of classicism against the state's takeover of cultural life, and especially the all-cultural state of Jack Lang. Fumaroli's polemic against the French state's long-standing policy of involvement in culture appeared somewhat paradoxical: he was a specialist on the (monarchical) golden age. But as an aspirant for membership in the highly traditionalist Académie Française, the author of *L'État culturel* rejected Lang's understanding of culture. The book's timing, coinciding as it did with the Socialist government's precipitous decline in support, gave it great resonance despite its patently false central thesis, namely, that historically the arts in France had flourished best when independent of the state. Few noted that Fumaroli had adapted his main arguments from the ideological arsenal of American neoconservatives, especially from that of his friend Alan Bloom, whose *Closing of the American Mind* (1987) had produced a sensation on the intellectual right and attacks from the cultural left.

Lang had begun his tenure with great claims about what the state could do to encourage creation in popular culture, improvement in society, and enhancement of France's international prestige. But by the end of his time in office (1993), he had assumed a more defensive posture. He had successfully defended small bookstores and some publishers against big vendors and commercial houses by prohibiting price competition in the sale of new books. But paradoxically, it was the Mitterrand-Lang governments that first opened the door to the licensing of private and for-profit radio and TV stations whose effects on culture Lang would later condemn.

Meanwhile, beginning already in the 1980s and increasingly in the 1990s and the following decade, the movement to decentralize French politics and society meant that, more and more, regional councils and municipalities rather than the Ministry of Culture dispensed funds for cultural uses. From the mid-1980s to the mid-1990s, Paris still received approximately half of the budget for culture—this was the era of Mitterrand's huge and expensive building projects in his own honor—but the regions and cities gradually gained control of the other half. The largest part of the ministry's own budget was now spent on protecting and maintaining the nation's architectural and museological treasures. It could mobilize little money for the kinds of great initiatives of cultural politics dreamt of by Malraux; in the emerging more pluralist, technologically oriented, and globalized society, it became increasingly unclear what such initiatives could, or should, be.

In this context, the Culture Ministry's own periodic surveys, *Les pratiques culturelles des Français* (of the years 1973, 1981, 1989, 1997), cast further doubt on the effectiveness of the state's ability to shape cultural practice, much less make it more democratic. Although public funding for culture had risen significantly in the Lang years, the ministry's data showed that concerts, opera, and dance drew only 3 to 7 percent of the population; 85 percent of French people never set foot in a museum or visited an art exhibit, and 33 percent read not a single book in the year queried. There was little, wrote Philippe Urfalino (82), to the idea that culture, as understood by the successive leaders of the ministry, could serve as a "lever" to "strengthen democracy, sustain citizenship, and battle inequality." If the state's ability to give cultural direction from on high had proven negligible, this did not, of course, mean that the French public eschewed cultural activity. The ministry's surveys had asked only about cultural practices that came, more or less, under its official purview. It neither measured nor encouraged the presumably large amount of time French people spent listening to music at home, playing word games en famille, doing art, pursuing hobbies, or making music with friends—the dense culture of everyday life, if anything, intensified by modernity.

By the early 1990s, with the domestic battle for culture clearly not going well, a new united front formed to combat an external enemy, blamed in part for the failures of "L'État culturel." Lang and his successors—on the left and the right—turned their attention to blocking, or at least diminishing, the impact of what Malraux had called the "culture industries," specifically, the United States' culturally imperial expansion in the realms of film, packaged television series, and popular music. In 1996 a new law required French radio stations to program French songs for 40 percent of the music they played. With the breakdown of the Malraux-Lang project for a national cultural policy, the various cultural activities increasingly decentralized, and the American media menace growing stronger, the Ministry of Culture increasingly occupied itself with what Marc-Olivier Padis called its "Maginot lines" (*Esprit,* March–April 2002).

Although the American-led culture industry was not without its effects, the cultural impotence of the French state resulted at least as much from failings internal to the Hexagon. The Ministry of Culture's lack of systematic collaboration with either the educational system or other state agencies concerning young people, immigrants, and recreation limited the Malraux-Lang approach to representing, at best, the interests of artists vis-à-vis the state and the needs of the already advantaged groups. Even had such collaboration occurred, it is unclear that it could have overcome the cultural primacy of commercialized television programming, the asphyxiation of the ministry's budget, and the regionalization of cultural expenditure. Still, not all large cultural projects ground to a halt. If the ministers of culture under the Socialist premier Lionel Jospin (1997–2002) did very little, President Chirac (1995–2007), a man not lacking in taste and cultivation, succeeded in building a monumental museum on the Quai Branly dedicated to the arts of Africa, the Pacific, Amerindians, and Asian village cultures.

The accession of President Nicolas Sarkozy perhaps marked a low point in the Fifth Republic's cultural policies. An economic and political liberal in the European sense, he has shown scant interest in resurrecting anything like a state-directed cultural policy. He has occasionally intervened to make an appointment that would play well in the media or make a statement showing that, after all, he was concerned about the nation's culture. The sole cultural project he has announced so far (2010) will be a new museum of French history to open in 2015. Sarkozy plans to house it in the seventeenth-century Hôtel de Soubise, which will require the eviction of the parts of the National Archives currently stored in that landmark of the Marais. But for the most part, he has left cultural activities to local governments, with mixed results at best.

It can be asked, finally, what tasks French political authorities can, and will, undertake in the future to save, foster, and spread French culture in an age when electronic media—not the state—are increasingly the centers of cultural invention and diffusion. Largely in reaction to Google's project of creating an online international library of books, in 1998 the French National Library created its own rival public site, Gallica.bnf.fr, "privileging works in the French language," but including other world literatures as well. Funding and energy for this vast project have not been noteworthy. In 2005, the Ministry of Culture launched its own initiative to encourage the development of French culture via the Internet. Since then, however, most of its actions have been defensive rather than expansive. On its website the ministry describes its interest in digitalization of cultural information first as a "way to safeguard our cultural heritage when it is threatened," and only second—echoing the old Malraux language—to give access to that heritage and encourage interest in it. But since a common culture remains central to French republican ideals, we can hope, in the future, to see rich, imaginative, democratic, and even pluralist initiatives for revitalizing the unity of a French people.

References

Bourdieu, Pierre, et al. *The Love of Art: European Art Museums and Their Public.* New ed., trans. Caroline Beattie and Nick Merriman. London: Polity, 1997. [original French ed., Paris: Minuit, 1966]

Chartier, Roger. "Trajectoire et tensions culturelles de l'Ancien Régime." In Roger Chartier et al., eds., *Histoire de la France: Les formes de la culture,* 307–92. Paris: Seuil, 1993.

de Baecque, Antoine. *Crises dans la culture française: Anatomie d'un échec.* Paris: Bayard, 2008.

Dubois, Vincent. *La politique culturelle: Genèse d'une catégorie d'intervention publique.* Paris: Belin, 1999.

Lebovics, Herman. *Mona Lisa's Escort: André Malraux and the Reinvention of French Culture.* Ithaca, NY: Cornell University Press, 1999.

Mainardi, Patricia. *The End of the Salon: Art and the State in the Early Third Republic.* Cambridge and New York: Cambridge University Press, 1994.

Martin, Laurent. *Jack Lang: Une vie entre culture et politique.* Paris: Complexe, 2008.

Moulinier, Pierre. *Politique culturelle et décentralisation.* Paris: CNFPT, 1995.

Ory, Pascal. *L'aventure culturelle française, 1945–1989.* Paris: Flammarion, 1989.

Poirrier, Philippe. *Histoire des politiques culturelles de la France contemporaine.* Dijon: Presse Université de Bourgogne, 1996.

Urfalino, Philippe. "L'Epopée culturelle en sédiments." In Antoine Vitez, et al., eds., *Culture publique, opus 1: l'imagination au pouvoir.* Paris: Sens and Tonka, 2004.

And of course, *Le Monde, Le Débat, L'Esprit, Le Canard Enchaîné, La Revue Internationale des Livres et des Idées,* and *Charlie Hebdo.*

Conclusions

American Perspectives on the French Republic

Edward Berenson

Writers on both sides of the Atlantic have long referred to France and the United States as "sister republics." In these two nations, modern democratic politics was born. But despite this fundamental commonality and a great deal of mutual interest and admiration, France and the United States have been marked by sharp political and ideological differences. A classic statement of these differences is Tocqueville's *De la démocratie en Amérique,* a work that in many ways remains unique. If Americans have adopted *Democracy in America,* first translated in 1840, as one of their sacred texts, no American book about French politics has achieved equivalent status in France.

The absence of such a sacred text in France is no measure of Americans' interest in French democracy or the French Republic. During the United States' first century of existence, American political and intellectual leaders wrote regularly, even obsessively, about French politics and particularly about French revolutions and the republics that followed in their wake. So central was France's republican experience to the United States that Americans used the pivotal events of the Hexagon's history to define their identities as Americans and to understand the meaning of their own democratic society.

Americans' particular fixation on France remained intense until the 1870s, when the racially charged outcome of the Civil War, rising immigration, and rapid industrialization focused attention inward and shook many people's democratic faith. The more Americans worried about the dangers of majority rule, the less appealing their sister republic seemed to be. Such was especially the case after the Paris Commune, as conservative and moderate Americans identified more with monarchical England than with republican France. Only a small, albeit vocal, American Left continued to draw inspiration from the French republican tradition, with its promise of a more egalitarian society and a centralized, interventionist state.

Americans' fin-de-siècle indifference to French republicanism stood in stark contrast to the fascination they had felt a century earlier. In 1789, inhabitants of the United States greeted the French Revolution with almost universal approval. Conservatives found reassurance in French efforts to write a constitution like their own, and radicals were thrilled by the advent of liberty, equality, and fraternity and the rights of man. Americans shared a general feeling that they no longer stood alone as a nation of free people.

Such near unanimity was not destined to last. In 1792–93, Americans divided into supporters and opponents of the French Revolution, and that division did much to create the foundational cleavage of U.S. politics. Supporters of the French Revolution coalesced around Thomas Jefferson and his emerging Republican Party, while opponents of the Revolution sided with the Federalists John Adams and Alexander Hamilton, both hostile to the Jacobin regime. Jefferson's group sought a democratic republic inspired by France; the Federalists believed in government by a gentlemanly elite.

In many ways, the French Revolution was just as crucial to the elaboration of American democracy as the American Revolution itself. Thanks in large part to French military support, the American colonies achieved independence from Great Britain in 1781, and that successful independence movement laid the foundations of the American Republic. But it was the example of the French Revolution that enabled Americans to define their political culture as democratic. However paradoxical it may sound, the French Revolution retrospectively transformed the American War of Independence into a democratic revolution.

Contrary to schoolbook mythology, which presents American colonial society as an incipient democracy, the thirteen colonies, like the mother country, were ordered hierarchies ruled by landed gentlemen. Those who articulated the bases of their status did so in terms of what recent historians have called a "classical republican" model. Political authority, according to this model, inhered in individuals whose wealth and property freed them from the need to pursue their selfish interests. They were thus *disinterested* enough to see what was best for the whole community and to govern in ways that served the public good. This conception of politics was consonant with an understanding of wealth not as an end in itself, but as a means to secure the standing and independence necessary to participate in public life.

This classical republican conception of government and society remained dominant until the 1790s, though by 1776 it coexisted, and in some ways overlapped, with a newer liberal politics that stemmed from the philosophy of Hobbes and Locke. Lockean liberalism was individualist and egalitarian; it saw government as a voluntary arrangement devised by individuals who sought a formal mechanism for the protection of their natural rights to life, liberty, and property. For Lockean liberals, political leaders were the arbiters of competing interests rather than, as before, those who governed as if private interests could be overcome. The new liberal philosophy was at once hierarchic and egalitarian, capitalist and democratic. It no longer stigmatized the pursuit of self-interest and thus offered huge rewards to those able to amass substantial wealth. But since freedom from the need to pursue self-interest was no longer a condition of entering public life, it opened politics and political leadership to all citizens, a category that until the twentieth century meant adult white men.

Despite the liberal, even democratic, ferment of the American Revolution, the first decade after independence in 1781 saw the reemergence of leaders who believed in the classical republican model. Wealthy, cultivated men such as Adams, Hamilton, and Washington accepted the idea that ordinary people could vote, but only for candidates chosen from among those "fit to rule." The ratification of the Constitution in 1787, and with it the emergence of a unified American nation, momentarily strengthened America's traditional elites. From the new political center of Philadelphia, they could now operate on a grander, national scale. But just as they were settling into their new positions of authority and power, the shock waves of the French Revolution swept their political world away.

A pivotal moment in this process was the arrival in April 1793 of the new French Republic's first ambassador to the United States, soon to be derided or hailed as "Citizen Genet." Landing in Charleston, South Carolina, where he debarked to extraordinary public acclaim, Genet journeyed overland to Philadelphia. His four-week trek provoked a series of parades, banquets, bonfires, and other celebrations proclaiming enthusiastic support for republican France.

In the wake of Genet's triumphal march, Americans formed some forty democratic clubs, whose Jacobin-style organization gave ordinary citizens the experience of political participation. That experience reinforced the Federalists' disdain for "people of no importance," as Hamilton indelicately put it, and intensified the democrats' growing hostility to Hamiltonian rule. These rival views of popular democracy now hardened into an all-encompassing ideological divide, with Federalist opponents of the French Revolution on one side and Republican supporters on the other.

By the late 1790s, the tones of American politics had become so dissonant that Hamilton accused Jefferson of conspiring with French revolutionaries to "new model our constitution." Meanwhile, Federalist newspapers denounced the former ambassador to France as a "sans-culotte" whose party exuded a "French mania" and "the irreligious sentiments of France." Jefferson did, at times, sound like Marat or Robespierre, declaring: "The liberty of the whole earth was depending on the issue of the [Revolution]. Rather than it should have failed, I would have seen half the earth desolated." There is no evidence the secretary of state wanted to bring the guillotine to Philadelphia, but statements such as these served as pretexts for the Alien and Sedition Acts of 1798.

This extraordinary attack on civil liberties resulted in the temporary closure of virtually every Republican newspaper.

Despite such anti-Republican repression, the democratic spirit unleashed by the French Revolution proved impossible to contain. Members of democratic clubs refused to be silenced, nor would Jeffersonian journalists and the militant farmers whose antitax Whiskey Rebellion of 1794 challenged the authority of the federal government itself. Although French democracy succumbed to Napoleon's coup of 1799, American democracy triumphed a year later, as Jefferson defeated the incumbent Adams in the presidential election of 1800. The party forged in the crucible of the French Revolution now promised to replace America's classical republicanism with a new form of republicanism that was liberal and democratic at heart.

Though inspired by France's revolutionary Republic, American republicanism was ultimately influenced far more by Locke than by Rousseau; American politics would retain few of the illiberal elements rooted in the French system. Still, American democracy had embedded within it the terrible contradiction of human slavery, and the increasingly violent conflicts over the "peculiar institution" would shape the U.S. response to France's Second Republic of 1848.

American reactions to the Second Republic resembled those toward the French Revolution. At first, there was a nearly unanimous chorus of support, as Americans rejoiced in the resurrection of their sister republic. Later on, when the socialist currents of the new French Republic became more evident, American opinion began to divide along ideological lines. But what proved especially controversial in the United States was the decision of the Second Republic's Provisional Government to free all slaves held in French colonies. This decision cheered American opponents of slavery, known as abolitionists, who used France's humanitarian and eminently republican gesture to criticize their own government for keeping black people in chains. Defenders of slavery, by contrast, criticized the French move as dangerous and rash, fearing it might incite slave revolts in the United States and strengthen the abolitionist cause.

The most positive reaction to the French Revolution of 1848 came from New York, which by the mid-nineteenth century had developed a rich civil society, replacing Philadelphia and Boston as the commercial, intellectual, and cultural capital of the United States. The city's dozens of newspapers, many sold for a penny a copy, powerfully shaped public life not only in New York itself but in hundreds of other cities and towns whose local papers reprinted verbatim articles from the New York press.

The *New York Herald* greeted the revolution with twenty-two successive headlines, one of which read: "The Establishment of a French Republic on the Model of the United States." The *Morning Courier* called the Second Republic "the most brilliant and most marvelous accomplishment of our century," and the

American Fourierist Albert Brisbane dubbed republican France "the Christ of nations." A variety of journalists noted, as the *Courier* put it, that "France and its revolution continues to attract the full attention of the American public." A huge outdoor celebration on April 4 drew some twenty-five thousand people, who shouted, "Vive la République!" and heard their mayor wax enthusiastic over the new French regime. In its ecstatic coverage of the demonstration, the *Daily Tribune* claimed: "Our city has not seen such a spectacle for an entire generation, and perhaps even a century."

Why such joy over political changes in a country three thousand miles away? The most important reason was doubtless the satisfaction of seeing a powerful European country appear to follow America's lead. Crucial as well was the newfound power of a popular press sympathetic to the views and concerns of working people and to the French regime's commitment to freedom of the press. Finally, New York's large communities of Irish, German, and Polish immigrants harbored a great many ardent nationalists who embraced the European revolutions of 1848.

There was some conservative dissent, as for example the *Commercial Advertiser*'s hostility to the Second Republic for promoting a "social revolution" rather than a "political revolution." And a great many commentators endorsed the Second Republic on the *Herald's* mistaken assumption that the French have "copied our constitution, imitated our institutions, followed our models and adopted our political principles." Still, New Yorkers from all walks of life appeared to agree with the future presidential candidate Horace Greeley, who applauded the French Republic for recognizing "the absolute incompatibility of its principles with the tolerance of human slavery." Equally important for Greeley, if not for his more moderate colleagues, was the willingness of French republicans to consider "the government as an organ of the People," unlike American republicans, who "glory in the negative axiom of laissez-faire." Thus, for Greeley, the Second Republic was significant, not because it showed that the American model had taken hold in France, but because it gave the Americans a superior form of republicanism to which they could aspire.

Such enthusiasm for the Second Republic was largely absent from Washington, D.C. The reason for different reactions in the two cities can be expressed in a single word: slavery. As a northern commercial and industrial city, New York had neither slaves nor prominent advocates of the "peculiar institution," formally abolished there in 1827. Washington, by contrast, was not only a southern town, but as the nation's capital it was the one place where advocates and opponents of slavery confronted one another every day.

The American defeat of Mexico in 1847–48 had placed the question of slavery at the forefront of national concern. Southerners sought to make slavery legal in the vast territory seized from Mexico, while northerners wanted at all costs to prohibit the expansion of the slave regime. By making slavery illegal in French colonies, the leaders of the Second Republic had injected a sense of urgency into the American debate.

Washington's *National Intelligencer,* the official organ of the Whig Party, worried that the immediate liberation of French slaves would "lead to the bloodiest scenes in the French colonies and provoke elsewhere"—especially in the American South—"the gravest disorders." Abolitionists, meanwhile, sought to exploit the general American approval of the new French Republic by pressing the issue of slavery. In the House of Representatives, the abolitionist congressman George Ashmun proposed that his colleagues recognize "the essential republican principle that there must be neither slavery nor involuntary servitude." This language evoked a howl of protest from those like the Virginia representative Thomas Bayly, who declared: "There has never been an abrupt emancipation of slaves... without conflagrations, pillage, and the massacre of every white person." In the end, the House, like the Senate, could agree on only an extremely narrow statement congratulating the French on their new Republic, but ignoring the issue of slavery altogether.

Though advocates of slavery rejoiced in the fall of the Second Republic, most other Americans expressed sadness and regret, albeit tinged with George Ticknor's conclusion that "republics cannot grow on French soil." For northerners, this emotion turned bitter when Napoleon III sided with the South during the Civil War. Eager to establish French rule in Mexico, Louis-Napoleon preferred a weak and divided United States to a unified continental power dominated by the industrializing North. Given the emperor's sympathies, it is no surprise that most northerners supported Prussia in the war of 1870, while most southerners sided with France.

This division of American opinion lasted only until the fall of the Second Empire. With the advent of a Third Republic, most U.S. citizens instinctively reverted to the support they had expressed early in the French Revolution and in the spring of 1848. This time, however, American enthusiasm was more muted than it had been for the two earlier Republics. Though President Grant applauded "the spread of American political ideas in a great and highly civilized country like France," Congress merely acknowledged that country's "suffering poor."

If the advent of the Third Republic evoked only a modest American response, the Paris Commune became an object of fascination, even obsession. The Commune was, of course, far more dramatic than any European development since 1848. But part of that apparent drama came from the new media of communication that had transformed the ways Americans followed European events. In 1848, it still took three or four weeks for news to cross the Atlantic and reach New York. This delay made it impossible for Americans to apprehend European affairs as an unfolding and unbroken daily narrative of events. For this reason, observers in the United States understood the Republic of 1848 not as a story, but as an idea or set of ideas illustrated by reports or letters, each separated from the others and frozen in time.

By 1871, everything had changed. The United States now produced 43 percent of the world's periodicals, including 574 daily newspapers, with an aggregate circulation of 2.6 million copies a day. And the completion of the Atlantic cable in 1866 gave Americans nearly immediate access to information from Europe. American readers, like their European counterparts, were now hungry, as one editor put it, for a steady stream of "conflagrations, calamities,...revolutions, wars, fallings of dynasties...strifes [*sic*]...and an unceasing round of exciting, thrilling, and astounding events."

In the spring of 1871, the Paris Commune received more newspaper coverage in the United States than any story except the battle over political corruption in Washington. Americans were particularly avid for illustrated journals, whose crude woodcuts depicted the (mostly imaginary) scenes of Communard violence and mayhem. Such scenes were reproduced in commercial spectacles like New York's "double stereoscopicon," a sort of diorama that depicted "Paris en Feu" for popular consumption.

Beyond the sensational, novelistic appeal of the Commune story, Americans found themselves drawn to the French event for a variety of political reasons. As they had done with earlier French revolutions, Americans used the Commune as a means for thinking through their own political and social conflicts. In the aftermath of the Civil War, when former slaves received the right to vote, a great many Americans displaced onto the Commune newfound reservations about democracy and popular government. The Commune was especially useful for certain northern Republicans whose ardor for black suffrage had cooled but who, as former abolitionists, were reluctant to say so directly. As the radical editor of *Leslies Illustrated Weekly* maintained, criticism of the Commune had become "a pretext for persecutions and violent and irresponsible repression of liberal sentiments...here in the United States."

Though most American commentators painted the Commune in the bleakest tones, finding it a "melancholy example of universal republicism [*sic*], cosmopolitan revolutions, and misdirected intellect," a minority of leftist republicans gave it wholehearted support. The militant abolitionist Wendell Phillips maintained that the "Commune of Paris...embodies all republican institutions [and] had our fathers as a precedent."

That such views were extremely rare in 1871 provides a good measure of American changes since 1848. During the 1790s and again after February 1848, American opinion was largely favorable to French revolutions and the republics they spawned. Both times, there were joyous public demonstrations in favor of their sister republic and the sense that the French had confirmed the wisdom and superiority of American ways. In 1871, by contrast, there was precious little support for French republicanism, even in its moderate non-Communard form. The *San Francisco Morning Bulletin* summed up the new American view by condemning the Commune for "destroying genuine republicanism and individual liberty" and for committing what the *New York Times* called "the crimes of the Parisian socialistic Democracy."

Before long, American writers would discover that same "socialistic Democracy" within the borders of their own country. Explaining the unprecedented strike wave of 1877, James A. Garfield declared: "The red fool-fury of the Seine" has been "transplanted here, taking root in our disasters and drawing its life only from our misfortunes." Once an inspiration for a great many Americans, French revolutionary and republican culture was now blamed for social conflict in the United States. Those Americans with left-wing views continued to admire the French republican tradition, and as the Third Republic stabilized politically, Americans in general adopted more favorable attitudes toward France. But the U.S. elite never regained its earlier enthusiasm for the French Republic. What distanced them from that Republic also distanced them from their own.

In the 1870s, Americans had not yet recovered from the bitter hatreds of the Civil War and Reconstruction, and the blatant corruption of President Grant's administration did little to win people's allegiance to a new, unified republic. Meanwhile, the impressive successes of American capitalism had created greater inequality than the country had ever seen. In this atmosphere of political disillusionment and economic antagonism, many Americans lost enthusiasm for their own republic—and all the more so for their sister regime.

The difficulties surrounding the Statue of Liberty are a case in point. The monument had, of course, been conceived and designed by two Frenchmen, the republican senator Édouard de Laboulaye and the sculptor Frédéric Auguste Bartholdi. Both men were enamored of the United States and disappointed with the failures of French republicanism. They imagined their statue as a French gift to the United States on the hundredth anniversary of American liberty in 1876. Laboulaye and Bartholdi financed the building of the statue by organizing a public subscription that brought in the impressive sum of $400,000. The Americans were asked to provide the pedestal, estimated to cost $250,000.

The problem was that New Yorkers expressed only lukewarm interest in a Republican monument conceived by the French; fund-raising efforts fell far short of their goal. Meanwhile, the governor of New York vetoed a measure to appropriate $50,000 from the state treasury, and the U.S. Congress rejected a bill to award $100,000 to the project. By early 1885, when a crated *Liberty* landed on Bedloe's Island, many thought it would never go up. Some journalists endorsed just such a denouement, while others chortled over the inability to give the statue a base. One paper pictured the goddess turned upside down and "drowned" in the Central Park Reservoir. A prominent critic likened the statue to "a bag of potatoes with a stick projecting from it." And Catholics condemned Bartholdi's monument for proclaiming that "mankind receives true light, not from Christ and Christianity, but from heathenism and her gods." Resisting the tide, the *New York Times* ran an editorial satirizing the statue's opponents. The *Times'* editors put their collective finger on a budding American appreciation for Bartholdi's work. They understood the statue's moderate, unthreatening political valence and sensed that it would be a unique asset for their city. Perhaps they also registered the growing influence of the illustrated press, which in the late 1870s took handsome advantage of the monument's visual lure—just as their Parisian counterparts had a few years earlier.

Although the *Times* made little material contribution to funding the pedestal, its lowbrow competitor, Joseph Pulitzer's *New York World,* succeeded in raising the cash—mainly through tiny contributions from people of modest means. In October 1886, the great statue took its place in New York harbor. During the ceremony on Bedloe's Island, the American speakers largely ignored French contributions to liberty and democracy, calling the Third Republic a regime "founded upon the American idea." Amid this official self-congratulation, members of the Woman Suffrage Association sailed a chartered boat into New York harbor. Excluded from the ceremony, the group denounced the hypocrisy of "erecting a Statue of Liberty embodied as a woman in a land where no woman has political liberty."

The decline of a once-enthusiastic American interest in French republicanism found a compelling analyst in W. C. Brownell, a literary critic and longtime editor at Scribner's. In *French Traits: An Essay in Comparative Criticism* (1889), Brownell argued that America's traditional democratic culture had been "obscured by the struggle with slavery," with the result that "democracy, as an ideal, almost wholly disappeared." With waning interest in their own pragmatic, libertarian democracy, it is small wonder, Brownell suggested, that Americans now had even less fondness for France's abstract, philosophical, and mildly coercive Republican regime.

Americans' relatively lax institutions, Brownell maintained, allowed great individual liberty, but at the expense of growing inequality. The institutions of French democracy, by contrast, provided a bulwark against inequality, considered "undemocratic and uncivilized." To those who considered French republicanism too authoritarian, Brownell responded that France needed a strong state to protect working people and defend democracy against the clerics and aristocrats who want to bring it down. Even so, he added, "the logic of republican tolerance has...completely counteracted the tendency to tyranny springing naturally from excessive state action."

With this argument, Brownell, like Horace Greeley a generation earlier, expressed admiration for the sort of muscular republican state that the United States had never enjoyed: "The sense that you are protected is much greater in France than either in England or among ourselves." To this claim, Brownell added a defense of the French revolutionary tradition, which resists "submission and servility" and "delights in…carrying out new ideas." As for the Commune, Americans failed to understand that "much of the violence was animated by a certain loftiness of political purpose." Concerning the French Revolution itself, Brownell wrote that "the Republic was engaged in a life and death struggle, and if it had not been defiant it would have been destroyed."

With statements such as these we have come full circle, back to the enthusiasm Thomas Jefferson had expressed a century earlier for the French Revolution. Such enthusiasm had been transformed from a majority to a minority position during the century following 1789 and would remain so until today. But Brownell's unheralded work reminds us not only of the differences between the French and American republican traditions but of an egalitarianism embedded in the French Republic that some Americans have wished they could claim for themselves.

References

Agulhon, Maurice. "Bartholdi's *Liberty* in the French Political Context." In Joseph Klaits and Michael H. Haltzel, eds., *Liberté/Liberty: The American and French Experiences,* 87–98. Baltimore: Johns Hopkins University Press, 1991.

Appleby, Joyce. *Liberalism and Republicanism in the Historical Imagination.* Cambridge, MA: Harvard University Press, 1992.

Bailyn, Bernard. *The Ideological Origins of the American Revolution.* Cambridge, MA: Harvard University Press, 1967.

Bertier de Sauvigny, Guillaume de. *La révolution parisienne de 1848 vue par les américains.* Paris: Commission des Travaux Historiques de la Ville de Paris, 1984.

Curtis, Eugene N. "American Opinion of the French Nineteenth-Century Revolutions." *American Historical Review* 29, no. 2 (Jan. 1924): 249–70.

Davis, David Brion. *Revolutions: Reflections on American Equality and Foreign Liberations.* Cambridge, MA: Harvard University Press, 1990.

Katz, Philip M. *From Appomattox to Montmartre: Americans and the Paris Commune.* Cambridge, MA: Harvard University Press, 1998.

Nash, Gary. "The American Clergy and the French Revolution." *William & Mary Quarterly,* 3rd ser., 22, no. 3 (July 1965): 392–412.

Rogers, Daniel T. "Republicanism: The Career of a Concept." *Journal of American History* 79 (1992): 11–38.

Trachtenberg, Marvin. *The Statue of Liberty.* New York: Viking Penguin, 1976.

Beyond the "Republican Model"

Vincent Duclert

Translated by Arthur Goldhammer

Both the *Dictionnaire critique de la République* (2002) and the present work take as their common goal the effort to combine a critical deconstruction of past historiography with an empirical reconstruction of a new historical object, which we call the "Republic in France." This approach has enabled us to escape the impasse produced in French historiography by the promotion of a "republican model," a notion that received perhaps its fullest expression in Serge Berstein and Odile Rudelle's aptly titled volume, *The Republican Model* (1992). Their book—and countless others—reproduced, rather than analyzed critically, an ideology that portrayed the Republic as imprinting itself on both the French nation and French society. According to that ideology, the Republic succeeded in resolving both the social question and the national question, making it a uniquely successful regime.

This view of the Republic did much to shape French historiography, and it reinforced in society at large the idea of "republican exceptionalism." Republicanist ideology has thus permeated both public discourse and scholarly research, driving a wedge between the Republic and its verifiable history In this book, like the *Dictionnaire critique,* our goal has been to bring the two back together by focusing on the dimension of collective political experience, on actual political practice and the effects of politics on French society. The result is a pluralistic history of France, a history enriched by the critical, transnational perspective represented here.

It is not easy to write such a history, because the Republic does not reveal itself as a perfectly constituted object defined by immutable texts, recognized traditions, and stable practices. As Christophe Prochasson noted in "The Undiscoverable Republican Model," "it was only slowly and gradually, with much hesitation and uncertainty and perhaps a certain superficiality, that the republican message permeated French society in the last third of the nineteenth century." The reifying, overly confident notion of the "republican model" was therefore imposed on a changing and often-contradictory reality, a reality that resists the model's efforts to encase the Republic in a mechanistic system that endows people and structures with an excessive rationality.

These developments produced a variety of troubling consequences, as Prochasson explains:

> Two contrasting but complementary views of the Republic have emerged from this model. The first of these views stresses the virtues that supposedly characterize "French exceptionalism" and the miraculous success of republican social integration (inclusion of foreigners, minority religions, women, etc.). The second indicts "the Republic" on charges of Jacobinism, centralization, and statism. Both views are unreliable guides to history because they avoid examining "what actually happened" and instead gravitate toward certain pre-established discourses (which are not without interest). That these discourses effectively serve a social function is beyond dispute. That they are even a crucial part of our social reality will come as a surprise only to the most unworldly scholars. But historians cannot leave it at that. Our job is to understand how different rhetorical conventions, how republican "discourses" and "projects," figured in the history of republican practice and how ideas were appropriated by social and political actors.

As our contributors show, to move beyond sterile analyses of the "republican model," we must historicize the Republic, that is, study the political experience of society in the period during which the republican regime consolidated its position in France. To that end, we must adopt a more open concept of the Republic, abandoning its narrow legal definition as a regime founded by the constitutional laws of 1875, the existence of a Jacobin state, and the regular functioning of institutions such as the electoral process and governmental policymaking. The Republic should not be identified with any specific republican model or order. In the middle of the nineteenth century, Alexis de Tocqueville identified the republic's risks of mob unreason, state power, and imperial temptation (in Europe as well as in the colonies). From 1871 to 1879, the Republic defined itself through its battles with monarchical conservatism and its affinity for law. It was therefore more than a constitutional regime. It gained adherents as a common good that unequivocally deserved to be defended, despite disappointment with the regime or its leaders. At times it was necessary to protect the Republic from itself, against its temptation to sever its historical ties to democracy. To understand its relation to democracy, historical inquiry—*historicization*—is essential, as shown by Philip Nord's important work (not yet translated into French) on the politics of the "republican moment" as it was shaped by the struggle for democracy in nineteenth-century France. For the majority, the Republic emerged from these struggles as an experiment in liberty.

The founding principles of the Republic, established by the revolutionary rights of man in 1789, were reaffirmed throughout the nineteenth century and enshrined in law at the beginning of the twentieth. This higher law, transcending any constitutional definition of the republican system, entered into what we might call the "antibodies" of the Republic. These ideas, symbolic as well as philosophic, enabled the Republic to remain on a democratic path through difficult moments in its history (the Commune, World War I, the defeat and collaboration, the war in Algeria), including periods of social violence. Thanks to these antibodies, the revolutionary extreme Left ultimately accepted republican legal norms, and the moderate Right agreed to save the Republic in order to "save France," doing so on several occasions, from the post-Dreyfus "republican defense" of Waldeck-Rousseau in 1899 to the Free France of General de Gaulle in 1940. The antibodies were not always effective, but ultimately they defined the Republic in France, just as the Constitution defines the limits and possibilities of the American Republic. Hence to study the French Republic, we must approach it by way of the philosophical and symbolic content of this higher law. In establishing the value and character of the republican higher law, authors such as François Furet, Marie-Claude Blais (2000), and Sudhir Hazareesingh (2001) have identified certain "founding fathers," men able to express the democratic spirit of the Republic and the political dream it has embodied through the ages. As for the symbolism of the Republic, the work of Maurice Agulhon on the representations and uses of Marianne (the female goddess that came to represent the Republic), and of Avner Ben Amos on funerary practices and honoring the dead, have taught us a great deal about what the Republic has meant in different times and places and the different ways French men and women have responded to it emotionally.

The conception of the Republic as the ground of a political morality born in history but ultimately liberated from it to become a philosophy of liberty has led a number of scholars to explore the terrain between history and philosophy: these include Mona Ozouf, François Furet, Marcel Gauchet, and Pierre Rosanvallon. It has led others to argue that the Republic continued to exist even when the republican regime did not. During the time of Vichy, for example, Free France preserved a form of legal and moral continuity. Still others have envisioned a history of the Republic in exile: in this volume Lloyd Kramer examines the Republic's exile abroad, as does Sylvie Aprile in other work. But one can also speak of internal exile in periods during which the republican regime severed its ties to democracy and experimented with the exclusion of racial and sexual minorities. Additional periods of internal exile occurred when republicans were forced underground, as during the Restoration (1815–30) and Vichy, or simply when repressive conditions required them to be discreet, as Sudhir Hazareesingh shows in his contribution to this volume. Beyond these matters, the historical development of republican liberty took a variety of other forms, especially in art, which Philip Nord studied in *The Impressionists and Politics* (2000). For certain French Impressionists, the importance of individual and collective experiences associated with the Republic infused artistic creation with the spirit of liberty. Avant-garde art in the late nineteenth century did not separate aesthetics from politics, and neither can be properly understood without the other.

As the republican spirit increasingly permeated practice and imagination, republican citizens acquired an effective sovereignty that counterbalanced the sovereignty of institutions and authorities. The citizen as political actor, social figure, and democratic symbol achieved a durable existence and gave his or her own definition of the Republic, recognizing its fragile but necessary capacity for liberty. Stanley Hoffmann alludes to this process in his preface to the 1990 edition of Marc Bloch's *L'étrange défaite* (Strange Defeat), a book written amid the "debacle" of 1940 and containing a history of the Republic in France at once immediate and philosophical. "The republican citizen," Hoffmann wrote, "is above all a liberal."

> Not in the conservative liberal sense of so many French thinkers of the nineteenth and even twentieth century, more conservative ultimately than liberal—but rather in the sense that Marc Bloch himself defined to perfection: 'The state, in serving individuals, must neither constrain them nor use them as blind instruments for ends of which they are unaware. Their rights must be guaranteed by a stable legal order. The tribe that is bound to its chief by a collective passion is here replaced by the rule of law.'

This collective adhesion, together with its imperative critique—the one reciprocally depending on the other—explains why the Republic cannot produce dictatorship within itself, especially not a dictatorship like Vichy. For this reason Gérard Noiriel's essay of 1999, *Les origines républicaines de Vichy,* is a pure oxymoron. The Republic remains a realm of democracy despite the deep failings that its scholarly history reveals. The American authors of *Why France?* (2007) understood as much in maintaining a view of France as a nation that kept its democratic doppelgänger alive even during the darkest periods of its history. "There was always the other France," concluded Robert Paxton, "the France of the *Declaration of the Rights of Man* and of the Resistance." For Herman Lebovics, that "other France" was less evident than it was for Paxton, so Lebovics set out "to sketch an alternative vision present in French history," a vision of "a pluralist, more open France." Although rarely articulated or championed, this was a France that rejected the notion "that there was but one way to be French." Like the earlier essays by Paxton and Lebovics, the chapters in our book, especially those by Philip

Nord on the Third Republic and by Jeremy Jennings on the values of liberty and equality, demonstrate the force of democracy—complex and conflicted as Patrice Gueniffey here shows it to be—within the French Republic.

Throughout its difficult history, the Republic has existed as a collective experiment that has allowed society to define itself democratically while fighting the temptation to justify exclusion and even tyranny in the name of some supposed "true France" (Lebovics). What binds the French together politically is their social and intellectual attachment to this experience, and that is why history is essential for understanding the present and future of the Republic. But we need a genuine history, a history with all its messy reality, not an artificial "republican model" that impoverishes the past rather than explaining it. It is a matter of some significance, moreover, that what François Furet and Mona Ozouf have called the "invention of republicanism" in the crucible of the Enlightenment has been of particular interest to American and British historians, as Johnson Kent Wright and Jennings, among others, show here. Though historians of the United States have largely shed their earlier fixation on republicanism, the French experience continues to raise questions pivotal to the fate of democracy in the United States.

References

Ben Amos, Avner. *Funerals, Politics, and Memory in Modern France, 1789–1996.* Oxford: Oxford University Press, 2000.

Bloch, Marc. *L'étrange défaite: Témoignage écrit en 1940.* With a preface by Stanley Hoffmann. Paris: Gallimard, 1990.

Duclert, Vincent. *La République imaginée, 1870–1914.* Paris: Belin, 2010.

Furet, François. *Jules Ferry, fondateur de la République.* Paris: Éditions de l'École des Hautes Études en Sciences Sociales, 1985.

Furet, François, and Mona Ozouf, eds. *Le siècle de l'avènement républicain.* Paris: Gallimard, 1993.

Hazareesingh, Sudhir, ed. *From Subject to Citizen: The Second Empire and the Emergence of Modern Democracy.* Princeton, NJ: Princeton University Press, 1998.

———. *Intellectual Founders of the Republic.* Oxford: Oxford University Press, 2001.

Lebovics, Herman. *True France.* Ithaca, NY: Cornell University Press, 1992.

Machelon, Jean-Pierre. *La République contre les libertés?* Paris: Presses de la Fondation Nationale des Sciences Politiques, 1976.

Noiriel, Gérard. *Les origines républicaines de Vichy.* Paris: Hachette, 1999.

Nord, Philip. *Impressionists and Politics: Art and Democracy in the Nineteenth Century.* New York: Routledge, 2000.

———. *The Republican Moment: Struggles for Democracy in Nineteenth-Century France.* Cambridge, MA: Harvard University Press, 1995.

Prochasson, Christophe. "Introuvable modèle républicain." *Cahiers français* 336 (January–February, 2007): 3–7.

Rosanvallon, Pierre. *Le modèle politique français: La société civile contre le jacobinisme de 1789 à nos jours.* Paris: Seuil, 2004.

Contributors

ANNE-CLAUDE AMBROISE-RENDU is maître de conference at the Université de Paris X. Her books include *Peurs privées, angoisse publique: Un siècle de violence en France* (1999); *Petits récits des désordres ordinaires: Les faits divers dans la presse française des débuts de la Troisième République à la Grande Guerre* (2004); and *Crimes et délits: Histoire de la violence de la Belle Époque à nos jours* (2006).

STÉPHANE AUDOIN-ROUZEAU is directeur d'études at the Ecole des hautes etudes en sciences sociales, Paris. His recent books include *Les armes et la chair: Trois objets de mort en 14-18* (2009); *Combattre: Une anthropologie de la guerre moderne, XIXᵉ-XXIᵉ siècle* (2008); *France and the Great War, 1914–1918* (with A. Becker and L. Smith (2003); and *Cinq deuils de guerre, 1914–1918* (2001).

JEAN BAUBÉROT is professor emeritus of history and sociology and honorary president of the École Pratique des Hautes Études at the Sorbonne. His books include *Une laïcité interculturelle: Le Québec, avenir de la France?* (2008); *Histoire de la laïcité en France* (5th edition, 2010); and *Les laïcités dans le monde* (3rd edition, 2010).

EDWARD BERENSON is professor of history and director of the Institute of French Studies at New York University. His books include *The Trial of Madame Caillaux* (1992); *Heroes of Empire* (2010); *Constructing Charisma* (coauthored and coedited with Eva Giloi, 2010); and *The Statue of Liberty* (2011).

JOHN R. BOWEN is the Dunbar-Van Cleve Professor in Arts and Sciences at Washington University in St. Louis. His books include *Islam, Law, and Equality in Indonesia: An Anthropology of Public Reasoning* (2003); *Why the French Don't Like Headscarves* (2007); and *Can Islam Be French?* (2009).

HERRICK CHAPMAN is associate professor of history and French studies at New York University. He is author of *State Capitalism and Working-Class Radicalism in the French Aircraft Industry* (1991) and coeditor of *The Social Construction of Democracy, 1870–1990* (1995) and *Race in France: Interdisciplinary Perspectives on the Politics of Difference* (2004).

ALICE L. CONKLIN teaches history at the Ohio State University. Her publications include *A Mission to Civilize: The Republican Idea of Empire in France and West Africa, 1895–1930* (1997); "Civil Society, Science, and Empire in Late Republican France: The Foundation of Paris' Museum of Man," *Osiris* 17 (July 2002); and *France and Its Empire since 1870* (coauthor, 2010).

VINCENT DUCLERT is professeur agrégé at the École des Hautes Études en Sciences Sociales. He coedited the *Dictionnaire critique de la République* (2002). His most recent books are *La République imaginée: La France de 1870 à 1914* (2010) and *L'avenir de l'histoire* (2010).

STEVEN ENGLUND is the NYU Distinguished Professor of History at The American University of Paris. He is author of *Napoleon, A Political Life* (2004) and is working on a comparative study of political anti-Semitism in Germany, Austria-Hungary, and France.

ÉRIC FASSIN is professeur agrégé in the Social Sciences Department at the École Normale Supérieure in Paris. His books include *Le sexe politique: Genre et sexualité au miroir transatlantique* (2009); *De la question sociale à la question raciale? Représenter la société française* (coedited with Didier Fassin, 2006); and *Cette France-là,* (editor, 2009–2010).

STÉPHANE GERSON is associate professor of French and French studies at New York University. His publications include *Why France? American Historians Reflect on an Enduring Fascination* (coedited with Laura Lee Downs, 2007); *The Pride of Place: Local Memories and Political Culture in Nineteenth-Century France* (2003); and (as guest editor) "Alain Corbin and the Writing of History," special issue of *French Politics, Culture, and Society* 22, no. 2 (Summer 2004).

NANCY L. GREEN is professor of history at the École des Hautes Études en Sciences Sociales. Her major publications include *Ready-to-Wear and Ready-to-Work: A Century of Industry and Immigrants in Paris and New York* (1997); *Repenser les migrations* (2002); and (with François Weil) *Citizenship and Those Who Leave* (2007).

PATRICE GUENIFFEY is directeur d'études at the École des Hautes Études en Sciences. He is author of *Le nombre et la raison: La Révolution française et les élections* (1993); *La politique de la Terreur: Essai sur la violence révolutionnaire, 1789–1794* (2003); and *Le 18 Brumaire: L'épilogue de la Révolution française* (2008).

SUDHIR HAZAREESINGH is a Fellow in Politics at Balliol College, Oxford. His books include *From Subject to Citizen* (1998); *The Legend of Napoleon* (2004); and *Le mythe gaullien* (2010).

IVAN JABLONKA is associate professor at the Université du Maine (Le Mans) and associated scholar at the Collège de France. He is author of *Enfants en exil: Transfert de pupilles réunionnais en métropole (1963–1982)* (2007) and *Les enfants de la République: L'intégration des jeunes de 1789 à nos jours* (2010).

JULIAN JACKSON is professor of French history, Queen Mary University of London. His books include *France: The Dark Years, 1940–1944* (2001); *The Fall of France* (2003); *De Gaulle* (2003); and *Living in Arcadia: Homosexuality, Politics, and Morality in France, 1945–1982* (2009).

PAUL JANKOWSKI is the Ray Ginger Professor of History at Brandeis University. His books include *Communism and Collaboration: Simon Sabiani and Politics in Marseille, 1919–1944* (1989); *A Confidence Man in the Republic of Virtue: France in the 1930s* (2002); and *Shades of Indignation: Political Scandals in France, Past and Present* (2008).

JEREMY JENNINGS teaches in the School of Politics and International Relations at Queen Mary University of London. His recent publications include *Tocqueville on America after 1840* (with Aurelian Craiutu, 2009) and *Revolution and the Republic: A History of Political Thought in France since 1789* (2011).

DOMINIQUE KALIFA is professor of contemporary history and director of the Doctoral School of History at University of Paris 1 Panthéon–Sorbonne. His books include *L'encre et le sang* (1995); *Naissance de la police privée* (2000); *Crime et culture au XIXᵉ siècle* (2005); and *Biribi: Les bagnes coloniaux de l'armée française* (2009).

LLOYD KRAMER is a professor and chair of the History Department at the University of North Carolina, Chapel Hill. His publications include *Threshold of a New World: Intellectuals and the Exile Experience in Paris, 1830–1848* (1988) and *Lafayette in Two Worlds: Public Cultures and Personal Identities in an Age of Revolutions (1996).* He is also a coauthor of *A History of the Modern World* (2007).

CÉCILE LABORDE is professor of political theory at University College London and (in 2010–11) Fellow of Princeton's Institute for Advanced Study. Her most recent book is *Critical Republicanism: The Hijab Controversy and Political Philosophy* (2008).

HERMAN LEBOVICS is State University of New York Board of Trustees Distinguished Professor of History at Stony Brook University. His books include *Imperialism and the Corruption of Democracies* (2006); *Mona Lisa's Escort: André Malraux and the Reinvention of French Culture* (1999); and *True France: The Wars over Cultural Identity, 1900–1945* (1994).

MARY DEWHURST LEWIS is professor of history at Harvard University. She is author of *The Boundaries of the Republic: Migrant Rights and the Limits of Universalism in France, 1918–1940* (2007), as well as several articles on immigration, empire, and citizenship in Third Republic France. She is currently working on a book titled *Divided Rule: Sovereignty and Empire in French Tunisia.*

PHILIP NORD is professor of history at Princeton University. He is the author of *Paris Shopkeepers and the Politics of Resentment* (1986); *The Republican Moment: Struggles for Democracy in Nineteenth-Century France* (1995); *Impressionists and Politics: Art and Democracy in the Nineteenth Century* (2000); and *France's New Deal: From the Thirties to the Postwar Era* (2010).

KAREN OFFEN is senior scholar at the Michelle R. Clayman Institute for Gender Research, Stanford University. Her publications include *European Feminisms, 1700–1950: A Political History* (2000); *Globalizing Feminisms, 1789–1945* (2010); and "Surveying European Women's History since the Millennium: A Comparative Review," *Journal of Women's History* 22, no. 1 (Spring 2010).

CHRISTOPHE PROCHASSON is directeur d'études at the École des Hautes Études en Sciences Sociales. He coedited the *Dictionnaire critique de la République* (2002). His most recent books are *L'empire des émotions: Les historiens dans la mêlée* (2008) and *La Gauche et la morale* (2010).

EMMANUELLE SAADA is a historian and sociologist and teaches at Columbia University and the École des Hautes Études en Sciences Sociales. She is author of *Les enfants de la colonie: Les métis de l'empire français entre sujétion et citoyenneté* (2007). An English translation is forthcoming.

MARTIN SCHAIN is professor of politics at New York University. He is author of *The Politics of Immigration in France, Britain, and the United States: A Comparative*

Study (2008) and *French Communism and Local Power* (1985); and editor of *Comparative Federalism: The US and EU in Comparative Perspective* (2006) and *Shadows over Europe: The Development and Impact of the Extreme Right in Europe* (2002).

JOAN WALLACH SCOTT is Harold F. Linder Professor in the School of Social Science at the Institute for Advanced Study. Her books include *The Politics of the Veil* (2007); *Parité* (2005); and *Gender and the Politics of History* (1999).

JERROLD SEIGEL is the William R. Kenan, Jr., Professor of History emeritus at New York University. His books include *Marx's Fate: The Shape of a Life* (1978); *Bohemian Paris: Culture, Politics, and the Boundaries of Bourgeois Life, 1830–1930* (1986); and *The Idea of the Self* (2005).

TODD SHEPARD is associate professor of history at the Johns Hopkins University. His publications include *The Invention of Decolonization: The Algerian War and the Remaking of France* (2006); "L'extrême droite et mai '68: Une obsession d'Algérie et de virilité," *Clio: Histoire, Femmes et Société* 29 (Spring 2009); and "Excluding the *Harkis* from Repatriate Status, Excluding Muslim Algerians from French Identity," in *Transnational Spaces and Identities in the Francophone World* (2009).

DANIEL J. SHERMAN is professor of art history and adjunct professor of history at the University of North Carolina, Chapel Hill. His books include *The Construction of Memory in Interwar France* (2000); *Museums and Difference* (editor, 2008); and *French Primitivism and the Ends of Empire, 1945–75* (forthcoming).

BONNIE G. SMITH is Board of Governors Professor of History at Rutgers University. Among her works are *Ladies of the Leisure Class* (1981); *The Gender of History* (1998); and the *Oxford Encyclopedia of Women in World History* (editor, 2008).

FRÉDÉRIC VIGUIER is a sociologist and assistant director of New York University's Institute of French Studies. He coauthored *Travailler pour être heureux?* (2003) and was guest editor of "The Lost *Banlieues* of the Republic?" special issue of *French Politics, Culture, and Society* 24, no. 3 (Winter 2006), to which he also contributed the article "Maintaining the Class: Teachers in the New High Schools of the *Banlieues*."

ROSEMARY WAKEMAN is professor of history at Fordham University. She is author of *The Heroic City: Paris, 1945–1958* (2009); *Modernizing the Provincial City: Toulouse, 1945–1975* (1998); and editor of *Themes in Modern European History, 1945 to the Present* (2003).

François Weil is directeur d'études and president of the École des Hautes Études en Sciences Sociales. His recent works include *A History of New York* (2004); *Citizenship and Those Who Leave: The Politics of Emigration and Expatriation* (co-edited with Nancy L. Green, 2007); and *Empires of the Imagination; Transatlantic Histories of the Louisiana Purchase* (coedited with Peter J. Kastor, 2009).

Johnson Kent Wright is associate professor and head of the Faculty of History at Arizona State University. He is author of *A Classical Republican in Eighteenth-Century France: The Political Thought of Mably* (1997) and articles on Montesquieu, Rousseau, and the Enlightenment in modern historiography.